The Bond of the Furthest Apart

The Bond of the Furthest Apart

Essays on Tolstoy, Dostoevsky, Bresson, and Kafka

SHARON CAMERON

The University of Chicago Press
Chicago and London

The University of Chicago Press, Chicago 60637
The University of Chicago Press, Ltd., London

Published 2017
Printed in the United States of America

26 25 24 23 22 21 20 19 18 17   1 2 3 4 5

ISBN-13: 978-0-226-41390-7 (cloth)
ISBN-13: 978-0-226-41406-5 (paper)
ISBN-13: 978-0-226-41423-2 (e-book)
DOI: 10.7208/chicago/9780226414232.001.0001

Figure 2.1: Hans Holbein the Younger, *The Dead Christ in the Tomb* (1521-22). Oil and tempera on lime wood, 32.4 × 202.1 cm. (acc. no. 318). Photograph: Kunstmuseum Basel. Photography by Martin P. Bühler.

Library of Congress Cataloging-in-Publication Data

Names: Cameron, Sharon, author.
Title: The bond of the furthest apart : essays on Tolstoy, Dostoevsky, Bresson, and Kafka / Sharon Cameron.
Description: Chicago ; London : The University of Chicago Press, 2017. | Includes bibliographical references and index.
Identifiers: LCCN 2016034769 | ISBN 9780226413907 (cloth : alk. paper) | ISBN 9780226414065 (pbk. : alk. paper) | ISBN 9780226414232 (e-book)
Subjects: LCSH: Bresson, Robert—Criticism and interpretation. | Tolstoy, Leo, graf, 1828–1910—Criticism and interpretation. | Dostoyevsky, Fyodor, 1821–1881—Criticism and interpretation. | Kafka, Franz, 1883–1924—Criticism and interpretation.
Classification: LCC PN1998.3.B755 C35 2017 | DDC 809—dc23 LC record available at https://lccn.loc.gov/2016034769

♾ This paper meets the requirements of ANSI/NISO Z39.48-1992 (Permanence of Paper).

Contents

Abbreviations

AG Leo Tolstoy, "Alyosha Gorshok"

B Franz Kafka, "The Burrow"

BK Fyodor Dostoevsky, *The Brothers Karamazov*

CP Fyodor Dostoevsky, *Crime and Punishment*

D Fyodor Dostoevsky, *Demons*

DFK Franz Kafka, *The Diaries of Franz Kafka, 1910–1923*

E Michel de Montaigne, *The Complete Essays of Montaigne*

FC Leo Tolstoy, "The Forged Coupon"

I Fyodor Dostoevsky, *The Idiot*

I Franz Kafka, "Investigations of a Dog"

II Leo Tolstoy, "The Death of Ivan Ilych"

IM Franz Kafka, "An Imperial Message"

L Leo Tolstoy, *On Life*

LM Franz Kafka, *Letters to Milena*

MM Leo Tolstoy, "Memoirs of a Madman"

N Robert Bresson, *Notes on the Cinematographer*

SS Franz Kafka, "The Silence of the Sirens"

WP Leo Tolstoy, *War and Peace*

Introduction

The essays that follow can be read with an eye to a set of shared concerns, or they can be read separately; their coherence does not depend on a single argument. Nonetheless, recurrent, if uneven, connections dictate the logic of the essays' collection in the same volume, which should be illuminated for the reader, who certainly deserves to know what the iconoclastic Catholic French filmmaker Robert Bresson (1901–1999), recognized for his aesthetic of minimalization and for the cultivation of automaticity and affectlessness in the nonprofessional actors he routinely called "models," could have to do with the histrionics of the nineteenth-century Russian novelists Fyodor Dostoevsky and Leo Tolstoy, never mind with the cosmic hopelessness of the enigmatic creatures in the Czech Franz Kafka's twentieth-century parables and stories. Of course Bresson filmed Dostoevsky and Tolstoy, though he insisted on the departure of his cinematography from its aesthetic origins: "Even if I make a film from Dostoevsky, I try always to take out all the literary parts. I try to go directly to the sentiments of the author and use only what can pass through me. I don't want to make a film showing the work of Dostoevsky."[1] Bresson's *L'Argent,* which takes Tolstoy's "The Forged Coupon" as its basis, transforms that story's ending, thus revealing "what can pass through me" as in fact recovering Tolstoy's own earlier "sentiments."

Bresson might extract "the literary parts" of the novels he adapts, excising the language that anatomizes motive, intention, feeling—excluding whatever insinuates access to inwardness, since such access is precisely what Bresson insists cannot be signified or visualized.[2] But he preserves the metamorphic, oppositional quality that informs Tolstoy's and Dostoevsky's writing. In Bresson's films anything at all (one could therefore say *everything*) has an irreducible truth value only when it is perceived as extra-individual, far-reaching, and even antipodal, as my essays will elaborate.

Thus what draws Bresson, Tolstoy, and Dostoevsky together in the thinking of my essays is not primarily Bresson's specific adaptations (which are only a focus in my discussion of Tolstoy's story), but rather the way in which Bresson's revision of the norms and conventions of cinematography runs parallel to certain suppositions about narrative; individuality; ontology; the demystification of human privilege; and, above all, the congruence of incommensurable entities and phenomena in the philosophical fiction of Tolstoy and Dostoevsky. In one aspect of this parallelism, in the work of all three, intensity rips apart the conventions of polite conversation, giving way to ultimate questions that erode the boundaries of individuality, as when Prince Myshkin in *The Idiot*, who has just met Aglaia, avidly answers her question, "you know how to be happy?" by launching into an exposition of a state of well-being we call happiness.[3] In Dostoevsky's writing, such conversations are impersonal—happiness being as much a concern of Natasha (characterized by "derangement and beauty"); of Aglaia (characterized by "modesty"); of Myshkin (by "idiotism"); of Ippolit (by "vanity"); and of course of the fatuous Lebedev, who patters on about the nineteenth century's ignominious indifference to universal happiness.[4] An analogous abrasion of personality is perceptible in *War and Peace*, where it is not only Prince Andrew who asks, "Can this be death? . . . I cannot, I do not wish to die," but also Nicholas Rostov, and Princess Mary, who, appalled by the "dreadful, terrifying, and repellent mystery" that is her dead father, Prince Bolkonsky, shrinks from what she sees: " 'No, he's not dead—it's impossible!' she told herself."[5] Like the collective deliberation on happiness in *The Idiot*, in *War and Peace* such expressions of incredulity are also impersonal. The narrator insists "anyone" (*WP* 152) struck by "the line dividing the living from the dead" (*WP* 151) would feel the welter of dismay and dread these characters do.[6] Such obsessive anticipations of death—which are specific without being personal—disrupt narrative and characterological intrigue across Tolstoy's writing.

But here I must back up. The idea for these essays began not with Tolstoy and Dostoevsky, whose work I had read for years in translation, but with—and then after—an astonished initial viewing of Bresson's *Au hasard Balthazar*, seen belatedly for the first time in 2006. In *Balthazar* fragmented images brought together rhythmically seemed to compete with, and to supplant, the spell cast by the film's narrative, a perception later validated for me as a first principle of Bresson's cinematography.[7] (In *Notes on the Cinematographer*, he wrote: "Fragmentation" is "indispensable if one does not want to fall into

REPRESENTATION" [*N* 93]).[8] At the same time, in *Balthazar* the affectless faces and mechanized movements of Bresson's nonactors similarly ask to be read against the ledgers of story, character, and exegesis (in ways that prompt analogy to the aspects of impersonality that distinctively mark Tolstoy's and Dostoevsky's writing).[9] "Unusual approaches to bodies" make it possible to be "on the watch for the most imperceptible, the most inward movements" (*N* 45), Bresson wrote, apparently describing his own approach, especially the strange automatism he cultivated in his models. One could only wonder what the vigilant beholder is being asked to *glean*, though not to *identify*, in those inexpressive faces and involuntary movements. Not to identify, because how could the "imperceptible" and the "inward" ever be more than intimated?

Some such question also emerges at the macro level in *Balthazar*, because Bresson subjects the essence of animal and human being to cinematic probing, so that the juxtaposed images of animal and human bodies are not only, or even primarily, legible within the binary of a species distinction, a state of affairs that divergently characterizes Kafka's animal stories. In Bresson's films what we discern of the relation of animal and human bodies is momentaneous and improvised. Also enigmatic is *Balthazar*'s allusion to Dostoevsky's valorization of the ass in *The Idiot*, which inclines us to consider a glancing connection between the beast that restores Myshkin to his senses and the film's noncompliant donkey. And then, since nothing can be made of that almost spectral reference (it has no significance, is not developed), the allusion (is it an allusion?) resists its own suggestibility, almost as though the hinted link between novel and film is meant to be insinuated and is then meant to fade. Such provocations to recognize and to resist recognizing what we see and hear across Bresson's films became for me a lens through which to re-see pivotal (and for each unique) nondiegetic moments in Tolstoy's and Dostoevsky's fiction that pull away from, or subordinate, narratives of plot, character, and destiny.

My considerations of Bresson press on the disparity between fictional episodes that unfold in what Mikhail Bakhtin called a "chronotope," a zone where "space becomes charged and responsive to the movements of time, plot, and history"[10] and a second zone where moments of narrative rupture are marked by spectacle, epiphany, rhythmic oscillation, or augmentations of intensity—and in the work of Dostoevsky, by interludes that break out of a redemptive theology to expand on non-Christian manifestations of joy and suffering; while in Tolstoy's writing I examine obsessive, if intermittent, visions of death that could not be narrativized, since they both portend and epitomize the end of narrative. However one describes these cinematic and literary elements (not like each other and not like other aspects of the aesthetic works of which they are part), for a reader or viewer they have the contrastive feel of Jacques Rancière's "*opsis*" (narrative disruption) and "*muthos*" (narrative coherence)[11] or, from another vantage, of Laura Mulvey's punctuated distinction between stillness and the moving image,[12] something extracted from the flow of the diegetic, even when, as in *Pickpocket* (described below), the medium shots of Michel's hands could also be regarded as the pivot on which the narrative turns. I take Mulvey's distinction between stillness and the moving image as an analogy for aspects of cinematic and literary texts that pause, retard, turn away from, choke off, overwrite, or otherwise resist the temporalities of plot and narratives of character in which they are embedded, and which also have their own mobility, even though in Bresson's films, in distinction to those discussed by Mulvey, accentuated images are not given to us as freeze frames, as slow motion blurs, or through manipulations of the DVD, but rather by rhythmic disruptions that are adjacent to the stories from which they can't entirely break free.

One obvious instance of Bresson's contrapuntal writing is visible in *Pickpocket*, which has a double allegiance to the theme of *Crime and Punishment* (in Bresson's variant: Michel, a nihilist and would-be superman who is a petty thief rather than an axe murderer, falls in love, thus taking his first step toward redemption) and to a fantasia on the virtuoso reach of his wandering hands, which, pulled out of narrative in medium close-ups that fill the screen, almost steal the show as the camera flashes those hands before us. When hands become instruments of pure fragmented motion, their italic relation to narrative lifts them into a register illusorily governed by rhythm alone, which Bresson approvingly called its "omnipotence" (*N* 68). Thus although Sergei Eisenstein explained that all cinema contrasts rhythmic and depictive elements in an antithesis he called "*optical counterpoint*,"[13] Bresson's films visually accentuate that polarity. In repelling the very mimesis he was bound to implement (except in experimental cinema, what is film without a story?) Bresson's "cinematography" becomes what he called a "new way of writing, therefore of feeling" (*N* 38).[14]

In this "new way of writing," as with the fiction of Tolstoy and Dostoevsky, access to what something is can't be identified independently.[15] The repeated juxtaposition of disparate, even antithetical phenomena, of what one could call "ripped-off pieces of reality"[16]—in *Balthazar*, beauty and cruelty, animal eye and camera eye, sentience and the extinction of sentience—reveal that for Bresson, as I have begun to indicate, essential aspects of something can only be gleaned by discerning what lies outside its boundaries. Such nonautonomy also governs Bresson's appropriation of religious paradigms: in *Balthazar* an archetypal framework of the crucifixion is allusively constructed to interpret the donkey's fate (the donkey, continuously brutalized, is killed on a hillside surrounded by sheep), but that frame of reference is then bent out of shape—is made to seem scandalous—so that it no longer retains its signifying power, since the film also flagrantly shows us deaths that cannot be thus universalized. In the same way, at the end of *Mouchette*, Monteverdi's *Magnificat* sounds in the background against (but is it against?) the logic of the girl's suicide. Dostoevsky in *The Idiot* also employs such subversions of Christian conventions, in Ippolit's ekphrasis of Holbein's *The Body of the Dead Christ in the Tomb* (in profile an "anti-icon"),[17] contraries that will be examined in my essays. Moreover, Bresson's films go further: as I have intimated, they rethink ontology. The taxonomies that distinguish one *kind* of entity from another—human from animal, animal from object, object from natural phenomenon—are eroded, so that fixities of classifications fall away. In the dissolution of categorical norms, animals, humans, and material objects are drawn toward each other through a sort of relay of images into a relation that both enthralls and resists formulas of intelligibility. For instance, *Balthazar* establishes a consonance between camera eye and animal eye, both illegible, both grounded in manifestations of nonsubjectivity. But how could such a kinship ever be demystified?

At the same time that Bresson baffles us, he insists on the affinity of images and ideas we suppose have nothing to say to each other, as when in *A Man Escaped* the imperative "you must be born again" (John 3:7) is exemplified not by divine spirit infusing human being, but by the material life of objects that are disassembled and reincarnated—through fantastic metamorphoses we are asked to visualize—into original entities whose new life is put to novel uses. In this way, the emancipation of objects from the constraints that confine them epitomizes, and rhymes with, the hero's freedom whose attainment their altered states realize. Such kinetic energy in which things are reborn by being liberated from what they were—or what we think they are—is the heart of Bresson's cinematic project. He explained the dynamism this way: "To move people not with images likely to move us, but with relations of images that render them both alive and moving" (*N* 89), a gloss inadvertently close to how Eisenstein defined "pathos,"[18] as when an action, a state, an emotion, an object breaks through its apparent boundaries to reveal a new quality, intensity, or affinity—a new vision of being, but not a new identity, since the characteristics of the latter, always the same, could only be immobile. A crisis of determination analogously occurs in reverse in *The Idiot* (in reverse, because the denatured creatures in Ippolit's nightmare are unrecognizable). Specifically, Ippolit can't decipher the ontology of the figures that appear before him: a Christ that is not a Christ, a scorpion that is not a scorpion, a beast that is not a beast, and a man that is not a man. Are they actual or apparitional?

Notwithstanding the historical particularities that infuse their singular aesthetics, such formal and philosophical questions are routinely asked by Dostoevsky, Tolstoy, and Bresson when they characterize an "actual" outside of and against conventions of identification. Thus in response to the public's outcry that the characters in *The Idiot* are "fantastical," Dostoevsky famously replied: "I have a totally different conception of reality and realism than our novelists and critics. My idealism—is more real than their realism. God! Just to narrate sensibly what we Russians have lived through in the last ten years of our spiritual development. . . . This is realism, only deeper; while they swim in the shallow waters."[19] Bresson located what he called the "real" in the vision of the mechanical camera's eye, and in the automaticity inflicted on his models, which could capture what the human eye and will blocked. He clarified the former this way: "Two sorts of real: (1) The crude real recorded as it is by the camera; (2) what we call real and see deformed by our memory and some wrong reckonings" (*N* 78–79). The narrator of "Memoirs of a Madman" claimed "death is the only real thing,"[20] but after Tolstoy's conversion this "real" crossed over to the other side, embracing eternal life—though not the eternity of an afterlife—contradictory assertions, each articulated with the same passionate certainty. Such counterpoints explain my book's title, drawn from Bresson's description of his cinematography: "The insensible bond, connecting your furthest apart and most different images, is your vision" (*N* 37), a vision shared by Tolstoy and Dostoevsky.

In Kafka's writing, there is no extra-diegetic space, no region but that of apparently infinite plot (and thought in the micro-spaces of Kafka's fiction, with its endless speculation about what is actual or possible, also has its boundless plot), in distinction to the registers in Tolstoy's, Dostoevsky's, and Bresson's work, in which, it is emphasized by each, truth variantly reveals itself, making Kafka a curious choice for inclusion in this book. Yet in representing ontology as nothing but illegible event and outcome, as narrative without the chance of breakthrough[21]—an alternative to the contrapuntal writing that I have argued differently characterizes the works of Tolstoy, Dostoevsky, and Bresson—Kafka's stories implicitly hold up a mirror to the dialectical relation between story and what escapes its grip, whether this be the spectacle of Bresson's rhythmic montage, Dostoevsky's interludes, or Tolstoy's conflictual understandings.

From a converse point of view, although the amalgamated features of Kafka's *sui generis* creatures are nothing like the humans and animals whose kinship Bresson asks us to contemplate, they are very like the animal Kafka calls himself in his letters to Milena. In the far reach of such a congruence, and in Kafka's reflections on interiors that cannot be penetrated and exteriors that cannot be enclosed, Kafka, the outlier, the "furthest apart," almost shares a "bond" (*N* 37) with the other three, since in a different context, what is within and outside, in this case of the diegetic, remains central to the ontology of each. To bear down on this near-affiliation from another vantage still, when Kafka associates himself less with human beings than with "the penholder in [my] hand," his self-exile from the human "species"[22] unsentimentally deflates human privilege, as Bresson's films also do. Kafka thought hope was not intelligible in relation to our human circumstances. When asked if he thought there was hope for the universe, he famously replied: "Oh, plenty of hope, an infinite amount of hope—but not for us."[23] Tolstoy and Dostoevsky exhibit a like skepticism that disputes the centrality of persons—our prospects, entitlements, distinctions—humanism's animating fiction. We see such skepticism in the visions of Tolstoy's terrified characters when death unbuilds human advantage; in Dostoevsky's meditations on the "here eternal"[24] of joy which sweeps away the future and our aspiration for its changes; and of course in Bresson's nonanthropomorphic reframing of experience, in which the ethical capacity of the animal to respond to suffering demonstrates that ethical need not be subjectivized.[25]

Below I summarize the concerns of each essay:

"Animal Sentience" examines Bresson's *Au hasard Balthazar* in which, through the filmic congruence of animal and human bodies that are brought together rhythmically rather than narratively, we are made to rethink the meaningfulness of the distinction that separates animal and human forms of embodiment—specifically, we are asked to rethink the roles of reason and will in making us who we are.

"Outside Christ: Dostoevsky's Joy" considers nondiegetic representations of joy and suffering in *The Idiot* and *Demons*—fragmentary interludes that have a contrapuntal relation to the constraints of narrative, character, and duration. In distinction to *Crime and Punishment* and *The Brothers Karamazov*, the representations of suffering and joy considered in my essay are not based on an exchange economy in which "happiness is bought by suffering."[26] Joy is "nothing earthly; not that it's heavenly" (*D* 590); it is a "here eternal" (*D* 236), without recourse to theology.

"The Sight of Death in Tolstoy" engages two strains of Tolstoy's writing. In the first, the sight of death is the foundation of ethical understanding; in the second, if ethical understanding is practiced, there is no death of any consequence. The latter half of the essay turns to Bresson's *L'Argent*, a filmic adaptation of Tolstoy's "The Forged Coupon," which transforms Tolstoy's Gospelized ethics to an immanent ethics, raising the question of whether ethics is phenomenal and embodied (as in Emmanuel Levinas and Jacques Derrida) or whether it is evental (as in Alain Badiou). An examination of aspects of Ludwig Wittgenstein's writing on ethics, T. J. Clark's *The Sight of Death,* and Tolstoy's fable "Alyosha Gorshok" sharpen the question of whether ethics is natural or supernatural.

"Robert Bresson's Pathos" examines how Bresson's cinematography captures phenomena outside a situating placement, specifically the ways in which *Procès de Jeanne d'Arc*, *Mouchette*, and *A Man Escaped* dismantle characterological, ideological, and taxonomic understandings of the essence of a thing. Gilles Deleuze's concept of the abstract face[27] and Eisenstein's theory of "pathos" (the ecstatic leap whereby a thing breaks out of its boundaries, as well as the leap out of the self experienced by the spectator when he witnesses this transformation)[28] enable me to ask how Bresson contests categories that treat being as though its manifestations could be split and apportioned into separate compartments.

"Kafka's No-Hope Spaces" focuses on the disjointed spaces in Kafka's writing, regions that can be neither penetrated, consolidated, nor abandoned. The estrangement of such spaces is then replicated in another register by Kafka's unidentifiable animal stories, in which *animal* designates the experience of being unrecognizable to oneself, in any system of classification.

The method of my essays is to isolate crucial images, sequences, topics, and questions from the literary and cinematic diegetic from which they partially break free, and my focus further extracts them from their contexts in that I sometimes no more than glance at the narrative or characterological structures which they breach. Yet I differentiate my analysis from postmodernist practices of reading that rest on ambiguity, undecidability, or aporia to explain why a text resists exegesis.[29] In distinction, my mode of reading draws close to and ponders elements that appear to reside outside of narrative and characterological structures, but also, paradoxically, to recede from visibility (like the "imperceptible" and "inward movements" [*N* 45] Bresson described behind the effaced expressions of his models) that would enable either analytic conclusiveness or a theory about why such conclusiveness is thwarted. In addition, the incommensurability of the extra-diegetic manifestations my essays consider could not be grasped by one interpretive account, since a question about the relation of camera eye, human eye, and animal eye ("Animal Sentience") differs from a question about an impersonal affect—if joy *is* an affect ("Dostoevsky's Joy"); and from visions of death that supplant each other—but do they supplant each other? ("The Sight of Death in Tolstoy"); as well as from the sense of how categories are optically and acoustically dismantled by the incongruent elements Bresson draws into relation ("Robert Bresson's Pathos"); and from the split-off realms of Kafka's writing ("Kafka's No-Hope Spaces"), even as the considerations of these problems are linked by a consistent method of reading that does not grasp at certain kinds of closure. For the imponderables Dostoevsky, Tolstoy, and Bresson call "real" do not add up either collectively *or* individually.[30]

How the real is captured by "a machine's scrupulous indifference" (*N* 36) in Bresson's cinematography of course differs from Kirillov's celebration of an eternal present that, in his view, could be actualized by anyone, and from Tolstoy's epiphanic claim *this* is "the only real thing" (MM 308)—a *this* that refers to antipodal understandings. Bresson thought the real could not be signified. Such a conviction is also attested by Dostoevsky in *Demons*. When Kirillov identifies "a leaf" (*D* 237), and ultimately adds "there isn't any more" (*D* 238), he means no more than deictic pointing to indicate how the vision of a leaf could open into timeless ecstasy. "There isn't any more!" (*D* 238) thus refers to his epiphany about the end of time; to the leaf as sufficient proof of timelessness—nothing more by way of proof is needed (though his discovery can't be extricated from his being so "happy" and from a conviction, arising from this happiness, that "everything is good," including violent suffering [*D* 237]). "No more" also points to the end of exegesis, which, it could be said, in Kirillov's ramble never began in the first place. Analogously Bresson's cinematography involves a juxtaposition of "*obvious*" meaning and "*obtuse*" meaning. In Barthes's definition, an "*obtuse*" meaning subverts narrative by being at once "persistent and fleeting."[31] Notwithstanding their opacity, as well as their cryptic temporality—since endurance and ephemerality would seem to exclude each other—I will argue that for Bresson's films, as for Barthes's descriptions of Eisenstein's films, "obtuse" meaning remains the "seal endorsing the whole of the work."[32]

These essays were guided by the thinking of Maurice Merleau-Ponty's *The Visible and the Invisible* (especially "The Intertwining—The Chiasm"), by Deleuze's *Cinema I* and *II*, and above all by Bresson's *Notes on the Cinematographer.* In his philosophy of cinema, which is also a disquisition on filmic practices he found indispensable for drawing out and fortifying awareness, he repeatedly contemplated the relation between the cinematographer's eye and the indifferent camera's eye (*N* 36). The negotiation of the two is what Bresson might have been considering when he bluntly wrote: "Retouch some real with some real" (*N* 88). Yet since Bresson does not specify a context for the directive, it could also indicate a contrary thought about his cinematographic intervention: "The true is not encrusted in the living persons and real objects you use. It is an air of truth that their images take on when you set them together in a certain order" and that then "confers on these persons and objects a reality" (*N* 80–81). Another specification of that relation is expressed in this aphorism: "Face to face with the real, your taut attention shows up the mistakes of your original conception. It is your camera that corrects them. But the impression felt by you is the sole *reality* that has interest" (*N* 104–5). A page later he added: "The crude real will not by itself yield truth" (*N* 106). The numerous and contradictory reflections on the deviation of camera eye and human eye demonstrate Bresson's unceasing deliberations on their unwritten and, in any definitive sense, unwriteable relation, since the word "real" does not express or endorse an aesthetic practice, but rather marks Bresson's shifting sense of how to discern an ethics and an ontology. In conclusion I stress this crucial point touched on too briefly earlier.

The conceptual disturbances in Bresson's cinematography arise from incongruous couplings (a Schubert andantino and a donkey's braying, a car's lights and a baby's eyes) that insist that ostensibly independent entities can neither be identified as discrete, nor associated in predictable ways with like entities. Bresson's cinematography everywhere effaces the distinction between phenomena thought to have a relation to each other and phenomena thought to have no relation. In Bresson's montage, fragmented images are linked and inimitably made penetrable; in this way heterogeneous phenomena come into being contingently in "*any-relation-whatever*,"[33] a practice that challenges our conviction that we know what things are, or the infinite ways they may be attuned or entangled. Bresson's genius is not therefore merely formal; rather, in his films an aesthetic principle becomes an ethical instrument to carve out—or, rather, to lay bare—an ontology in which the truth of categorical fixities is menaced. A similar, if tacit, assault on distinctions of nomenclature is perceptible in Kafka's letters and stories where the terms "animal" and "human" are drawn into relation not to enforce a taxonomic distinction, but rather to indicate the impossibility of doing so. Dostoevsky undertakes a revaluation in a different register when joy is extracted from circumstance and use value—shown to spring not from happiness or happenstance, but rather from the shock of an immanent vision in which time falls away and things are seen to be what they are, while in Tolstoy's writing ethics and death are fantastically made contingent in that one is said to determine the existence of the other.

Such visionary rethinkings, which assault conventions of understanding that segregate aspects of reality (gouging away at categories, taxonomies, and concepts), are each unique. Yet in the works I consider the aesthetic project opens to an ethical insight: that experience glimpsed close-up, in its intimate particulars, is more astonishing than any explanatory apparatus could fathom. In Bresson's films, for instance, this insight is ethical because it contests the implicit claim that certain beings count, while others don't (and things don't) by displacing such aggrandized reasoning with (quite varied) contrary images that demolish its bias and assault our certainty that knowing is the right word to describe the spectacle of world that is before (or in) us. In Spinoza's account, elucidations of why things happen, of what things are ("*good*," "*evil*," "*warm*," "*cold*"), and of how they should be valued are no more than "modes of imagining" what is adventitious to us and "do not indicate the nature of anything."[34] The "insensible bond" (*N* 37) to which my title alludes thus not only refers to the antinomies within each of the works discussed. It also refers to the bond perceptible beneath the strains of these vastly different works, which are nonetheless kindred in their resistance to all forms of abstraction that prevent us from seeing the welter of things that cluster around us that are not referenced to our distinctions, that, to adopt Kafka's words, are "not for us."[35] Although my book's critical and theoretical grounding lies in Bresson, then, it also implicitly reaches beyond Bresson (and beyond Tolstoy, Dostoevsky, and Kafka) toward intensities and mute presences that, saturated in vitality, evade the strictures of knowledge and expression, but that magnetize attention and lure us toward them, even, or rather especially, in the absence of an orienting perspective that would make what is seen precisely recognizable. Not to know how to express what is perceived may be not to know how its parts go together; what the parts are; or the frame that would make the whole legible,[36] a state of affairs that does not attenuate the question of how to regard aspects of the world that can't be grasped and that may even leave us speechless, a question I take to be ethical. Moreover, although inclination might make us prone to react a certain way (to back away, to be enthralled), the affect behind any predisposition could itself be seen as malleable, subject to reflection on how we might feel, or how we might relate to feeling, or might cultivate its abandonment, or might simply perceive feeling, the most insubstantial of all that identifies us, as only a precursor to what matters or remains to be decided in encounters with things we can't encompass or penetrate. What hangs in the balance in such a confrontation is how to respond—how to be in relation—to aspects of world with which we are not affiliated, but from which we are also not estranged, which call to us, the way voiceless things, or things that lack our voice, can be said to call to us to see them, unobstructed by the shadow of categories and ideas.

1

Animal Sentience: Robert Bresson's *Au hasard Balthazar*

In Robert Bresson's *Au hasard Balthazar* a young girl, who we discover is dying, looks on without expression, one might almost say without interest, or with interest dulled by her invalidism, from a supine position on a couch as the camera shifts to two still younger children, the objects of her attention: Marie and Jacques taking a pinch of salt to feed Balthazar, a baby donkey.[1] In a second scene—while Marie and Jacques, on a swing, gaze infatuatedly at each other—again on the sidelines, the young girl sits upright on a stretcher and herself feeds the donkey salt. But the carefree mood of the beautiful summer day suddenly darkens when the girl, given a spoon of medicine by an attendant, puts her head in her hand and cries at its bitter taste (fig. 1.1).[2] In a third scene the girl's father bids farewell to her as she lies fully dressed, as if laid out for burial. As the attendant props up the body so that a rimmed hat can be removed, we see she isn't dead, but has only fallen asleep in Sunday clothes (fig. 1.2). Although the girl is a minor character (whose actual death is reported later), what she models isn't minor.[3] She is the image of mourning at the taste of the bitter medicine. She is an image of death, which *is* the bitter medicine. She is at once a spectator looking on from the sidelines and the spectacle being regarded. Death is what the girl cries at when she takes the bitter medicine. Death is what she mimics when she falls asleep in her clothes. The scene in which the girl sleeps prefigures her death and recalls the tears she sheds at its anticipation. Yet the fate that is the dying girl's is not in fact unique. Rather, its manifestations—the deaths of Arnold (the film's vagabond), Marie's father, and Balthazar—are those of the fate that is anyone's, even as the versatility of these representations (death from illness, death from grief, death from drink, death from a bullet) resists universalizing. Moreover, the space of death occupied by the girl in her Sunday clothes is also occupied

FIGURE 1.1

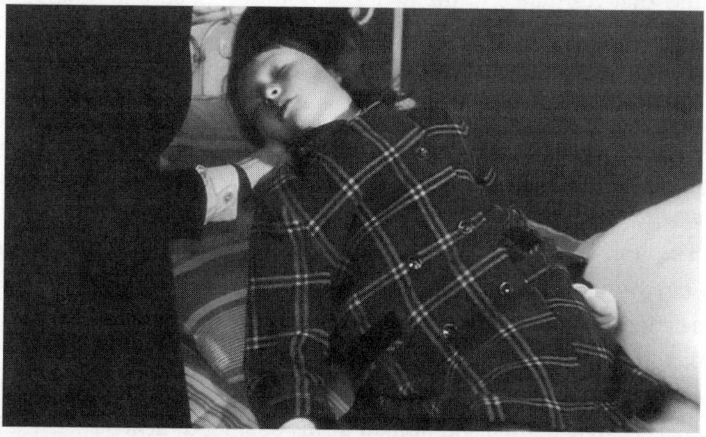

FIGURE 1.2

FIGURE 1.3

by Marie at the film's end, kneeling and naked, with her back to the camera, after Gérard's gang has stripped and beaten her (fig. 1.3). These inverse images (dressed up and naked) are drawn together and linked to death by the objectification of the body in the lifelessness of the countenance immobilized by sleep and in the blankness of the naked back, which registers Marie's effacement.[4]

I have begun by looking at images of sentience and its extinction (the dying girl, and Marie, in her nakedness, another dying girl), because they immediately indicate how *Balthazar* fastens images into a relation that subtends the film's donkey story. Such representations of embodiment reveal Bresson's film to be incongruously elemented of a reductive, yet enhanced, hence mysterious, materialism. To anticipate the strands my argument will draw together: in Bresson's film, materialism radiates from all embodied forms—the human and the animal—revealing a similitude so unthinkable (so appalling to think) that resistance to the identification of human and animal bodies provokes cruelty to the animal, even as its beauty at other moments fascinates with an allure apparently devoid of human counterpart.

"Images will release their phosphorus only in aggregating," Bresson wrote, capturing his belief that in cinematography, "an image must be transformed by contact with other images. A blue is not the same blue beside a green, a yellow, a red."[5] The aesthetic of juxtaposition and recomposition is of particular interest in *Au hasard Balthazar*, in which a donkey is acquired by different owners at whose hands he suffers and ultimately dies, because through the filmic congruence of animal and human bodies that are brought into relation rhythmically rather than narratively, we are made to rethink the meaningfulness of distinctions that separate animal and human forms of embodiment—specifically, we are asked to rethink the roles of reason and will in making us who we are.[6] One aspect of Bresson's genius involves the decoupling and reassociation of images to form novel relations. It could be said of film in general that, in Steven Shaviro's words, its "dematerialized images . . . are the raw contents of sensation, without the forms, horizons, and contexts that usually orient them. And this is how film crosses the threshold of a new kind of perception . . . non-intentional and asubjective."[7] But Bresson's films italicize this fracturing and relinkage of images. Such "parcelling," writes Gilles Deleuze of montage in the films of Bresson, Alain Resnais, Benoît Jacquot, and André Téchiné, produces "a whole new system of rhythm. . . . Instead of one image after the other, there is one image plus another"—a strategy Bresson identified with unforeseen manifestations of extremity: "Dismantle and put together till one gets intensity" (*N* 55).[8]

What has not been remarked upon, however, is that this technique in which independent images are linked in a fragmented virtual space, visible in all Bresson's films, has a specific effect in *Au hasard Balthazar*, where it becomes a resource for an exploration of the kinship between human and animal forms of embodiment. In the film's transplanted images and in the radical ellipses between narrative sequences (which cross and become entangled without being integrated), characteristics that separate the animal from the human are at once scrupulously italicized and paradoxically weakened, or rather, notwithstanding such distinctions, the animal and the human are brought right up against each other for the spectator to examine the meaningfulness of such distinctions. In visually and aurally associating animal and human beings, Bresson participates in a debate about what kind of alterity animal and human beings reflectively constitute for one another. Bresson does not take up the question of the animal in relation to Martin Heidegger's famous disparagement: "The stone . . . is *worldless*; . . . the animal is *poor in world*; . . . man is *world-forming*."[9] Nor does he engage in an effort like Jacques Derrida's to reclaim an honor for the animal in which the latter's difference is not "privation."[10] And, unlike Giorgio Agamben, Humberto Maturana, and Francisco Varela, he does not explore the traces that affiliate the animal with the human or that bind discrete species in an alliance outside of filiation.[11] (Needless to say, these characterizations of complex philosophical positions ought ideally to be elaborated.) Rather, as I explain, Bresson visually holds the animal up to the human in a series of rhythmic gestures without discursive argument. Or, if the film explores a common ground shared by the animal and the human, such a foundation could be specified in relation to the involuntary and to the "matter [men and women] are made of" (*N* 47) that compels it, to which Bresson inimitably discovers a corollary—even an essence—in the materiality of the animal.[12]

But I also want to suggest that in *Balthazar* the filmic proximity of animal and human forms of embodiment has a frictive relation to the film's frame narrative.[13] What is stunning about the contesting of the film's narrative is that it is not any story that is challenged in Bresson's *Balthazar*. Rather, insofar as the film begins with a mock baptism of the donkey and concludes with his brutal killing on a hillside surrounded by herds of sheep, the narrative puts into question the archetypal story of the crucifixion.[14] The film's Old Testament narrative of law and debt (there is a miser; the film's two fathers quarrel over money; there is an accusation of larceny, a sudden inheritance, and, throughout, courts and police, who officiate over charges of murder and changes in monetary fortune) and its New Testament framework of crucifixion and salvation, alluded to at the film's beginning and end, are, respectively, punctured and displaced by an investigation of the congruence between animal and human manifestations of embodiment and sentience that the film conducts rhythmically. While it is possible to describe the narrative as absorbing into a content the rhythmic elements I shall discuss—the donkey treated cruelly by its different owners ultimately dies a death so pitiless it could be regarded as a crucifixion—the film creates an aphony between these rhythmic congruences and the Christian frame so that they are unable to speak to each other. Let me press on why they cannot do so.

A death that can be redeemed suggested by the sacrificial frame (He died for all) is juxtaposed to and subsumed by the film's multiple representations of a death that is nontransferable. In *Balthazar* "the non-relational character of death individualizes" being "down to itself" (as Heidegger formulates it).[15] Yet, in a counterphilosophical claim, the film also curiously suggests that if no other can redeem or experience one's death, death also lies beyond the bounds of one's own experience. Death renders one passive to a fate that can't be universalized, that can't be transferred, and that also can't be owned. It could even be said that Bresson's attempt to recover the involuntary dictates that render the body will-less, discussed in the following pages, continually prefigures death as that state that only ultimately punctures the illusion of a body that is one's own. In *Balthazar* the dying body is rendered as a singularity that belongs to no one. This anonymous state of dispossession is also the animal's, is the donkey's at the film's end (where the mass of sheep overwhelms and visually negates the unique fate of a single lamb in their midst, contesting the Christian story at its most unambiguous). Starkly figured against the mass of moving sheep, Balthazar, a non-lamb, remains, like the girl on the sidelines, a solitary figure of unredeemed materiality. Such juxtapositions—which are, in Bresson's special sense, rhythmic—lock animal and human forms of embodiment and sentience into relationship, penetrating the enigma of each outside of a common understanding of either.

By rhythm, Bresson understood the recurrence of sounds and images (and the camera's movement between them) as they repeat and vary. Bresson elaborated: "Nothing is durable but what is caught up in rhythms. Bend content to form and sense to rhythm" (*N* 68). The rhythms are all-powerful. "The meaning arrives last."[16] Rhythm, and even the special case of rhyme, is perceptible in the film's title, *hasard/Balthazar*—in French a perfect syllabic homophone, putting the accident or hazard back in all characterization. It is perceptible in the constant cries "Marie, Marie" (whom Jean-Luc Godard called "another donkey"), at once a summons and a cry at the fact that the one who is summoned can't be made to come and stay, and can't be saved by the care that underscores the call's urgency, as well as in Marie's reiterated "Balthazar"—variously a greeting, a designation, an expression of love, and a powerless importuning.[17] And the film rhymes objects in space; as has been

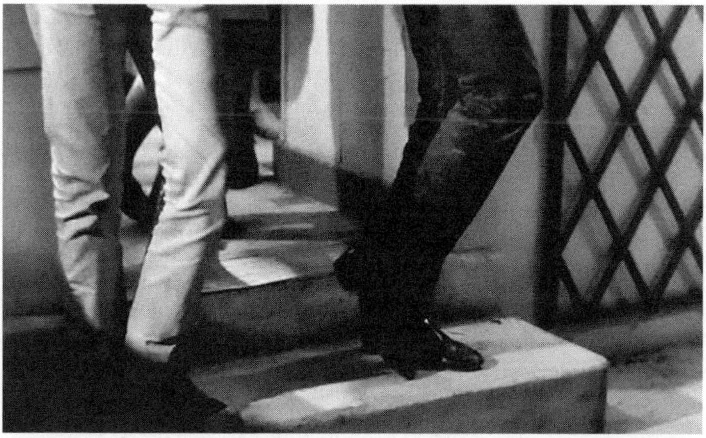

FIGURE 1.4

FIGURE 1.5

FIGURE 1.6

much discussed, the camera is as interested in the expressiveness of legs, feet, arms, and torsos—which are disarticulated from the image of the whole body and juxtaposed to each other—as in the human countenance (fig. 1.4). Animal bodies are similarly fragmented and juxtaposed: thus, in the circus scenes the hind portions of donkey and horse are set against trailer cars in back of them (whose rear we also see)—constructions of matter, in their piecemeal appearance without compositional integrity (fig. 1.5). In *Balthazar* one point of this filmic disarticulation is to shatter and even demolish an illusory image of embodiment, one constructed by thought rather than one perceived as inhabited. In the reduction of human and animal bodies to isolated parts—to a crude materiality that is partialized—Bresson is reimagining forms of embodiment so that they appear as strange as they really are (and as they sometimes feel): unthinkable as wholes and unthinkable apart from each other (fig. 1.6).

In section I of the following pages I examine the congruence of animal eye and human eyes, and the eerie consonance between the involuntary movement of Bresson's untrained actors, whom he called models, and the instinctive movement of animals. In section II, I turn to an allusive juxtaposition of Bresson's donkey with his precursors in Dostoevsky's fiction, and to the rhyme established by the film's intercutting of the donkey's braying and a Schubert andantino. The versatility of the film's representations of cruelty constitutes its most pervasive rhythm. Yet one of the most unaccountable features of *Balthazar* is its ecstatic conjoining of beauty and cruelty. An identification with the animal body incites cruelty, even as its beauty (with which identification is impossible) unmistakably compels rapture. I conclude by pressing on the relation between rhythm and representation across Bresson's films.

I

The donkey's liquid eye haunts the film (figs. 1.7–1.9). That eye is passive, beautiful, seemingly omnipresent in its witnessing of events, and in the camera's dwelling on it, repeatedly discoverable as an opacity, an eye that could be profound, but that is in fact unfathomable. Sometimes Balthazar's vision (what he *might* see as he gazes in a certain direction) indicates what we *will* see, as when Balthazar, decked in flowers, gazes at Marie who sits across from him on a bench in the middle of the night, while Gérard, coming into view, creeps up behind her. In other scenes, the donkey is treated as if he were inanimate, a stone or a ledge (Marie and Gérard chase each other around him and use his body to steady themselves), while the camera, framing his eye, rather records him as an experiencing presence.

FIGURE 1.7

FIGURE 1.8

FIGURE 1.9

FIGURE 1.10

The camera moves away from the donkey's eyes when, as in illness, sentience flows out of him. Distance from the eye is also perceptible in the camera's record of his death. But Balthazar's eye in health and viewed close-up epitomizes sentience, in contrast to Arnold's drunken stupor when he rides away from the bar slumped over the donkey's neck. And when Arnold falls off the donkey—dying from an immediate blow to the head—the camera juxtaposes the side of Arnold's lifeless head and face to Balthazar's leg and hoof, which it has landed beside, as if the sentience registered moments earlier in the animal's eye has now suffused his whole body and is most palpable in his leg, which sways as the animal stands, and visibly pulses with life (fig. 1.10).

The camera's relentless close-ups of that liquid eye, its recurring to the eye in relation to the human interchanges it reveals the donkey witnessing, as well as in its recording of his reaction to the elements, presses us to seek meaning in the donkey's gaze—a seeking that would confer agency—even as the seeking is consistently rebuked by being thwarted. Pertinent to this allure is Maurice Merleau-Ponty's idea of "tacit . . . expression" in relation to what he calls "style"—the contrary of formulas that can be translated into statements and conventions—in that it privileges mute forms of expression. Such muteness "dwells and makes us dwell in a world we do not have the key to . . . [within] *matrices of ideas* . . . symbols whose meaning we never stop developing."[18] In *Balthazar* what we most lack a key to is the liquid eye that, in its suggestiveness, is a depth, a plenitude, hence a condensation of attributes we ascribe to it—judgment, neutral witness, innocence, beauty (notwithstanding the incompatibility of these traits with one another)—and, at the same time, a placeholder, an absence, because the eye repels these attributions. The pull toward attribution and the pull away from it catch the spectator up into a mobility, an inconsistency, an improvisation, a repetition with a difference that is itself a rhythm. This being compelled and being refused by the camera's vigilance—being compelled despite being refused—invests the eye with depth (though depth that is impenetrable), as if what the eye holds to be revealed is not just vitality (indistinguishable from sentience), but responsiveness itself, a responsiveness eerily mirrored in the eyes of the animals in the circus. Moreover, in an apparent reflection of our own absorptive interest in that eye when we behold the animals in the circus seeing, their glassy eyes take Balthazar as their object.

This is the narrative: Balthazar, pulling a cart of hay, is led by a handler past animals in their cages. As the latter goes about a task, he leaves the donkey standing—we don't know standing where until we see Balthazar stare, and then we see a caged tiger stare. Although we never see the tiger and the donkey in the same frame, the shot/reverse shot suggests they are looking at each other.[19] The stripes made by the vertical bars of the tiger's cage throw into relief the stripes of the tiger's pelt. And the visual echo of iron and flesh precipitates a half-implicit sense that something internal to the animal's flesh has been extracted and deformed into the very mechanism of his prison. Though we see the tiger's body fully—he is lying in his cage—a bar crosses in front of and obstructs one of his eyes (fig. 1.11). Or rather, it is unclear whether the bar that blocks our vision also blocks the tiger's eye, a singularity mirrored with a difference in the camera's shot of Balthazar's single eye.

When Balthazar, pausing before the cage of a polar bear, looks at the latter, we discern an interest that, in the bear's downward glance, might not be

FIGURE 1.11

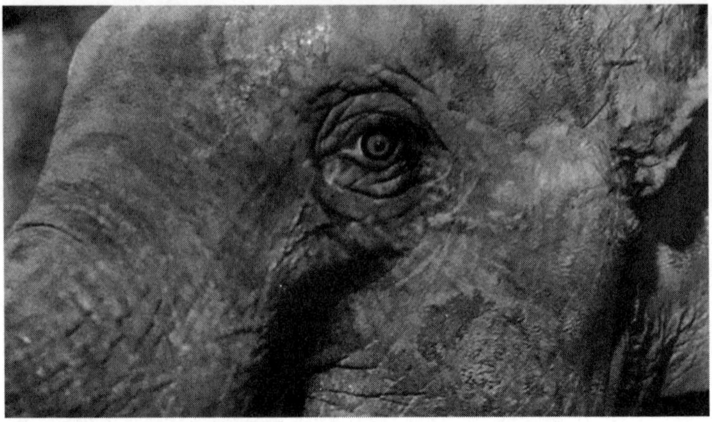

FIGURE 1.12

reciprocated. When the donkey stops before an ape's cage, the ape, exchanging glances with him, emphatically shakes his arm and speaks. In Balthazar's vision of an elephant's scopic presence, there is a fierceness, even a wretchedness, contrasted to the donkey's passive visage. Unlike the shot of the tiger (with one eye blocked by the bar from our view, but nonetheless present in its entirety), this shot cuts out the elephant in order to depict it synecdochically, being a shot of a single eye buried in massy folds of flesh whose radical foreshortening renders trunk, mouth, ear a mere plane of wrinkled skin from whose midst the eye flashes (fig. 1.12). (It might seem that these encounters are progressively humanized—fierceness and wretchedness hint at meaningfulness—even as the evanescent glimpse of that eye insists that reading is what the camera fails at.)

The series of encounters between the donkey and the circus animals, which concludes with Balthazar's vision of the elephant as a Cyclops—or rather, with our vision of this—initiates an interpretive crisis. Is the point, like the effect, of the animal's interpenetrated gazing a purity of communication, not compromised by the fact (even founded on the fact) that the animal is impervious to human understanding? Is there a presumptive content to the communication generated by the different fates of being caged and being free? Or is the point rather our voyeurism: we are looking at a spectacle we can only be outside of? Is the point to represent the eye as a vital, animate force, as vital as Balthazar's breath—visible from the cold—weirdly linked by the alternating images of donkey and tiger, to the tiger's inhalations and exhalations (the only movement in the frame) on its own muscular flank? The instigating of questions that can't be addressed and hence fall away returns us to the exaltation—the sublimity—of scopic exchanges whose grandeur and power arise out of their inscrutability. Human presence—including ours—is thus made so marginal to the animal scenes that they are in effect neutralized or purified of that presence. We see into a space from which humans have been exiled, even as the camera eye is the mechanical presence that performs this subliming.

The evocativeness of Balthazar's looking—looking that seems acute and, in Bresson's term, even "ejaculatory"—at human beings as well as at the animals in the circus depends on the camera's repeatedly shooting him from the side, revealing one eye, not both simultaneously.[20] Although there is a logic to these shots (Bresson, commenting on the fact that the donkey looks sideways, wrote that the camera had to be "not a millimetre too much to the left or to the right"), the effect is in excess of the mechanics of this decision.[21] In the camera's excision of it, the single eye in *Balthazar*—the donkey's, the elephant's, the tiger's—is that ocular particularity associated with animal, not human, vision. Bresson's insistence on this distinction seems repeatedly to press on a meaning to the difference. (Thus, when Marie arrives at the miser's house, his lamp held high, he attentively examines the girl. But the miser's inspection of her face is supplemented, even superseded, by Balthazar's vision of the same encounter, but reversed, a mirror image, with the donkey's eye on the *miser's* visage—a look we are invited to read as something decisive, rather than incidental, a judgment or an understanding, even as the scene underscores the inscrutability of the animal's vision.)

If the camera eye makes Balthazar's eye its focus, and simultaneously disallows the eye of the animal any interpretable depth, in the character Marie, "another donkey," to recall Godard's designation, Balthazar's eye has a human counterpart.[22] Comparatively, Marie's ocular expressions are legible, as the donkey's are not. Thus, the glances she casts at Gérard when she returns to her car to sit with him indicate submissiveness, something she has assented to as well as something she will endure, a curiosity as well as a wretchedness, suggesting that her interest, supplanting her outrage, will predict the outcome of their encounter. But though there is a versatility to the moods conveyed by Marie's eyes—and a language that can express it—the relentlessness with which the camera focuses on those eyes comparatively trivializes such meaningfulness. Scene by scene, the camera haunts her eyes, summoning forth—and bequeathing to them—a nuance, a mercurialness, an absorption without affective equivalent. This nuance is heightened by Bresson's containment of emotions because in Bresson's films emotions are not projected or expressed but are rather inimitably contained.[23] If we see in Marie's expression something piercingly felt—for instance, Marie's joy at Balthazar when, driving in the car, she catches sight of him—this is oddly discernible, because joy is not an extravagance that is demonstrated by her face's lighting up; it is perceptible rather as a concentration or an inwardness. Bresson's antitheatricality, his voiding of a model's expressiveness, which he associated with the exaggerations of Kabuki, weakens any link between a model's countenance and an interiority ("No psychology [of the kind which discovers only what it can explain]" [*N* 82]). Even when in the car, next to Gérard, Marie's eye tears and the tear spills onto her face, the camera treats this more as a documentary event—more as a "physics" than as a "psychology" of emotion.[24] We can connect the tears to what might incite them, Gérard's forced presence in the car, or Marie's capitulation to it. But the camera's oxymoronic record of those tears (they fall on a virtually expressionless face) simultaneously abstracts them from such domestications (fig. 1.13). The camera, therefore, repeatedly lingers on Marie's eyes as if it had discovered not the expression of an affect, but rather a tactile feel to retinal impressions, and were itself a surface in contact with the surface of her eyes and of the objects that engage them, rendering vision itself almost palpable, as the properties of the objects Marie regards are made indistinguishable, in the camera's back and forth, from her absorptive looking at them (fig. 1.14). Though the film preserves the difference between animal and human vision (animal vision being an exhibition of what we can see without seeing into), it makes both contributive to a world envisioned rather than a world rendered meaningful, even though the human eye (in distinction to the animal's) could never fully achieve the state of being nonsignifying.

Moreover, the film's plurality of points of view—the camera's, Marie's, Gérard's, Balthazar's—saturates objects, creating the illusion of something like a "total visible," not reducible to any one point of view.[25] In *The Visible and the Invisible*, Merleau-Ponty's metaphor for such a visible is that of two eyes that form "the channels of one sole Cyclopean vision."[26] Unlike the terrible Cyclops presented in Bresson's elephant eye—terrible because it suggests something riven, something cut out and missing—Merleau-Ponty's image of eyes that form a single vision rather suggests something integrated: first, the unification of monocular visions that form a single sight ("one sole body before one sole world"), and second, a more inclusive unity in which "the little private world of each is not juxtaposed to the world of all the others . . . all together are a Sentient in general before a Sensible in general."[27] Yet for Bresson, unlike Merleau-Ponty, the sentient in general is not a close-bound system, but, as I have noted, is rather expressed by bodies that are fragmented. ("*Fragmentation* . . . is indispensable if one does not want to fall into REPRESENTATION"

FIGURE 1.13

FIGURE 1.14

[*N* 93], Bresson wrote, distinguishing the *being* of his models from the *seeming* of actors.)[28]

One way to understand the single animal eye is as synecdochic of materialized being. *Balthazar* insists that to see animals as they really are is to see materiality as it really is (including our materiality), not as a constituted integrity but as concentrated intensities, not as a system of parts working as one, but as a series of fragments (neck, hands, hoof, torso, feet, ear, along with eye and eyes), sites where inarticulate sentience also grounds itself. In a *counter*-phenomenological vision, to see the materiality of being is to see the enigma of Balthazar's eye as our own. Such a perception of identity is based not on identification but rather—like Jean Genet's discovery "at the slaughterhouses" that "the fixed, but not sightless eyes of the sheep's heads, cut, piled in pyramids on the sidewalk" are equivalent to his own tangible corporeality—on materialization.[29] To recognize Balthazar's eye is not to familiarize what we see, but to defamiliarize what we are.

At the same time, therefore, that the circus animals' scrutiny of each other suggests the incomparability of animal and human vision, other parts of Bresson's film draw the animal and the human toward each other. They do so specifically, also, through the film's representation of what is reflexive rather than what is reasoned. In radical exercises meant to circumvent his models' thinking about the meaning of their roles and even about the meaning of their words, Bresson made them learn their lines as if the words were just syllables: "We keep repeating lines fifty times if necessary until the mind no longer intervenes in the dialogue or the gestures," Bresson wrote.[30] He explained: "Models who have become automatic . . . their relations with the objects and persons around them will be *right*, because they will not be *thought*" (*N* 32). "The real, when it has reached the mind, is already not real any more" (*N* 78). And he elaborated: "Nine-tenths of our movements obey habit and automatism. It is anti-nature to subordinate them to will and to thought" (*N* 32). One could say that the automaticity of the models—and of the camerawork itself—gives us the thought and the unthought together in something like the realm of the virtual or the latent.[31] What cannot be reasoned or thought, Bresson asserted, is gesture:

> I think that most of our gestures, and even our words, are automatic. If your hand is on your knee, you didn't put it there. . . . Montaigne wrote a wonderful chapter on this subject, about how our hands go where we don't tell them to go. Our hands are autonomous, you see. Our gestures, our limbs, themselves are autonomous; they're not under our command.[32]

Although he does not specify it, the chapter Bresson evidently had in mind is the extensive analysis of gesture in Montaigne's "Apology for Raymond Sebond," which extraordinarily discourses on the posture and bearing of the body as a whole, as well as on its movements, attitudes, and expressions in the context of the relation between animal and human forms of communication.[33]

"How does he know," Montaigne asks contemptuously of man, "the secret internal stirrings of animals?" (*E* 331). Turning first to a characterization of a mutual misunderstanding between animal and human species ("We have some mediocre understanding of their meaning; so do they of ours, in about the same degree. They flatter us, threaten us, and implore us, and we them" [*E* 331]), Montaigne pauses on the incontrovertibility of animal communication, which does not depend on speech or even on voice. But this elaboration of the absolute adequacy of animal communication that proceeds without word or sound leads Montaigne to consider the absolute adequacy of its human equivalent:

> Lovers grow angry, are reconciled, entreat, thank, make assignations, and in fine say everything with their eyes. . . . What of the hands? We beg, we promise, call, dismiss, threaten, pray, entreat, deny, refuse, question, admire, count, confess, repent, accuse, condemn, absolve, insult, despise, defy, vex, flatter, applaud, bless, humiliate, mock, reconcile, commend, exalt, entertain, rejoice, complain, grieve, mope, despair, wonder, exclaim, are silent, and what not, with a variation and multiplication that vie with the tongue. With the head: we invite, send away, avow, disavow, give the lie, welcome, honor, venerate, disdain, demand, show out, cheer, lament, caress, scold, submit, brave, exhort, menace, assure, inquire. What of the eyebrows? What of the shoulders? There is no movement that does not speak both a language intelligible without instruction, and a public language; which means, seeing the variety and particular use of other languages, that this one must rather be judged the one proper to human nature. (*E* 332)

In Bresson's film the language "intelligible without instruction"—the "public language"—is gesture, what the body makes visible when it slips the mind's yoke. Gesture and posture can't be fully governed, and often they can't be governed at all. When Marie, chased by Gérard, falls on the ground, her prone body, legs seductively bent, extends the consent that her words, and her eyes, have withheld. Gérard's identifying gestures are always thrusts outward: slaps; punches; kicks; and, in the bar where Arnold is celebrating his inheritance, the sweep of a hand with which he brushes bottles and glasses off the counter into pieces. Arnold's timidity or cowardice (waiting for the police to come, he pulls the covers over his head), his capitulation to the bullies around him, is epitomized by his slouch, a gait or manner of walking that is commensurate with his manner of dying. The body whose muscles are so relaxed that it gives the appearance of drooping or sloping downward (whether he walks or whether he stands) is a short reach to the unconscious body, slumped over the neck of Balthazar (fig. 1.15), and from that to the dead body lying beside the donkey's leg.

But if Arnold is continuously represented by degrees of a single stance—a body that is lowered (and that is flung by Gérard, and falls at his death) to the ground—Marie's gestures and postures have no uniformity. Rather, they reflect her mercurial moods: as, for instance, when she slaps Gérard and a moment later puts her arm around his back and as when she kisses Balthazar and then calmly watches him being kicked. And when she slams the door to walk away from Gérard in the car, it is the bend of her foot to which the

FIGURE 1.15

spectator's eye travels, the camera having isolated that flex as something like a natural force whose impetus propels her return to him. (Marie's fleetingness, and Arnold's death and decomposing, capture flesh in the two states that indicate its range: change and nothingness.)

Although "Apology for Raymond Sebond" begins by defending animals' capacity to communicate with each other and with us, and their ability to reason, it then turns in another direction, devastatingly asserting that reason has no capacity to give knowledge of the world.[34] Montaigne concludes: "Knowledge is nothing else but sensation" (*E* 444).[35] And sensation is not ours alone. Rather, "Hardness, whiteness, depth and bitterness" is knowledge also possessed by the animals (*E* 452).[36] Though Bresson does not comment on those aspects of Montaigne's essay that draw together animal and human forms of communication and knowledge, his notes on cinematography similarly invert the value of reason and sensation: "Stick exclusively to impressions, to sensations. No intervention of intelligence which is foreign to those impressions and sensations" (*N* 42); "It is [the model's] non-rational, nonlogical 'I' that your camera records" (*N* 84). In humans the involuntary has to be excavated from "intelligence itself," as the trainer facetiously dubs Balthazar's potential to impersonate rationality. In the animal, sensation—and the instinct that conducts it—are unobstructed and omnipresent. Thus *Balthazar* registers a fascination with the involuntary as that "language proper to human nature" that is modeled by the animals.

Balthazar, captivated by the handlers of a circus, can be trained to represent a mathematical calculation by tapping his hoof to indicate the solution to a multiplication problem posed by numbers provided by the circus audience and written on a board—as if he were not only computing but also reading. Of course such training only *represents* mathematical ability. Balthazar is not reasoning. He is *performing* a process of reasoning. When he and Arnold recognize each other—Arnold is sitting in the audience, drinking a bottle of alcohol, and, with a show of his teeth, Balthazar recognizes Arnold first—Balthazar refuses to be restrained by the animal trainers. He would prefer to go off with Arnold, the owner who sometimes beats him, than to remain with owners who make him engage in ludicrous tricks. Mathematical reason is a trick that has no meaning—no reality—for the animal. The interest of that (apparently banal) recognition, even its thrill, is that in the complexly different worlds of Montaigne and Bresson, reason is equally a trick—not a ground or a cause, but an explanatory tissue that is fraudulent—for the human equivalents.

Bresson continues to switch back and forth from the depiction of the animal to the depiction of the human, defining one against the other, until not only their features but also their outcomes are rendered inseparable. "She won't come back," Marie's mother proleptically says—a prediction realized in Balthazar's death. The sustained negotiation between his eye and Marie's eyes renders the donkey's death the visualization of a fate that could be the girl's. "A gaze" that is bottomless, "at the same time innocent and cruel perhaps, perhaps sensitive and impassive, good and bad, uninterpretable, unreadable, undecidable, abyssal and secret"—Derrida's rhetorical tour de force for the inexplicability of the animal's eye—in Bresson's film is given a correspondence in Marie's.[37]

Balthazar's "enigma," its oddity, is not therefore that it discovers the "automatism of real life" to penetrate to a "true nature" (*N* 39; the source of Bresson's fidelity to it in all of his films), but rather, specifically, that automatism (Montaigne's language "proper to human nature") links the human to the animal, even seeming to reside on the line between the two species, because the coerciveness of bodily dictates resembles the plight of animals whose governance by such forces remains unparalleled in its extremity.[38] Thus while Bresson generally extols "the power" of "images" to be "other than they are" (*N* 42)—to be "transformed by contact" with unrelated images (*N* 20)—in *Balthazar* the transformation that emerges from the "contact" of unlike images is specifically rendered as a question about a species difference. To put this in the most radical terms suggested by Bresson's film: the human is most fully expressed by a nature that is alien to it. At the same time, unlike the equivalence between the animal and the human announced in *Une femme douce* when a couple visit a natural history museum and one of them exclaims that the vertebrae of the human and the animal are made of the same material, distinct only in being arranged a different way, *Balthazar* can't arrive at such a conclusion, since the involuntary of the human—in distinction to that of the animal—has cruelty (and even criminality) at its foundation.

In fact, murder lingers over the film's events.[39] Because there is no conviction, nothing to anchor the charge, it reads as false with regard to the murder for which the police round up Arnold and Gérard. Rather, it attaches itself amorphously to Gérard's brutal treatment of Marie, as well as to his inventive cruelty to Balthazar (when the donkey won't move, setting his tail on fire); to the unidentified man ready to club Balthazar to death; to the miser who takes away the animal's food while he is eating; to Arnold in his drunken rage; and finally, literally, to the border guard whose bullet kills the donkey.

"Not the guillotine," Arnold says, waking terrified from a dream in which a conviction for a murder carries the death penalty for a crime he personalizes as *his*. But an abstract debate about criminality, which emerges among three men—two artists and a psychologist, traveling on Balthazar and another donkey—to whom Arnold is giving rides for hire ("The criminal may awaken unaware that he's a criminal. . . . Can one be held responsible for a crime one commits involuntarily but forgets out of nervous shock or due to alcohol?") raises speculative questions about the relation between the criminal and the involuntary.[40] In this way criminality is theoretically deliberated among aesthetes and intellectuals, even as it explodes within the film's bursts of cruelty. Yet if the involuntary is linked to cruelty and to criminality, it is not linked to a particular crime, and it is not linked to one rather than to another character. Arnold, the gentle man, and Gérard, the vicious man, are both driven by murderous rage.[41] Just as Bresson treats the human face as equivalent to the limbs, the trunk, the feet—there is no exception for the face that can be counted on—he equally attacks other privileged sites of the individual. For Bresson, the criminal, like the involuntary, is discoverable in everyone.

II

In *The Idiot*, Myshkin—who suffers from seizures, from sadness, and most of all from "strangeness"—is restored to his senses by "the bray of an ass" that suddenly clears his head ("my melancholy passed completely" [*I* 53]).[42] The mysteriousness of the donkey who, heard and then seen, can make one recover one's senses invests Myshkin with rapture of which the ass is the object, because being struck by the ass is immediately equated with knowing how to see things, and then, in a leap, with happiness itself ("You know how to be happy?" [*I* 55], Aglaia asserts in an interrogative that is really a statement).

The ecstasy associated with the ass, the seeing of it as a revering of its beauty that transforms the way everything else is seen, is incorporated into Bresson's (and sometimes Marie's) view of Balthazar, as in the scene in which she garlands, kisses, and then gazes blissfully at the animal. Thus, even though Bresson dissociates Balthazar from the ass in Dostoevsky's novel—that "is not the idea of the film. The idea came, perhaps, visually. . . . The head of a donkey seems to me something admirable"—the very expression "something admirable," echoes Myshkin's "I was . . . extraordinarily pleased with it" (*I* 53), just as the camera's rapturous attention to Balthazar's body echoes the ecstasy that Myshkin both identifies with the ass and disclaims understanding of ("I used to go to bed very happy and get up happier still. But it would be hard to say why" [*I* 55]).[43]

But if the transport occasioned by the animal in Dostoevsky's fiction is voiced through Bresson's film, so is the cruelty. An unparalleled cruelty underscored by its senselessness arises not in *The Idiot* (where cruelty takes human objects) but in *Crime and Punishment*, in Raskolnikov's dream of the "small, skinny, grayish peasant nag" being whipped to death by the drunken Mikolka, who explains himself as follows: "This little runt of a mare breaks my heart—I might as well kill her. . . . I'll whip her to death!"[44] I think Bresson combines these elements—the rapturous love of the donkey in *The Idiot* and the cruelty to the nag in *Crime and Punishment*—in effect establishing rhythms by repeatedly drawing together beauty and cruelty, love and mercilessness, for the beating of the donkey is always in excess of the fact that he is not dutiful.[45]

Moreover, the convergence in Bresson's film of rapturous love and barbarous cruelty strikingly underscores the gratuitousness of both responses—adoring and abusing—that the animal inspires. In Dostoevsky's novel, as in Bresson's film, it is not only the animal's powerlessness—the fact that it can feel pain without inflicting pain—that precipitates cruelty. But also the animal's embodiment (his fully inhabiting his body without resisting the habitation), *un*like our own relation to embodiment, renders his incarnation beautiful (hence inspiring rapture) and, *like* our own embodiment in its inescapability, also renders incarnation terrible (hence the object of human rage). Cruelty erupts as violence against the gleaned kinship of that inescapability: "This little runt of a mare breaks my heart—I might as well kill her."[46] The chains that clank throughout *Balthazar* and bind the animal to fence, post, and stable exteriorize constraint. But a prior constraint, and not only for the animal, is the body itself, which enchains through and through. Moreover, if the animal instigates rapture (because its embodiment is thicker than the human, deeper, it could even be said, purer, hence not conflictual) and violence (because its embodiment exemplifies an imprisonment in flesh analogous to that of the human), that is, if the animal body occasions both an estrangement and a recognition, the latter (the similitude) is underscored in *Balthazar* by Bresson's representation of the human will's subjection to the body's involuntary dictates—a subjection Bresson's film radiates.

At the same time that Bresson draws the animal and human body and eye into relation, he also establishes an auditory correlative in the mysterious exchanges incongruously initiated by a sort of relay between the sound of the donkey's braying and the sound of the andantino in Schubert's Piano Sonata no. 20 in A, D. 959, which the film treats as voices in a dialogue. At the film's beginning, while the credits appear on the screen and prior to any other image, we hear first the Schubert andantino, then the donkey's braying, then again the andantino. This colloquy—the insertion of the braying between the bars of music, first extracted from image and then permitted to introduce and to follow it—conditions the film's viewer to hear the donkey's cry in relation to the music, even over prolonged intervals and even when each sounds independently.[47]

The braying and the Schubert are fully distinct (a cry is distinct from a musical composition) even as each implies the other as an equal element also associated by being nonlinguistically signifying. The equality accorded the cry and the andantino, however subliminally, also pertains to their source, the animal and the human, so that, albeit in a fully inconsequential auditory register, the hierarchy whose distinctions permit the film's cruelty to the animal is transiently leveled. Even though in some sense it is absurd to compare the complexity, the versatility, the genius of the Schubert with the donkey's loud, harsh, doleful cry, the film daringly precipitates this comparison, just as in its privileging of the involuntary over the rational, the gestural over the willed and reasoned, it compels a comparison between human and animal bodies, and, notwithstanding the respective degrees of impenetrability, between human and animal eye. In the braying and the Schubert the essence of the human and the essence of the animal are reduced to sound, as the rhythms established between the animal and the human eye reduce both to scopic presence. In the irrelevance of the human's words in relation to his involuntary movements, Bresson ascribes to him a virtual dumbness, mirrored in the animal's muteness.[48] In the intensities of sound (as in the tactile immediacies of seeing), the animal and the human come together in the film's nondiegetic elements—in the representation of sensation, where indiscriminately for both, Montaigne located "knowledge" of the world (*E* 444). The point of that convergence is not a reductiveness, but rather a mysteriousness—animal embodiment being a touchstone for the mysteriousness of our own embodiment—which, in this film, gazed at, is alternately adored and hated.

I could leave it at that. Bresson's episodic story of the donkey's cruel owners, framed by a religious symbology, is subverted by intensities—the animal eye/ human eyes; the braying and the Schubert; the manifestations of rapture and cruelty toward the animal that Dostoevsky isolates in the ass and the mare and that Bresson rethinks as a complement. But I am inclined to press harder on the congruences I have examined. What are they? One way to think of them is in terms of what Roland Barthes calls "obtuse meaning," which he defines as "a signifier without a signified . . . an *accent* . . . rased of meaning." Obtuse meanings simply come and go. They can be located but not necessarily described because they "do not represent anything." (An obtuse meaning is "outside [articulated] language while nevertheless within interlocution" like the stare of the animals in the zoo.)[49] Of course the convergences I have described are conveyed in shots and sequences; they are assemblages of nonverbal units, hence syntactic. They are not free of story, but nor are they precisely part of it. Rapturous love of the the animal's beauty (Marie gazing at Balthazar) and cruelty (Marie turning away while Gérard kicks the donkey) are treated less as elements of a story that could develop than as elements in a rhythm, which recur and fluctuate much as Gérard and Marie, who chase each other around the donkey, run first one way and then the other until it can no longer be discerned who is chasing whom. In being what Philippe Lacoue-Labarthe calls "pre-specular . . . even pre-figural . . . ," such rhythms are also "finally untheorizable" because, since rhythm is "improvised and momentaneous," it "has no organic consistency," but is rather constellated by oscillations and inbetweenness.[50]

Moreover, although the rhythmic elements in *Balthazar* contrast with the depictive or narrative elements—it is not in Sergei Eisenstein's understanding of that relation. For, although Eisenstein describes montage in terms of "*optical counterpoint*," opposition, and even "collision" in which rhythmic and depictive elements are not only juxtaposed but are also "inevitably in conflict," this dialectical sense dissolves in Eisenstein's explicit definition of rhythm as "the ultimate means of generalising about a theme, as being the very image of the internal dynamics of its content."[51] In such a formulation rhythmic elements are re-understood as *constituting* the depictive elements—"the very image of [their] internal dynamics"—rather than as sustaining the frictive relation to the narrative that Eisenstein articulates elsewhere.[52] In distinction, for Bresson the "omnipotence of rhythms" plays no collaborative role; rather, if there is a primacy, it is narrative that the cinematographer is enjoined to subordinate, as when Bresson imposes this prescription: "Bend content to form and sense to rhythm" (*N* 68). (In fact, image and sound "must not support each other" but "work each in turn through *a sort of relay*" [*N* 62], while sound itself—for instance, the "noise of a door opening"—exists purely "for the sake of rhythm" [*N* 52].) This virtual dissociation of the narrative and the rhythmic constitutes one aspect of *Balthazar*'s strangeness. In *Balthazar* the rhythmic element that fascinates resides, it is made to seem, outside of, or detached from, the narrative element and cannot be assimilated to its interests or—be these associated with provincial or Christological figures—to its stories. It is the perverse and rigorous strangeness of *Balthazar* to place side by side figuration that implies the Christian narrative and rhythmic elements that remain like hard insoluble facts, outside of, and irreducible to, its mediation. To amplify, or rather complement, my earlier remarks: it is as if the redemptive story had not yet emerged, or as if it had emerged but could not become intelligible, as if it remained unclear how to get from a story of law and debt to a story of love and how to avert a story of love and beauty from becoming a story of cruelty. In less sweeping terms: Balthazar does not belong to the Old Testament world of law and debt. That is why he has to be kicked. He is beautiful, not dutiful. He has no sense of obligation. But he also does not belong to the New Testament world where his ordeal could be defined in terms of martyrdom under cruel provocation. Rather, the film is captivated by something that might more dimly be defined in terms of patient sentience, as it continuously holds up the bottomless gaze of that cool impassivity.

Balthazar's eye is like a Buddha eye, or like a neutral camera eye, or, in being just the donkey's eye, like any enigmatic animal eye. We can't penetrate that eye. Thus the eye finally becomes a figure for a sentience that is illegible—an unreadability also perceptible in relation to the body itself, whose surface of flesh reveals something irremediably visible and irremediably hidden. (In putting it like this, I am proposing a genesis for the cruelty that arises in relation to the experience of one's own body when one regards another's, even though in *Balthazar* it is the other's body, not one's own, that is cruelty's recipient. That genesis would include the half-implicit, if phantasmatic, sense that what enrages about the body, as about the eye, is its illegibility, though for matter to be intelligible would be for matter not to be what it is.) Human cruelty in relation to that mute sentience takes not only the animal as its object, but also its human counterpart. When Gérard, at the bar celebrating Arnold's inheritance, looks at Arnold's indecipherable eyes (fig. 1.16), he first tries to provoke him: "Not breaking anything? Not going mad? Drink up, you retard! Jerk, moron, leech," he continues, and then, swept into a fury at eyes

FIGURE 1.16

that, like the donkey's, he can't read, he systematically and savagely begins to break all the bottles and glasses in the bar—the first in a series of devastating acts of destruction that culminate in Arnold's death. Such cruelty is outside any narrative impetus that could instigate it and equally outside any story that could compensate for it.

Although it may be counterintuitive to argue that representation does not occupy a significant role in Bresson's film, even while rhythm, which is central, escapes figuration—for these marginalizations and evasions would seem to leave the film inhabited by nothing—my claims are consistent with Bresson's description of cinematography as "the art, with images, of *representing* nothing" (*N* 116). Bresson's passionate accounts of cinematography redefine filmic interest outside of representation. Or they aim to do so ("Ideally, nothing should be shown, but that's impossible").[53] They redefine it also outside of significance ("See your film as a combination of lines and of volumes in movement apart from what it represents and signifies" [*N* 90]). What replaces representation and significance is the intensity that rhythm makes durable, incarnating itself most breathtakingly, because most fundamentally (as with the dying girl) in a *fort-da* movement between sentience and its extinction—embodiments free of story, which, in his other films, too, as I now indicate, Bresson never stopped representing as fully transporting objects of attention.

At the beginning of *Lancelot of the Lake* we are shown a horse's eye so close up that we can see the sheen of light on the pupil and the red capillaries against the whites, while at the film's end, near a pile of armored men, another horse

FIGURE 1.17

FIGURE 1.18

(Lancelot's), pierced by an arrow above the eye, lies dying. In the movement of the horse's eye (in the reflected image on the pupil, in the quiver of the lashes), the first eye depicts pure unstoried sentience, while at the film's end, the dull eye (from which light has all but been occluded), then the closed eye, depicts its extinction (figs. 1.17, 1.18).[54] When in the film's final moments Lancelot, in his death throes, leans against the arrow obtruding from his horse's flesh, bending and twisting it (the horse is still alive) as, in half-conscious lurchings, he struggles to stand, so powerfully do we experience the sentience of the horse—but not of the man—that although both are dying, it is the *horse's* presumed sensation that arouses the spectator's horror, since it is the horse, and not the man, whose body seems penetrable, even as the meaning of the scene (which contains the fleeting detail I have dwelled on) is not this comparison.

In *Mouchette* a young girl, to drown herself, rolls down a hill toward a lake. She is not initially successful, however, her body coming to a stop twice before, in the third try, she drowns. Mouchette's matter-of-fact commitment to her goal—she is undeterred by the initial failures and undisturbed by any sadness that might change her mind—contributes to the singularity of the recurrent attempts, which are as compelling as any story that precedes them. Questions about what motivates the determination with which the girl ensures her fate are subsumed by the rhythm in which the body, set into motion, rolls down the hill. The astonishment of that rhythm arises from the way in which a purpose so deliberated, so fully willed, could become easy, even effortless, a force that Mouchette sets into motion but that, no longer hers, sweeps her up in its momentum. Thus, a rhythm is established between something willed and something involuntary, between an intention that holds the girl in its thrall, and—in the pull of gravity—a release and freedom from it. Similarly, in *Lancelot* a rhythm is established between the contrasting images of the horse's eye—powerful not in relation to a significance but rather in relation to the optic of another monocular, impersonal eye, the camera's, which makes visible/visceral the quick involuntary movements of the horse's pupil, lashes, eyelid (and then their quiescence), in which, juxtaposed, we chillingly see the absolute distinction between sentience and its negation.

And when Arnold falls off Balthazar and lies dead with his head by the donkey's leg, which visibly pulses with life, the thrill of this moment is something like a rhyme—one of Bresson's master rhymes—between the animal body that is sentient and the human body that has relinquished sentience, a contrast also visible in *Procès de Jeanne d'Arc* when the spaniel runs toward Joan who, tied to the stake, is consumed by flame. In his passionate attention to the transfiguring difference between sentience and its extinction—the latter of which only the animal never seeks—Bresson turns a banality into a mystery.

At the same time that the film delivers the spectator to a crushing view of cruelty, it is suffused by the beauty of Bresson's cinematography. Thus the degradation in *Balthazar* constituted by the unremitting brutality is rhythmically brought together with the beauty captured by the camera, by its rapturous attention to animal and human eyes and the embodiments of which they are synecdochic. Or rather: what the camera reveals is not beauty but sublimity, when the ordinary of flesh is astonishingly perceived as marvelous. In *Balthazar* the animal eye, the animal flesh, the sentience of the animal (a mirror almost for human sentience seen purely) are transfigured by being revealed in their commonplace radiance, but only to the film's spectator. The characters remain oblivious of it. In *The Idiot*, a novel as chaotic and dark as

Bresson's *Balthazar*, the atheist Ippolit plans his own suicide, explaining his logic thus: "I could not go on living a life which was taking such strange, humiliating forms" (*I* 398). Analogously, Bresson, when asked how he regarded the suicides in his films, cryptically responded: "For myself, there is something which makes suicide possible—not even possible but absolutely necessary: it is . . . the feeling of void which is impossible to bear. . . . There is not one kind of suicide that I could not agree with."[55] But if unredeemed materialism—incarnation from which no supernatural relations can free one—compels despair and rationalizes suicide, the camera's vision is otherwise.

The camera's vision is otherwise not because of its immediacy but because of its access to a real that is not our real, an access conferred by automaticity that indifferently catches by chance (*hasard*) what eludes the discriminating eye.[56] But more: for Bresson's insistence on "two sorts of real: (1) the crude real recorded by the camera; and (2) what we call real and see deformed by our memory and some wrong reckonings"—poses a "problem. To make what you see be seen, through the intermediary of a machine that does not see it as you see it."[57] In this way the mechanical eye provides something like a transport, even an ecstasis born of automaticity, which opens to a space outside our "wrong reckonings." The camera's mechanical eye and the materiality that is Bresson's subject subvert not simply the model's intentions but also the cinematographer's. Thus of the donkey, he remarks:

> [I did not want] a performing donkey. . . . I wanted that animal to be, even as an animal, crude matter. . . . So I took a donkey that knew how to do absolutely nothing. Not even how to pull a cart. I even had a great deal of difficulty getting him to pull the cart in the film. In fact everything that I believed that he would give me, he refused me, and everything that I believed he would refuse me . . . he gave me. Pull a cart, for example, one says to oneself: a donkey will do that. Well, not at all! . . . During the last scene, that of the death of the donkey . . . I had enormous difficulty to get the donkey to do what . . . I wanted him to do. And he did it only once, but in the end, he did it. Only, I had to provoke him to do it, in another way than the one I had thought about. In the film that is situated at the moment when the donkey hears the bells and pricks up his ears. It was by catching something at the last moment that things worked: he had the reaction that was necessary. He did it only once, but it was marvelous. That is the kind of joy that filming sometimes gives you! One is in terrible difficulties, and, all at once, the miracle occurs.[58]

The marvelous of *Balthazar* is inseparable from *hasard*, from a real outside of intelligence and thought—a real we do not dictate, do not expect, and do not ourselves directly see. The camera catches spontaneous relations, sounds, and images that exert pressure on each other—the Schubert and the braying;

animal eye and human eyes; and what such congruences (most expansively) epitomize: the splendor of undiscriminated objects whose dignity Arnold recognizes when, drunk, he formally bids farewell to road-marker, donkey, and telegraph pole before falling to his death. If Bresson surprisingly asserts of *Balthazar*, "This humanity that you find so bleak I don't see that it's any less loveable than a humanity that's less dark," this is because, notwithstanding a judgment like Ippolit's—"I could not go on living a life which was taking such strange, humiliating forms"—the mechanical eye divines a mystery: life inimitably yet innocently given, outside of assessment and design ("all at once, the miracle occurs"), to which the discerning human eye is blind.[59]

2

“Outside Christ”: Dostoevsky’s Joy

In *Crime and Punishment* Raskolnikov dreams of “the small, skinny grayish peasant nag” being whipped to death by the peasant Mikolka, as he shouts: “It’s my goods!”[1] What is astonishing about the dream is that Raskolnikov’s wild sorrow at the mare’s suffering (“the poor boy is beside himself. . . . in a frenzy [he] flies at Mikolka with his little fists” [*CP* 58]) immediately transforms itself when he awakens into a question about whether *he* will inflict suffering as callously as Mikolka did (“can it be that I will really take an axe and hit her on the head and smash her skull . . . ?” [*CP* 59]), even as it ultimately hardens into a *commitment* to inflict suffering. For if the intention to murder the crone precedes Raskolnikov’s dream, it is inexplicably strengthened by the dream whose anguish (it could be supposed) might impede it. What the boy imbibes from the mare is torment (“there is such strain, such strain in his chest” [*CP* 59]), from which—axing the old crone—the man will free himself. Or, rather, for an “ordinary” (*CP* 259) person there is one kind of suffering if he has a conscience and obeys laws (*CP* 264), while there is another kind of suffering for “true geniuses—the ones who are granted the right to put a knife into others” (*CP* 264).

A somewhat different economy underscores Liza’s psychology—the crippled girl, the “little demon”[2] in *The Brothers Karamazov*—who confesses to Aloysha:

> “I have a book here, I read in it . . . that a Jew first cut off all the fingers of a four-year-old boy, and then crucified him on the wall, nailed him with nails and crucified him, and then said at his trial that the boy died quickly, in four hours. . . . Sometimes I imagine that it was I who crucified him. He hangs

> there moaning, and I sit down facing him, eating pineapple compote. I like pineapple compote very much. Do you?" (*BK* 583–84)

Liza's indifference to others' suffering can be distinguished from Raskolnikov's because, as expressed in her flamboyant image, she takes pleasure in torment rather than being excruciated by it, and because she loves only to read and dream about it. (Her voyeuristic sadism is not equivalent to Raskolnikov's murderous cruelty, which, devoid of pleasure, is not sadism.) The enjoyment she derives from reading about torture is augmented and heightened by the enjoyment she derives from her exuberant taste for pineapple compote. Differently understood: the boy's suffering is so delicious for Liza that it is synaesthetically indistinguishable from the pleasure of a sweet. Yet if Liza revels in extravagant expressions of guilt (unlike Raskolnikov who disclaims guilt), when she qualifies the statement "people love crime" (*BK* 582) by adding, "I'm the first to love it" (*BK* 583), she construes her fascination, if not her exhibitionism, as ordinary. Such examples of two different forms of an economy in which to inflict or enjoy another's suffering is implicitly to avert, or to heighten, one's own suffering, infuse Dostoevsky's novels.[3]

And there is an inverse—a salvific—side to this convertibility best expounded by Porfiry Petrovitch, the prosecutor in Fyodor Dostoevsky's *Crime and Punishment*. "Suffering . . . is a great thing," he tells Raskolnikov: "don't look at me, fat as I am, that's no matter, but I do know—don't laugh at this—that there is an idea in suffering" (*CP* 461). The idea Porfiry has in mind is vehicular. Suffering "will carry you straight to shore and set you on your feet" (*CP* 460). In such a conception suffering is a means of passage. Elsewhere suffering is currency: "Happiness is bought by suffering. . . . It is possible to pay for it by years of suffering."[4] In *The Brothers Karamazov* suffering that is a vehicle, a form of payment, a condition required for a compensation is a Christian idea, powerfully condensed in "Cana of Galilee" when Alyosha falls asleep next to the Elder Zosima's corpse and dreams of a wedding where water is made into wine (*BK* 359–62); in Dimitri's resolve to go to prison for "the wee one" (*BK* 507–8); in Zhuchka's, the dog's, rebirth as Perezvon (*BK* 544); in the novel's theoretical chapters rigorously balanced to counter the pain endured by children with the enduring task of "active love" (*BK* 56).

In distinction to these examples, in the following pages I examine forms of suffering and joy that do not participate in the economic exchanges that substitute suffering for joy, someone else's suffering for one's own joy (or, as in the violence of masochism, for a more intense and pleasurable form of one's own suffering). I am interested in asking how ideas of suffering and joy that are not based on an exchange economy, and that sometimes even seem aneconomic, are shaped in Dostoevsky's novels, joy being the more remarkable of the two phenomena by virtue of its scarcity.[5] One such example of a joy that is not measured emerges in Myshkin's story of a peasant woman who devotedly crosses herself the first time she sees her infant smile, explaining "God has just such gladness every time he sees from heaven that a sinner is praying to Him with all his heart, as a mother has when she sees the first smile on her baby's face."[6] Yet the bounty of gladness in this religious fable—from which Myshkin deduces "the essence of Christianity" (*I* 213)—also differs from the instances of joy I examine in the following pages, which are dissociated from any doctrinal exemplification.

In *The Idiot* and in *Demons* (novels on which I focus), I mean to distinguish joy from happiness.[7] Happiness is a region Dostoevsky's characters, who have a thirst only for states at the limit, rarely inhabit. Joy, by contrast to happiness, which implies good luck that issues from happenstance, is eschatological, arising in a disclosure of the immanent end of a present order, as the experience of immediacy provoked by a limit. Happiness follows social success (another form of chance), but joy requires the awakening to a reality that, though perpetually present, is only suddenly *perceived* as extraordinary—as if it were an elsewhere, a transcendental contact—and is always a shock. From the vantage of joy, the answer to the questions, is the manifestation of reality perceived as extraordinary actually extraordinary? is every single thing extraordinary? is yes. In these novels, joy is sharp, distilled, and instantaneous, while happiness suffuses being as a sensation that is or could be protracted. In distinction to *Crime and Punishment* and *The Brothers Karamazov*, in *The Idiot* and *Demons* joy is "here eternal";[8] "it is nothing earthly; not that it's heavenly" (*D* 590)—a natural phenomenon perceived in astonishment, a marvelous more inclusive than the divine, whose ground is wonder without recourse to theology.

The representations I consider have an agnostic, atheistic, and sometimes even indifferent relation to Christianity, and this is the case even though *The Idiot*, in particular, recurs to a Christian image (Holbein's *The Body of the Dead Christ in the Tomb*) and to a text appropriated by Christianity (the Apocalypse). No one would dispute Dostoevsky's Orthodox Christianity. But "the haphazardness of the action," which Joseph Frank observes in *The Idiot*—in his characterization the novel "most difficult to see in any unified perspective," implicit, for instance, in "the contradictory imperatives of [Prince Myshkin's] apocalyptic aspirations and his earthly limitations"[9]—radiates through the novel, touching all its aspects, including certain representations of joy and suffering that contest the Christian context, and even break free of it. In the following pages I claim these passages are not merely foils for the values of Christian love and religious faith, but rather must be examined as independent strains in Dostoevsky's writing. Therefore I shall be arguing for a heterogeneity in Dostoevsky's representations and stressing the disjointed strains in his thinking. In doing so, I take Hannah Arendt's discussion of Augustine as a model, when in *Love and Saint Augustine* she explains how philosophical ideas of late Antiquity were not excised from Augustine's thinking when he became a Christian; rather, "Neoplatonic rudiments, though hidden, remain active in each set of Christian problems, peculiarly transforming them (even concealing them) from a purely Christian point of view."[10] Analogous contradictions in Dostoevsky's writing have long been acknowledged, first by Dostoevsky himself—in the notion that the atheist is one step away from the believer—even as the conceptual tensions that run through his work have been smoothed over. Although the passages I consider may move through Christ to get outside His purview, I argue that we should take the idea of an "outside" seriously. Its formulation is Dostoevsky's. "If someone proved to me that Christ is outside the truth, and that *in reality*, the truth were outside of Christ," he famously wrote, "then I would prefer to remain with Christ rather than with the truth."[11] *Crime and Punishment* and *The Brothers Karamazov* attest to this preference. An alchemy in which suffering and joy first combine and then reduce to leave salvific joy the strange remainder is the story of *The Brothers Karamazov*. In *The Idiot* and *Demons*, where there is no linkage between torture and rapture, Dostoevsky's allegiance is otherwise—joy being discoverable not in an elsewhere but rather in a here and an inherence, not in what endures but in what could not do so, not in something transformed, but in common objects so fully present that their truth is plain, even to God-tormented characters like Kirillov and Ippolit, a truth often realized in an awakening to the death sentence.

In *The Idiot* Dostoevsky is obsessed with representing different experiences of the death sentence, because when death is imminent time suddenly stops, and joy, the absorption in immediate experience, ruptures the fabric of unconscious life with the thrill of awareness. In that moment of awakening, in which the past is "no more" and the future is "not yet" (Arendt's distinction),[12] the pure present of no time and no space (which also means all time and all space) unfolds or, more precisely, is manifest as unimaginably long, yet nothing from a temporal perspective. Such a paradox of infinity is of course at the center of Christian eschatology (the end of time—eternity—being conventionally understood as time without end). But as discussed in section I it is differently understood at the heart of Dostoevsky's non-Christian representations of earthly joy: when life to which a character has been inattentive is identified as immanent—as Life—that intimacy shatters oblivion, and time suddenly stops. Implicit in such a present, as represented by Dostoevsky, is the discovery that, if before we exist we are nothing, and afterwards nothing, too, there is an existence that goes on all the time, which is also ours. While being is only perceptible in the suspension of time,[13] nonbeing is associated with duration that is endless, with a negative infinite: not everlasting joy but everlasting doom, with suffering that arises in time that can't be put to an end, and in which nothing can properly be identified (exemplified by passages examined in section II). As discussed in section III, in *The Idiot* Dostoevsky represents these perspectives through the atheist Ippolit, whose genius lies in his capacity to inhabit both perceptions. In section IV I suggest that if *The Idiot* is a failed novel (the conventional verdict), it might be because these episodic expressions of suffering and joy are estranged from the novel's plot and characters, whom they inhabit impersonally; rather, they reside as insets in the novel's expressive fragments, and, with the exception of the Ippolit interlude, are essentially lost to view after Myshkin's first seizure. In fact, when joy reemerges it is as a topic—not a manifestation—toward the novel's conclusion, during the Epanchin party, where it is mechanically given expression by Myshkin in something like a patter ("can one really be unhappy? Oh, what does my grief, what does my sorrow matter if I can be happy? . . . I don't know how one can walk by a tree and not be happy at the sight of it. . . . Look at God's sunrise! Look at the grass, how it grows" [*I* 537]), whose banality horrifies, even before he falls into an epileptic stupor, for in *The Idiot,* as in *Demons,* joy, not Christian, is also not social.

I

"You know how to be happy?" (*I* 55), Aglaia exclaims to Myshkin incredulously at the beginning of *The Idiot* after she has elicited a reply to her request that he recount to the Epanchin family his first impression of Switzerland. Myshkin prefaces his response by recalling the illness whose confusion clouded his mind: "I was all the while lost in wonder and uneasiness. What affected me most was that everything was *strange.* . . . I was crushed by the strangeness of it" (*I* 52–53).[14] What shocks Myshkin to his senses—so he can have an impression of Switzerland—and brightens his mind (a state subsequently understood as a recovery that involves knowing "how to see things" [*I* 54], which could be called joy) is "the bray of an ass" (*I* 53). While the ass has specific properties whose contemplation are conducive to equanimity ("I understood at once what a useful creature it was—industrious, strong, patient, cheap, long-suffering" [*I* 53]), it is also a random creature whose harsh, indecipherable sound draws Myshkin to the animal with a fascination indistinguishable from appreciation. Hearing becomes so inseparable from valuing that the donkey's rude cry can no longer be extricated from wonder ("I was immensely struck with the ass, and for some reason extraordinarily pleased with it" [*I* 53]). The mix that makes for joy—sentience, even absorption indistinguishable from cherishing the object that compels attention—transforms the ass into a conduit for how to hear and see other things: "And so, through the ass, all Switzerland began to attract me, so that my melancholy passed completely" (*I* 53). If it is impossible to specify what aspect of the ass occasions joy and what aspect of the world as seen "through the ass" (*I* 53), seen as rapturously as the ass is seen, intensifies it ("every day became precious to me. . . . I used to go to bed very happy and get up happier still. But it would be hard to say why" [*I* 55]), for unlike happiness, which is explicable in relation to the fortunes of the social world, joy can't be reasoned or explained, it as inexplicably disappears. When it does, Myshkin abandons his interest in the ass; in Switzerland; in any perceptible region. Rather he comes to pine for "a new life" (*I* 55) at the limit "where sky and earth meet" (*I* 55), for a place analogized to "Naples" (*I* 55) but beyond the experienced world. Yet although the world is vast, it has no elsewhere.

For the prisoner in Myshkin's story of the man about to be executed, joy is differently precipitated by the threat of a death sentence, which gives onto a true limit—an eschatology that could not be banished by any dreams or imagining. Just as Myshkin experiences the ass in an otherworldly light (that is why the Epanchins laugh at him), but an otherworldly light that electrifies his recognition of the actual astonishments of the ass, so the prisoner's perceptions before the eternity of the death sentence are stunning not because they drive away the ordinary, but because they compel its recognition with the same rapt attention as if it were an elsewhere:

> "He had only five minutes more to live. He told me that those five minutes seemed to him an infinite time, a vast wealth; he felt that he had so many lives left in those five minutes that there was no need yet to think of the last moment, so much so that he divided his time up. He set aside time to take leave of his comrades, two minutes for that; then he kept another two minutes to think for the last time; and then a minute to look about him for the last time. He remembered very well having divided his time like that. He was dying at twenty-seven, strong and healthy. As he took leave of his comrades, he remembered asking one of them a somewhat irrelevant question and being particularly interested in the answer. Then when he had said goodbye, the two minutes came that he had set apart for *thinking* to himself. He knew beforehand what he would think about. He wanted to realise as quickly and clearly as

> possible how it could be that now he existed and was living and in three minutes he would be *something*—someone or something. But what? Where? He meant to decide all that in those two minutes! Not far off there was a church, and the gilt roof was glittering in the bright sunshine. He remembered that he stared very persistently at that roof and the light flashing from it; he could not tear himself away from the light. It seemed to him that those rays were his new nature and that in three minutes he would somehow melt into them. . . . nothing was so dreadful at that time as the continual thought, 'What if I were not to die! What if I could go back to life—what eternity! And it would all be mine! I would turn every minute into an age; I would lose nothing, I would count every minute as it passed, I would not waste one!' " (*I* 57)

What is alien about these moments is their sufficiency—so that, for instance, the man could be absorbed in the answer to the "irrelevant" question. In the collapse of the disparity between the idea of irrelevance and the idea of interest, Dostoevsky dramatizes the dislodging of a perspective dulled by discriminations, irrelevance being a category that has no meaning in the prisoner's circumstances. The prisoner's division of time into moments is a distribution of attention into what is intuitively understood as valuable: taking leave of comrades, thinking, and looking. Dwelling within the moments gives them their plenitude, even as the brevity of the time allotted would seem to prohibit dwelling, determining ("the two minutes . . . that he had set apart for *thinking* to himself" [*I* 57]), or intending ("He knew beforehand what he would think about. . . . He meant to decide" [*I* 57]). That thinking and intending—which are transitory—could even be considered states in which it is possible to dwell, insists on the depth of the man's experience, his capacity to sink into what is apparently without dimension, even as the urgency of his sense of time ("He wanted to realise as quickly and clearly as possible" [*I* 57]) would seem to deny the luxury of such penetration. In this way the passage aggregates temporal states that preclude each other, repeatedly compacting duration and no more duration. Moreover, although the man resides within the space of the moments that remain to him, this does not preclude his capacity to wonder what being might become when he can no longer identify it as his own ("he would be *something* . . . . But what?" [*I* 57]). Thus the capacity to value loving, thinking, looking is perfectly continuous with—might even be the precondition for—the relinquishing of those human attributes in an identification with a nature that can't be recognized as his: "those rays were his new nature" (*I* 57).

The man has lamented the gratuitousness of his discovery ("What if I were not to die! What if I could go back to life—what eternity! . . . I would count every minute as it passed" [*I* 57]), but when he is suddenly reprieved, he can't sustain his attention, as with Myshkin's penetrative vision of the ass, which fades. Although the death sentence tears the prisoner out of his daze by intoxicating him with the reality before him, the moment his life is assured of duration, immanence has no endurance. He is restored to an obtuseness precipitated by the illusion that there is no longer anything immediately necessary for him to see or feel. "So it seems it's impossible really to live 'counting each moment,'" Alexandra, one of the Epanchin sisters, concludes; "For some reason it's impossible" (*I* 58).

While the joy Myshkin experiences when he awakens from madness vivifies ordinary objects, and while the prisoner's joy inheres in plumbing—and in dispelling—the very idea of the ordinary, in the aura that precedes Myshkin's epileptic seizure, no discriminations remain to be dispelled because nothing divides the experience of being from a totality. Thus the following passage calls to mind an ecstasis more selfless than Myshkin's fellow-feeling for the ass, and more extensive, if more fleeting, than "rays" of light understood to be the prisoner's "new nature" (*I* 57):

> he always had one minute just before the epileptic fit . . . when suddenly in the midst of sadness, spiritual darkness and oppression, there seemed at moments a flash of light in his brain, and with extraordinary impetus all his vital forces began working at their highest tension. The sense of life, the consciousness of self, were multiplied ten times at these moments which passed like a flash of lightning. His mind and his heart were flooded with extraordinary light; all his uneasiness, all his doubts, all his anxieties were relieved at once; they were all merged in a lofty calm, full of serene, harmonious joy and hope. . . . Thinking of that moment later. . . . he often said to himself that all these gleams and flashes of the highest sensation of life and self-consciousness, and therefore also of the highest form of existence, were nothing but disease . . . and if so, it was not at all the highest form of being, but on the contrary must be reckoned the lowest. And yet he came at last to an extremely paradoxical conclusion. "What if it is disease? . . . What does it matter that it is an abnormal intensity, if the result . . . turns out to be the acme of harmony and beauty, and gives a feeling, unknown and undivined till then, of completeness, of proportion, of reconciliation, and of ecstatic devotional merging in the highest synthesis of life? . . . Yes, for this moment one might give one's whole life!" . . . "At that moment," as he told Rogozhin one day . . . "I seem somehow to understand the extraordinary saying that *there shall be no more time*. Probably," he added smiling, "this is the very second which was not long enough for the water to be spilt out of Mahomet's pitcher, though the epileptic prophet had time to gaze at all the habitations of Allah." (*I* 218–19)

The passage's uncontingent joy, joy without an object—elemented of "tension" and "lofty calm" (*I* 218); a heightened "consciousness of self" (*I* 218) and its simultaneous dissipation ("merging" [*I* 218]); sudden bursts of light nonetheless contributive to the "proportion" (*I* 218) and order that its intense flashes would seem to destroy—culminates in a figure that temporalizes these paradoxes, and that underscores the fact that time falling away can only be represented through temporal marks.[15] In Richard Pevear's gloss of the legend "Muhammad was awakened one night by the archangel Gabriel, who in the process brushed against a jug of water with his wing. Muhammad then traveled to Jerusalem, from there rose into heaven where he spoke with angels, prophets, and Allah, visited the fiery Gehenna, and came back in time to keep the jug from spilling" (*D* 731).

The "*no more time*" (*I* 219) that Myshkin analogizes to the fraction of a second—the twinkling of an eye—in which the water does not spill, is no more time that can be counted, not even as the prisoner, whose counting is a savoring, counts it; that is, no more division of one part of an experience from another. Not counting and also not absorbed into a vision that dissipates counting by a singular focus (the "ass" [*I* 53]), which can be expanded to another singularity ("Switzerland" [*I* 53]), but which cannot be sustained, the manifestation of joy before the fit does not contain its own negation or undoing. And this is true although when the blissful moments end, Myshkin is harrowingly plunged into the darkness of the epileptic seizure (even leading, when he recovers, to the devastating question of whether the sensation of joy is nothing but disease). For the final emblem that expresses joy—"not long enough for the water to be spilt out of Mahomet's pitcher . . . time to gaze at all the habitations of Allah" (*I* 219)—in its frictive conjunction of the instant and the apparently infinite or, in any case, the inclusive ("all the habitations"), is not comprehensible in terms of time, being rather as conceptually illegible as the no more time of the Apocalypse (Revelation 10:6) to which Myshkin implicitly compares it, and of which it is a rewriting. Joy ends for Myshkin just before the epileptic "fit" (*I* 218), but perhaps it does not end for Mahomet. For both, the obliteration of time is implicitly made inseparable from something like a prophetic vision of "undivined . . . completeness" (*I* 218) revealed in domestic circumstances at the brush of an angel's wing.

In *Demons*, where Kirillov rewrites the same Apocalypse passage, his exegesis produces not only a phenomenological account of the joy he is expounding, but also something like its logic. Thus when Stavrogin asks the atheist Kirillov, "You've started believing in the future eternal life?" Kirillov corrects him: "No, not future eternal, but here eternal. There are moments, you reach moments, and time suddenly stops" (*D* 236). Time made gratuitous because of the diffusion of joy will ultimately disappear for everyone. Thus Kirillov predicts: "When all mankind attains happiness, time will be no more, because there's no need" (*D* 236–37). In a crude literalization that expresses his skepticism at the improbability of time's disappearance, Stavrogin bluntly inquires:

> "And where are they going to hide it?"
>
> "Nowhere. Time isn't an object, it's an idea. It will die out in the mind. . . ."
>
> "You seem to be very happy, Kirillov."
>
> "Yes, very happy," the latter replied, as if making the most ordinary reply.
>
> "But you were upset still so recently, angry with Liputin?"
>
> ". . . Then I didn't know I was happy yet. Have you seen a leaf, a leaf from a tree?"
>
> "I have."
>
> "I saw one recently, a yellow one, with some green, decayed on the edges. Blown about by the wind. When I was ten years old, I'd close my eyes on purpose, in winter, and imagine a leaf—green, bright, with veins, and the sun shining. I'd open my eyes and not believe it, because it was so good, then I'd close them again."
>
> "What's that, an allegory?"
>
> "N-no . . . why? Not an allegory, simply a leaf, one leaf. A leaf is good. Everything is good."
>
> "Everything?"
>
> "Everything. Man is unhappy because he doesn't know he's happy; only because of that. It's everything, everything! Whoever learns will at once immediately become happy, that same moment . . ."
>
> "And if someone dies of hunger, or someone offends and dishonors the girl—is that good?"
>
> "Good. And if someone's head gets smashed in for the child's sake, that's good too; and if it doesn't get smashed in, that's good, too. Everything is good, everything. For all those who know that everything is good. If they knew it was good with them, it would be good with them, but as long as they don't know it's good with them, it will not be good with them. That's the whole thought, the whole, there isn't any more!" (*D* 237–38)

Kirillov's ecstasy (joy rather than happiness), because outside of time, indifferent to circumstance, depends on a way of thinking about what is happening—"Everything is good . . . . For all those who know that everything is good" (*D* 237–38)—rather than on what is happening. (In this sense, joy is an extravagant indifference to violence that is *itself* a violence, since catastrophe is a fate before which joy radiates imperviousness: "And if someone's head gets smashed in . . . that's good, too!" [*D* 237].) The idea of knowing as an agreement with a present state of affairs is implicitly its own value, and is meant to rectify a habitual if tacit feeling that immediately penetrates to the unsatisfactoriness of every moment—loosely conceived as a moment of suffering—which some other moment will cure or recompense. Supposing the absolute adequacy, the goodness, of everything that occurs renders experience timeless, there being nothing outside of the moment that would need to compensate for its insufficiency. Because there is no need for compensation, there is "no need" (*D* 237) for time (which "suddenly stops" [*D* 236]) when plenitude is everywhere perceptible. But perception is not quite the right word for the determination which Kirillov calls "know[ing]" (*D* 237), which is a judgment inseparable from a perception of brute facts. Moreover, because goodness arises from a general state of consent, more comprehensive than a particular feeling, Kirillov can explain how he could have been "upset" with Liputin while also being "happy" (*D* 237).

Of course one way to understand how Kirillov can be "upset" and also "very happy" is to see being "upset" as existing in a past that happiness succeeds. But in Kirillov's ambiguous tense ("didn't know I was happy yet" [*D* 237]), happiness also refers to a past in which being "upset" would not contradict (if one knew of it) being "very happy." That is, if happiness were a feeling cultivated in relation to an understanding that "everything is good," Kirillov's "didn't know I was happy yet" might describe not only a shift of emotion from being "upset" to being "happy" but also a more fundamental change from regarding the first feeling (being "upset") as important to regarding it as irrelevant, a correction on which what I am calling joy is based. Thus Kirillov's assent is capacious because it hospitably contains the very elements—being "upset," being "happy"—that would seem to render it incoherent. Yet if Kirillov's perception of a happiness so rapturous that, in its transport, it must be called joy is meant to vanquish being upset (if it is meant to dispute the habitual error of regarding all moments as ones of suffering), one could say it makes a new mistake in supposing *no* moments are ones of suffering—even as to make such an objection is to miss the extremity of Kirillov's claim that joy can be what it is ("here eternal" [*D* 236]) only because "*everything* is good" (italics mine).[16] The outrageousness of the claim (its radical logic) renders *is dead* ("if someone dies . . . if someone's head gets smashed in" [*D* 237]) compatible with "is good." There is, perhaps, in addition, a half-implicit sense that time stopped by bliss and time stopped by death could even coincide. That of course is the real stretch, for if "is good" also applies, at the outside limit, to the speaker's *am dead* (which one would have thought required consciousness as its ground), as well as to the prisoner's *will be dead*, joy is constructed as an experience to which death is no impediment.

Although it might initially look as if the examples of joy I have been considering are fundamentally unrelated, they are not, since being "extraordinarily pleased" (*I* 53) with the ass is a condensation of the idea that "everything is good" (*D* 237). Thus Myshkin, caught up in the wealth of that singular vision, sees it diffused everywhere: "I used to go to bed very happy and get up happier still. But it would be hard to say why" (*I* 55). The insufficiency of any explanation for joy, which is always in excess of the conditions that could generate it (the ass) or to which it randomly attaches (going to sleep, waking up), is perilously close to Kirillov's claim that goodness (and the joy that its recognition instigates) is, in principle, indifferent to the sorrowful conditions that might be expected to dispute it. This "harmony" (*I* 218) with a present state of affairs described by Myshkin in terms of a "completeness" and a "merging" (*I* 218) is therefore more like a mode of being than like an assent to a set of conditions. For "melt[ing] into" "rays" of "light" (*I* 57), "merging in the highest synthesis of life" (*I* 218), which the prisoner and Myshkin respectively describe feeling, imply a permeability of person to light and calm in the face of which it would no longer make sense to speak of any threshold between them from which an assent could be proffered. Similarly, although Kirillov tells Stavrogin that in his "here eternal," time is not "an object, it's an idea" (*D* 237), it is an idea that has no place to insert itself, since there is no longer any division between person and world in which time could make itself intelligible. Such an elision of person and world, "upset" and "very happy," *am dead* and "is good" almost erodes the distinction between phenomena (and between phenomena and experiencer) that would constitute a perspective. Yet what is remarkable about the rapture of this near-seamlessness is not its genesis in an exceptional state of consciousness, though as Kirillov insists, consciousness alone is the source of bliss ("Man is unhappy because he doesn't know he's happy" [*D* 237]; when he learns, he will "immediately become happy" [*D* 237]), but rather the claim that accompanies this recognition: to see integratively ("through the ass, all Switzerland" [*I* 53]) but essentially ("simply a leaf" [*D* 237]) is to see in a way that eradicates incongruity ("my melancholy passed completely" [*I* 53]), to see things neutrally reveal what they are.

II

While the death sentence precipitates joy when this world is glimpsed by dint of an eschatology that bathes the real in a recognizable light, it precipitates suffering when the illumination is indecipherable, when what is seen cannot be identified except as "a presence of the negative."[17] That negation is what Ippolit, the eighteen-year-old consumptive atheist, witnesses when he stands

FIGURE 2.1

before Holbein's painting, the *Dead Christ* (fig. 2.1), represented as the "corpse of a tortured man" (*I* 396) whose violent and disfiguring death—contorted hand, eyes rolled back in the head, gaping mouth—seems so definitively natural that it could never be transcended.

Moreover, as Rowan Williams explains, Holbein's image is a negation—an "anti-icon" in "a purely formal sense." For while "classical Orthodox iconography. . . . seeks to confront the viewer/worshipper with a direct gaze informed by the divine light Holbein's painting shows . . . a corpse seen from alongside . . . a dead man in profile, a double negation of the iconographic convention."[18] Williams's claim that Holbein's *Dead Christ* is an image "emptied of divine content," hence "a 'diabolical' image,"[19] illuminates the source of a different aspect of the painting that I want to argue Dostoevsky stresses: its pervasive suffering:

> "It's true it's the face of man *only just* taken from the cross—that is to say, still bearing traces of warmth and life. Nothing is rigid in it yet, so that there's still a look of suffering in the face of the dead man, as though he were still feeling it. . . . the face has not been spared in the least. It is simply nature, and the corpse of a man, whoever he might be, must really look like that after such suffering. I know that the Christian Church laid it down, even in the early ages, that Christ's suffering was not symbolical but actual, and that His body was therefore fully and completely subject to the laws of nature on the cross. In the picture the face is fearfully crushed by blows, swollen, covered with fearful, swollen and blood-stained bruises, the eyes are open and squinting: the great wide-open whites of the eyes glitter with a sort of deathly, glassy light." (*I* 395–96)

Although in most representations the beauty of the crucified Christ mutes the visceral sense of His suffering, in Holbein's painting, as glossed by Ippolit, suffering unnervingly lingers in the features of the corpse ("as though he were still feeling it" [*I* 395]). Thus there is a tension in the painting between "the laws of nature so mighty" (*I* 396) they cannot be vanquished or "overcome"

(*I* 396) and a preternatural sense that suffering has a potential that survives death. Ippolit attributes the appearance of suffering to the fact that He is "*only just* taken from the cross" (*I* 395), but his account does not fully explain the diffusion of that suffering lodged first in the features of the corpse and then spreading to infect onlookers "not one of whom is shown in the picture" (*I* 396). To see that the man who raised others from the dead could not apparently Himself be raised "must have . . . crushed all their hopes, and almost their convictions" (*I* 396). And Ippolit reaches further into the invisible space off the canvas to disseminate to Christ's disciples and to Christ Himself despair so extreme at the apparent gratuitousness of suffering unredeemed by transcendence that, could it have been anticipated, it might have unwritten history: "if the Teacher could have seen Himself on the eve of the crucifixion, would He have gone up to the cross and died as He did? That question too rises involuntarily, as one looks at the picture" (*I* 396). Thus in Ippolit's excursus the suffering actually made finite by death is reinvigorated everywhere.

Suffering is also manifested in the compressed space of the rectangular canvas only twelve inches high, which is in the shape of a long narrow box that contains the bier on which Christ lies. The claustrophobia of the coffin-like space surrounding the body (the ribs come close to, though they do not actually touch, the top frame of the painting, and they protrude at one point above the gravestone that lies to the body's side and along its length) accentuates, by compelling the viewer to see—without recourse to any space that would alleviate misery—the paradoxical features in which death vivifies rather than obliterates the manifestations of suffering. At the same time, the muscular body that lies on the draped bier, notwithstanding the bruises and marks of the crucifixion, with its fleshy hue, its luxurious shock of hair falling over the slab, betrays a vitalism though not a vitality, since what "glitter" (*I* 396) are the whites, the unseeing parts, of the eyes. The painting's vigor, its power not only to represent suffering, but to proliferate and diffuse it, renders suffering omnipresent—as if it had a life of its own beyond a person's life—and this is anticipated earlier in the novel when Myshkin looks at a print of Holbein's painting and instantly remarks: "Why, that picture might make some people lose their faith" (*I* 211).

Antithetical elements characterize not only Ippolit's description of Holbein's *Dead Christ* but also his reflection on the agent that killed Him: "Looking at such a picture, one conceives of nature in the shape of an immense, merciless, dumb beast, or more correctly, much more correctly, speaking, though it sounds strange, in the form of a huge machine of the most modern construction which, dull and insensible, has aimlessly clutched, crushed and swallowed up a great priceless Being" (*I* 396). That "insolent, unreasoning and eternal

Power to which everything is in subjection" (*I* 396) is then climactically analogized to a "huge and loathsome spider" (*I* 396). The terror of Ippolit's aggregate entity—mechanized, doubly analogized to natural forms (an arachnid and an animal), and, a paragraph later, again identified as supernatural (an "infinite Power," a "dull, dark, dumb force" [*I* 396)])—lies precisely in its ambiguous essence. Moreover, and this connection has heretofore gone unremarked, the anomaly of the Christ and of the composite entity that crucified Him links Ippolit's exegesis on Holbein's painting to the "awful animal" (*I* 377) in his nightmare, which precedes it by some twenty pages.[20]

The creature in Ippolit's dream also resists recognizability, even as it radiates doom and injury. Its grotesqueness is a feature of its indecipherability. "It was like a scorpion, but was not a scorpion" (*I* 377), Ippolit explains, then referring to it as a "reptile" (*I* 378) with features of an arachnid (elongated body; segmented tail with stinger; four pairs of legs), and with other menacing attributes. Though Ippolit's dream "beast" (*I* 378) is an amalgamation of several animals, it is most terrifyingly like no animal at all. This beast is "more disgusting, and much more horrible" than a scorpion, "and it seemed it was so, just because there was nothing like it in nature, and that it had come *expressly* to me" (*I* 377). Although the "beast" (*I* 378) is not recognizable, then, it can itself recognize; this is what Ippolit means when he says the creature has singled him out. Its manner of locomotion is what, in a visceral reaction, Ippolit calls "revolting" (*I* 378), because its resolute motion insists it has a purpose, even as its failure to disclose that purpose tortures and repels him. While the creature's motive remains dark, its inexplicable menace is perceptible even to Ippolit's dog Norma, the "huge, shaggy, black Newfoundland" (*I* 378) (dead five years), notwithstanding the fact that "Animals cannot feel terror of the mysterious" (*I* 378)—the extravagance of the beast's venom compelling Norma to a clairvoyance that live animals do not possess. As Ippolit elaborates his description of this "beast"—of its grotesque physical characteristics and of its metaphysical aura of pure malignity (which emanates more from its power to terrify and to mystify than to sting)—we see that a question he will ask about the "beast" that "crushed" (*I* 396) the Christ ("Can anything that has no shape appear in a shape?" [*I* 396]) was anticipated by the creature of his nightmare. Yet Ippolit is horrified to learn that these incomparable creatures—creatures of different magnitude—could incongruously be identified with each other: "I remember that some one seemed to lead me by the hand, holding a candle, to show me a huge and loathsome spider, and to assure me, laughing at my indignation, that this was that same dark, dumb and almighty Power" (*I* 396)—could be diverse manifestations of the same fantastic malevolence. For if the awful dumb beast that kills the Christ and the repellent diminutive creature of Ippolit's nightmare are embodiments of a single indiscriminate force, then His death is a mockery, as well as a catastrophe, by virtue of a kinship so ignominious.

While Ippolit connects the "eternal Power" (*I* 396) of the beast that ravages the Christ to the dream creature that repulsively "dart[s]" (*I* 379), "crawl[s]," and "wriggl[es]" (*I* 378), he simultaneously caricatures the mega-beast by an opposite, more novel, and truly terrifying compounding: for the beast that destroys the Christ also seems to have assumed His properties. Its malice and its horror lie in its incorporation of the "infinite," the "eternal," the "almighty" (*I* 396), attributes ordinarily associated with divinity. The assumption of divine properties suggested by Ippolit's designations deadens the Christ and enlivens the beast—in both its incarnations, for the beast in Ippolit's room is also characterized by him as a mysterious, other-worldly, and even providential, messenger ("who had sent it into my room . . . and what was the secret of it?" Ippolit marvels [*I* 378])—while the Christ, a mere corpse, is evacuated of mystery. In Ippolit's linguistic transfer of attributes from the Christ to the beast with "almighty Power" (*I* 396), transcendence is not simply obliterated. This would be its fate if Holbein's *Dead Christ* had no connection with the beast. Instead, transcendence discloses itself as a travesty when what "has no shape appear[s] in a shape" (*I* 396), both as the dream creature and the machine-like power, in a material manifestation of infinite godlessness.

"And what if there are only spiders there [in a future life], or something of that sort?" (*CP* 289), Svidrigailov asks in *Crime and Punishment,* in a speculation that shrinks the infinite to an image whose denigration can be recognized, and even recoiled from:

> "We keep imagining eternity as an idea that cannot be grasped, something vast, vast! But why must it be vast? Instead of all that, imagine suddenly that there will be one little room there, something like a village bathhouse, covered with soot, with spiders in all the corners, and that's the whole of eternity." (*CP* 289)

While Svidrigailov introduces the contraction of eternity to "one little room . . . covered with soot" (*CP 289*), his imagining accomplishes the reduction from "vast" to confined and airless (or to an enclosure with fetid air: the bathhouse) without expressing affect at the degradation. In distinction, Ippolit is appalled by the dream in which an "infinite Power" (*I* 396) takes the form of a repellent beast. Yet the ultimate object of his dismay is neither the Christ nor the beast but, rather, an apparently (but not actually) alien entity introduced precipitously by Ippolit into his "Explanation"—a phantom, a specter that *looks* like Rogozhin (the novel's most dangerous character) but could not *be* Rogozhin: "Rogozhin in the flesh could not have come in, as all our doors are locked at night" (*I* 398).[21] Why does Ippolit's inability to distinguish transcendence from its debasement become intolerable only in relation to a seemingly anti-climactic vision, an invisible being so like—but not—Rogozhin? The "apparition" (*I* 397) of Rogozhin,

> "which I have described so minutely was the cause of my making up my mind [to kill myself]. What helped to bring about that 'final decision' was not logic, not a logical conviction, but a feeling of repulsion. I could not go on living a life which was taking such strange, humiliating forms. That apparition degraded me. I am not able to submit to the gloomy power that takes the shape of a spider." (*I* 398)

Unlike the beast which is unidentifiable, and the Christ who cannot be identified with the transcendence that historically defines His essence, what is horrible about the apparition is its *in*distinguishability from Rogozhin. The apparent lack of similitude between the threat posed by the specter of Rogozhin and that posed by the Christ and the beast raises a question about the relationship between what cannot be recognized because it does not look like something known (the Christ, the beast), and what cannot be recognized because it does (the specter of Rogozhin).

The specter of Rogozhin is neither mysterious, like the beast, nor stripped of mystery, like the Christ. Yet Ippolit's terror at the phantom specifically derives from its categorical indecipherability, from the fact that the figure, neither clearly vital nor clearly spectral, evades classification. Thus "Rogozhin" belongs to the same family as "the merciless, dumb beast" (*I* 396) that crushes the Christ and the awful animal in Ippolit's room, even as he strikingly elucidates the source of their common horror. Rogozhin's contested identity precipitates Ippolit's "repulsion" (*I* 398), because (the antithesis of the states described in the previous section) it thwarts the capacity to identify a principle or ground according to which a thing can be said to be what it is.[22] What characterizes Ippolit's suffering is horror at entities that, neither vital nor spectral, mortal nor immortal, natural nor supernatural—*sui generis*—cannot be classified. What cannot be classified also looks like this:

> And locusts came out of the smoke onto the earth, and power like that of earthly scorpions was given to them. And they were told not to harm the grass of the earth or any plant or any tree but only men who had not God's seal on their foreheads. . . . And the appearance of the locusts was like horses prepared for war, and on their heads they wore what looked like wreaths of gold, and their faces were like the countenances of men, and they had hair like women's hair, and their teeth were like lion's teeth and they had scales like

> iron breastplates, and the sound of their wings was like the sound of chariots with many horses rushing into battle. Also they had tails and stingers like scorpions, and the power to harm men for five months abides in their tails. (*The Anchor Bible,* trans. J. Massyngberde Ford [Garden City, NY: Doubleday & Company, 1975]: Rev 9:3–11)

In this passage from Revelation which *The Idiot* incorporates as its center (for the beasts, the Christ, the specter that is and is not Rogozhin are all composite entities with indeterminate features), locusts can't be sorted into one species or another; one gender or another; one element or another because they have men's countenances, women's hair, teeth like lions', scales like breastplates (Rev. 9:7–9), being aggregates that prohibit identification. More striking than particular passages called to mind from Revelation by Dostoevsky's novel is their shared pattern in which nothing separates eschatological justice from eschatological vengeance. In that pattern some manifestation of purity is hollowed out, travestied, or lethally polluted, as when in a reversal of Exodus 15:22–25, where Moses throws a tree into bitter water and thereby sweetens it, men die of bitter water because the "star . . . called by the name, 'The Wormwood'" falls into a third of the rivers and poisons them (Rev 8:10–11). The apparent indistinguishability of a theophany of God from an infernal epiphany in central passages of Revelation is replicated at the heart of the hallucinatory emblems that Ippolit contemplates, which permit God's attributes to radiate from a beast that negates Him. Yet, as the passages I have discussed powerfully demonstrate, *The Idiot* not only weaves Revelation's conjunctions into its own nightmare fabric, but also deepens their horror by reversing Revelation's logic. In distinction to the Biblical book where ultimately "world" will be "transfigured, for ever immune from the threat of chaos . . . for ever immune from ageing, disease, and death,"[23] in Ippolit's analysis redemption could not be secured but is insistently thwarted: there is not endless life but endless death, not a cessation of suffering but rather its surfeit. In one further instance Dostoevsky augments Revelation's unholy congruencies by inscribing a reversal into his own reworking of a passage from Revelation that is initially free of it. For the "*no more time*" (*I* 219) of Myshkin's joy is bitterly rewritten by Ippolit to indicate the end of time for him personally ("tomorrow there will be 'no more time'" [*I* 372]) when he kills himself (the "final moment of full determination" [*I* 398] to which his exegesis refers) because he cannot discern an apocalyptic vision—the no more time of unmitigated bliss—distinct from its mockery.

In the passages I have considered in this section Dostoevsky links Ippolit's experience of a negative infinite ("everlasting gloom" [*I* 381]) with his incapacity to recognize the figures he scrutinizes—time being experienced as a mere postponement, an interminable waiting for encrypted images to be revealed. The protracted torment of apocalyptic images that cannot be deciphered leads to the immediate anguish of Ippolit's inability to identify even the form of Rogozhin directly in front of him. This production of a visible that withholds disclosure, never revealing its essence but always provoking the supposition that it could be divulged, though not in any present, is epitomized in Dostoevsky's recurring trope—the spider which irreducibly embodies opacity as its *sine qua non*. In its several incarnations, the spider is a creature with discernible physical properties, but always also more, the more being emitted as something like an aura whose intimated essence might forever mesmerize but (unlike that of true apocalyptic figures) could never be unsealed.

The categorical indecipherability of a thing that looks like itself but is not itself—a scorpion that is not a scorpion; a man that is not a man; a Christ that is not a Christ—is rendered most appalling in the third instance, where death that ought to end duration is rather composed of more duration. If joy is that state in which everything is immediately recognizable—hence is suffused with agreement—suffering is that state of affairs in which assent is inconceivable. The need to identify what stands before one, and the impossibility of doing so, might be the very definition of suffering. In the nightmare realm, as in the world of plotted narrative where discoveries require time to unfold, nothing in the present is scrutable. Or rather nothing is what it is, but is always only what it might be revealed to be in some future moment of disclosure. In this state of expectation, as Ippolit explains, there is no legible being in the present, but only its deferral.

III

In *The Idiot* the transcendence—not of the actual but of the temporal—is joy, in which perception breaks free of indifference and postponement. We see such a release in Myshkin's rapturous vision of the ass, which is liberated from the stupefaction that constitutes the ordinary way of seeing it; in Kirillov's joy which breaks loose from the limits that assign value to certain experiences and withhold value from others. At the moment that time burns up, in Georges Bataille's words, "distinctions melt in the intense heat of intimate life." He writes: "It is precisely the disappearance of duration, and of the neutral behaviors associated with it, that uncovers a ground of things that is dazzlingly bright (in other words, it is clear that the need for duration conceals life from us, and that, only in theory, the impossibility of duration frees us)."[24] What is consumed in such freedom is individuality ("those rays were his new nature" [*I* 57]), but what burns in its wake is the "*invisible* brilliance" of "intimate life."[25] The revelation of death identified as one's own discloses life's plenitude, obliterating anticipation, that prolepsis that is being's displacement.

Ippolit's genius lies in the sweep of his analysis of such paradoxes, only perceiving the joy that could make living rapturous once he learns from the doctor "I had about a month left to live . . . but I may die much sooner" (*I* 377).[26] As in the case of the reprieved man, the experience of his own death sentence is required to make living real to him. Yet if, from one point of view, death releases Ippolit to an immediacy, from another point of view, his desire to remain personally alive turns death into anguish. "Why did I actually *begin* living, knowing that I couldn't begin it now? Why did I try it, knowing that it was useless for me to try anything?" (*I* 380). If Ippolit can't live until he sees that living is prohibited, he also can't live in the shadow of death's imminence. The apprehension of "*no more time*" (*I* 219) introduces this impossibility: living as a finishing. Hence he can't learn Greek grammar because, as he explains, "I shall die before I get to the syntax" (*I* 382). Once he has only "two or three months left to live, perhaps four" he can't contemplate "a good deed which requires a great deal of work, activity, and bother" (*I* 393), but only one "on a smaller scale . . . (if I am still so drawn to good deeds)" (*I* 393), he qualifies to Bakhmutov, because "I haven't time enough left" (*I* 393) to complete it.

Ippolit sees his fate as absurd: his life is experienced as dreamlike until he is awakened to its reality by the imminence of a death sentence that will deprive him of that reality. The incoherence of such a plight can be analogized to his inability to distinguish the antipodal creatures of his nightmare, since its chiasmic logic converts the condition for something being possible to the condition for its being impossible. The joy Ippolit experiences only when he discovers he is passing away is the very joy that he cannot experience because he is passing away. Thus he apprehends suffering as a bitter condition that culminates in dying, but which is first perceptible in a vision of nature's splendor from which he sees himself outcast:

> "What use to me is your nature, your Pavlovsk park, your sunrises and sunsets, your blue sky, and your contented faces, when all this endless festival has begun by my being excluded from it? What is there for me in this beauty when, every minute, every second I am obliged, forced, to recognise that even the tiny fly, buzzing in the sunlight beside me, has its share in the banquet and the chorus, knows its place, loves it and is happy; and I alone am an outcast." (*I* 400)

Myshkin reiterates the anguish of that exclusion from a different vantage when he recalls a memory that echoes and even, in his dreamy reverie, counterintuitively occasions (since it was never spoken by him), Ippolit's expression ("those very words . . . that phrase about the 'fly' Ippolit took from him" [*I* 410]), when, "in Switzerland . . . he was almost like an idiot" (*I* 410) and "once went up into the mountain-side, on a bright, sunny day" (*I* 410):

> Before him was the brilliant sky, below, the lake, and all around an horizon, bright and boundless which seemed to have no ending. . . . What tortured him was that he was utterly outside all this. What was this festival? . . . Every morning the same bright sun rises . . . every "little fly that buzzes about him in the hot sunshine has its part in the chorus; knows its place, loves it, and is happy." Every blade of grass grows and is happy! . . . Only he knows nothing, and understands nothing, neither men nor sounds; he is outside it all, and an outcast. (*I* 410)

Exile inspires the feeling of idiocy and a perception of its uniqueness—a knowing that, in distinction to the fly, is different from a being, as well as a relation to nature defined by an end that is known, even before it is experienced, as a grief. Yet this consciousness, experienced as unique, is in fact disseminated throughout *The Idiot* so that it is impossible to have a proprietary relation to it. It stretches across the novel as a backdrop, articulated by Myshkin and Ippolit, but in the series of characters and exemplary figures who died long ago, or who in Ippolit's expression now are "going *over yonder,* and this time I believe I really am going" (*I* 542), amorphously belongs to everyone, each of whom experiences the exile made definitive by the death sentence as solitary: "I alone" (*I* 400), "Only he" (*I* 410).[27] If Myshkin's language echoes Ippolit's, it can do so because their fate is univocal rather than individual, even as Myshkin's response to the exclusion is melancholy, while Ippolit's is outrage.

Notable about the "everlasting" (*I* 410) joy Myshkin and Ippolit attribute to the sentient fly and the nonsentient blade of grass is that it has no personal equivalent. This is not only because there could be no forever to joy for the dying man, since his life is perceptible as a vanishing. It is also, more categorically, as Kirillov expounds it in *Demons,* that joy is unendurable, is a completion—"eternal harmony, fully achieved . . . clear and indisputable" (*D* 590)—in the presence of which man could no longer be what he is:

> "There are seconds, they come only five or six at a time, and you suddenly feel the presence of eternal harmony, fully achieved. It is nothing earthly; not that it's heavenly, but man cannot endure it in his earthly state. One must change physically or die. The feeling is clear and indisputable. As if you suddenly

> sense the whole of nature and suddenly say: yes, this is true. God, when he was creating the world, said at the end of creation: 'Yes, this is true, this is good.' This . . . this is not tenderheartedness, but simply joy. You don't forgive anything, because there's no longer anything to forgive. You don't really love—oh, what is here is higher than love! What's most frightening is that it's so terribly clear, and there's such joy. If it were longer than five seconds—the soul couldn't endure it and would vanish. In those five seconds I live my life through, and for them I would give my whole life, because it's worth it. To endure ten seconds one would have to change physically. I think man should stop giving birth. . . . It's said in the Gospel that in the resurrection there will be no birth, but people will be like God's angels." (*D* 590–91)

As with the prisoner's ecstatic rendering of the five minutes before the execution, Kirillov's analysis opens to an elaboration that would seem to defy the instantaneousness of the experience, and sinks into its clarities: as in the difference between "joy," which Dostoevsky explicitly names here as such, and "tenderness" or "love"; as in the assent that miraculously unites the vantage of a God ("this is good") with a person's vantage ("this is true"), but a person's vantage razed of grievance ("no longer anything to forgive"); as in a glimmer of what would differentiate being as it *is* from futurity: no more "birth" being a radical expression of being that did not bring forth more being, of being that could withstand becoming. Yet the astonishments of Kirillov's analysis repeatedly give way to this plain fact: joy cannot be humanly lived for more than a few seconds. That is what it means for joy to be what it is. For rapture to endure—to be registered in consciousness as definitive—it, and the moment of death, would need to be coterminous. Just such an impossibility instigates the desire for a timelessness produced by suicide. Although Kirillov and Ippolit both court death (dismayingly from Dostoevsky's vantage), behind their thirst for sovereignty lies a more blameless craving for a state of affairs in which "is good," "fully achieved," "no [more] birth" inhabit consciousness with a nothing further.

If joy is not legible in terms of an "everlasting" (*I* 410), or even a persisting, Ippolit explains, human suffering is. Counterpointed to the "endless" happiness enjoyed by the fly and by "every blade of grass" is the "everlasting" preoccupation and worry, the "everlasting sullen spite" (*I* 381) for which Ippolit berates those around him. While "the everlasting story!" (*I* 381)—the human story of continuing—is one of discontent, Surikov especially provokes Ippolit's ire because his misfortunes ("he's poor, destitute, starving, his wife died, he couldn't buy medicine for her, his baby was frozen to death in the winter; his elder daughter is a 'kept mistress' " [*I* 381]) only epitomize Ippolit's point, which he claims no degree of adversity could alter: "If he's alive he has everything in his power! Whose fault is it he doesn't understand that?" (*I* 381)—a question Ippolit can ask only once he distinguishes his adversity as a dying man from Surikov's. But in fact the living man *is* the dying man who has not yet discovered his plight. Hence, inconsistently (from the vantage of the claim that "If he's alive he has everything in his power!" [*I* 381]), Ippolit derides life as an impotence. Ippolit, despising not simply Surikov's meekness but also Surikov's helplessness, brutally accuses the latter of killing his baby—"Surikov 'froze his baby,' about the middle of March" (*I* 384)—because, in a flickering of empathy with Surikov, he believes that violence (Surikov's killing his child) would confer on such a tragedy the dignity that he thinks meekness denies it. In this twisted expression of compassion, Surikov's fate fleetingly becomes an image of Ippolit's own fate, which neither meekness nor rage can ameliorate. In *The Idiot* the man before the death sentence he cannot avert is the man without agency.

Unlike that of characters for whom the threat of dying is transient, Ippolit's capacity to dwell within death's near-immediacy permanently shatters his obliviousness to the universe he is taking leave of. His centrality to the novel depends on his capacity to press on questions that illuminate the contradictions his dying epitomizes. In inquiring what gives life ("the sun's the spring of life, isn't it? What's the meaning of 'springs of life' in the Apocalypse?") and what, like "Wormwood," poisons it (*I* 361), he would unencrypt emblems from Revelation and the nightmare equivalents of his allegory, which promise but withhold transparency. In the same way, he is drawn to contemplate the phenomenal world, "Meyer's wall" (*I* 400), the brick wall outside the window of Ippolit's room, and "all that is so openly and simply written on it" (*I* 400)—the stony, blank, unyielding nothing, without hope, vitality or meaning—and, its converse, the "everlasting 'trees'" (*I* 375), trees being for Ippolit what "a leaf" (*D* 237) and "the sticky little leaves" (*BK* 263) that come out in the spring are for Kirillov and Ivan, a natural miracle:

> "The prince . . . persuaded me . . . that it would be 'easier to die among people and trees.' . . . I asked him what he meant by his everlasting 'trees,' and why he keeps pestering me with those 'trees,' and learnt to my surprise that I had myself said on that evening that I'd come to Pavlovsk to look at the trees for the last time. When I told him I should die just the same, looking at trees, or looking out of my window at brick walls . . . he agreed at once." (*I* 375)

The constellation of images—"Meyer's wall" (*I* 400) and its prophetic corollary in Revelation, "the star that is called Wormwood" (*I* 361); the Prince's "everlasting 'trees'" (*I* 375) (here colloquially indicative of the trees he keeps talking about), which are unmistakably allied with originary influences, with "springs of life" so pure they can "produce a physical change in me . . . and *my dreams* will be affected and perhaps relieved" (*I* 375)—form a pattern Ippolit is trying to read. How should he interpret the relation between experiential poles so extreme—the "trees of Pavlovsk" (*I* 400) (in Ippolit's grudging acknowledgment, "the last semblance of life and love" [*I* 400], objects drenched in immanence) and "Meyer's wall," their converse—that, like living and dying, can be seen, but not, by Ippolit, simultaneously?

If these tropes represent alternative points of view between which space is ineradicable and if any point of view is irrelevant to dying (since the contents of consciousness could not thwart its obliteration), point of view is not irrelevant to the stance that could be inhabited in relation to a dying that others seem spared. For Ippolit, who awakens from the nightmare of duration to behold the splendor of greenness from which he sees he is outcast, the joy he recognizes is not his joy, even though it is precisely his awakening to the death sentence as *his* that first aroused his discovery that joy could be fleetingly inhabited. For Ippolit the question is how to feel toward a joy that could not be sustained—a question of how to see a joy of which he is being dispossessed. When he asks, "Can't I simply be devoured without being expected to praise what devours me?" (*I* 401), the petulance of the question does not compromise its nobility, since Ippolit is considering the stance that *could* be chosen to give meaning to a fate that *cannot* be chosen, even as it also cannot be interpretively penetrated. In his identification of life as a spectacle he can only gaze at—in distinction to the fly imagined as so fully one with nature that it personifies that unity—Ippolit incarnates the problem of how to live (and die) in relation to a joy that is "everything in his power" (*I* 381) experienced from the outside.

Although Dostoevsky wrote in his notebook "*Ipolit—the vanity of a weak character*," he also insisted: "Ipolit—the main axis of the whole novel. . . . Write tersely and powerfully about Ipolit. Center the whole plot on him."[28] Ippolit is central to the development of other characters.[29] But his autonomous contribution to the novel resides most powerfully in his obsessive meditation on a death sentence, a topic to which all his spitefulness and all his hope refer. More than for any other character in Dostoevsky's oeuvre, nothing else is real to him. So that when, for instance, Myshkin praises his manuscript—"even the most absurd points in it . . . are redeemed by suffering" (*I* 505)—he brightens at the praise, even as the brightness quickly fades: " 'Yet I must die all the same!' he said, almost adding, 'a man like me!' " (*I* 506). The egotism betrayed in his incredulity does not compromise his dignity but gives it a foundation—"a man like me" being a man like all contemplating an end that cannot be countenanced. For the man before the death sentence—Surikov with his "'frozen' baby" (*I* 384); the man on the scaffold kissing the cross (*I* 61); the prisoner, before he is reprieved; the consumptive Ippolit; and especially for Christ, who, in Ippolit's horrified eyes, is impartially meted out the same indiscriminate destiny—*The Idiot* repeats: what is the right way to live (or die) in relation to a joy that isn't yours and a suffering that is?—Dostoevsky's most passionately deliberated question. This is partly an ethical question (Ippolit applies to it a standard of virtue [*I* 507]), but it is first an affective question. When Ippolit asks, "what do you think would be the best way for me to die?" (*I* 507), Myshkin exhorts him: "Pass by us, and forgive us our happiness" (*I* 507). *The Idiot* thus seems to be advising a hopelessness without rancor and a benevolence without hope—a state of mind (or heart) that endures experiences of suffering and joy that can be neither transformed nor understood. This is what it might mean to be exiled from joy without inflicting suffering.

IV

On March 14, 1868, Apollon Maykov wrote to Dostoevsky: "How fine the Idiot is! . . . all the characters are very strong, very vivid, only they are lit with an *electric light*, in which the most ordinary face and the most ordinary colours have an unnatural glow . . . it is the lighting of *The Last Day of Pompeii*."[30] Maykov does not elaborate his observation. Yet in pointing to the unnatural aura that illuminates *The Idiot* he might have been responding to the novel's overwrought theatricality (as in the scene in which Nastasya throws the bundle of a hundred thousand rubles into a fire and dares Ganya to retrieve it with his bare hands), and to the violent emotional conflagrations that scorch Dostoevsky's characters, igniting and fuelling their conflicts. Even the novel's debates about faith are intense, elemental, and fiery: "faith," Dostoevsky writes, "is a red color."[31] Thus it is easy to see what instigates the comparison between the harsh brightness of Karl Briullov's painting and Dostoevsky's flamboyant novel. Yet also contributive to the eerie light of *The Idiot* is the contrast between such conflagrations and the nontransitive moments of joy and suffering that are not causally related to each other; that are not subject to the calculations that determine the novel's scarcity of love; that are outside the tumultuous upheavals engineered by the characters—and that are even, as I have intimated, outside of character—claims I take up in the remaining pages. As a consequence, *The Idiot*'s plot—the Aglaia/Nastasya/Myshkin/Rogozhin contest—is virtually independent of the inset pieces (at once autonomous and fragmentary) in which the novel's very different brilliance lies.[32] Roland Barthes writes on the fragment:

> Each piece is self-sufficient, and yet it is never anything but the interstice of its neighbors. . . . The man who has best understood and practiced the aesthetic of the fragment (before Webern) is perhaps Schumann; he called the fragment an "intermezzo"; he increased the intermezzi within his works as he went on composing: everything he produced was ultimately *intercalated*: but between what and what? What is the meaning of a pure series of interruptions?[33]

These fragments recur to suffering and joy prismatically, in interludes (I shall return to this point), rather than sequentially—perspectivally, from different angles—a mode of structuring that could also describe the images in the Apocalypse.[34]

In *The Idiot* convertibility—the rapid-fire exchange of words and states—defines Nastasya, whose high spirits can be transformed to despair in a single instant, and whose quicksilver changes of mood shape, even warp, the actions of the other characters who, exhilarated by her passion, immediately turn their lives upside down. "I love you! I would die for you. . . . I won't let anyone say a word about you. If we are poor, I'll work" (*I* 158), Myshkin says to Nastasya the first time he meets her. Moreover, unlike the diffusion that is joy (Kirillov's "everything is good" [*D* 237], Myshkin's "Switzerland," apprehended "through the ass" [*I* 53]) which mirrors and includes what surrounds it (a pervasion that also characterizes Ippolit's misery, touching all he sees), the plotted narrative of *The Idiot* is marked by a very different management of resources. Thus the climactic moment when Myshkin, engaged to Aglaia, but challenged by Nastasya to "throw [her] up at once, and stay with me for ever, and marry me" (*I* 554), hesitates, something changes forever: "She could not endure even the instant of his hesitation" (*I* 555). Myshkin's hesitation recapitulates the negotiations in which the happiness of one character is the anguish of another. Yevgeny's scornful analysis ("I will show you to yourself as in a looking-glass" [*I* 563]) lays bare the novel's paradigm in which choosing one woman is repudiating the other, in which equivocating about one's choices (hesitating) unmakes those choices; or to put it as Yevgeny does, in which Myshkin's ostensible love of both women—his capacity to love one and then, instead, the other one, really means "you've never loved either of them!" (*I* 567)—reveals a system of exchange that the novel does not so much develop as it again and again repeats. Moreover, if Myshkin chooses Nastasya and then again Aglaia and then again Nastasya, this "*yes/no*"—in Barthes's words "ultimately the pure form of any paradigm"—is echoed by Nastasya ("the same story told in . . . variations" [*I* 557]), who exercises her capricious will, first in clinging to Myshkin, then in casting him away.[35] Variants on these exchanges, transacted with cash, also swirl around the novel's secondary characters, as Kolya exclaims, "all money-grubbers" (*I* 128), experts in bribery, thievery, and usury.[36]

The political nature of both *Demons* and *The Idiot* would seem to repel the idea that any autonomous state could be exempt from the "whirlwind movement of events" that blows through those novels.[37] Yet there is no relation between characters' manic operations (whether Lebedyev's petty conniving, thieving, and lying or the more ambitious machinations of *Demons'* revolutionaries) and those threshold moments, which are detached from the politics that characters instigate. Although Dostoevsky would never advocate quietism, the "topsy-turvydom" and "chaos" (*I* 276) of the particular political ideas in both novels (liberalism and nihilism)[38] only recapitulate "the right of might . . . of the individual fist and of personal caprice" recognizable in all systems (*I* 284), whatever the idealism that might generate them.[39] For Dostoevsky, metaphysical manifestations of suffering and joy are obduracies no politics, however ideal, and no personal supplanting of torment by love, could rectify. Though politics could relieve the suffering that arises from social inequity (hence determine conditions more propitious for happiness), it could never confer joy, since joy, these representations insist, inhabits being impersonally.

A character like Ippolit might seem fully immersed in the particulars of personality and ideology: when he and Burdovsky (not Palishtchev's son); Keller (the boxer); and Doktorenko (Lebedyev's nephew) come to blackmail Myshkin, they are promptly recognized as "nihilists" who are "first of all men of business . . . a sort of sequel to nihilism, not in a direct line, but obliquely, by hearsay" (*I* 249). Yet though Ippolit is part of the plot, he is immediately distinguished from "the spectacle of strange young people" (*I* 282), not only because of his consumptive appearance (his "glittering . . . eyes" [*I* 281]), but more explicitly because he starkly identifies himself as a near-"dead man" who "came . . . to see the trees" (*I* 286). Thus what might individuate his character is immediately subordinated to his condition, dying ("these people here, there never will be any more of them, never!" [*I* 286]), and an alternative vision ("the trees"), on which he discourses permissively because "the dead may say anything" (*I* 286). Ippolit's "anything" is his exasperated diatribe. Yet as he holds forth against a "Nature" that is "ironical" (*I* 287) ("I do not want this life!" [*I* 402]), he passionately evokes its power over him: "When I reach these lines, the sun will, no doubt, be rising . . . and its vast immeasurable power will be shed upon the earth. So be it!" (*I* 402). Ippolit might wish to take his life but he cannot negate his attachment to its source, manifested by the trees (*I* 286) whose immediacy dazzles him. It could even be said that Ippolit's indignation, his resentment and his disdain—particulars that, cumulatively, constitute his character—are momentarily consumed by rapture, and are ultimately trivialized by an attachment whose primacy Dostoevsky metaphorizes. For at the conclusion of Ippolit's "Explanation," the narrator fleetingly proposes an analogy for Ippolit's oneness with nature (glimpsed by the narrator in retrospect or in some imaginary speculation) from which he will be separated (*I* 402). "This eighteen-year-old boy, exhausted by illness, seemed as weak as a trembling leaf torn from a tree" (*I* 402), an image that both recalls and vivifies, it could be accidentally, were Dostoevsky a lesser writer, those "everlasting 'trees'" (*I* 375) that awaken Ippolit's ecstasy ("the last semblance of life and love" [*I* 400]). In Ippolit's being analogized to a living part of the tree, he is figured as adhering not to joy but, more directly, to its source, even as the absolute union implied by the analogy does not avert the absolute violence implied by its rupture. Although there could be no way to reconcile the incommensurability of Ippolit's joy (or his suffering) with his character, the leaf, a figure of attachment/severance, albeit transiently, embodies Ippolit's fate stripped of his deforming response to his circumstances, petulance.

If rapture is embodied in a simile that is a fragment (Ippolit like "a trembling leaf torn from a tree" [*I* 402], first a living part of the source of joy and a second later the emblem of a rending), it stands contiguous to the representation of Ippolit's character as revealed in his dialogue. Readers of Mikhail Bakhtin would insist on the impossibility of such isolation which could allow any character to disentangle himself from a relationship with the other characters by which he is elemented, to rise up out of the novel's plottedness, hypostatically, as an avatar of joy or the release from it. Yet I am suggesting that the is-ness of the leaf is at once identified with Ippolit and also breaks free of the aggregate of features that individualize him and render him legible only in affiliation with the tangle of the novel's other characters.

A more radical image of partitioning—first, of joy from suffering, then both from the person they occupy—can be glimpsed in Kirillov, a character who, like Ippolit, believes, since God does not exist, that he is obliged to kill himself.[40] As with Ippolit, one could say of Kirillov, with Verkhovensky's incredulity: "The swinishness is that he believes in God worse than any priest" (*D* 623). Kirillov's outrage and his suffering—that Christ was not exempt from death ("this man was the highest on all the earth. . . . if the laws of nature did not pity even *This One*, did not pity even their own miracle . . . then the whole planet is a lie, and stands upon a lie" [*D* 618])—however apparently incompatible with his exultant happiness ("Everything is good" [*D* 237]), peacefully coexist with it. These two antithetical reactions neither cancel nor moderate, in fact barely impinge on, each other. Thus when Stavrogin says to Kirillov "you also love life. . . . yet you've resolved to shoot yourself," the latter answers: "So what? . . . Life's separate, and that's separate" (*D* 236). This separation—this autonomy of phenomena that would seem to encroach on each other—is equally perceptible in the peculiar relation between Kirillov and his actions. He can confess to crimes, can agree to be implicated in the plot (as with Ippolit in *The Idiot,* even be discernible as its "axis") without being touched by what he brings about.[41] "I could be useful if I killed myself, and . . . one day when you got into some kind of mischief and they were looking for culprits, I could suddenly shoot myself and leave a letter that I had done it all" (*D* 375), he promises Verkhovensky. In the end he signs a document confessing to actions that exonerate the revolutionaries, complying with Verkhovensky's instructions without being affected by what he admits: "it makes no difference to me" (*D* 375).[42] It makes no difference to him (specifically under discussion is the timing of his suicide), because his resolve to take own life (*D* 374) is a pure act of will ("There was just my will, and now there is just my will" [*D* 373]) which could not be disturbed by any contingency. Thus he insists on a spectacular freedom ("there is not and was not any agreement . . . I'm bound by nothing" [*D* 373]), whereby nothing he confesses implicates or even interests him. Because Kirillov is a figure whose experience of suffering does not press on his experience of joy, whose pivotal role in the novel's action does not engage his motive and intention, he can be used in the plot without being sullied by that use, being a figure of pure exemption.[43]

Kirillov's enduring peculiarity, his cryptic strangeness, emanates from such separations (of suffering from joy, of action and articulation from a will that is free of these), and it is given a physical corollary in Dostoevsky's representation of the moments before his death when, grabbing the revolver with which he will kill himself, he disappears inside a closed room, sequestered from Verkhovensky's scrutiny. We see the enigma of this vanishing character, from Verkhovensky's point of view, first as the latter "ponder[s] . . . the door" (*D* 621); then "listened cautiously; not the slightest sound could be heard" (*D* 622); then, when opening the door, he immediately slams it as "something bellowed and rushed at him" (*D* 622). Finally, gathering courage, Verkhovensky reopens the door to see "no one was in the room. . . . exactly no one" (*D* 623). Yet in the corner by the wardrobe and wall, he suddenly perceives "Kirillov was standing, and standing very strangely—motionless, drawn up, his arms flat at his sides, his head raised, the back of his head pressed hard to the wall, in the very corner, as if he wished to conceal and efface all of himself" (*D* 623–24). As Verkhovensky stares at "the protruding parts of the figure" (*D* 624), he cannot "make out the whole of . . . the riddle" he calls

"Kirillov" (*D* 624). The riddle that is Kirillov, half-visible and half-illegible, cannot be disclosed or penetrated. Or rather, to put it as the novel does, if he is not seen but rather sensed, he is most viscerally—and blindly—perceptible as "a terrible pain in the little finger of [Verkhovensky's] left hand" (*D* 624), as pure piercing sensation, when "something so hideous" (*D* 624) occurs and Kirillov leans down to bite it. Unlike Svidrigailov before *his* suicide in *Crime and Punishment,* whose lucid and sensuous dreams transparently reveal his torment, Kirillov is uninterpretable, less someone whose motivation could be deciphered than a sequence of ferocious lunges and postures of arrested stillness. In his deranged frenzy, this detachment of Kirillov from himself relates him to us as a trope of ecstasis or rapture—an embodiment of transport, a state of being carried away, as a being lifted out of himself. (In Kirillov's contorted immobility Verkhovensky sees him as a "figure" that is "made of stone or wax" [*D* 624].) Or rather: the subsumption of Kirillov by impassioned bursts of suffering and joy, worked up to a state of rage that alternately freezes and propels him, evacuates or nullifies what in other instances we would call subjectivity and attribute to character, so that, more completely than Dostoevsky's other vehicles for the impersonal expression of suffering and joy, Kirillov is exactly "no one" (*D* 623).

Ippolit, like a "trembling leaf torn from a tree" (*I* 402), is the product of nature that nourishes and then releases him, while Kirillov is that character whose character is nullified, each becoming a vehicle for the transport of a joy that passes through and leaves them. Joy is the immanence to which Martin Heidegger attests with inadvertent recourse to Ippolit's greenness: "We stand before a tree in bloom . . . and the tree stands before us. . . . The tree and we *are*." To stand "face-to-face" with the tree is to spring from a conceptual world, unreal, ideational to "firm soil. . . . upon which we live and die."[44] Like Ippolit's wonder-struck experience of those "everlasting 'trees,'" Heidegger's trees are miraculous because they attest to an ecstasy perceptible here: "A curious, indeed unearthly thing that we must first leap onto the soil on which we really stand."[45] In distinction to the encrypted images that Ippolit cannot decipher—nightmare congruences that Lebedyev supposes he alone could interpret, "for I am clever at it" (*I* 194)—in *The Idiot* and *Demons* joy is a transparency in which nothing is hidden that *could* be explicated. Kirillov's leaf is not an allegory or a symbol—not something penetrable—but is rather a manifestation of being joyfully discovered both within and around it, hence the widening exaltation ("Everything is good" [*D* 237]) of that blissful perception. "The 'what' of being," Heidegger continues, "its essence . . . *is*" (emphasis mine)—is nothing that can be isolated: "Where in the tree or on the tree or behind the tree, is this thing named by the 'is'? . . . the 'is' does not keep within it a weightiness that we can hardly ever weigh."[46] The tree in its bloom condenses the ubiquitousness of being—being is everywhere the tree is—into a particular manifestation (greenness) that arrests Ippolit's attention because it strikes him as unique: being revealed by being brought forth in the lushness that is foliage, even though greenness is no more constitutive of the tree than its bark or its dying leaves are. Although it may seem perverse to suggest a relation between Heideggerian immanence and Dostoevsky's Russian Orthodoxy, in certain moments of *Demons* and *The Idiot*, outside plotted narrative, outside character, and outside theology, joy may be seen to dwell, strangely (since this is not precisely Dostoevsky's emphasis), in the consciousness that constitutes it. But not in quotidian consciousness. Rather in consciousness become the site of being that impersonally reveals itself. This receptiveness to being, this "presence," as Heidegger calls it, is "a gathering. . . . the coming-to-the-fore" of "the radiance issuing from unconcealedness."[47]

We see how thoroughly consciousness creates and structures joy and suffering by its striking omission, when in the contest at Nastasya's nameday celebration Epanchin, Aglaia's father, ends his story of the worst thing he has ever done—abusing an old landlady for keeping a bowl of his—with this deliberated image:

> "I was beside myself . . . when I got to the old woman's. I saw her sitting in the passage, huddled up in the corner all alone, as though to get out of the sun, her cheek propped on her hand. I poured out a stream of abuse, calling her all sorts of names . . . as I looked at her: she sat with her face turned to me, her eyes round and staring, and answered not a word. And she looked at me in such a queer way, she seemed to be swaying. At last I calmed down. I looked at her, I questioned her—not a word. I stood hesitating: flies were buzzing, the sun was setting, there was stillness. . . . So that at the very time I was abusing her she was passing away. . . . at last God had brought her to the end, as the sun was setting, on a quiet summer evening my old woman too was passing away." (*I* 143–44)

Although in Epanchin's account the woman's "passing away" is made pervious to his abuse of her (he half-heartedly accepts blame for her death and half-heartedly offers recompense for it), it must more strikingly be observed that in her rapt and solitary engagement with her dying as he paints it ("left alone like . . . some fly accursed from the beginning of time" [*I* 144]), she remains unaffected by him. Even though the old woman is central to the story Epanchin tells against himself—the object of his abuse, she could not technically be outside of it—her dying is isolated, like the many such scenes collected by the novel and set against the plot, moments that are flooded with unknowing and that could not be further narrated. The juxtaposition of his "violent swearing" (*I* 144) and her disengagement ("eyes round and staring . . . not a word" [*I* 143]), her apparent obliviousness to him, is analogous to the parceling of the economic moments that grind out the plot and the fragmentary moments, both ultimate and intermittent, that interrupt and punctuate it with strains that are foreign. Although Epanchin theatricalizes and sentimentalizes the moment, implying a causal relation between his cursing and his agency ("Why she should have taken it into her head to die at that moment?" [*I* 144]), nothing disturbs the interest that underscores the autonomy of the scene. If Epanchin gives voice to the old woman's dying—an uncanny moment marked by his estrangement from it—the old woman, the only one whose utterance could count for anything, is speechless. The illegibility of the old woman's state of mind illuminates by contrast how completely consciousness is the ground of the representations of joy and suffering which have no space to emerge outside it. The old woman's silence, even her stupor, permits us to ask: Could one have joy without being conscious of it? Could one perceive another's suffering or joy while she remained unconscious of it? If one died in a stupor, where would joy or suffering be? With a nod to the logic of Kirillov's exegesis, could one be joyful if one were dead?—questions that fall away before the opacity of the old woman's consciousness (blocked to her also?) while she is passing away.[48] This lodging of suffering and joy in the space of the mind's perception of it rather than in the social space where dialogically Dostoevsky constructs the preponderance of his novel punctuates the discrepancy between the drama of character and event that Epanchin's story merely epitomizes and those recognitional states in which being is "unconcealed" and "lying-before-us."[49]

Yet Ippolit associates joy with *un*consciousness, because joy detached from awareness is joy that does not fade, a proposition exemplified for him in the image of a fly, which, unlike the malevolent spider, is innocent. The fly is innocent because it is construed to have no consciousness—no perceptible mental state. The fly, first an emblem of joy Ippolit cannot experience ("even the tiny fly . . . is happy" [*I* 400]), oddly recurs as an emblem of his extinction ("the dark and obscure lot . . . was to crush me like a fly, and, of course, with no reason" [*I* 380]). The fly is also inscribed in the old woman's dying ("flies were buzzing, the sun was setting" [*I* 143]). In the fly's shifting associations (with joy, with extinction, with Ippolit's awareness of these), the fly does not signify or mean, even as its immersion in nature is elevated in Ippolit's narrative to a value above anything that *could* signify. The beauty of the fly is that it is so interpenetrated with a nature of which it is unconscious that it could be singled out to be extinguished but, as in Georges Bataille's account below, not afflicted by that extinction:

> [A] biologist can separate a fly from the swarm, all it takes is a brushstroke. But he separates it *for himself*, he does not separate it for the flies. To separate itself from the others a fly would need a monstrous force of the understanding; then it would name itself and do what the understanding normally effects by means of language, which alone founds the separation of elements and by founding it founds itself on it, within a world formed of separated and denominated entities. But in this game the human animal finds . . . precisely human death. . . . The only true death supposes separation and, through the discourse which separates, the consciousness of being separated.[50]

In Dostoevsky's novel, as in Georges Bataille's account, immune to the perception of death, or to the perception of any boundary that would alienate it—a counterimage to the novel's reiterated expressions of solitude ("I alone" [*I* 400], "Only he" [*I* 410])—the fly is a figure for the absorption that is joy oxymoronically purged of the consciousness that could register it. Its felicity does not abide within the constraint of consciousness.

The fly is also a synecdoche of harmony, a figure detached from the larger narrative—like the passages I have discussed, something like a fragment. *The Idiot*'s intense fragments—the ass, the leaf, the trees—isolated, interruptive, and apparently incidental, in addition, preside over the novel, parts apart from the whole, which loom over it: "The fragment figures . . . the outside-the-work . . . that is essential to the work," Jean-Luc Nancy and Philippe Lacoue-Labarthe assert; "it always operates both as a sub-work and as a super-work. . . . it is inscribed outside the work, and it completes it."[51] The fragment involves "*Witz* . . . an immediate, absolute knowing-seeing," specifically, knowledge that is received at "lightning speed"—something that could be described as a "spiritual faculty, and a type of spirit."[52] Bursting with ungoverned energy—with energy free of agency—these fragments embody a fullness without a futurity. They are essential to the work because they immediately aggregate the joy that characters cannot personally realize. Such moments of transport, the fragments suggest, extreme and anonymous, could be anyone's.

In concluding, I touch on states of mind—over which characters attempt to exert agency—that Dostoevsky's novels set side by side with joy, to press on the differences illuminated by that proximity. Thus Stavrogin grandiosely theatricalizes a vision of an "earthly paradise. . . . for which prophets have died on crosses and been killed, without which people do not want to live and cannot even die," into which "a tiny red spider" (*D* 703) intrudes—its incongruity an emblem of Stavrogin's torment.[53] While the spider is Dostoevsky's recurrent emblem of the mysterious baseness that displaces joy, it is here transposed into an image of *Stavrogin's* baseness, since that torment is interwoven with an account of his crime—the violation of the ten-year-old child, Matryosha. Stavrogin claims to kill himself because "what poured out of me was only negation" (*D* 676). An alternative would be "magnanimity" (*D* 676): courage to embrace joy even in its evanescence.

Joy is more banally driven away by the appetite for pleasure (the converse of Stavrogin's revulsion), which *Crime and Punishment*'s Svidrigailov embodies to a near-perfection. Although Svidrigailov delights in sensuous refinements ("One all but requires pleasant sensations!"), those "pleasant sensations" (*CP* 505), which, in being sought and cultivated, are joy's displacement—his thoughts, like Stavrogin's, are irredeemably spoiled by nastiness. Either pleasure leads to common satiety or to uncommon grief and ruin. Thus in Svidrigailov's fantasy of "a rich, luxurious country cottage in the English style, all sunk in fragrant flowerbeds, with rows surrounding the entire house . . . a bright, cool stairway . . . adorned with rare flowers in Chinese jars . . . bouquets of white and tender narcissus, in jars of water on the windowsills, bending on long, bright green, fleshy stems, with their heavy, sweet scent" (*CP* 506), an image of oppressive surfeit their fragrance makes pervasive—fantastic, lush, exotic—bloom into their fatal opposite. "He went up the stairs and entered a large, high-ceilinged room . . . everywhere there were flowers. . . . in the middle of the room" of the resplendent house with which Svidrigailov consoles himself against the stormy night, his last before he kills himself: "a coffin. . . . Garlands of flowers twined it on all sides. All in flowers, a girl was lying. . . . The girl was a suicide—by drowning" (*CP* 506–7). In distinction, joy can vanish but can never spoil or be defiled.

Svidrigailov crafts his death with exquisite care—unlike Kirillov, who is indifferent to the effect of *his* death, before which he virtually fades away—remaining most himself in ruminating his extinction. "Never in my life have I liked water, not even in landscapes" (*CP* 504). But contemplating where to kill himself, he thinks: "It will be daybreak in an hour! . . . I'll leave now, go straight to the Petrovsky: somewhere there I'll choose a big bush doused all over with rain" (*CP* 508). Actually, he hopes to shoot himself by "the water of the Little Neva" (*CP* 510) where he imagines "wet paths, wet grass, wet trees and bushes, and finally that very bush" (*CP* 510) so that even nature looks compliant to his sensuous plan, "a big bush doused all over with rain" (*CP* 508), and to its details, "so that if you barely touch it with your shoulder, millions of drops will shower down on your head" (*CP* 508). In this aesthetic, beauty, or, if not beauty, splendor—a magnificent display—would redeem even the water Svidrigailov finds distasteful, and make it dazzling, so that, were he not dead, it might be pleasing to him.

"What sort of beauty will save the world?" (*I* 370), Ippolit asks. *Demons* and *The Idiot* suggest that no beauty but a joy could—the antithesis of the opulence that drives Stavrogin's and Svidrigailov's fantasies, and whose lavish disappointments justify their suicides—something uncompounded, like Christ in its absoluteness, but devoid of that narrative, hence free of its economies in which joy is a compensation for suffering. If joy arises in consciousness, its presence there is not simply impersonal but also foreign to the commonplace idea of consciousness and to character—so much so that Ippolit associates it with unconsciousness, even with obliviousness ("Every 'little fly'" [*I* 410]). In these ways joy is alienated, made strange, even made unrecognizable. Without attributes ("not tenderheartedness, but simply joy" [*D* 590]); without forgiveness ("You don't forgive anything, because there's no longer anything to forgive" [*D* 590]); and even without love ("You don't really love—oh, what is here is higher than love!" [*D* 590]), the nothing of joy, its evanescence and its insubstantiality, can only be indicated in notations so fleeting as to be virtually gestural: "five seconds" (*D* 590), "Muhammad's jug" (*D* 591). Joy is without content, contour or duration, what the characters in Dostoevsky's novels cannot endure, but for which they would forfeit the stories they enact and tell ("I would give my whole life" [*D* 590]) and which Dostoevsky amazingly constructs around them, even as the stories they tell postpone or dispel joy. For story is always someone's story, and to be in time is to rush past the present moment, which, vanishing, has no story.

These interludes—fragments—could never find a place in *Crime and Punishment* or *The Brothers Karamazov*, where bliss emerges from a conversion narrative, "Cana of Galilee," which is reenacted anew in transformative understanding when Alyosha, bitterness dispelled, "water[s] the earth with . . . tears of . . . joy" (*BK* 362). In distinction, in *The Idiot* and *Demons* the redemptive story can't be grasped. The fragment acts as "a sub-work" or "super-work,"[54] in that it distills antitheses to isolated plus and minus tropes (which neighbor the curve of story): joy and no more joy; transparence and illegibility; the green leaf and Meyer's wall; Myshkin and Rogozhin; "everything in" your "power" (*I* 381) and no agency; the old woman's speechlessness and Epanchin's invective against her while she is passing away; "Everything is good" (*D* 237) understood without the tincture of Kirillov's lunacy and, of course, its inverse. If such fragments do not drive the plot, they inflect it, since it is out of such plus and minus tropes steeped in time and narrative that *The Idiot*'s and *Demons*' fatal stories (fatal, for *their* bliss is otherworldly) are woven as a counterpoint.

3

The Sight of Death in Tolstoy

Rainer Maria Rilke, whose fascination with death could not be severed from his discovery of its germinating origin ("if a tree blossoms, death blossoms in it as well as life, and the field is full of death . . . and the beasts go patiently from one [to the] other"[1] [brackets in the original]), might have been describing his own maturing understanding of that relation when he elaborated on Leo Tolstoy's writing:

> [H]is enormous experience of Nature . . . made him astonishingly able to think from a sense of the whole and to write out of a feeling for life which was so permeated with the finest particles of death, that death seemed to be contained everywhere in it as an odd spice in the strong flavor of life—, but for that very reason this man could be so deeply, so frantically frightened when he discovered that somewhere there was pure death, that bottle full of death . . . out of which one was compelled to drink bitterness of undiluted death. This man observed in himself and in others many kinds of fear of death, for through his natural composure it was given him to be the observer even of his own fear, and his relationship to death will to the last have been a fear permeated with grandeur, a fugue of fear, as it were, a gigantic structure, a tower of fear with corridors and flights of stairs and railless projections and sheer edges on all sides—only that the force with which he experienced and admitted the very extravagance of his own fear may—who knows—at the last moment have changed over into unapproachable reality, was suddenly this tower's sure foundation, landscape and sky and the wind and a flight of birds around it—(150–51)

Rilke's wealth of images, at first loosely gathered together, then formed into the conceit of a single edifice with differentiated parts ("structure," "tower," "stairs," "edges"), would not have been Tolstoy's, whose stark figures for death—a disembodied "voice," a neuter "*It,*" a mass of color and shape: "red, white, and square,"[2] could never dissolve into Rilke's consolatory vision of transport (the "wind," the "flight of birds"). Yet Rilke's determination of "particles of death" that become "pure death" and then the "sure foundation" of "unapproachable reality" excavates the stages—brings to light the essential conversions—plotted by Tolstoy's late short stories.

Tolstoy's stories render death a presence that can be experienced as well as contemplated, and that evolves in the consciousness of Tolstoy's characters so that its foretaste is made integral to the vitality that would seem to be its antithesis, even as Tolstoy preserves the strangeness of such an invigoration, for it would seem that death could no more be animated than a stone could be brought to life. Yet for Tolstoy, death is never only a blow whose violence is future. Tolstoy's endless writing on death is something like an endless knowing that is also a *not* knowing that the fate that seems elsewhere is here "in a room nearby"[3]—a realization whose dawning is subverted by resistance: "Can this be dying? No, I don't want to!" (II 127). This interpenetration of something seen and simultaneously blocked constitutes the thickness, the texture, the feel of death in Tolstoy's writing—which continually turns into the feeling of not feeling it.

Tolstoy's stories written between 1882 and 1905 dwell on the impossibility of mitigating death's fact (or what he calls its truth). But Tolstoy's didactic writings—roughly contemporaneous with these stories—propound a different understanding. In the words of Simonson in *Resurrection* (1889–1900), "everything in the world is alive, and nothing can be described as 'dead.'"[4] Yet if Tolstoy's didactic writing is religious, it is not conventionally Christian. For Tolstoy's denunciation of the blasphemy of the Orthodox Church, which is "ablaze with the fire of false doctrine," is also an invective against the core teaching of Christianity itself: including the doctrine of the Trinity ("that God . . . would melt like ice before my eyes"), the Incarnation, and the Atonement—specifically against the "fairy tales" of Christ's resurrection.[5] The latter point is crucial to emphasize, for Tolstoy's conviction of deathlessness is severed from any belief in redemption through "a life beyond the grave," being, rather, iconoclastically founded on "eternal life and retribution here and everywhere, now and for ever."[6] In some stories there is a hinge between the two strains of writing, for instance, as I shall suggest, in "The Forged Coupon" (1904). Its paradigm is "Memoirs of a Madman" (1884); in that story the narrator proclaims, "Death is the only real thing, and death ought not to exist" (MM 308), but, in its conclusion, the narrator, on the spur of the moment, seeing beggars at the door of a church in which he has been worshiping, gives away all he has (MM 313)—an inspiration whose charity, like nothing else, dispels his torment at the death-charged core of everything: "if this was not, then neither was there death or fear."[7] The stark contrast of the two claims is highlighted when the perception that "Death is the only real thing" of "Memoirs" confronts *On Life*'s claim (1887) that, through a special relation to the world constituted by augmentations of love, there is no death of any consequence.[8]

It could be argued that there is nothing perplexing about the relation between the two strains of writing that overlap, in the sense that the great stories on death conclude with the protagonist's being importuned by, or acknowledging, the God of the didactic writing.[9] Yet although the conclusions of "Memoirs of a Madman," "Death of Ivan Ilych," and "Master and Man" are in one sense compatible with the claims of *On Life*—that "true life" (*L* 393) is love, understood as the striving toward the happiness of others; that such love "annihilates" the "fear" of death (*L* 372); and, in *On Life* , also annihilates its fact (*L* 405)—this consonance is not the sense of the two strains of writing, which allocate their persuasive forces to objects inherently hostile to one another: the realization of death as absolute for oneself personally and an ethical project that renders death insubstantial. Thus the overlap that exists between the two kinds of writing is trivialized by the disparity between characters who, tortured by death, embrace its actuality, and characters whose ethical practices are marshaled to dispel that actuality. My interest in the following pages can be specified as a desire to examine the ethical consequences of these frictive beliefs (that death is "real," that death is "fantastic"),[10] and to press on how access is gained to the ethical in each kind of writing. In the death-obsessed writing, the realization that death is *your* death, or the death of another that demands your witness, opens into an ethical assent to the world as it is, *however* it is, or into right conduct. Though one cannot save oneself from a force that will neither be abstracted nor banished, a valid object of effort spontaneously emerges as what it might be possible to do for another.[11] Or, the ethical might more simply be discerned as wonder at the mere existence of the other and at existence itself, which dying throws into relief. Thus no formula reveals how the ethical incarnates itself (it could be in an action, a feeling, an affirmation, a vision, the *refusal* of vision, or it could register viscerally); this indeterminacy is a thrill for the reader, since the ethical discovery that relativizes death's suffering (but not of course its fact) can issue only from the specific torment of experiencing it, whose effects could not be anticipated. In the writing that vanquishes death, the ethical is "brain-spun"[12]—revealed by "rational consciousness" (*L* 346) and the cultivation of love it prescriptively dictates.

In section I, focusing on Tolstoy's writing of the 1880s, 1890s, and early

1900s (with some look-back moments to the earlier novels), I examine the protean manifestations of death's insistent claim that "*It* alone was true" (II 130). In II, I turn to a counter-notion espoused by *On Life* and enacted in "The Forged Coupon," a story in which a character first preempts his own death by appropriating its aggression and turning it on others by murdering them, and, in the second half of that fable, by penitently immersing himself in the love prescribed by Tolstoy's treatise. Section III considers Robert Bresson's 1983 film *L'Argent*, an adaptation of "Coupon," to examine the implications of Bresson's against-the-grain rendering of the ethical moment in that story. I interpret *L'Argent* as a critique of the placement of the ethical insight in Tolstoy's didactic fiction, to which it supplies a correction; it ends not with "Coupon"'s redemptive "love," whose "augmentation" is said to be "life" (*L* 417) but with the enigmatic moment that precedes the protagonist's confession, on which Bresson lingers. In his reworking, Bresson obliquely sheds light on the ethical underpinnings of Tolstoy's two kinds of writing. I conclude by asking in what sense the ethical in Tolstoy's writing is supernatural. Of interest for Tolstoy, as for Ludwig Wittgenstein (who first associated ethics with the supernatural), is what could be meant by that designation which gestures toward something beyond the world, but not beyond imagining. "Every one knows the life of the spirit," Tolstoy wrote in *The Gospel in Brief*, quoting Jesus: "You all know it; but you do not do that which you know. . . . you are drawn away from the true life."[13] Tolstoy's scathing characterization of shallow knowledge raises the question of how the ethical might be realized. What awakens a character to a universe he does not recognize? How does the ethical grip a character so that it changes him?

I

In Father Sergius's fantasy of self-recrimination, his own death is lovingly engineered. The monk's atheism, his hypocrisy, his coldness, his sensual attraction to Marie, a "feeble-minded" girl (he permits her to put his hand on her breast), reminds him of Pashenka, another "insipid, insignificant, and pitiable" girl whom he tormented when she was a child, by commanding her to lie on the floor and to move in such a way as to prove she knew how to swim.[14] These pleasurable reminiscences give way to a temptation of another stripe, Sergius's seductive thought of suicide. For the thought of suicide will regulate or vindicate his unseemly reflections: "'Is she still as unhappy as she was then when she had to show us how to swim on the floor? But why should I think about her? What am I doing? I must put an end to myself.' . . . So he lay for a long time, thinking now of his unavoidable end and now of Pashenka."[15]

If the alluring thought of suicide alternates with the alluring thought of Pashenka "swimming" on the floor, this is because death by suicide is a punishment Father Sergius can imagine inflicting on himself and can also refrain from inflicting on himself—his death being an outcome he metes out, judiciously deliberates, and then withholds, so he can embrace a more provocative daydream.

Less crude than the fantasy in which one's own death can be erased by a titillating reverie, or in which death is so unsolid that "freehold land" could usurp it,[16] is the supposition that death can be superseded by intelligence about it. " 'What is it all for?' " Levin asks in *Anna Karenina*[17]—a question echoed by Pierre in *War and Peace*, by "Three Deaths" 's uncomprehending invalid, and, of course, by Ivan Ilych. To ask " 'what . . . for?' " is to suppose that death is a problem that adroitness could decipher, a supposition analogous to the reasoning that Nekhlyudov in *Resurrection* queries: "why, by what right, does one lot of people lock up, torture, exile, flog and put to death other people, when they are no different from the ones they torture, flog and put to death?"[18] Nekhlyudov's question is rhetorical, since it implies a logic in which those who put to death are blinded to their interchangeability with those put to death. The point to their blindness—its efficacy—lies in the establishment of a difference on the basis of which death might become the destiny of others. In this way, they are relieved of their fate because it is inflicted on others whose difference from themselves can bear it.[19] Similarly, when Ivan Ilych justifies his life as good ("I did everything properly" [II 145]), he does not see that appropriateness and even virtue are irrelevant to a finality that is indifferent to the distinctions on the basis of which such a characterization is founded. It is only when death's imminence eradicates the meaningfulness of good, as a correct assessment (from one vantage) and as a distinction having bearing (from another), that Ivan Ilych becomes someone he was not prepared to be, and comes to glean the nature of his strange torment.

Let me first specify what that torment is not: it is not the image of the body without integrity seen from the outside, as in "A Prisoner in the Caucasus," when Zhilin's horse, felled by a bullet, lies "its legs in the air, unable to touch the ground. There was a hole in its head, and black blood was pouring out, turning the dust to mud."[20] It is not the anguish of a man being dispossessed of the qualities that make him who he is, as when Hadji Murad, dying from a wound in his side, no longer moved, and "felt nothing more," while "his enemies kicked and hacked at what had no longer anything in common with him."[21] And torment is not visible in the corpses of Vasily Andreevich, Nikita the peasant, and Mukhorty the horse in "Master and Man," which, though spared human violence, have become mere receptacles for the elements:

> Mukhorty, buried up to his belly in snow, with the breeching and sacking hanging down, stood all white, his dead head pressed against his frozen throat: icicles hung from his nostrils, his eyes covered with hoar-frost as though filled with tears, and he'd grown so thin in that one night that he was nothing but skin and bone.
>
> Vasily Andreevich was stiff as a frozen carcass, and when they rolled him off Nikita his legs remained apart and his arms stretched out as they had been. His bulging hawk eyes were frozen, and his open mouth under his clipped moustache was full of snow. But Nikita though chilled through was still alive.[22]

Though the horse's visage is humanized—for the horse's eyes, not the man's, simulate the sorrow that neither can feel—and though the man's eyes are likened to those of a diurnal bird of prey, and *his* body, rather than the animal's, is described as a "carcass," any attempt to differentiate these creatures (or to associate each with characteristics of the other's species) is rendered gratuitous by the fate that renders all identifications meaningless. Vasily's "open mouth . . . full of snow" most aggressively violates our conception of a living being (as the icicles that hang from Mukhorty's nostrils introduce by negation the image of breathing). These vestiges of speech and breath only italicize Tolstoy's determination to render lifelessness everywhere, however such a representation necessitates distinctions—"dead head pressed against . . . frozen throat"—as though only such discriminations between two kinds of immobility could awaken us to their irrelevance.

In distinction to these static representations of death seen from the outside, the torment of Ivan Ilych's dying is incredulity that does not exhaust itself: "In the depth of his heart he knew he was dying, but not only was he not accustomed to the thought, he simply did not and could not grasp it" (II 129). And in distinction to Tolstoy's mesmerizing descriptions of the corpses in "Master and Man," which astonish with their detail, death glimpsed from within has no attributes for perception to fasten on. The heart of Tolstoy's story lies in his capacity to bear down on this nothingness and to intensify it—to ask: what can be grasped when "could not grasp" (II 129) gives way? One aspect of the collapse is the rapidity with which formulations about death encounter their own meaninglessness. Ivan Ilych's "I was here and now I am going there!" (II 127) is barely articulated before it is rebuked as illegitimate. "Where?" implicitly contests even the category of the placeholder "there." Ivan Ilych's not grasping, grasping, and then again failing to grasp, churningly repeat themselves in waves that ripple through the story.[23]

Unlike a painting, Tolstoy's narrative unfolds a sequence in words and time. Yet, in its sustained recurrence to Ivan Ilych's fright, Tolstoy's story could be said to act on us very like a visual image, in terms I adopt from a remarkable discussion by T. J. Clark of Nicolas Poussin's *Landscape with a Man Killed by a Snake*. Clark's analysis is pertinent not only because of the analogy between the panic-stricken vision of death in Tolstoy's story and Poussin's painting, but also because Clark's insight orients us to ask how, in another medium, Tolstoy balances that terror with an ethical counterweight that makes it bearable. In writing about *Snake*, in which a "running man" catches sight of a "corpse in the grip of" an "anaconda," Clark characterizes the narrative as "the story of the world interrupted." This "deadness" is "the key to what it is the running man cannot take his eyes off—the particular form in which the world rears up in front of him, looking like nothing anyone can say."[24] Clark, then, inquires how the nothing-like-it of death touches those who behold it from outside the painting's frame, arguing that what gives the painting's beholders the equipoise to endure the terror of the running man's eyes is an equilibrium conferred by a second perspective, that of an "imperturbable" "woman on the path," whose equanimity takes stock of the horror without being devastated by its extremity. Clark associates the perspective with an "ethics."[25] The beholder, Clark argues, requires the woman whose serenity in the face of death sustains his own capacity to see what the running man sees. Who occupies the woman's position in "The Death of Ivan Ilych"? It would seem this ethical agent could only be Gerasim, "the butler's young assistant . . . always cheerful and bright" (II 132), who shrugs off sleeplessness and who performs tasks that would repel the other characters (drawing up his master's trousers, lifting him from the commode, leading him "to the sofa," raising Ivan Ilych's legs; "he felt better while Gerasim was holding up his legs" [II 133]).[26]

There is an ethical charge in "Ivan Ilych," but it is not linked to a second perspective manifesting composure—as in Clark's discussion of *Snake*'s "imperturbable . . . woman's sanity and balance, her wide embrace of the world, her having it rest stably on her shoulders"[27]—however this image might be a metaphoric corollary to the weight Gerasim literally shoulders. Rather, Tolstoy's countervision, unlike an image that arrests the eye at once, dawns only gradually, and from the same vantage as Ivan Ilych's pain and terror—there being no other foundation in Tolstoy's story that is afforded such legitimacy—as these are dealt out to Ivan Ilych in a progression of passages that come so rapidly upon each other as almost to breach decorum. When Ivan Ilych asks of his impending death, "How is one to understand it?" (II 129), the question is immediately driven up against impossibility: "He could not understand it" (II 129). Instead, "the former current of thoughts that had once screened the thought of death from him" (II 130) gives way:

> *It* would come and stand before him and look at him, and he would be petrified and the light would die out of his eyes, and he would again begin asking himself whether *It* alone was true. . . . And what was worst of all was that *It* drew his attention to itself not in order to make him take some action but only that he should look at *It,* look it straight in the face: look at it and without doing anything, suffer inexpressibly. And to save himself from this condition Ivan Ilych looked for consolations—new screens—and new screens were found and for a while seemed to save him, but then they immediately fell to pieces or rather became transparent, as if *It* penetrated them and nothing could veil *It.* (*II* 130)

The vision stripped of mediation—there is nothing but a bare presence indicated by a neuter pronoun—is juxtaposed to moments that flesh out Ivan Ilych's physical torture (the "gnawing, unmitigated, agonizing pain [*muchit' bol'*],[28] never ceasing for an instant" [II 136]), his mental agony at "the deception, the lie . . . that he was not dying but was simply ill, and that he only need keep quiet and undergo a treatment and then something very good would result" (II 134), and his irritation, as at the disagreement between his wife and daughter on "the elegance and realism" of Sarah Bernhardt's acting (II 142)—conversation that chokes off acknowledgment of his extremity. These have a substantiality on which the mind can dilate, whereas the *It* is void of properties, but not void of the capacity to grip the attention and rivet it on that vacuity. Tolstoy marks the distinction between the "it" that is physical and the *It* without properties by setting them against each other, and italicizing the latter.[29] Ivan Ilych's naked encounter with the unfeatured *It* is most powerfully brought into focus by this rejoinder that is the inverse of nothingness: " 'But I am not guilty!' he exclaimed angrily. 'What is it for?' " (II 145). For guilt is an alloy, a welter of mental concessions and rebuttals—did this, did not do that—and of feelings.

"Not guilty" has always seemed to me the fulcrum on which the logic of Ivan Ilych's ethical understanding falsely pivots. Ivan Ilych's protest may also provide the grounds of the reader's purest identification with him. In the wake of "agony" unstintingly parceled out to Ivan Ilych, and preceding his own "What if my whole life has really been wrong?" (II 148), the introduction of guilt implies that suffering (still "dreadful" but no longer "incomprehensible" [II 146]) is a punishment for life lived as a betrayal of its essence (Georg Lukács' reading). A contravening understanding emerges in the retort to Ivan Ilych's question: " 'Why these sufferings?' And the voice answered, 'For no reason—they just are so' " (II 145). The latter exchange would suggest guilt and retribution are part of a punitive logic the mind dreams up to gloss experience's meaninglessness—its inexplicability—since only under pressure of death could life be seen authentically (Lev Shestov's reading). As with Dostoevsky's prisoner counting the minutes before his execution, to be sundered from a habitual point of view depends on the violence of near-extinction. Yet when Ivan Ilych repeats, "An explanation would be possible if it could be said that I have not lived as I ought to" (II 147), Tolstoy's didacticism again seems unequivocal. Which is true?[30] In constructing two explanatory planes on which the answer to "Why these sufferings?" is staged, Tolstoy explores the relation between the powerful but incommensurate logics that grip his antihero. As Tolstoy ultimately insists, the alleviation of suffering lies in the vitality of the moment (on this both interpretations agree), a recognition that, however fleeting, exerts the counterweight to suffering, whether its meaning can be grasped or whether it cannot be, whether the affliction could have been averted, or could not have been averted because it is given ontologically.

This breakdown of distinction between guilt ("What if my whole life has really been wrong?" [II 148]) and meaninglessness ("For no reason—they just are so" [II 145]), which intersect in the rectification of the present moment, is a paradigm for the dissolution of other disparities. Thus the "peculiar flavour and the flow of saliva" around the "stones" of the "raw shrivelled French plums" (II 146) Ivan Ilych sucked as a child are more like the terrible *It* that cannot be screened than either are like the "damasks, dark wood, plants, rugs, and dull and polished bronzes" (II 114)—the material pleasures of Ivan Ilych's "drawing-room where he had fallen and for the sake of which (how bitterly ridiculous it seemed) he had sacrificed his life" (II 131). Though the flavor of plums and the *It* are, in one sense, antitheses, they are, in their irreducibility, pure metonyms for the life and death elsewhere figured categorically: "all that for which he had lived . . . was not real at all, but a terrible and huge deception which had hidden both life and death" (II 149). The thought of the "French plums of his childhood," and the feel in "the present" of "the button on the back of the sofa and the creases in its morocco" (II 146) are like death in being "self-luminous," nothing the mind could embellish or even reflect on, taken in instinctively as things that are "lived" rather than things "conceived,"[31] and as things that may even be relished. In Tolstoy's story immediacy is deeper than either guilt or meaninglessness, and deeper than the opposition that life and death might signify. This convergence of life and death, which meet beneath the surface of unlikeness, risks the appearance of banality to disclose its actual, essential strangeness.

Similarly, the intoxicating good health and power of those surrounding Ivan Ilych, attributes that also once were his ("power" being the "consciousness" of "being able to ruin anybody he wished to ruin" [II 109]), are brought up against the cramped space of the sickroom, where the diminishments of "illness, suffering, and death" (II 141) brook no commerce with strength or buoyancy. These realms would seem to have no more kinship with each other than Ivan Ilych's emaciated, enfeebled body has with his daughter's "fresh young flesh" (II 141), exposed by her evening dress. Yet the story's ethical point depends on permeating the walls—on disputing the logic of partition that its representation has seemed to make inevitable. Thus the cool analysis, "Ivan Ilych's life had been most simple and most ordinary and therefore most terrible" (II 102), delivered from a distant vantage, whose sweeping conclusions apply indiscriminately to everyone who has lived as he has—that is, in kind if not degree, to everyone—is brought right up against his individual experience of that "terrible" rendered from the inside. This experience is so solitary, because unacknowledged ("none of them know or wish to know" [II 127]), as to be unbearable ("he had to live thus all alone on the brink of an abyss" [II 124]), even though Ilych's life is typical. Not until the story's end can Ivan Ilych himself assent to that "terrible," so he, too, is divided from his experience. The logic of partition breaks down when the question "What is it for?" (II 143) opens into a radically different understanding: "it was revealed to him that though his life had not been what it should have been, this could still be rectified. He asked himself 'What *is* the right thing?'" (II 151), a question that comes into contact with and dismisses "What is it all for?" (II 131), whose implicit *it is all for nothing* depends on an assessment of a past so filled with suffering that it can only be dismissed as worthless.

This convergence of the two questions is the triumph of Ilych's experience of pain, which destroys his resistance and his endurance, thus demolishing a personhood built on the foundation of what he refuses to countenance. Specifically, the pain-space deprives Ivan Ilych of any operation in which a "current of thoughts" (II 130) could assuage what he sees. "He would go to his study, lie down, and again be alone with *It:* face to face with *It*. And nothing could be done with *It* except to look at it and shudder" (II 131). There is no way to grasp the "*It*" so incomprehensible it is devoid of name. This "nothing . . . except to look," and, in looking, nothing to see, is the ground of the ethical insight of Tolstoy's story; pain permits the intrusion of that insight. In pain's indifference to agency—and to distinction—which it wears away, the world is offered whole, to take or not on the basis of a risk: to accede without resistance to experience whose equality—the same for everyone—cannot be appropriated or personalized, and without knowing the consequence of relinquishing resistance. The risk is that there is no difference between assent and the withholding of it. Thus Ivan Ilych's helplessness tears him away from the fiction that he has agency.

At the end of "The Death of Ivan Ilych" there is a dissolution of Ivan Ilych's despair at "the cruelty of God, and the absence of God" (II 143), which also displaces the travesty of God who can effect a "cure" "by a wonder-working icon" (II 122) that could perform miracles. The God that remains, stripped alike of sadism and sensational agency, and fleetingly evoked in Ivan Ilych's confidence that, even if the humans don't, "He whose understanding mattered would understand" (II 152), is almost nothing but a manifestation of acknowledgment. What supplants the fear of death ("In place of death there was light. . . . 'What joy!'" [II 152]) is Ivan Ilych's *own* acknowledgment: pity that wells up, seemingly out of nowhere, when Ivan Ilych gleans his family's misery ("I am making them wretched" [II 151]) and sees how to ameliorate it without recourse to the miraculous, but through a common wonder—his capacity to feel for them. Ivan Ilych's presence to what is called God depends on that compassion and on the request for forgiveness that slips into a wish that they surrender the pleasures that have constituted his anguish ("He tried to add, 'forgive me,' but said 'forgo'" [II 152]).[32] Thus God's unexpected presence, which Tolstoy introduces as a surpassing (of atheism, of guilt, of death, though not of torment, which remains—"'And the pain?' he asked himself. . . . 'Where are you, pain?'. . . . 'Yes, here it is'" (II 152)—is itself surpassed by an everyday triumph in which Ivan Ilych turns outward from the impasse of his suffering to see his own family. "He opened his eyes, looked at his son, and felt sorry for him. His wife came up. . . . He felt sorry for her too" (II 151). At the edge of death Ivan Ilych discovers kindness in a beyond as remote as any supernatural. One could almost say that "God" is a transient name for that discovery, did Tolstoy not insist that compassion is its own sufficiency—"'How good and how simple!'" (II 152)—an amplitude that does not require anything extraneous to validate it.

The story's immense authority issues from the way in which incommensurate threads—guilt, the irrelevance of guilt; the *It*, the prune stones; pain, joy—are woven into a single fabric. Of course, in line with the incongruity between Ivan Ilych and those who estrange themselves from him, the experience of the dying man is not equivalent to that of those who witness it (and insofar as "joy" emerges from the welter of pain, Ivan Ilych's experience is not self-congruent). They only hear sounds that are themselves waves of torment—"'Oh! Oh! Oh!' he cried in various intonations" (II 150)—a sound that is itself a reduction of complexity: "He had begun by screaming 'I won't!' and continued screaming on the letter *O*" (II 150), for however excruciating the sound, the within-ness of that agony is bounded. The container into which Ivan Ilych is shoved ("It seemed to him that he and his pain were being thrust into a narrow, deep black sack" [II 143]) is in part a trope for the obstacle to ascertaining agony from any place exterior to it—suggesting even a materiality to the suffering that envelops Ivan Ilych, hence an inside and outside to its structure. There is also an additional "suffering"—Ivan Ilych's resistance to the pain that dying metes out to him, so that, though he "co-operated," he also "struggled" (II 143): "He was hindered from getting into" that black hole "by his conviction that his life had been a good one. That very justification of his life held him fast and prevented his moving forward" (II 151). At the same time, the story insists, there is a surplus of suffering irreducible to cause.

By surplus I mean that for Tolstoy's reader, drawn up close to this narrative, anguish is so intensely concentrated, but also so excessive, that it spills over the borders of any explanatory confine. Suffering which is sometimes allied with terror and sometimes floats free of it; whose object is at once physical (his "bare, enfeebled thighs" [II 132]) and metaphysical (the "death" of Tolstoy's title); which incessantly occasions Ivan Ilych's question "Why these sufferings?" (II 145) (even as that question is itself an obstacle to sinking into pain's inescapability, that is, its fullness), leads me to return to Clark's insight into what occasions horror in Poussin's painting: "What is it the running (and not running) man recoils (but does not recoil) from? Not from death pure and simple . . . and not just from the snake's endless, formless liveliness, but from the obscene mixture of the two—from the way one state feeds on the other."[33] In "The Death of Ivan Ilych" some such admixture characterizes experience seen in its entirety. "Suffering," "terror," "death," "pain"—and the "joy" that, at the end, rises from their midst—give onto each other, are often conjoined, and are sometimes even represented as interchangeable. These words follow from one another—are textually associated in the same or proximate paragraphs—and cannot be pulled apart from the aggregate "this awful horror" (II 127) that they constitute.[34]

Tolstoy creates a narrative whose temporality distinguishes these designations and continually draws them into relation so that pain arises from the thisness, the immediacy of the "*It*," but no less from the "more . . . life" (II 146) identified with the "the raw shrivelled French plums of his childhood," which occasions Ivan Ilych's recoil: "No, I mustn't think of that. . . . It is too painful" (II 146) [ellipsis in original], since the sensuous "flavour and the flow of saliva when he sucked their stones" (II 146) also has the feeling of an inevitability that can be neither recovered nor altered. In the permeability of everything fresh and vital to death, which, in this story, has its own vitality, the "black sack" (II 143) both bounds the agony and could not do so. Tolstoy's unstinting descriptions of "the gnawing, unmitigated, agonizing pain" (II 136) surpass any logic—and any object—that could account for this pain which, in its permutations, is virtually everywhere the narrative is. To put this in other terms: if there were no guilt and no vindication—there would still be pain. The subtlety of the story's didacticism is thus its inclusiveness (not its prescriptiveness): "justification" (II 151) may be the "suffering" that hinders "moving forward" (II 151) and that proliferates pain. But the freedom that releases Ivan Ilych from that suffering leaves pain in its wake, purified, as it were, of anything gratuitous. " 'And the pain? . . . Yes, here it is. . . . Let the pain be' " (II 152). At such a moment one could ask: if Ivan Ilych's compassion changes "death" to "light" and "joy," what of the story's own mercilessness in drawing Ivan Ilych closer and closer to the "terrible" he has refused to see? Only unflinching, helpless—stripped of vindication, acquiescent to the pain, himself naked—can Ivan Ilych see through "the deception" hiding "both life and death" (II 149) from him. Are the sensuous taste of the "the raw shrivelled French plums" (II 146) and the "*It*" unmediated by screens, bare of consolation, worth it? In 1908, Tolstoy wrote in his diary "It's bad that a stone is hard if you want to break it up, but if you need a stone to sharpen something on, the harder and stronger the better."[35]

In *War and Peace*, though initially blocked from view by Pierre's articulation of a principle, *another*'s death is so fully absorbed that in a revelatory dream, the death he could not countenance becomes inseparable from the spectacle of his own death. After the burning and looting of Moscow, while the French army is demolishing itself by its "convulsive stampede" (*WP* 1136) from the capital—and Moscow is being destroyed not by "the barbarity of the French" (*WP* 999), but by its "inhabitants [who had] abandoned it" (*WP* 1000)—Pierre Bezukhov and Platon Karataev, a peasant whom Pierre has idolized since their imprisonment together after the latter's arrest as an incendiary, are marched away from Moscow under "incomprehensible" and "revolting" conditions (*WP* 1175). If the "Russians . . . froze and lagged behind on the road . . . the order was to shoot them" (*WP* 1175). Yet Pierre cultivates "in proportion to the efforts of [a] fatal force" that would crush him personally "a power of life independent of" fatality (*WP* 1129). His obliviousness to the likelihood of his own death, and also to the dying men strewn along the road on which the convoy moves, appears to contest the ethical principle advanced in "Ivan Ilych": Pierre "did not see and did not hear how they shot the prisoners who lagged behind, though more than a hundred perished in that way" (*WP* 1177). If Pierre's refusal to be devastated by the suffering that surrounds him is initially no more than animal instinct—he seems as indifferent to horror as the blue-gray dog who cavorts among the corpses ("the dog was merrier . . . than it had been in Moscow. All around lay the flesh of different animals . . . [it] could eat all it wanted" [*WP* 1177])—his detachment then becomes an axiom, founded on a "consolatory truth" (*WP* 1176) shocking under any circumstances, and virtually inconceivable under *these* circumstances: "nothing in this world is terrible" (*WP* 1176). Pierre's apparent indifference to "the convoy of prisoners . . . rapidly melting away" (*WP* 1175) as they fall sick or are executed does not depend on a belief in the compensations of an afterlife.[36] It issues from his understanding that the mind can regulate what it sees by turning away from what would destroy it: "Only now did Pierre realize the full strength of life in man and the saving power he has of transferring attention from one thing to another, which is like the safety valve of a boiler . . . when the pressure exceeds a certain limit" (*WP* 1177). By this mechanism, "there is no condition in which man can be happy and entirely free" and "no condition in which he need be unhappy and lack freedom" (*WP* 1176).[37] What further drives apart mental and empirical conditions so they are apprehended independently is the liberating insight at the core of Tolstoy's writing that "suffering and freedom have their limits and . . . those limits are very near together" (*WP* 1176).

This relativism is breathtakingly translated into Pierre's hyperbole: "Nothing . . . is terrible" (*WP* 1176)—a blessing on the world, notwithstanding the "terrible," which, from one point of view (though not, I must stress, Tolstoy's), betrays the severity of the "terrible" by devising strategies that mitigate it. Thus even though, in the flight from Moscow, Pierre is repeatedly assaulted by the grotesque and the piteous (a "corpse smeared with soot for fun" [*WP* 1128]; a sick man left to die [*WP* 1125]; "women with rouged faces" incongruously "dressed in glaring colors" [*WP* 1128]), "All that he now witnessed scarcely made an impression on him" (*WP* 1128). Pierre's refusal to see the overwhelming suffering all around him most remarkably applies to the sickness and death of Karataev, since Pierre's response is incompatible with the man's importance to him.[38] When Pierre hears a shot near a "birch tree" under which "Karataev had been sitting" (*WP* 1180), he resists perceiving the murder of the man who had himself anticipated the death that the gunshot achieves. Karataev's death, always on the verge of revealing itself to Pierre, is repeatedly displaced, first by a calculation ("Pierre heard" the shot "plainly, but at that moment he remembered that he had not yet finished reckoning up how many stages still remained to Smolensk" [*WP* 1180]); then by the "howling" of the dog "behind him, where Karataev had been sitting" (*WP* 1181), whose distress only irritates him ("'What a stupid beast! Why is it howling?' thought Pierre" [*WP* 1181]); even the guilty expressions of the French soldiers, "one of whom carried a . . . smoking gun" (*WP* 1181) remain illegible to him. Later, awakened to "a crowd of memories" ("the shot . . . the dog's howl . . . the guilty faces of the two Frenchmen . . . Karataev's absence at this halt" [*WP*

1182]), Pierre seems unable to continue forestalling awareness from dawning on him, even as it is once again supplanted: "he was on the point of realizing that Karataev had been killed, but just at that instant, he knew not why, the recollection came to his mind of a summer evening he had spent with a beautiful Polish lady on the veranda of his house in Kiev. And without linking up the events of the day or drawing a conclusion from them, Pierre closed his eyes" (*WP* 1182). Thus Karataev dies virtually unnoticed by Pierre.

Pierre can survive only by not seeing, not hearing, not detecting the sea of deaths that swells around him, but at the same time he viscerally absorbs the death that does not touch his senses. Earlier in *War and Peace* Pierre's repeated susceptibility to deception has grown out of the naive belief that he *does* see what is before him. Hence his disastrous first marriage to the chilling Hélène; hence his decision to become a Freemason—two punishing choices that derive from the mistaken trust in his own acuity. In distinction to these misperceptions, on the march away from Moscow Pierre incorporates the savagery he does not hear or see with no idealism, no sentimentality, and no self-deception, until the devastation is so fully absorbed that, as I shall explain, though it bypasses his senses, no knowledge could be more penetrative.

Ivan Ilych is condemned to look unremittingly at the death he cannot bear to see, while Tolstoy valorizes Pierre's capacity to impose screens between himself and the barbarous fate that is Karataev's. Yet this distinction is irrelevant to the amplification of Tolstoy's ethical point: both characters are made to dwell within a torment that seems to have no boundary, until each arrives at the brink of the extremity that envelops him, that is, with a vision of its outside. Ivan Ilych's joy arises from his ability to see outside his travail the importance of easing the suffering of his family, which is suddenly as genuine to him as his own agony. Pierre's "nothing in this world is terrible" (*WP* 1176) implies a consent to experience based on the capacity to reach outside the boundaries of the terrible (itself unalterable) to what the "terrible" can't assimilate—his dream of the "summer evening he had spent with a beautiful Polish lady on the veranda of his house in Kiev" (*WP* 1182) and the peace it epitomizes.[39] It could in fact be said that Pierre's serenity arises from closing his eyes to evidences of death that are so pervasive that all his negations of it ("He made as if he did not notice" [*WP* 1180]; he "did not know" [*WP* 1181]; he "did not look round" [WP 1180]; he "did not finish" [WP 1182]; he did not "understand" [*WP* 1182]) are mere reminders that death is everywhere he is. When Pierre asks about the "blue-gray dog" (*WP* 1182) "Why is it howling?" (*WP* 1181), what he cannot fathom, what he is always only "on the point of realizing" (*WP* 1182)—but never realizes as an endpoint—is that "Karataev had been killed" (*WP* 1182). The protraction of Pierre's experience of that death in effect never terminates. Rather, in an awareness more comprehensive than consciousness, it widens to include everything so that death becomes temporally and spatially omnipresent.

This ubiquitousness is literalized in a dream fragment that precedes the recollection of the "summer evening" and the "beautiful Polish lady" (*WP* 1182), when Karataev's death is explained by Pierre's old Swiss geography teacher, who shows him a "globe . . . a vibrating ball. . . . Its whole surface consisted of drops closely pressed together" (*WP* 1181). The teacher explains: "each drop. . . . grows, merges, disappears from the surface, sinks to the depths, and again emerges. There now, Karataev has spread out and disappeared" (*WP* 1181–82). The ball's oscillations could not come to rest in any static finish, and its totality ("God is in the midst" [*WP* 1181]) includes beauty, death's other side. One gloss of the lesson is to say that, in Rilke's words, "particles of death" ("drops closely pressed together") become "pure death"[40] ("Karataev had been killed" [*WP* 1182]), and then, in the recollection, pure beauty (the "summer evening," the "Polish lady"), while never requiring Pierre's acknowledgment of that distillation or that alchemy. Although the dream pedagogy seems to universalize Karataev's death—and thereby to exempt Pierre from being touched by it personally—in a reverie that immediately follows the geography teacher's lesson, Pierre interpolates himself into the geography teacher's exegesis, since vanishing from the surface is not what happens to Karataev, but rather what happens to *Pierre*, who implicitly "changed places" (*WP* 1181) with his friend: "without linking up the events of the day or drawing a conclusion from them, Pierre closed his eyes, seeing a vision of the country in summertime mingled with memories of bathing and of the liquid, vibrating globe, and he sank into water so that it closed over his head" (*WP* 1182).

The phrase that the teacher uses to explain what happens to the drop that is Karataev is *ukhodit v glubinu*; he undergoes a process (and thus all the verbs in the sentence from which the phrase is taken are in the present imperfective form), part of which is a sinking into the depths (*glubina*), which can also mean into a deep interiority. Although in the instructor's lesson it is "each drop" that "departs into the depths [and] again reemerges" (*WP* 1181–82), rather than explicitly Karataev who does so, insofar as Karataev is one of the drops indicated in the exegesis, the immersion must also be imputed to him, and is so attributed when, in the next sentence, the geography teacher says "There now, Karataev has spread out and disappeared (*razlilsia i izchez*)." A different verb is used by the narrator to specify what happens to Pierre (*opustilsia*, which is the reflexive form of the past perfective verb that means to lower or to let oneself go; translated literally it would be "he let himself go, sank somewhere in the water"). Yet something imitative occurs in Pierre's internalizing of Karataev's death: the deep interiority (*ukhodit v glubinu*) into which *Karataev* sinks is linked to *Pierre's* going under ("so that [the water] closed over his head"), however briefly. Aylmer Maude implicitly notes the congruence of these different words when he translates *ukhodit v glubinu* and *opustilsia* by linking each to the infinitive "to sink."[41] In Pierre's mimetic immersion in the watery "globe" among drops that "changed places," "several of them merging into one"—drops that are "sometimes destroyed," that disappear "from the surface," or that sink "to the depths, and again" emerge (*WP* 1181–82)—a more harmless image arises than that relayed by the geography teacher, and than that exemplified by the execution that the teacher's lesson ameliorates. For Karataev's death could not be experienced more fully or, since Pierre awakens, more mildly, though what is being experienced (but not recognized as experienced) is fatality. In this way Karataev's death, which Pierre initially could not countenance, "mingle[s]" (*WP* 1182) with the dream spectacle of his own prospective death, to which Pierre proleptically also gives consent, since Karataev's death can't be extricated from the holistic pedagogy of the geography teacher's imagined lesson, from the beauty of the summer evening, which does not need to be imagined since it has been so fully lived, and from the dream's benignity, which inexplicably washes over everything.

For Ivan Ilych and for Pierre what precipitates the ethical insight is not routine, not utilitarian, not redemptive (not consequential for a future life). Without duration, it can barely be narrated. Located in a split second, what enables the flash of the ethical insight is the edge of what can be expressed, being something the reader can barely identify, and can't train for or emulate. In that sense, it eludes categories. For Ivan Ilych the ethical insight lies in the recognition of what is outside his own pain, in the perception of his family's suffering. For Pierre it lies in the incorporation of Karataev's death momentarily experienced as his own, though not, in Pierre's case, experienced with agony. What precipitates the flash of the ethical impetus is registered *in* the body *against* the body's resistance to it, as when Ivan Ilych is pushed into the black sack, and as when the dream-water closes over Pierre's head. When the body begins to take each character down (or in Pierre's case, to overwhelm his resilience), something visceral replaces ideas. Granted, there is a disparity between Ivan Ilych's experience of his death (he is so swallowed up in pain, he can't glimpse its outside) and Pierre's registration of Karataev's death (he can't see outside his own willed blindness). The lack of awareness that comes from being submerged in pain is not the same lack of awareness that keeps pain at bay—is, in fact, its inverse.

To experience death's extremity figuratively (fleshed out in a dream image that embodies a dream exposition of a dream logic supplied by a dream teacher to explain what happened to Karataev) is not the same as being at its mercy. Yet in Tolstoy's writing when the body sinks into death, however it might be realized (the black sack, the water's surface), shock opens to ethical understanding: as in the involuntary question "What *is* the right thing?" (II 151) and as in the revisioned perception "nothing in this world is terrible" (*WP* 1176) in which Pierre sees outside the "terrible," now for the first time, by being immersed in it. If Pierre owns Karataev's death by appropriating it—without, it could be argued, ever recognizing specifically what happens to *Karataev*—the elaborate drama in which not seeing turns into an incorporation of what is not seen remains in striking contrast to a different logic still that, as I shall suggest, repels death's terror by disputing its actuality.

II

In distinction to "The Death of Ivan Ilych" and *War and Peace*, Tolstoy's 1887 *On Life* explains how one gains access to the ethical when death is not a stepping-stone. In the treatise the sight of death is not only irrelevant to an ethical vision, but if such a vision is practiced, there *is* no death. The treatise thus insists there is a life "independent of time and space," the only real one (*L* 337). Although one should not be terrified of bodily or mental changes, which have occurred "scores of times . . . muscles and inward parts, and bones, and brain" alter and evolve (*L* 395), often agreeably.[42] By these transformations we are "borne irresistibly, by every movement, by every breath, toward suffering . . . toward death, toward annihilation" (*L* 303). But this "constantly perishing" (*L* 350), in the end, definitive, that afflicts Ivan Ilych and to which Pierre blinds himself—this annihilation of the individual—is in fact incidental to existence that matters, to be lamented only by "the thronging of the unintelligent crowd about the doorway of life" (*L* 318), that is, on its outside. Real life is not to be found in the body, in the consciousness, or in the "seething activity" (*L* 317) whose aim is "the impossible bliss of personality" (*L* 318).[43] Nor—Tolstoy vigorously argues—is life discoverable in any hereafter: The life that counts is not an afterlife ("Onesided eternity is an absurdity"),[44] but rather an endless life. "True life *is*, and therefore it cannot either begin or perish" (*L* 354). *Is* what?

Tolstoy's answer is "rational consciousness" (*L* 348)—which is more like a set of conclusions about what is imperishable than a capacity to reason analytically or intuitively about what is not empirical. Though Tolstoy buttresses his argument—that "true life" begins only when we discount animal existence—with Biblical testimony ("whoso saveth his life shall lose it" [*L* 352]) and corroborates it with epigraphs from Kant on the "true eternity" of "moral law" and from Pascal on "thought," which gives us the "principle of morals" beyond "space and duration" (*L* 286), Tolstoy's eccentric idea of "rational consciousness" is not assimilable to other religions or philosophies. In *A Confession*, Tolstoy had explicitly "reject[ed] all the efforts of humanity" and the "concepts that have been worked out in history" to grasp religious or philosophical matters.[45] One extravagant name for such heterodoxy is "spiritual autism,"[46] for Tolstoy insisted: "I, rejecting all the efforts of humanity, wanted to do it all over again, alone, in my own way."[47] Thus, for instance, Tolstoy's "rational consciousness" (like Immanuel Kant's pure reason) is transcendental—we know it *a priori* and it is, as for Kant, a regulative principle, but in *On Life*'s reworking the only things reason regulates are degrees of love, which it enjoins us to amplify.[48] "Rational consciousness" is not a soul, not a spirit, but is rather an inclination that provokes a capacity to love. And love alone—"the fact that each one . . . loves and does not love, and in what degree each loves and does not love" [*L* 399]), as well as the propensity to know that love should be increased and made impartial (*L* 404–5)—defines one's "special relation to the world" (*L* 399).[49] Love opens the understanding ("like a key made for this one lock alone" [*L* 371]) to the realization that this "happiness" is "the only possible one" (*L* 371) destroying not only the "phantom" of death (*L* 392), but its actuality. "According to this view, death does not exist" (*L* 392), since love withstands it.

For love to be "genuine" it must be indiscriminate ("only [were] men . . . gods . . . could the preference of some over others be true love" [*L* 376]); it must not be occasioned by "an accidental frame of mind" (*L* 373) or by an unnatural state of mind. Specifically, love must not appear "disturb[ing] . . . like what it must seem to the owl when the sun rises" (*L* 373). Nor should love emanate from an impassioned mind—from "a burst of feeling, clouding the reason." Rather, love should be "luminous," "tranquil," and "joyous" (*L* 380). Above all, "love is, in truth, a preference of other beings to oneself" (*L* 381). For Tolstoy (as for Jonathan Edwards)[50] this preference can be calculated: "The amount of love is the amount of the fraction whose numerator, my partiality, my sympathy for others, is not in my power; but the denominator, my love for myself, can be augmented or diminished by me, to infinity, in proportion to the significance which I attribute to my animal personality" (*L* 381).[51] Tolstoy's heretical Christianity (not grace nor faith, which Tolstoy associated with habit,[52] but rationality alone is its basis), is most iconoclastic when it propounds the thesis for eternal life here.[53] The ego constituted by accumulated love (the only true "life" of the person, that which alone differentiates him [*L* 417]), extracted from the dying animal body and carried forward from birth to birth, is "on his entrance into the world . . . well-defined" (*L* 398), according to whether in a prior existence, the "denominator" posited by Tolstoy's "fraction" has been increased or diminished—very like the Buddhist notion of reincarnation. If "love for myself" can be either "augmented or diminished by me, to infinity" (*L* 381),[54] the love that *replaces* my feeling for "myself" merely passes through me. So that the "I" becomes only a conduit or an implement: "Animal personality is, for man, the spade given to a rational being in order that he may dig with it, and, as he digs, dull and sharpen it, and wear it out, but not in order that he may polish it up and lay it away" (*L* 352). Tolstoy here proposes a different system for moral development than the sight of death, which, for Ivan Ilych and Pierre, awakens the ethical on the other side of suffering. Rather, the ethical is an aggregation that can be calculated and which itself accumulates. In this way, though the animal personality and the embodied consciousness die, "true life" thrives ("I never begin anywhere . . . I shall never end anywhere" [*L* 392]) in the transmission of impersonal love to another incarnation: "A man, having received his life from a past that is invisible to him, and recognizing its constant *and* unbroken growth, transfers it also to the unforeseen future" (*L* 405).[55] Thus the truly ethical person who lives eternally is and has nothing, including subjective interest in what he loves. In the image from Tolstoy's diary: the "spider" who "spread[s] out from [him]self in every direction . . . a whole spider's web of love" so he can "catch in it everything that comes along"[56]—like the actual arachnid, which must take care not to be snared by the sticky strands of its own silk—never entraps himself in the glue of love's entanglement.

III

To move closer, from a different angle, to the split that divides Tolstoy's writing—one strain based on reasoned love, the other requiring the sight or the experience of death, and an intimation of its certainty for oneself personally—I turn to Tolstoy's "The Forged Coupon," itself bifurcated by a dynamic conflict between serial representations of death and an ethical vision that unleashes serial manifestations of reasoned love that vanquish death, a dynamism that Bresson's filmed adaptation reworks. I read "Coupon" through the theoretical lens of *On Life* and by implicit analogy to "Memoirs of a Madman," whose own bipartite structures oppose death to a compensatory ethics of love and charity. "Coupon" is a variation on the paradigm of these works, because the death that permeates part I is brought about by murder: killing is how the protagonist wards off his own mortality; he dispenses death rather than agreeing to be its victim. Yet in "Coupon" the death-dealing violence of part I and the love that aggressively supplants it in part II are, as in the paradigm, also structural complements, arising from antithetical understandings of what is true.[57] In "Coupon," the drive to exterminate is an impersonal counterforce to that of love, which, as in *On Life*, is also compelled by an impersonal energy.[58]

In "Coupon," characters presume that they should live within the confines of conventional morality until they are lied to, cheated, and themselves made to lie, cheat, or kill. Then each becomes remorseless. The hero Stepan Pelageyushkin is an industrious man, "a tall, stooping, long-armed muzhik" who "was starting to do quite well. . . . By working for a year in the mines Stepan managed to set himself up with two horses." When these are stolen, Stepan threatens to murder Ivan Mironov, the "accomplished, daring and successful horse-thief," unless he confesses to the crime. But though Stepan "struck him in the face, and broke his nose, from which the blood started to trickle . . . Ivan still did not speak."[59] So Stepan becomes a killer: "Stepan took hold of a stone from a pile he had ready, and he smashed Ivan Mironov's head in" (FC 905). Killing retaliates against an aggression whose violence feels like dying, because the theft deprives Stepan of his livelihood and of the restraint that makes him recognizable to himself. I am thus arguing that Stepan experiences being deprived of his living as equivalent to being deprived of his life, an equation that provokes the violent murder of Mironov. The domino effect of such provoked rancor sweeps the characters of "Coupon" into a torrent of crime.[60]

If Stepan's barbarous murder of Ivan Mironov is motivated by a particular event, killing soon becomes an aimless practice that keeps dying at bay. His indiscriminate murders suggest he also kills on principle, adhering to the logic that life means nothing except what you make it mean, once conventional ideas of morality, conventional notions that life is good or that human relations have value, are rendered insubstantial. Killing is the routine that Stepan substitutes for meaning. Killing is a counter-ethical, a way of making meaning that invigorates his industry. As *On Life* puts it, "every living being . . . must be ready, for the sake of his petty happiness, to deprive all other beings of greater happiness and even of life" (*L* 301). Although Stepan is sent to prison for a year for the murder of Ivan Mironov, he is nonchalant about his crime.[61] Released, he stops for the night at an inn kept by a "fat tradesman." But the innkeeper's kindness (supposing the stint in prison is the result of "bad luck" [FC 907] he lets Stepan stay for the night) and that of his consort, Matryona, who offers him tea, only aggravate him, since kindness contradicts the evidence that legitimates his nihilism. Once he lies down to sleep, his thoughts immediately turn to butchering them. When the fantasy of "slashing" the tradesman's "paunch wide open and letting out the fatty intestines" (FC 908) loosens its grip on him, "he would remember Ivan Mironov" and, whipped into fury by the fatal theft that precipitated his first murder, conclude: "he might as well kill them both" (FC 908). Before daybreak, he discovers a knife and an axe in the kitchen. When the innkeeper unexpectedly comes upon him, "he swung the axe up and brought it down, splitting the man's head open" (FC 908). He then went into Matryona's room—she "jumped up and stood there by the bed in in her nightshirt. Stepan killed her too with the same axe" (FC 908–9).

When the reader next encounters Stepan—intervening pages have recorded the life of Mariya Semyonovna, "a thin, wrinkled woman of fifty" (FC 909), who is so saintly that a crippled tailor who does her mending is "lost in wonderment for the life she led" (FC 909)—Stepan is savoring the innkeeper's murder: "he actually found himself returning to it in his mind several times each day. . . . he kept scrutinizing the people around him with the same thought always in mind: how he could set about murdering them" (FC 921). The horse theft that turns Stepan's life upside-down, and destroys his scruples, crazes him with a visceral certainty (like the one espoused in *On Life* as love's fraudulent counter-thesis) that, since "not one being or not half a score of beings only, but all the innumerable beings in the world, for the attainment, each of his own object, are ready every moment to annihilate" each other (*L* 301), "the best external arrangement" for any single person who believes life is his alone "depends upon the exercise of . . . violence" (*L* 387).[62] If the "law of reason" is love (*L* 387), lawlessness is ungoverned animosity, demonstrating that human life is nothing but individual existence in which ill will for others thrives. The impulse to kill gathers energy from unprovoked wrath whose own aggression propels it onward each time its history repeats itself. Stepan's impartial enmity toward all (which intensifies after each murderous episode) epitomizes the odium springing up in all the characters who commit crimes out of rage that the happiness of the individual life, certainly "destined to perish" at death (*L* 352), might be prematurely spoiled by others' venom. Love will be shown to be equally externally unmotivated (also propelled onward by its own augmentation), although it is, in *On Life*'s sense of things, "reasoned." Stepan's final murderous exploit draws the two propulsive forces together. For, of course, the angelic Mariya Semyonovna encounters the "exterminating angel."[63]

Overhearing a conversation in which he learns she has collected her pension, Stepan forces the lock on Mariya's house that night, climbs the stairs to the bedrooms, cuts the throat of her daughter, kills the son-in-law, and finally comes upon Mariya, who "raised herself on the bed and looked at Stepan with gentle, frightened eyes and crossed herself" (FC 922). In the split second before he slaughters her, she counsels: "Oh, what a great sin. What are you doing? Have pity on yourself. You think you are destroying others, but it's your own soul you are destroying" (FC 922). But her altruism only peeves him: "I haven't got time to waste chatting with you," Stepan replies, as he "slashed the knife right across her throat . . . soaking one of the pillows with her blood" (FC 923). The very words that provoke his derision will, of course, become redemptive seeds that germinate. For Tolstoy's polemic insists happiness cannot actually reside in the dream of annihilating everyone: "real life cannot be like that" (*L* 304). After Mariya's death this is also Stepan's conclusion. Combining Christ's command "Ye must be born anew" with Tolstoy's theory of "rational consciousness" (*L* 353), love becomes the weapon that irradiates death. Although "Coupon" does not advance an explanatory logic that links love and death, in the story as in the treatise, once love is introduced, there is virtually no more perishing.[64] Instead of the "senseless conflict of beings engaged in destroying each other," life lies in "constant, mutual service" (*L* 356). When Stepan takes this in, he becomes "a different man" (FC 931) and the domino effect of love comes full circle from the other direction.[65]

Such a surfeit of plot and counterplot—of entanglements that tie all the figures to one another in a collective karma—suffuses "Coupon." What is plotted is less the interplay of characters than a conflict between powers of aggression and of benevolence that pulls characters into redemption or its betrayal. Stepan kills repeatedly without reflecting on his carnage, and even when the narrator prompts us with a signal of inwardness—as in prison, when reading the Gospel, Stepan "sat deep in thought"—thinking is a force that instantly enlightens him: "So that is what the true faith is all about" (FC 930). In "Coupon" the seamless movement between "thought" and insight, or between "thought" and action, rids the story of all but consequence. The ethical, requiring no duration, has no development, but, rather, emerges as pure unchallenged reversal.[66] The ethical is a principle often exemplified by a Gospel passage (the model for the story's quicksilver conversions?), which "rational sense" illuminates—which inspires a character—and which he realizes. How fully consequence subsumes any consciousness that might have precipitated it is immediately illustrated by the moment after Mariya Semyonovna's murder, when Stepan takes refuge in a ditch. Stepan's recollection of her "thin, meek, terrified face" and her remonstrance, "You can't do this" (FC 923), eventually give way to "thoughts and memories" of "everything he had done to her" (FC 923). Since "memories" implies something specifically visual, the sight of death is intimated but not inhabited, because it is immediately effaced, caricatured by "one black devil, then another, and after them still other black devils with red eyes, all pulling hideous faces and all saying the same thing: 'You did away with her—now do away with yourself'" (FC 923). "Towards the evening of the second day," unable to banish the devils, "he got to his feet and walked to the tavern nearby" (FC 923). Asked to identify himself by a constable, Stepan replies, "I'm the one who cut all those people's throats at the Dobrotvorovs' house" (FC 924).

The moment that incites most curiosity in this narrative sequence precedes Stepan's confession to the constable. His breaking point, the story's climax and its ethical turn, arises when "however much he drank, he was quite unable to get drunk" (FC 924). Although the crisis is punctuated by a mind-state apparently so horrifying that alcohol can't intoxicate him, this decisive moment, which reverses not only Stepan's violence but his passive suffering (in the ditch "he suddenly felt so weary that he could hardly move a limb" [FC 923]), is withheld from us. Rather, we are drawn away from the vision that can't be dispelled and can't be revealed by his answer to the constable's question "who might you be then?" (FC 924). Why, asked this question, does Stepan suddenly see how to identify himself, and how to see the self he has identified? Something beyond Mariya's charity magnifies his misery, or deepens his inkling of *her* misery. In its condensation and concealment, the ethical turn of "Coupon" postulates the emergence of a discovery that crystallizes a seeing and a being seen, a being-visible to himself, a change that—we can only speculate what it elucidates to Stepan. Who he has become? His cruelty? All the deaths in which he is implicated, which must include his own, since the frenzy of killing almost conceals, but could not quite conceal the one death he could neither prevent nor experience callously?—even as the confession bars from view, and essentially makes irrelevant whatever mental picture might have preceded it. For in "Coupon" it is precisely the sight of death that is occluded.[67] Although death pervades every aspect of Stepan's story, his vision of it is made perfunctory. Tolstoy's representation of Stepan's transformation from callous murderer to ardent lover of mankind has no experiential foundation; he has a purely ocular—not a penetrative—sense of the deaths he's caused: he repents of the murders he has committed without *seeing* them.

In his adaptation of "Coupon," *L'Argent*, Bresson highlights this omission and amends it by restoring the sight of death so that—as though he were recalling the imperative of the nondidactic Tolstoy and perhaps also distinguishing "The Forged Coupon" from that other story of a penitent axe-murderer, *Crime and Punishment*, in which contrition requires rethinking a philosophical position (that there are "people to whom everything is permitted")[68]—the sight of death, rather, appears to be the foundation of *L'Argent*'s ethical understanding. In *L'Argent*, which transports Tolstoy's story from the nineteenth to the twentieth century—the "strange atmosphere [is] halfway between the era of banknotes and the era of credit cards"[69]—Yvon is also at the mercy of a crime set in motion by two schoolboys, which his violence perpetuates and makes fatal. Bresson wrote: "I saw the film immediately because it related to my wanting to make a film about a chain reaction leading to a major disaster. A banknote that ends up murdering loads of people."[70] Or as *L'Argent*'s lawyer puts it when he considers defending Yvon for the alleged intention to smash a guard's head with a kitchen skimmer: "A man who hasn't killed can be worse than a mass murderer."[71]

In "Coupon," Mariya Semyonovna's virtue is rendered second-hand, in the testimony of the tailor's awed impression of her (FC 909). Bresson animates that virtue so that Yvon is its direct recipient. After the killing of the hotel keepers when Yvon stops by the woman's house to ask for food, she also gives him shelter. When, in her kitchen, eating, he boasts about the killing ("I enjoyed it . . . I remember every detail"), she elucidates: "You'll be forgiven. If I were God, I'd forgive everybody." Though he derides the woman's industry, "You do everything, you wear yourself out for [your family]. How come you don't drown yourself? Are you expecting a miracle?" she flatly says: "I expect nothing." Later, he steals the woman's axe, murders her and her family, then throws the axe into a river. After the murder, *L'Argent* restores attention to what Yvon sees (which "Coupon" renders stereotypically by devils), when, standing immobile with his eyes cast down outside a bar, his imperturbability is shattered. Something he sees gets the best of him, compelling a self-betrayal that Bresson denominates as "moral."[72] For, in the next frame, Yvon follows a man into the bar, downs a drink, and finds a policeman: "I killed the hotel owners to rob them and I've just killed a whole family." In Bresson's film, unfettered benevolence does not follow: "I was unable to linger on Yvon's redemption . . . the rhythm of the film, at that stage, would not stand for it."[73] Rather, Bresson intuits the ethical moment in "Coupon" to be a moment of perception that Tolstoy almost effaces, dwelling upon its strangeness. "My characters are taken to the brink of themselves. I cannot do otherwise, or they would seem dead. If I were to paint a flower, I should not paint a bud, but a mature bloom, at its most mysterious."[74]

L'Argent no more discloses Yvon's vision than Tolstoy divulges Stepan's as each sits in his respective bar unable to be stupefied. In *L'Argent,* Yvon's vision outside the bar (like Stepan's in the ditch) precipitates his confession. But if the film *almost* ends there, it does *not* end there. Directly after Yvon confesses and, flanked by police, is ushered out of the bar, we view the bar's patrons streaming to the doorway, straining to see something off-frame to which our vision is also blocked (fig. 3.1) while, in a night-darkened outside, a

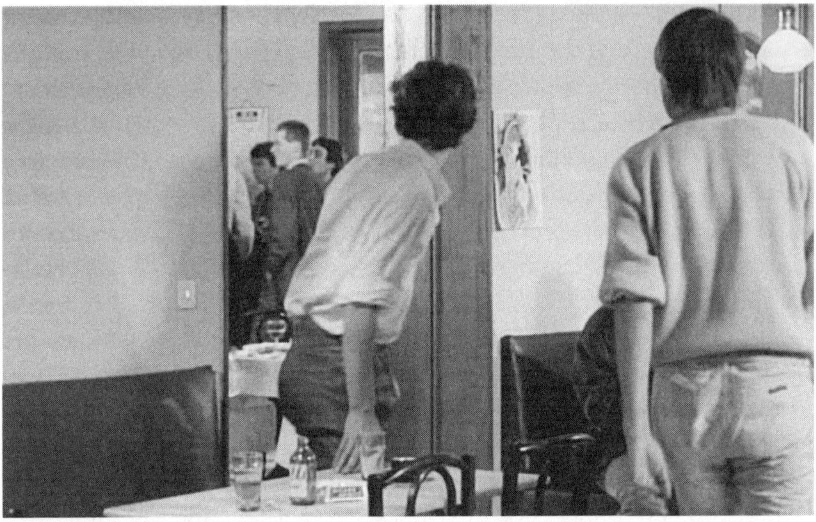

FIGURE 3.1

FIGURE 3.2

group of passersby (the ones in front in silhouette; one at the rear in profile), throng the door of the bar (fig. 3.2) from which Yvon, in handcuffs, is led away (fig. 3.3). In the next shot, in silhouette, the crowd peers into the lighted empty space behind him (fig. 3.4). Bresson wrote: "Doors opening and closing are magnificent, the way they point to unsolved mysteries." He added: "I love passers-by who stare into nothingness."[75] Thus Bresson takes Yvon to the threshold of himself, delivering him from violence, and turns our attention to his viewers' grasp of what can be discerned of such a crushing mystery—"crushing" because in an instant the killer, who boasted of his ingenuity, is eradicated, and Yvon, another man, is led away. Mingling our curiosity with that of the crowd hypnotically staring into the space from which Yvon is led away, Bresson occludes from view what Yvon sees, and also marks it.

Thus, while in "Coupon" the sight of death is effaced by a caricature (devils), what Yvon heeds in the still that frames him outside the bar's back

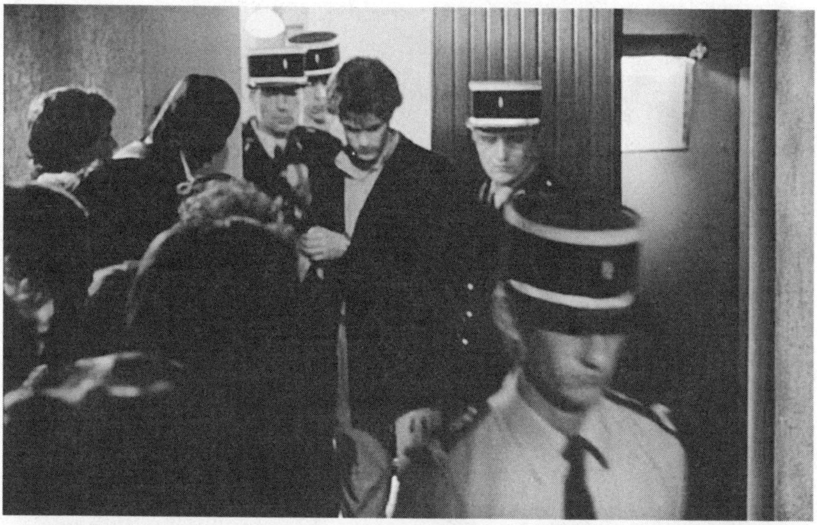

FIGURE 3.3

FIGURE 3.4

door is staged as crucial, and is accentuated by the crowd outside the bar's front door, straining to look at and past him. At such a moment the crowd's interest in what has gone on in the space behind him—in what Yvon has *done*—inevitably melts into our interest in what he has *seen*. In Bresson's film something like the sight of death becomes the ground of the ethical turn, for *L'Argent* dwells on what can't be seen by us or the crowd (Yvon's vision) and, in its obsessive attention to that blockage, almost cancels the obstruction of vision it underscores, whereas in "Coupon" the perfunctory sight of death is given such transience that it doesn't count for anything, almost as though it had not occurred at all.

Bresson's adaptation of Tolstoy's climactic moment, indicated by what we (and the crowd) do *not* see, obliquely calls attention to what seeing *is*, to what transforms Yvon, in Bresson's reconception of Tolstoy's writing, deliberated from a different vantage in the final murder scene, which aggressively adds a vision of death to Tolstoy's story. In "Coupon" there is no witness to the murders of the woman and her family. But in the film the camera follows a dog that barks after Yvon pries open the door of her house and enters with an axe. Earlier, sitting in the woman's kitchen, he had petted the dog. Now it rushes from room to room and up and down the stairs, first awakening the sister and brother-in-law (the camera frames them from the waist downward; standing at their bedroom door, barefoot, we see her nightgown and his pajama leg; fig. 3.5). Then the dog hastens to where the carnage is and will be, yelping and squealing, as he discovers the bodies: first the father on the floor of his

FIGURE 3.5

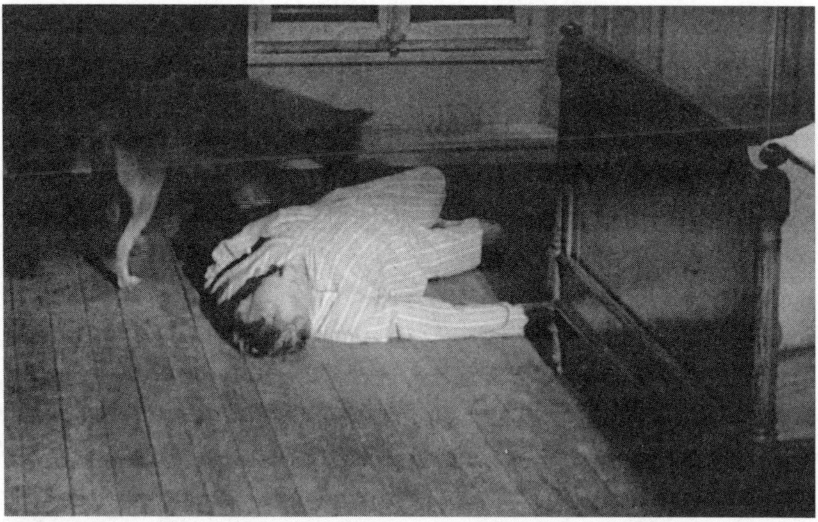

FIGURE 3.6

FIGURE 3.7

room (fig. 3.6); then the young sister and brother-in-law felled on the stairs (fig. 3.7); then a crippled boy, their son, the moment before he is killed, crying in his bed (fig. 3.8); and, finally, the woman who calmly looks at Yvon as he asks "Where's the money?" (fig. 3.9) and raises the axe, his hand bloody. In the entranceway to the room, the dog whines and barks. The camera moves back to the raised axe (fig. 3.10). Off-frame, without a reverse shot—acousmatically—the dog gives a piercing howl.[76] Yvon brings the axe down,

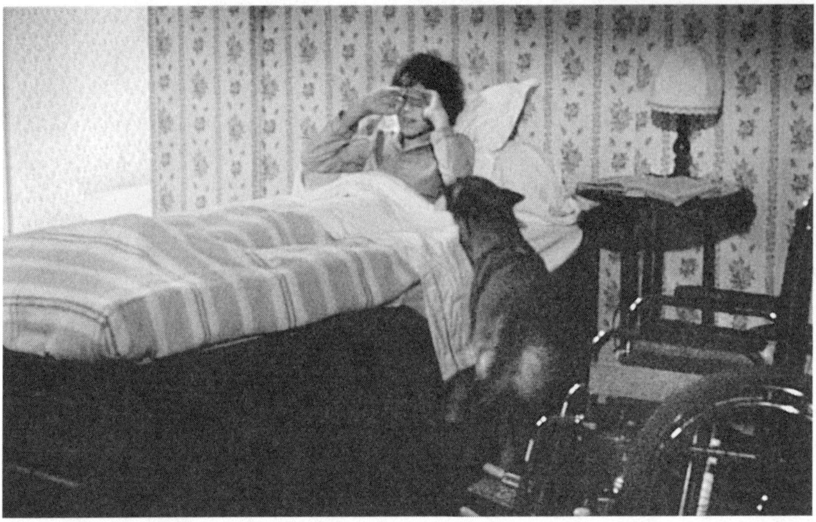

FIGURE 3.8

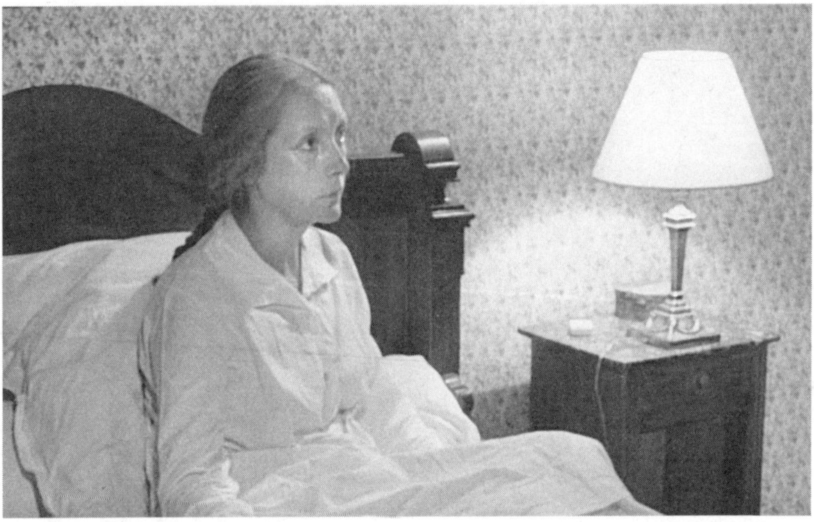

FIGURE 3.9

then swings it into a bedside lamp (fig. 3.11). Behind the crashing lamp, blood spatters on the wall (fig. 3.12).

Although "the beauty of the murder scene . . . is in the emotion of the dog's lament,"[77] the *power* of that scene differently issues from the film's assigning to the dog the task of bearing witness to a slaughter made visible, for Bresson intimates that in this moment an animal can fathom brutality better than a human. Of course the camera eye and the human eye behind it tracks (and elicits) the dog's anguish, and of course the dog, the sole survivor of Yvon's rage, *could* be the only witness, but these logical fundamentals do not dispel the film's unwavering sense of the dog's incomparable authority—his instinct, his seeming omnipresence, his vigilance and his discernment. A harbinger of disaster, he warns the living; he paces across the bodies of husband and wife

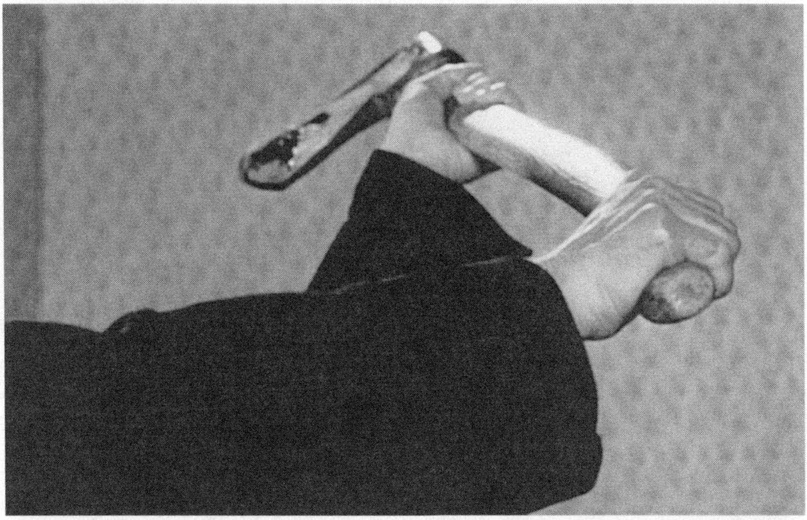

FIGURE 3.10

FIGURE 3.11

FIGURE 3.12

sprawled on the stairs, marking their fate, and—this is his real genius—he knows what makes the blow of the axe transgressive. For the howl that precedes the woman's death breaks off—is instantly silenced—when the stroke of the axe moves sideways to fell the table lamp; the stilled outcry implies that the dog sees the difference between the blow to the person and the blow to the object, an ethical distinction to which Yvon in his rage is blind.

"He is forsaken by society," Bresson writes of Yvon. "The carnage is an expression of his despair. What was interesting about his meeting the little lady was that it was a meeting between acceptance and revolt. What would come of it? What I want is to get at the moral core, not just tell a tale."[78] In Bresson's film the "moral core" is discoverable in the woman's goodness (her equanimity at how things are, when she is treated poorly by her inconsiderate family, and when Yvon's threat to kill her takes such treatment to the limit) juxtaposed with Yvon's revolt at how things are (set in motion by the thoughtless schoolboys). Standing outside the bar, is he assaulted by the disparity between her innocence and his convulsive rage (fig. 3.13)?

However we might formulate the image that Bresson both withholds and provokes us to contemplate (a vision that, in the crude language of causality, draws him to the policeman), it must include something dawning on him, though it might resist articulation: his agency in her extinction—a different perception entirely (if perception there was at all) than what he had when he indifferently brought the axe down to murder the woman and on the upswing struck and overturned the lamp, as though in the single sweeping motion of his arm, the blow to object and person delivered the same violence.

Who are those people in the film's last frame who strain to see through the empty doorway where Yvon has been, and what compels their interest? What are we meant to glean from the stark outline of those solid figures marveling at something they can't see? That they divorce themselves from Yvon's plight? But they seem riveted to, not severed from, what they gaze at. Their pleasure at the scene of his being led away? But we see only the back of their heads, and their profiles. Is it Yvon's downfall? Is it his salvation? Is it one become the other in the moment when Yvon stands motionless outside the bar (but *they* do not see this), as though literalizing Bresson's curiosity ("what would come of it?"). And ours. For if an audience can visibly be drawn into a scene they only thought to view, to recapitulate, in the anonymous crowd we also see the spectacle of our own inquisitiveness.[79] (It is not his fate that is of interest to us; his fate is clear: he will go to prison.) In this moment, Bresson's "what would come of it?" fuses with our interest in what Yvon sees and can't drive away, and with the crowd's rapt attention to its dénouement. This seeing but not seeing (theirs but also ours) is in *L'Argent* then not illuminated by love cast from "the sun of reason" (*L* 353). At the same time, the camera's lingering on the backs of these heads of the crowd gazing into Bresson's "nothingness" erodes the distinction between what grips Yvon (what does he see?) and the

FIGURE 3.13

FIGURE 3.13

FIGURE 3.4

spectators' curiosity (at what they see), because the latter is itself imbued with the very enigma at which they look. Bresson has arranged for us to see this congruence. For in his special sense of "rhythm," the still of the crowd at the film's end "rhymes" with—retrospectively glosses—the earlier scene outside the bar where Yvon also stands spellbound (figs. 3.13 and 3.4 again).[80]

Bresson wrote: " 'False Coupon' is a magnificent short story, but right at the start Tolstoy refers to God, to the Gospels. I couldn't go down that route."[81]

Thus Bresson's film not only discloses a different sense of the ethical than Tolstoy's story, but a different understanding of its placement and manifestation. Bresson's representation of the ethical force is extracted from Biblical prescriptions and lodged in vision, but not in any vision: in something seen of death, rather than something reasoned—and not in a unique or individual vision, though Yvon outside the bar is its repository, since the anonymous crowd, from a different vantage, is also on the outside (but by the bar's front, rather than its back door) and seems mesmerized by what magnetizes the police around Yvon, while we wonder about the mystery his vision makes of him, and the dog, with the instinctive prescience of his species, recognizes a horror that escapes Yvon. In *L'Argent* this marking of a vision from the inside and the outside—from several outsides—until the distinction between inside and outside falls away, extracts the ethical as surely from character as from the mechanics of salvation where Tolstoy places it. Rather the ethical diffuses itself across the film's canine star, its protagonist, its faceless crowd, and in our contemplation of what Bresson calls the "moral," the film's beholders, revealing the way in which—though such a reach seems inconceivable—in the film's final moments, the ethical vision indiscriminately penetrates the whole of the world.

Yet when Bresson, remarking on what transpires through the interlocking visions of the film's climax, writes, "It is not really sayable in words,"[82] he perhaps means to signal that the radical break in his filmic reconception of Tolstoy's story is not in the transformation from a Gospelized to an immanent ethics, but rather in the transformation from a Gospelized to an evental ethics. That is, Tolstoy's immanent ethics can be understood in terms of an acknowledgment of the other (as in Ivan Ilych's "Sorry for you" [II 152]). It can be understood in terms of the perceptual and embodied ethics of Emmanuel Levinas and Jacques Derrida. In distinction, *L'Argent*—where all that looking yields nothing that can be seen by us—might more radically call to mind Alain Badiou's eruptive ethics in which a "secularized conception of grace,"[83] an event out of this world but not classifiable in terms of any other world "punches a 'hole' "[84] in the knowable. An evental ethics could not be founded on image, perception, or any relation to the world, being rather groundless.

There is a tension between the pull of these two interpretive possibilities. The sequence of Bresson's concluding frames suggests that death seen penetratively enables Yvon to grasp the horror of his violence.[85] In distinction, all that looking in which nothing is seen by us suggests an evental force of grace devoid of image and foundation. Yet both interpretations agree that the ethical consequence is an incongruity arising in an inaugural moment that could not be anticipated, as a departure from what has gone before, taking shape as the discovery of a mistake, which is clarified, as when Prince Andrew, mortally wounded, suddenly grasps: "There was something in this life I did not and do not understand" (*WP* 906) that can be manifested only as an expression of wonder—the core of the ethical impulse Bresson touches on when he inquires what would come of Yvon's meeting with the murdered woman and obliquely lodges his question in the crowd's curiosity. If characters resist the sight of death because it terrifies (why Pierre turns his back on Karataev and Ivan Ilych can't endure the *It* that requires him to see it), it is on somewhat different grounds that in *L'Argent* the ethical insight can't be made transparent. How but formally—through a series of unencryptable images that mirror each other—could it be constituted, since any embodiment would scant its strangeness?

IV

In his well-known 1929 "Lecture on Ethics"—which I touch on as a prelude to a consideration of a correlative tale of Tolstoy's in which the ethical is preternaturally incarnated in a figure who, though he dies, escapes Ivan Ilych's torment—Wittgenstein presses on G. E. Moore's definition of ethics as "the general enquiry into what is good," expanding it to include common understandings: "I could have said Ethics is the enquiry into what is valuable, or, into what is really important, or . . . into the meaning of life, or into what makes life worth living, or into the right way of living."[86] However, as he elaborates, Wittgenstein runs up against the impossibility of expressing ethics in *any* formulation, since the propositions he has enumerated can be understood in a relative *or* an absolute sense, while the ethical is concerned with "absolute" rather than "relative" understandings of these expressions: "Nothing we could ever think or say" could formulate ethics, because propositions merely affirm or deny whether something is true or false—whether it is factual—and "no statement of fact can ever be, or imply, a judgment of absolute value."[87] Underscoring the radical nature of the transcendent value he designates, Wittgenstein famously writes: "Our words used as we use them in science, are vessels capable only of containing and conveying . . . *natural* meaning and sense. Ethics, if it is anything, is supernatural and our words will only express facts; as a teacup will only hold a teacup full of water."[88]

Wittgenstein no sooner establishes the limits of what it is possible to say about ethics than he pushes beyond the limits he has identified, for if "things" cannot be put into "words," into propositions that express facts—"They make themselves manifest"[89] here in analogies that evoke an unconditioned, an ethical absolute. "If I want to fix my mind on what I mean by absolute or ethical value"—the assumption being that each person would vivify it differently—then "one particular experience presents itself to me. . . . the best way of describing it is to say that when I have it *I wonder at the existence of the world.* And I am then inclined to use such phrases as 'how extraordinary that anything should exist' or 'how extraordinary that the world should exist.'"[90] This is an absolute statement, rather than a relative one, because wonder does not exist at the world's being a certain way, but rather at its being whatever way it is.[91] Though he calls it a "paradox" that the description of an experience should seem to have "supernatural value," since "no description" could express "absolute value"—and (implicitly) a paradox that only nonsense could get at the core of the ethical—he concludes by celebrating these expressions (even though they operate *like* similes or allegories; *like* because "the simile must be a simile for *something*," for a "fact," and if we "drop the simile . . . we find that there are no such facts").[92] "Wonder" comes closest to it—"the experience of seeing the world as a miracle" as does the feeling of being "safe . . . *whatever* happens."[93] The expression of such absolutes (like Levin's "wonder" in *Anna Karenina* when "lying on his back . . . gazing at the high cloudless sky" he sees "infinite space, and not a rounded vault,"[94] though such a statement also has no "sense" for Tolstoy) is a transgression Wittgenstein exalts. To draw Levin's thoughts about the ethical absolute toward those of "Lecture on Ethics," where they tend: when Theodore the peasant tells Levin that one should "live not for one's needs but for God!" Levin thinks nothing "could be more senseless."[95] Yet this "senselessness"—like Wittgenstein's "nonsense"—points to a "miracle, the one possible, everlasting miracle, all around me,"[96] whose "nonsensicality was" its "very essence."[97]

In Tolstoy's oeuvre there is a way to imagine an ethical absolute that emerges prior to the sight of death, but does not preclude death, and also is not founded on death. It is epitomized by Tolstoy's 1905 fable "Alyosha Gorshok," whose eponymous hero, a peasant, so fully incarnates the ethical point of view that his inclinations do not require death's governance. That is what makes "Alyosha Gorshok" a fable. The ethical vantage is first embodied in Alyosha's preternatural dutifulness. In his peasant family, though "not particularly strong . . . he had the knack of doing things."[98] "You would never hear anything but 'Run and fetch this' . . . or 'Alyosha, you sort it out' . . . or 'Look here, Alyosha, don't forget this.' And Alyosha ran, and sorted out, and looked, and didn't forget . . . and all the time he never stopped smiling" (AG 960–61). At the same time that he amiably performs these chores without discriminating their relative importance—importance resides everywhere unreflective dutifulness is satisfied—he also intuits an obedience of another order: "Of prayers, he knew none at all . . . but he still prayed morning and evening—he prayed with his hands, by crossing himself" (AG 962). Praying with his hands and then "his heart" (AG 965), Alyosha comprehends the essence of devotion: attention, love, and, above all, steadfastness—qualities differently contributive to Alyosha's capacity to cherish Ustinya, the kitchen maid, and to his awakening ardor for her.

But if Alyosha knows how to love as well as to obey and worship, what he does best is to die. Dying is his gift. Or rather, it is the surprise with which Alyosha dies that, in the narrative's emphasis, reveals the talent that we belatedly realize has also infused the ethical impulses of all the actions that precede it. "One day in Lent" climbing onto a roof to clean "frozen snow from the gutters," he slips and falls "on the iron-covered entrance gate of the yard" (AG 965). When the priest is sent for, Ustinya asks: "what if you should be going to die?" (AG 965). Alyosha shrugs off her alarm: "What if I am? We don't go on living for ever, do we?" (AG 965). Although it could be said that his acquiescence is founded on belief in an afterlife, his death is strikingly represented as something whose occurrence *startles* him: "He did not say very much. He just asked for something to drink, and as he drank it he looked as if he was surprised at something.[99] He looked surprised, stretched himself out, and died" (AG 965). In "Alyosha Gorshok" the novel response to dying is neither to see nor to resist seeing death, but, rather, to be surprised.

At a moment of surprise—we could call it wonder, as the neuter noun *udivlenie* is also translated—no foreknowledge can dispel his amazement when death, unprepared for, actually comes upon him. In fact, insofar as Alyosha is characterized by the radical innocence of wonder—which essentially involves *no* expectations of what will come next, in distinction to surprise, whose connotations suggest a response to expectations that are *subverted*—wonder, rather than surprise, more accurately delineates Alyosha's indiscriminate response to *all* experience. In "Alyosha Gorshok," astonishment has the feel of the ethical because it resides in not knowing the next of experience, which arises out of nowhere—pushing aside the shadow of what has come before; shattering the *thought* of that "before" and the action based on such a thought in a real that deprives the past of any substance. Only in such a present, which Wittgenstein, like Tolstoy, associated with the eternal,[100] could action be spontaneous and therefore fitting, rather than compulsive, accidental, or careless. In this way, Alyosha Gorshok is saturated with transcendence, while having nothing to transcend: he has no resistance to the ethical.[101] The story is so short because there *is* no story. Alyosha's death reiterates his pervasive spirit of astonishment, and is not a unique or revelatory event. "Alyosha Gorshok" thus differs from Tolstoy's death-haunted writing in which ethical understanding only emerges climactically once death is countenanced, since for

"Alyosha Gorshok," the ethical is omnipresent. And "Alyosha Gorshok" differs from Tolstoy's didactic writing where an ethics of love deprives death of consequence—in effect there is said to be no death—since Alyosha Gorshok dies. "Alyosha Gorshok" thus almost combines, or combines in a false synthesis (false because "terror" is missing), the two strains of Tolstoy's writing: the death-haunted fiction that dwells on the impossibility of escaping death and the didactic prose from which death has been dispelled.

Yet if from one point of view, Alyosha seems pure perfection, from another, there is an objection to Tolstoy's parabolic ideal from whom the zigzags, the obstacles, the whole spectacle of the inner life with its history, its outrages, its triumphs, and its betrayals are missing. Alyosha can servilely enact, but he does not deliberate, intuit, or even seem to fathom the ethical imperatives that he obediently fulfills, it could be said, heedlessly. Thus in Tolstoy's fable there is an incongruity between the incarnation of ethics and the deficiency of the ethical agent: how could ethics seriously be manifest in a simulacrum devoid of choice and human complexity? The friction in the "Lecture on Ethics" and in Tolstoy's fable, though not symmetrical (since Wittgenstein sustains an ironic point of view toward the wonder he valorizes, while it is Tolstoy's reader, not Tolstoy, who glimpses the disparity between Alyosha's blamelessness and what emerges, from a critical vantage, as the emptiness of his purity), underscores the problem of distilling ethics to certain "phrases"[102] and to the representation of an embodied ideal. For Wittgenstein the "phrases" are meaningless, because "Ethics, if it is anything, is supernatural"[103] and Tolstoy's representation could also be described as meaningless because Alyosha is a caricature, a mere instrument of compliant labor. To appropriate Wittgenstein's discrimination: ethics could make "sense" or have "meaning" only within a "natural" framework.[104] In distinction, *L'Argent*'s climactic moments, like Levin's insight that birth and death "were like openings in that usual life through which something higher became visible,"[105] suggest the "something higher" is only *simulated* by the personification of Alyosha Gorshok.

V

Across Tolstoy's writing, then, diverse instantiations of the supernatural starkly emerge in contrast. *On Life* identifies a realm that does not exist in the observable world, as well as a trajectory for arriving there that can be figured by an architecture.[106] In distinction, Ivan Ilych's vision at the story's end has the sense of the marvelous without being a literal miracle. What segregates these supernaturals is not an ethics that is "*latent*" versus one that is conspicuous (in Wittgenstein's characterization) or an ethics that is not "aestheticized" versus an aesthetics that is "ethicized" (in William Dean Howells's),[107] but an ethics wholly immanent in the world at hand, with no recourse to religious disquisition needed—rather than one in which the self exhibits the virtues of the Gospels, as though the only way to be ethical were not to be where we are, but always to be or require an elsewhere.

Tolstoy's ethics of *this* world is, in fact, more radical than any extraterrestrial counterpart: such an ethics dictates a break with the self, and an emancipatory relation to our own being. Some such self-transcendence is legible in "sorry for you" (II 152), "Nothing . . . terrible" (*WP* 1176), "I'm the one who cut all those people's throats" (FC 924); in recognitional states of mind and heart that arise in Ivan Ilych's "joy!" (II 152), in Pierre's dream of the water closing over his head (*WP* 1182), and, in Bresson's interpretation of Tolstoy, in Yvon's convulsion of guilt. We glimpse the latter not by access to what strikes Yvon (gleaned from the *outside*) and not in his action (which could be seen only *as* an outside), but in what we are pressed to intuit of what must have entered his mind to *change* him (though his being different, his being as such, cannot of course be seen at all). *L'Argent* thus renders what occurs to Yvon as *itself* the miracle—a redemption Bresson reclaims from the other world where Tolstoy locates it. ("I slip in the notion that the protagonist is redeemed, that he can save himself, which does not come at the same point in the short story.")[108] Bresson points to the mystery of the ethical—its supernatural quality—not by taking us out of the world, but by representing our world as habitable, a place where one *could* live.

The question of whether ethics has a special domain split off from the ordinary realm in which we live is debated in relation to conflicting interpretations of Wittgenstein's *Tractatus Logico-Philosophicus*. In conclusion, I touch on one aspect of this deliberation for what it inadvertently illuminates about Tolstoy's otherworldly writing.[109] In "What Ethics in the *Tractatus* is Not," James Conant provides a series of clarifying sentences that unintentionally highlight the rarefied features of Tolstoy's otherworldly ethics. Conant writes:

> what makes a sequence of signs an 'ethical proposition', for early Wittgenstein, is not its involving certain vocabulary—say, the words 'good' and 'evil'—which pick out ethical features of reality. . . . a proposition's involving specialized ethical vocabulary does not suffice as a ground for classifying it as an ethical proposition. What makes an employment of language-like structures ethical, for early Wittgenstein, is not the sort of content it is able to convey. . . . Ethics does not pertain to an independent subject matter.

Conant still: Although "the *Tractatus* as a whole . . . aims to change us," it does not seek to do so by "initiating us into ('logical' or 'ethical') truths to which we were previously not privy."[110] If ethics does not have a special vocabulary or an independent subject, or pertains only to certain aspects of reality, then in Cora Diamond's words: "What 'transcendental' means in the *Tractatus* is that the 'sign' for whatever is called transcendental is the general form of a proposition, not some particular proposition or set of propositions that says something in particular."[111] In the same spirit, "a moral concept seems less like a movable and extensible ring laid down to cover a certain arena of fact, and more like a total difference of *Gestalt*."[112] On such accounts, one could say that the problem with *On Life* and "Coupon" is the "ring drawn around" the arena of the ethical so that the prescriptive *ought* of love all but banishes vision, attention, deliberation, and feeling—since action and choice are predetermined by the special truth of love and deathlessness that Tolstoy's explicitly ethical texts inculcate.

But Tolstoy's death-haunted fiction *also* has its precondition: the sight of death that illuminates the urgency of the ethical, as nothing else does. Thus the question is "not whether there is life after death, . . . but actually whether there could be life before death."[113] Only the perception of death as mine—my fate, my limit, my joy, and my mystery (for the particulars of the death that will be mine are always concealed from me)—introduces, in Natalie Repin's words, "the constant choosing of priorities, so that every commitment must be worthy of the high price paid by the limited portfolio of human life."[114] "Life," Tolstoy's story implies, "is living with death or living on a death row, a dead man walking. Without the realization of that, there is no life, just as much as there is no death."[115] This is the case because, in a reformulation of Martin Heidegger's terms, the "logic of everydayness," a logic that undergirds Ivan Ilych's mediocre aspirations, and "the logic necessary to understand death are different and incompatible."[116]

Only in "Alyosha Gorshok" does the ethical permeate all points of experience, exacting the same attention as the moment of death does. Yvon in *L'Argent* marks the mystery of the ethical—the question of what precipitates "I'm the one who cut all those people's throats" (FC 924)—while Alyosha Gorshok sustains his vision of the ethical (*I'm the one called to see what is necessary to do*), across all the moments of that six-page story, so that, from one point of view, the perception of the everyday is continuously the perception of the ultimate, even though, from another, Alyosha Gorshok's stolid obedience must be seen as the antithesis of the ethical. At the same time, "Alyosha Gorshok" throws into relief the real contrast between Tolstoy's didactic and nondidactic prose, which is not just that one makes death an agon, the other, an irrelevance, but that the fiction puts death into narrative as traumatic telos, while the spiritual prose speaks proleptically from death's vantage from the start (recall all the plotted deaths of "Coupon" and *On Life*'s screed on death's inconsequence), dissolving life's plot into a prolonged epiphany. "Alyosha Gorshok" totalizes these strains—a virtual dead end for narrative—while the death-haunted fictions keep death in the realm of duration and experience, where the distinction between *zoe* and *bios*, life with and life without meaning, is plotted.[117]

In "Forged Coupon," *On Life*, and "Alyosha Gorshok" Tolstoy tried to get around the irreconcilability of what Heidegger distinguished as "everydayness" and "being for death" by immersing the quotidian in eternal life, so that "being for death" could morph into being that can survive it. But in his reflections Tolstoy could not dispel the menace of death his treatise had dismissed as spectral. From 1902 through 1910, in his diary, Tolstoy broods:

> Getting closer to death. . . . How fortunate that memory disappears with death and only consciousness remains. . . . Death is a window through which one observed the world, and which has been slammed shut, or lowered eyelids and sleep, or a walk from one window to another. . . . Death is becoming more and more simple, more and more natural. . . . Living is dying. To live well means to die well. Try to die well. . . . The whole difference between a man and an animal is that a man knows he will die, but an animal doesn't. . . . Death is the only place one can really go away to. . . . I feel death approaching nearer and nearer.[118]

Such ruminations vitalize *War and Peace*, "Ivan Ilych," *Anna Karenina*, and the explicitly ethical writings, as does no other animation. If death is the radical break—"the only place one can really go away to"—there might be nothing after ("a window . . . slammed shut"). Or there might be an elsewhere: "a walk from one window to another" with a different view.[119] In "Memoirs of a Madman" (1884)—a sequence of diary entries before they were a story—Tolstoy sided with the nothing:

> "I am living, have lived, and ought to live, and suddenly—here is death to destroy everything. Then what is life for? To die? To kill myself at once? No, I'm afraid. To wait for death till it comes? I fear that even more. Then I must live. But what for? In order to die?" I could not escape from that circle. (MM 310)

And earlier in the story: " 'There is nothing to life. Death is the only real thing, and death ought not to exist.' . . . Life and death somehow merged into one another" (MM 308). But in 1906, in the diary, Tolstoy understood the question this way:

> Thought today about what I, an old man, should do. . . . Several times in my life I've considered myself close to death. And—how foolishly!—I would forget, or try to forget it. . . . And now, because of my years, I naturally consider myself close to death, and there's no point in trying to forget it, and I can't forget it. But what should I, an old feeble person, do? I asked myself. And it seemed that there was nothing to do, that I had no strength for anything. But today I realised so clearly the clear and joyful answer. What should I do? It's already been revealed—I must die. This is my task now, as it always has been. And I must perform this task as well as possible: die, and die well. The task is before you, a noble and inevitable task. . . . This made me very glad. I'm beginning to get used to regarding death and dying not as the end of my task, but as the task itself.[120]

Between the dates of these two passages Tolstoy wrote *On Life* and "Forged Coupon." In the 1906 diary entry, the torment of "Madman" has faded, and Tolstoy can't pull apart the forces of life from their antithesis, because he sees the undertaking as unitary ("living *is* dying"[121] [emphasis mine]), "the end of my task," one with the "task itself"—the same from whatever vantage, or from whatever stage, it is regarded. "Living is dying"[122] also discloses a vitalism that refuses the kind of splitting—of mundane from eternal life, of life from a banished death—that bifurcates the doctrinal writing. In a like manifestation of integrity, the novel perception ("today I realised") of death's imminence for Tolstoy does not inaugurate an undertaking distinct from what was stipulated in the time that preceded the realization that his death is looming. "Always" in relation to "now" and "as it has been," rather, lights up a continuum, the same, there being no marker that would drive apart the "end" from the whole, since their imperatives are indistinguishable. Though this discovery slantly recalls the *always* of Alyosha Gorshok's enterprising attention (also unwavering), the ethical (if that's what it is) is so inert in Alyosha Gorshok's constitution that it could never be ambiguated or flower into a recognition.

Alyosha Gorshok's virtue could not develop, being always perfectly what it is, whereas the diary entry marks a breakthrough and the attainment of an unexampled understanding. In this way—after *War and Peace*, after "Ivan Ilych," after the ethical treatises—a year after he wrote "Alyosha Gorshok" (but in a reflective countervision), Tolstoy pushes past his own conclusions to the questions that besiege them, so that the task of questioning itself becomes the ethical enterprise. In "Ivan Ilych," *War and Peace*, and the continuous reflections on death in Tolstoy's late diary entries, Tolstoy creates a world unlike that of "Alyosha Gorshok," because it is perceived, is seen close-up, and because it *changes*. "An artist . . . must be a seeker," Tolstoy wrote in 1900. "His work must be a search. . . . Only if he is seeking does the spectator, the listener or the reader join with him in his search."[123] But if seeking is a process—is processual—the ethical insight that overturns the status quo occurs in a flash. In the works alluded to above, and in distinction to "Alyosha Gorshok," though this evanescent flash has no duration, it has consequences, in which something not possible or not *thought* possible *becomes* possible. In the late diary entry, the sight of death also has its compensations—not the "bliss of personality" (*L* 318), as *On Life* dourly names it, and not the imperishable love that collects in an eternal repository, but "joy" (akin to wonder, in that exaltation is its own, sufficient transport), here arising from the simplification—"I must die"—which is free of the agonizing deliberation of whether what follows is more of the same, is nothing at all, or is unrivaled. Thus when Tolstoy writes, "today I realised," we can't set vision and what transcends vision against each other in an antagonism I articulated earlier in relation to Yvon's perception (does he *see* death penetratively, or does what happens to Yvon surpass vision, description, and even content?), since whatever punctures complacency or agony, like Wittgenstein's "wonder," could not in some sense be naturalized.

4

Robert Bresson's Pathos

Robert Bresson's cinematography is an improvisation that captures phenomena without an orienting placement. "I never tried to settle in advance what I would do nor how I would achieve it," Bresson explained to Michel Ciment, his interviewer. "There has to be a shock at the moment of doing, there has to be a feeling that the humans and things to be filmed are new, you have to throw surprises on film. . . . Otherwise, I might as well have used a picture postcard."[1] The "shock" discoverable in film after film lies in Bresson's dismantling of ideas about what something is,[2] a divestiture accomplished by his reworking of filmic traditions.[3] This disassembly can be characterological as when in *Mouchette* the gamekeeper who protects animals and the poacher who destroys them are shown in parallel shots that erode the distinction of these respective dispositions. The dismantling can be ideological, as in *Journal d'un curé de campagne*, where a fundamental similarity underneath contested points of view connects the idealistic young priest with Dr. Delbende, the bitter doctor unacquainted with antiseptics. When the doctor is "found at the edge of the woods . . . with his skull blown out" because "he'd lost his faith and couldn't get over not believing," the young priest says: "I have never suffered so much and likely never will again."[4] The doctor's not believing and the young priest's not believing can't be separated from each other in the young priest's mind. In *Procès de Jeanne d'Arc*, Bresson presses on the question of what being is at its most rudimentary, before it is animated in facial expressions and before it is destroyed.

The pattern of cinematic probing is everywhere. When *Lancelot du Lac* juxtaposes armored knights, shielded from view, to the exposed flanks, heads, flashing eyes of horses, our uncertainty about why we are being shown such a radical contrast yields to a question of *what* we are being shown. Bresson addressed the question this way: "A thing expressible solely by the cinematographically new, therefore a new thing."[5] The juxtaposition of armored men to the sensuality of animals—birds, the shiny coat of horses, a furry creature Guinevere sees climbing a tree outside her chamber window—almost suggests that vitality is visible only in the lives of animals. But *Lancelot* also asks what human life is behind that visor, and answers sensationally, in arresting detail, when the headgear is struck off to disclose only a rush of blood pouring from the metal suits of knights decapitated in battle. That this vital fluid is the same in human and equine vascular systems seems counterintuitive, because in *Lancelot* human flesh is concealed by clothes and armor, while animal flesh, naturally, remains exposed to view, so that the visual disparity seems to mitigate the likelihood of their having a common life-force. "How little we know what a human life really is," the grieving countess muses in *Journal d'un curé de campagne*, punctuating a fact all of Bresson's films ponder.

In Bresson's cinema we are asked to see not only the relation between animal and human being, but also the mystery of the life of objects. For instance, in *L'Argent* when the glass on the piano ledge falls and shatters from the force of the saintly woman's father pounding out Bach on the keys, we discern the vibrations of life beyond the entanglements of plot and character, and also beyond *L'Argent*'s overarching contrast in which "money," the "visible God," is juxtaposed to an invisible god (call it sight or grace) that transforms Yvon. The drama of the glass more immediately revolves around images and sounds—the piano notes, the shattering, silence, the wet sponge against the floor—which constitute the last moment of the glass's history: its being what it is, and then its no longer being anything but shards.[6] Martin Scorsese put it this way: "Bresson focuses on the moments that happen between the ones that appear in most other movies. But he is also an incredibly dynamic filmmaker." Although for Scorsese that dynamism is felt in Bresson's "set-pieces," which are "some of the most breathtaking . . . in cinema": the thieves "at the racetrack in *Pickpocket;* Joan's burning at the stake in *The Trial of Joan of Arc*; the final massacre in *L'Argent*,"[7] the unpredictable occurrences sampled above ("moments that happen between the ones that appear in most other movies") have a subtler charge whose power is extraneous to the context (the saintly woman's relation to her difficult father) in which they occur, inciting curiosity about trivial objects, like the glass. In Bresson's films, even the backs of anonymous heads and empty doorways have a lure that draws us toward them. What is an opening through which one can pass? What are designations like *front* and *back*? What is being where we are—in which all moments are open and closed?

In what follows, I examine the way in which Bresson's cinematography exposes the being or essence of an entity—being with and without admixture and change[8]—through contrasting images. Gilles Deleuze's theory of the face which, at one extreme, can be seen as an abstract entity, helps me explain how in Bresson's montage, Mouchette's face reveals its kinship with nonhuman entities, while, from a second perspective, I consider what Sergei Eisenstein called "pathos"—an ecstatic leap in which a thing "goes out of" itself by transgressing limits that define it: as in the movement from a static condition to a dynamic one; from an affective or linguistic register to a material register; from a narrative exposition to an imagistic exposition; and so forth—a theory that has bearing on whether fixed boundaries around a phenomenon *could* visually or philosophically identify it.[9] Throughout I mean to ask how Bresson filmically subjects ideas about perceptible essence to unusual scrutiny. And Bresson is also interested in what we *can't* see. In his own specification of his subject matter, he told Michel Ciment: "The only things that matter are invisible. Why are we here? What are life and death? Where are we going? Who is responsible for the miracle of animal and vegetable life?"[10] Bresson wanted to make a film called *Genesis*, which would reveal the impossibility of even conceiving such unanswerables in a modern language, and, further, which would ostensibly record a time prior to the creation of language—cinema being implicitly a perfect medium for such a project because it is afferent, delivering insights to the senses in ways that skirt and even evade linguistically expressive communication. The film would end "either at the Flood or with the Tower of Babel and the invention of language"; it would be "spoken in Ancient Hebrew . . . with bits of Aramaic. Adam cannot speak in French or English," Bresson insisted: "he must speak in a language almost no one can understand."[11] *Genesis* was never produced, but all of Bresson's films ask essential questions in a language that is foreign, and that even seems prelinguistic, while the beholder's task is to take in what antecedes understanding, preconception, and sometimes vision.[12]

Our vision is conspicuously blocked in Bresson's filmic investigation—because we can't see what Bresson's models see.[13] In the eye—the horse's eye, the donkey's eye, Mouchette's eyes, Yvon's eyes—we see a portal to being's essence from the outside, but we see from a perspective that keeps us bearing witness to what is not visible *behind* what is seen, an invisible that catches the viewer's own eye and holds it. At the same time, the impediment to sight just as often extends to the whole optic field, because we can't isolate significance—can't penetrate the visual plethora on the screen which has the feel of not being sorted out or focused. For this reason, the philosophical question of whether the is-ness of something can be identified autonomously, or at all, overlaps with the cinematographic question of how, or if, something can be identified visually.

One can't get far with a question about the ontology Bresson's project both reveals and occludes (is that ontology a religion, a philosophy? and what philosophy?) before realizing the inefficacy of theory's binaries to address Bresson's cinematic complexity, as indicated in the long-standing critical debate about whether Bresson's films are materialist or spiritualist.[14] Thus, as noted, Deleuze's books on cinema enable certain ways of theorizing the *in*expressiveness of the human face in Bresson's films, but Deleuze's bipartite paradigm scants the norm of the model's blank countenance. While Martin Heidegger obsessively engages questions about Being, in his philosophy humans are separated from other beings because they alone possess *Dasein*, a distinction whose privilege Bresson's films resist when he draws together the kind of entity human beings are and everything else in the world there also is, including the sentient but not limited to it. Nor is Bresson's ontology phenomenological, because though his films valorize perception, it could never be an endpoint; Bresson repeatedly bring us up against perception's limits. Say, rather, Bresson's ontology is one of fragmentation and incompossibility—a momentariness and incompleteness that constitute a vision of the real that is his aesthetic. If the "is" of Bresson's "essence" keeps splintering before our eyes, this is also because (with the exception of Joan in *Procès*, as I'll elaborate) there is no single "is" of person, quality, or object. Essence, as such, can only be understood as plural and transient. At the same time, Bresson's films convey that each image, each sound—any image and sound—has the inextinguishable life which "Vinteuil's little phrase" conjures for Swann.[15] Yet Bresson's ontology is also not Proustian, since what we see and hear is nothing if not present. This long list of qualifications (not this, not that, but also not the exclusion of this and that) suggests that Bresson's ontology could be described as "queer" in Eve Sedgwick's use of that term: not monolithic, not structured by binaries; rather, fractured, momentaneous, improvised. Bresson himself identified the core of his cinema as rhythmic. It is rhythmic as Philippe Lacoue-Labarthe, quoting Émile Benveniste, defines that term to designate "form at the moment it is taken by what is in movement, mobile, fluid," with "no organic consistency."[16] How then could the visible not be fragmentary or governed by oscillation and in-betweenness—that which fractures, even as it portrays, the essence and identity we appear to see but can't see into (on the screen, and in our midst). The discussions that follow particularize these insights.

I begin with *Procès de Jeanne d'Arc* by asking how Joan's being—identified with what she sees—is obstructed and how the impediment is made visible. Section II turns to *Mouchette*, in which the essence of a phenomenon is revealed not as an elemental purity (as Joan's vision is), but as what could not be conceived as singular or autonomous. In *Mouchette* oppositions structure the film visually, characterologically, antonymically, and aurally, so that what something is remains open to what lies outside of it. Section III examines *Un condamné à mort s'est échappé*, in which the essence of objects is discoverable in their transformations. In sentences that offer another image for an aggregation of alien elements, Bresson wrote: "Proust says that Dostoevsky is original in composition above all. It is an extraordinarily complex and close-meshed whole, purely inward, with currents and counter-currents like those of the sea" (*N* 124). Bresson's recollection of Proust's description of Dostoevsky, which Bresson adds is "a thing that is found also in Proust" (*N* 124), illuminates the contrary impulses of his *own* compositional system. "Close-meshed . . . purely inward" points to elements that are hidden, as Joan's visionary world is (how could a "close-meshed whole, purely inward" be seen?), while the image in the second part of the description turns outward ("currents and counter-currents" flowing outward and inward, antiphonally). Thus the "close-meshed whole" initially figured as hermetic is drawn toward a visible surface whose pervasiveness is troped by the simile of the "sea."

In Bresson the "purely inward," where we think mind, spirit, vision dwell, transgresses the bounds of all enclosure, becoming a manifestation that eludes placement in that the blockage to inwardness is made omnipresent. That is the subject of *Procès de Jeanne d'Arc*, in which Joan's inquisitors would force her to reveal her mystical visions (but how could her apparitions and voices be seen or heard by others?), while, in another register, in the film's initial scene, the spectator is pressed to identify the cloaked, hooded, parceled figures whose folded robes fill the screen, thwarting him from doing so, a transient difficulty that reveals the tension between what coerces and resists disclosure sustained by the film as a whole. At the same time, Joan's face and her demeanor bear witness not to what she has seen but to who she is within the particular historical and religious circumstances that structure Bresson's film and also, impersonally, beyond that tragedy, in the film's specification of being revealed at its most minimal. By the film's end, the question *what is there?* in Joan's visions gives way to *what is the there is*? that discloses her being as she is, a question made visible in her burning at the stake, which a dog witnesses.

I

Bells ring out at the start of *Procès de Jeanne d'Arc*. On the screen, flanked by the shadow of two attendants, a robed figure with shiny black shoes comes into view. Everyone in the film's initial near-four minutes is visible only from the waist down. In the case of the robed figure, lower still. When the camera moves closer we see a woman's hands holding a sheet on which black letters are inscribed. In a medium close-up, she turns, her back to us. She is hooded.

FIGURE 4.1

One of the robed men (earlier, off-frame, he could only be made out as a black moving edge and a marginally legible shoe) comes to her side, and puts his hand around her arm. The other man lays his hand on her back.[17] These mantled figures (fig. 4.1), including a priest with a censer, another figure wearing a surplice, and a third cassocked figure holding a rule (visible only on one side and from below the shoulders), will contrast in the sharpest way to Joan's open face seen in its entirety.[18]

But she has not yet been introduced. Then the title *Procès de Jeanne d'Arc* scrolls across the image of the mother's cloaked back, accompanied by the beat of a drum (the same staccato beat will sound at the film's end when we see a bare stake, hugged by the chain that bound Joan's body, which has burned away); the credits appear; a bugle sounds, more beats of the drum. Bresson's words crawl down the screen in a textual scroll: "Joan of Arc died on 30th May 1431. She received no burial and no portrait remains of her. But we have a better portrait: her words before the judges of Rouen. I have used the authentic transcripts from the Condemnation Trial. For the last instants, I have used the witness statements from the Trial of Rehabilitation which took place 25 years later. When the film starts, Joan has been imprisoned for several months in Rouen. Captured at Compiègne by French soldiers loyal to her adversaries, she has been sold to the English (we know the interests at stake). She appears before a tribunal made up exclusively of members of the Anglophile University of Paris, and presided over by Bishop Cauchon."[19]

In the next frame the hem of a jacket and the top part of a woman's leg clothed in tight pants appear. A bible resting on a table in front of which she stands obscures her legs and feet. "My name is Joan. I am 19," we hear Florence

Delay—the voice that is Joan's—say. "Swear to tell the truth," a man's voice commands. Her chained hands touch the Bible. Not until she sits do we see Delay's face—the first visible countenance—and her downcast eyes. The cinematographer Léonce-Henri Burel complained that he couldn't capture Delay's eyes because she frequently looked downward. But in fact when she speaks to her questioner, her eyes always appear to meet his gaze (fig. 4.2) (there is no reverse shot).

Only then does she turn her eyes away in something like restraint—so she will not have to face the stares of her examiners. "I will tell the truth, but not all of it. . . . I come from God and do not belong here. Send me back to Him," Joan says, immediately establishing what decisively orients her outside the world in which the churchmen place themselves, and thus instigating the sparring that characterizes her exchanges with the Bishop. When he asks about the voices that commanded her, she replies: the voice "came from the right of the church. It was always accompanied by a bright light. I recognised the voice of an angel. It told me to raise the siege of Orléans and go to Vaucouleurs and what would happen there."[20] When asked if the saints make any promises to her, she differentiates what he has a right to know from what he does not: "It's not relevant to your trial." When pressed, "What proof do you have that your visions come from God?" she beseeches: "O gentle Lord, if you love me, tell me what to say to these churchmen." Joan is dangerous because of the intimacy of this colloquy to which the churchmen are not privy. The questions put to Joan—including whether she would try to escape if she could; whether she is a virgin; whether there is a bright light around the angels when they speak; whether she always obeyed the voices of St. Michael, St. Catherine, and St. Margaret;

FIGURE 4.2

FIGURE 4.3

whether St. Michael was naked (she responds: "Do you think God cannot afford clothes for him?"); by what sign the king recognized that Joan had been sent by God; whether God hates the English—sensational in their own right, even on the page, are eclipsed by Delay's breathtaking performance (which Pauline Kael peremptorily dismissed: she's like "a philosophy student taking an oral examination for which she's over-prepared"),[21] the antithesis of lifeless.

Joan's visage during her exchanges with the churchmen entices us to ask what compels our fascination with her. Is it her purity, her integrity? Is it that she is turned inward toward the visions and voices about which she is pressed to testify? Or is it inwardness itself, which for Joan is indistinguishable from divine witness?[22] *Procès* is unique in its insistence that, while Joan's divine revelations define her at the same remove and with the same inaccessibility as any hidden interior would, they are in another sense incomparable (how could subjectivity not be dwarfed or driven away by such visitants?), since her visions of saints and angels bequeath her inspiration and agency with sweeping historical consequences. Moreover, though in distinction to Bresson's other models, Joan is repeatedly forced to describe what she has seen, her statements do not make her experience legible, but instead provoke the churchmen's incredulity. If Bresson can't stop asking us to see her, it is because of the difficulty Joan poses for how to make the incorporeal credible (fig. 4.3).

Historically, Joan's answers to her interrogators' questions were said to stupefy them.[23] Bresson never again tried to depict a character's mental or spiritual recesses linguistically. His models are laconic and often mute. In *Procès*, the verbal exchanges between Joan and the churchmen are atypical, but they only technically provide transit to her visionary world of saints and angels, since words could neither make that realm perceptible, nor verify it.

Joan's countenance, on the other hand, seems immediately to place her in a supramundane realm. Although Delay never looks the same, her face also never deviates from a certain incommunicativeness—what Bresson would call its "automatism" (*N* 69)—registering something outside of will, intention, reason, and calculation.[24] At the same time, paradoxically, what appears as her openness in response to the questions by which the Bishop would ensnare her is so striking as to suggest a counterfactual: how Joan would appear if appearance did not count for anything, as if we saw her in solitude, rather than in the contested courtroom space where she is challenged. Other shots of Delay reveal her from angles that raise a question about how she is seen by the churchmen, what she is shown to see, and why we might see her as we do, as when we view Delay half-turned from us (her back and profile visible simultaneously, with sharp contrast created by the off-camera light source to the left), while she replies to the question of what the king gave her (fig. 4.4). We are looking at Joan at right angles to the light source through the heads of others (curious bystanders? or from the perspective of her interrogators looking at her through a peephole in the door of her cell?). Her words "war," "money," her staunch bearing (is she facing away from or toward her inquisitors?), and the light that frames her with uneven margins, a contrast to her crisp answers, seem antagonistic elements tensely drawn together. In shots like this the spectator wonders why Bresson wants us to see Joan from the side, through the lens of others' vision of her, with our view of her augmented by the shadows of those

FIGURE 4.4

FIGURE 4.5

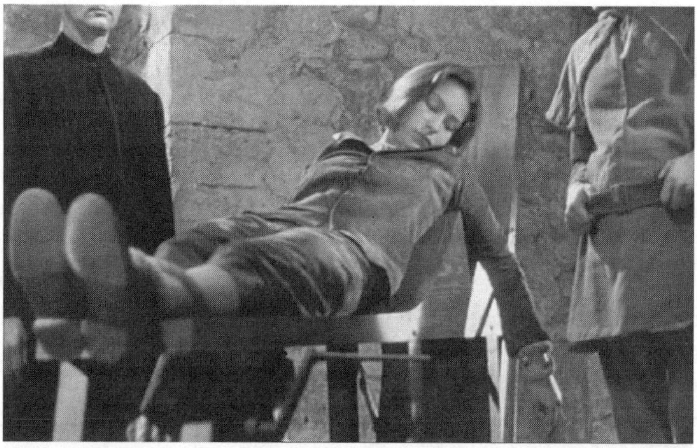

FIGURE 4.6

anonymous heads—as though we are seeing her through the distorted image of her captors' impressions, a distortion displaced onto thc jaggedly shaped light that frames her so that her body and the light vie for dominance in what amounts to a double vision. The image also reminds us of Joan's claim that the voice that commanded her was "always accompanied by a bright light"—not because the bright light around the voice and the bright light around Joan's body are congruent, but because they could not be so, since the former is not available to others' scrutiny.[25]

In figure 4.5, where we see Joan from below her knees, the light, bare legs, the single chained shoe render her defenseless—as though she has been optically dismembered by her captors' gaze—more than a shot of her full body would. Another medium shot (fig. 4.6) captures Joan from her soles to her head, her arms and legs bound. Since nowhere else in the film do we see her body extended in its entirety, the frame suggests that the churchmen cannot view her probity (here in in its manifestation of bodily completeness) without shackling what they see. The shot creates a split-second image of something like a displaced subjective vision of her captors' point of view, reflecting not that they have manacled Joan but why they been compelled to do so. Though Joan cannot be identified outside of what constrains her, the shackles that bind her also flesh out a wholeness made corporeal, an integrity discoverable in mere physical presence, not in personal identity, in this full-length medium shot of her, accentuated by contrast to the frame's fragmented images of her captors.

The film presses us to see Joan's harmlessness wherever the camera finds it: above, in her passive gaze, as she turns away from her oppressors; in her crossed arms when she maintains "I say I am [a virgin]. Too bad if you don't believe me"; in her unshakeable serenity when, suddenly awakened, she sits up in bed to see two guards stand over (fig. 4.7) her; in her consistency, her adherence to her visions: "If you tear me limb from limb, I will not speak differently. . . . If you throw me in the fire, I will not speak differently." Although the gripping drama of *Procès* also emanates from such intransigence, Delay's body and naked face, especially her face, more curiously compel attention. Delay's vigilant sentience—the reduction of her face to bare attention that supersedes all but fleeting expression and seems free of anything extraneous to neutral awareness (she appears neither to anticipate nor to forestall circumstance, but rather to meet it with a watchfulness uninflected by thought or anxiety)—is central to the film's interest in her.

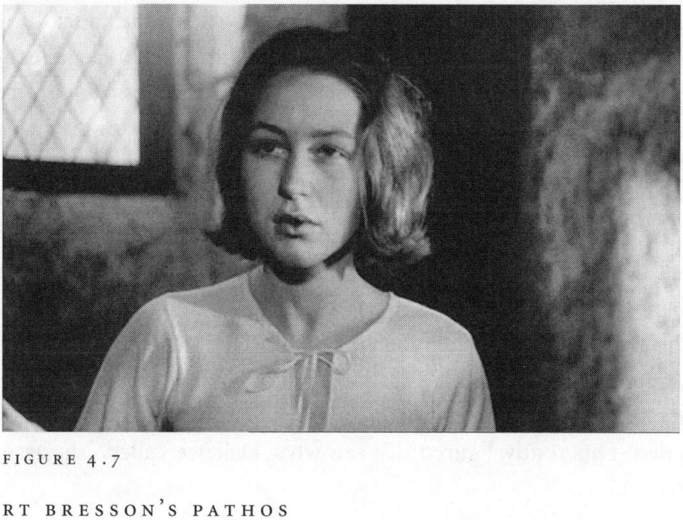

FIGURE 4.7

FIGURE 4.8

It is frequently reiterated, and Bresson himself insisted, that he depicted the "soul."[26] However, it is not the soul that Joan's face vivifies, but rather something more dimensional and fleshed. Yet the lure of gleaning an immaterial entity like the soul is again held before us when in *Procès*, as Joan is tied to the stake, a spaniel walks between two rows of witnesses (we see only their legs), pauses and, presumably, looks ahead at the figure chained to the post (there is no reverse shot), as though its regard, its long fixed look, in the film's penultimate moments marked the emergence of a countervision to the fallible human gaze, which could convey to the beholder what the churchmen cannot fathom. But Bresson avoids the sentimentality with which he here flirts. Something that passes across the dog's face or is revealed in its bearing also cannot be decoded. We see the animal perfectly, but cannot penetrate the image (fig. 4.8). The dog's elusive gaze (elusive not because it is unique; it is a mutt with ordinary features, but because those features are no more legible than any animal's would be) forms a slant rhyme with the elusiveness of Joan's countenance, although, in distinction to an animal's, we take the human face to be decipherable.

One aspect of the kinship of animal and human faces, established by their proximity, is that by analogy to our discernment of the contour of the spaniel's face, which supersedes its particular features, we see a like abstraction transform Joan's face. What lies beyond expression draws animal and human faces toward each other. When Joan is bound to the stake, we see not only her agony, but her endurance of it (fig. 4.9), as though anguish were no more impediment than a pane of glass through which, strange to say, her face remains unclouded. Differently figured, we see what Deleuze called "the face as an outline," its "unity"[27] beyond any expressive feature; section II will elaborate. What we see in Delay's face is nothing that can be recognized, isolated, or even fixed in present-tense awareness (I take that to be the force of Bresson's recognition that to watch the model is to witness his deviation from himself moment after moment: "All those things you could not conceive of him *before,* or even *during*" [*N* 57]), the model's "true nature" (*N* 39) continuously revealing itself as insusceptible to fixity and to any specific look. This nothing suffuses Delay's face, the first of Bresson's models to incarnate it. (In the earlier *Pickpocket*, Michel's identifying feature is his hands, not his body or face.) In the rhyme Bresson creates between the image of Joan bound to the stake (fig. 4.9) and the blackened stake with Joan's body burned away, Joan free (fig. 4.10), we see the contrast between the nothing that shows through Joan's flesh to characterize her (even as she is burned alive, she is protected from assault by the neutrality of looking inward, rather than being compelled to witness her own barbaric murder), and a very different nothing (her annihilation) that the latter frame literalizes. In drawing these together, Bresson implicitly asks, what is being at its most rudimentary—mere being, the most impersonal—not body, not soul, not animal, and also not impalpable, since it continuously registers in the flesh as an enigma before it is realized in particular features, or denatured?

Joan's integrity, born of her autonomy and her fierce will, appear to contradict (to say the least) the value Bresson places on "Models. Capable of eluding their own vigilance" (*N* 77). Yet, without parallel in his other films, in *Procès* Bresson renders these two sources of purity (reflection of mere being, willful defiance based on unyielding vision and principle) coincident—the film's extraordinary achievement—as though what Joan wills has been first discovered in her passive obedience to the voices that coerce her to become what she is. Joan's quiddity could never be disclosed—not by looking at her and not by penetrating the reflection in the dog's eyes—because it is inseparable from the body that shows it forth, while of course not being identical to that body. In watching the flames consume Joan, we see a burning figure, not an essence that is destroyed. Joan thus epitomizes Bresson's typical insistence on the unassailability of inwardness to scrutiny, while of course her fate (to be burned as a heretic, sorceress, adulteress) is inalienable and incomparable to that of Bresson's mundane characters.

At the same time, at the film's end, our perception of Joan is also constituted by the aggregate vision we discover at the juncture of her closed eyes, the dog's illegible gaze, and the churchmen whom we see from the waist downwards, at a right angle to the burning stake, turned away so they cannot witness the conflagration. From the beholder's point of view, these interpenetrated and

FIGURE 4.9

FIGURE 4.10

thwarted visions (what is not seen behind Joan's closed eyes and in the dog's indecipherable vision), as well as what the churchmen refuse to countenance, variously manifest inwardness as unsanctioned and inviolable.[28] Such multiple vantages (including the historical one, the "portrait" painted by Joan's "words before the judges at Rouen . . . and the witness statements that took place twenty-five years later") suggest that, in Maurice Merleau-Ponty's words, there is no "'pure' being" outside of the "system of perspectives that open into it . . . at the intersection of my views with those of the others," an intersection that "makes the sensible world and the historical world . . . interdependent."[29] From one vantage, then, at the film's end, Bresson insists that what Joan *is* can be discerned only in the nexus of such incommensurate visions that inequivalently fail to grasp her.

If *Procès* suggests there is no "zero point of Being," no "aerial view" of it,[30] nonetheless by virtue of the dog's emphasized gaze in *Procès*'s concluding frames, and, by contrast to the parceling and masking of the figures in the film's opening shots, the film asks us to intuit this "zero point" or ground state of being from an opposite vantage: its extermination. Specifically, the dog's gaze at the conflagration turns us toward the shock of beholding the extinction of Joan's vitality—of what Charles Dickens calls "the spark of life"; Giorgio Agamben, following Deleuze, "*a life*"; Merleau-Ponty, "'pure' being"; Simone Weil, the impersonal quality that epitomizes the sacred in a human being[31]—which we, displacing the dog's vision, but through its agency, its standing there, arresting our attention, are asked to apprehend, as though Bresson were pressing us to see, through the instrumentality of the dog's interest, something that might escape us. What might escape us is that in *Procès* this reduction of Joan to a vital minimum, is associated not at all with Joan's "singular" life, as in Agamben's and Deleuze's specifications; nor with the "impersonal" quality that constitutes the sacred for Weil; and not with what Merleau-Ponty calls "'pure' being," a characterization I had provisionally reiterated, but with Joan's vision, fidelity to which exacts her death—with the "close-meshed whole, purely inward" (*N* 124), and with inwardness itself, which Joan's visions signify.[32] Joan's vision exceeds her life, and her death does not exterminate vision—or the capacity for vision, or that which vision is—what we and the churchmen cannot see. Call her vision, then, a plenitude that cannot be destroyed, though, at the same time, since vision has no features and no substance, it is also nothing. These characterizations, plenitude and nothing, precisely identify the same phenomenon.[33] We cannot see the light around the voices; how St. Michael is clothed; whether Joan's visions are to the right or to the left; what angels or saints look like; what proof she has that her visions come from God. How extraordinary to shoot a film that has at its core what is noncoincident with, what repels, others' perceptions (and that also wards off *our* perceptions of Joan's inner world), and to make that impasse vivid.

What renders Joan's vision so perilous, what the churchmen seek to destroy, is not only her allegiance to what she sees, or the military triumphs in which her vision is realized, and not the actions that incite the charges against her of "indecency, sedition, idolatry and evil-doing," but rather her capacity to see what her inquisitors can't see—"The constant, the eternal beneath the accidental" (*N* 56)—thus provoking the reiterated dictate: no matter what she says or repudiates: "she must be burned."[34] Even when Joan concedes "I will submit to the Holy Council of Basel," even when she acknowledges "I will obey God and the Pope," her inquisitor insists: "This will not do." And when, in fear of the fire, she momentarily submits, signing the paper that recants her testimony, her danger for the churchmen lingers past her exhausted disavowal of it, since the very propensity to see what they are blind to could never be revoked or legislated. The churchmen can only literally constrain Joan by the "penance" of "perpetual imprisonment," though no discipline could force her vision into coincidence with theirs. Joan's repudiation of her testimony (which is itself recanted) does not sap her power or her peril for the churchmen. This is why, after Joan's retraction, the Bishop, still sensing her potent harm, insists that if Joan's virginity gives her strength, she must be divested of it. But Joan's innocence, her purity, resides not in her chastity (which could be sullied), but in her vision, which is immune to tampering. Her vision remains unmediated—driving back everything alien that would encroach on it—free of compromise, admixture, or compounding, and indestructible. Thus notwithstanding her singularity, or rather, because of the singularity of Bresson's documentary of Joan's incorporeal revelations, which seem to recede from view the more they are given utterance, Joan becomes a prototype for all of Bresson's models (even those who precede her), because her vision, her voices, her inwardness, that which vitalizes and makes her radiant, which cannot be apprehended, extracted from her, engaged, or even precisely identified, comprise a very different nothing—as I have been trying to say—than that produced by the conflagration whose marks are visible on the blackened stake after the body has burned away as vision, for instance, never could be.

II

Until its dénouement, *Mouchette*, which Bresson adapted from Georges Bernanos's novel, lures the beholder into supposing that no violence could adulterate its eponymous fourteen-year-old girl's innocence.[35] Although the film initially isolates Mouchette's innocence from the baseness that everywhere surrounds it, that segregation does not survive the film's scrutiny; the separation of discrete phenomena is menaced in all of the film's registers.[36] For instance, as I shall explain, a soundtrack (Monteverdi's *Magnificat*) that promises religious uplift frames the narrative, but the illegible treatment of the music compromises that elevation. The film suffuses the face of Mouchette, played by Nadine Nortier, with incandescence, but that brilliance is queered in the similitude the film establishes between Mouchette's bright countenance and luminous *inanimate* objects, which are counterintuitively made to share its traits. *Mouchette* counters the melodramatic plot by an accompanying if tacit philosophical investigation of whether persons, objects, natural entities have autonomous essences that could remain impervious to outside assault, an examination that Bresson

FIGURE 4.11

conducts filmically when the boundaries of categorically discrete entities are contested.[37]

Bresson's fascination with the congruences of unlike phenomena is immediately apparent in the film's opening sequences. After *Mouchette*'s credits, behind which we hear the strains of Monteverdi's *Magnificat*, we see a man, subsequently identified as Mathieu, the game warden, run through the woods and hide behind a tree. He is watching a second man, later identified as Arsène, the poacher, take a looped wire trap out of his cap, hang it on a branch he cuts from a bush, and lay it across the ground (fig. 4.11).

When a partridge's neck gets caught in the trap, the camera moves back and forth between the image of the bird's wings fluttering and an extreme close-up of Mathieu's eyes; one eye, half-hidden, is framed by leaves (fig. 4.12). He watches the bird flap against the bushes, fling itself on the ground to shake the branch loose, and turn on its back, legs in the air, flailing (fig. 4.13). Only when the bird hops away, still in the chokehold, unable to shake off the branch, does the gamekeeper—framed in two cut-away shots—move out from behind the tree, pick the bird up, slip the snare from around its neck, and free it (figs. 4.14, 4.15).

But in another extreme close-up, we see the second man, Arsène, who has set the trap, who is watching as the bird is snared and released (fig. 4.16). One eye, like that of his adversary (fig. 4.12), is obscured by a leaf. Although Arsène entraps the partridge and Mathieu frees it, both dispassionately observe the bird suffer. The viewer's inability to identify whose eyes watch (and whose hands entrap or liberate the partridge) visually entangles the two men

FIGURE 4.12

FIGURE 4.13

in a parceling out and paralleling of hands, eyes, legs, feet, torsos, however the diegetic elements oppose them. Not until he walks away toward the road, rifle in hand, do we see Mathieu, the mustached man, from his head to his shins, whereas the several shots of the bird always reveal its body whole, in the throes of agony.

A few scenes later Mouchette shuffles into a schoolroom. She is late. The teacher gives her a severe look. In a previous scene we have viewed Mouchette at home (fig. 4.17) put hot compresses on her dying mother's chest, and pick up a wailing infant while her father (if "you call that a father," the gamekeeper's wife will say) reclines on a bed holding a tweed cap in his hand and *drives* it. He turns the cap this way, then that, as he would the steering wheel of a truck, while making a droning engine sound (fig. 4.18), ignoring his dying wife and

FIGURE 4.14

FIGURE 4.15

FIGURE 4.16

FIGURE 4.17

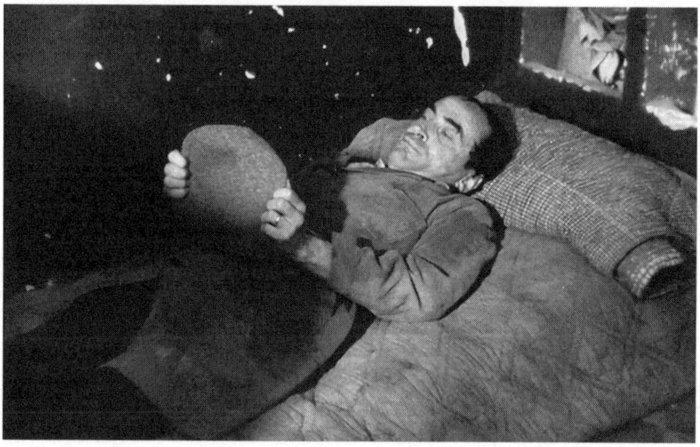

FIGURE 4.18

the bawling infant she cannot get up to quiet. Mouchette glances at her father steering his cap and humming engine sounds while the baby screams.

Mouchette now stands in a row of children. They are singing: "Hope! Hope is dead/Three days, Columbus said to them/Pointing to the vast sky ahead/ That stretched behind the horizon/Three days and I'll give a world/To you who have no more hope/Over the vast depths/He opened his eyes wide" to see it.[38] She is silent. The teacher comes from behind, puts her hands on Mouchette's shoulder and twists her around by the neck (fig. 4.19), much as Mathieu twisted the wire that ringed the neck of the partridge to free it (fig. 4.14), then pushes her toward the piano, and orders "Sing!" Just as Bresson has intertwined the two antagonists, Mathieu and Arsène, he also interweaves the near antonyms in the antiphonal response "Espérez!—Plus d'espérance! . . . qui n'avez plus d'espoir." Pressing Mouchette's neck and face to the keyboard (fig. 4.20) the teacher pounds out the notes and Mouchette, solo, sings. She is out of tune. The creatures grabbed by the neck, snared, pushed, beaten, raped, and killed are children, birds, animals—brutalities whose differences are marked and effaced by the malevolent indifference that undergirds them all.

In the film's central encounter Mouchette and Arsène bump into each other at night in a wood where Mouchette, leaning against a tree in the rain, her school bag next to her, has lingered into the dark to escape her classmates and her family (fig. 4.21). That is where Arsène, hunting Mathieu (they are fighting over Louisa, the barmaid), finds her, and asks: "What're you doing here?" When Arsène says to Mouchette, "I think I killed a man," she asks, "Mathieu

FIGURE 4.19

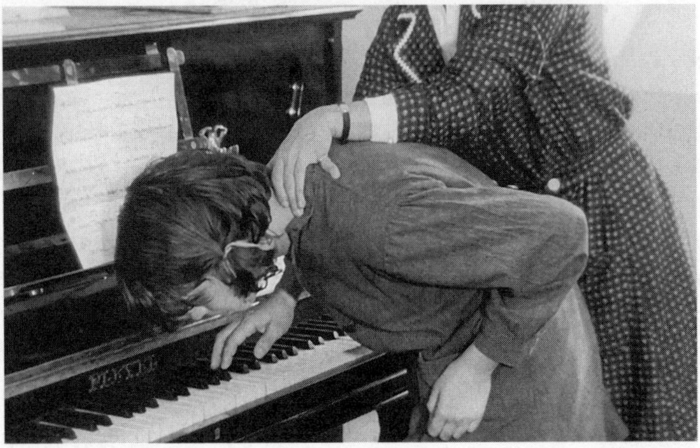

FIGURE 4.20

FIGURE 4.21

FIGURE 4.22

the gamekeeper?" Arsène, taking her to his hut, elaborates: "We rolled in the stream. . . . I can see myself holding a trap by its spring. . . . He was facedown in the water. It turned red." In an over-the-shoulder shot (fig. 4.22), Mouchette listens to his confession. The camera shots spatialize the temporary mobility of their positions: she is looking up to, across, then down at him. When Arsène tells Mouchette that Mathieu may still be alive, and may talk, she offers to help: "I'll say I was in the woods, that . . . he . . . attacked you. . . . Do I say he was drunk? . . . I hate them . . . all." Before he can answer, Arsène feels "a fit coming on" and begins to froth at the mouth. When he falls to the floor convulsing, and rolls from side to side, Mouchette kneels beside him (fig. 4.23) and puts her hands around his head (fig. 4.24), a different grip from that of the gamekeeper, the teacher, and the father steering his wheel-cap.

When the fit subsides, Mouchette sings the schoolroom song: "Hope! Hope is dead/Three days, Columbus said to them/Pointing to the vast sky ahead." In a voice that stays in tune, she finishes: "Three days I'll give a world/To you who have no more hope." In the novel, the narrator explains that Arsène's face "seemed to be the first human face she had ever really looked at."[39] In Bresson's film there is no cue that glosses her perception of him. Arsène's cornered plight may remind Mouchette of her own fate. But she's not credulous. When Arsène, recovered, stands and says "I'll take you home," she asks: "Where are we really going?" When she tries to leave, he blocks the door: "One word to anyone and I'll wring your neck." The neck, threatened by violence. "I'd rather die than hurt you," she reassures him. Misunderstanding her solicitude, he rapes her.

FIGURE 4.23

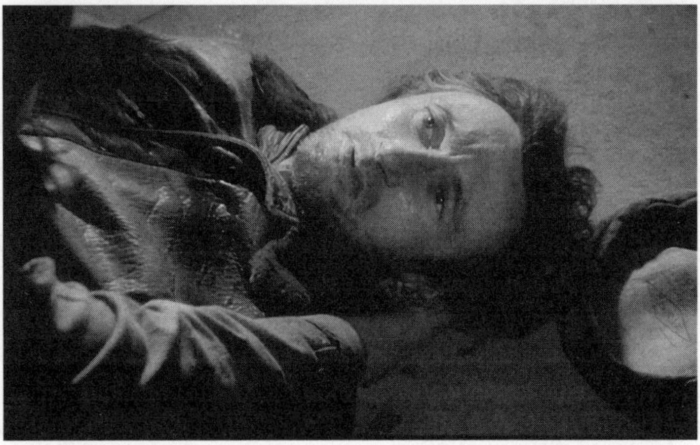

FIGURE 4.24

FIGURE 4.25

FIGURE 4.26

Bresson draws the trap and the face into antiphonal relation.[40] But while the cruel particulars of the trap are evident, Mouchette's impassive face, for all its sometime-plasticity—we see its mobility in the scream of joy when she rides the dodgem car; in shock, pushing Arsène away, as he caresses her arm; looking down at the dead rabbit killed by hunters out for a lark (is she watching its tortured body writhe from side to side, which *we* see before she comes into the frame and the camera shifts to a retroactive eyeline match of her view of it? [fig. 4.25]); in tears as she holds the baby to feed it a bottle warmed against her breast (fig. 4.26)—can't be read decisively. We see her face register feeling and sensation the way the texture of a surface would, denying access to anything beneath it.

The cinematic disparity between countenance and an inner world that isn't penetrable calls to mind Theodor Adorno and Hanns Eisler's explanation of the function of music as an "antidote against the [silent] picture. The need was felt to spare the spectator the unpleasantness involved in seeing effigies of living, acting, and even speaking persons, who were at the same time silent. The fact that they are living and nonliving at the same time is what constitutes their ghostly character, and music was introduced not to supply them with the life they lacked . . . but to exorcise fear or help the spectator absorb the shock."[41] When Adorno and Eisler add "*the talking picture, too, is mute*,"[42] I take them to mean that even though the speaking picture furthers the illusion that we are seeing persons living in front of us, their images are no more alive than those in silent films. Film's anachronistic celluloid images are as incapable of speaking directly to us as the "gesticulating masks"[43] that precede the talkies. When Bresson ascribes agency to the innovation of audio recording ("THE SOUNDTRACK INVENTED SILENCE" [*N* 48]), his words have a special application to his own films, in which dialogue often does not elucidate what we see on the model's face; in which this incommunicativeness is amplified by stretches of filmic time unrelieved by dialogue; and in which Bresson's practice of segregating aural and visual registers of a film is founded on a principle: "What is for the eye must not duplicate what is for the ear" (*N* 61). Thus sound, however striking, might at times illuminate neither a film's images nor its diegetic, rather throwing into relief something like the silence to which it gives way.

Mouchette's frequent dumbness is obliquely echoed in her own uncertainty about how to identify her experience. Is Arsène a rapist or a lover (during the rape, she fights him off and then puts her arms around his back, embracing him)? Is the storm she and Arsène are caught in caused by heavy winds from an ordinary rain or is it a "cyclone" they endure (how Arsène explains it)? When Mouchette tells her mother: "The wind shifted with the cyclone," the latter deprecates: "Where did you see a cyclone, you poor girl?" Replying to Mathieu's question about what she was doing with Arsène in his cabin the previous night, Mouchette explains, "I went there for shelter from the cyclone," and then corrects herself: from "the rain." Such ambiguity has an analogue for the spectator when, in a scene to which I shall return, Mouchette rolls down the hill at the film's end three times (the first time her body loses momentum, the second, it is stopped by a bush) before she falls into the pond and drowns. Should we see her suicide as her redemption or her doom? Is there hope or is hope dead? In impelling herself forward toward the water—clasping the long gossamer dress that the creepy old lady bequeaths her to wear in honor of her mother's death—is she amusing herself with "Russian roulette," or does she intend to drown in the quarry pool?[44]

Mouchette's effaced expressiveness is also legible as imperviousness. Losing her clog in the mud is the plight of a shoe; she does not react to it as a portent. When she is pushed by her father in the bar, we do not see his violence faze her. And death is, also, apparently all right, though if by chance her intention to kill herself had been averted (by an exchange with the farmer driving the tractor, whom she hails before he looks away), that too might have been a fine outcome. Thus Mouchette seems uncompromised by what she experiences—like Joan, though not from faith—immune to any assault against her integrity. Her expressions of erupted affect (whether anger, joy, tears) give the odd sense of touching her and leaving her as she is—as, Bresson implies, they would for anyone we could see impartially.[45] The film's particular interest in her countenance does not lie in its intense reactions, but in its impenetrability. The face sustains the assault of experience, while at the same time not being changed by it,[46] though from another point of view, of course, that same assault leads to Mouchette's suicide. Both are true. Such a disparity must have prompted Deleuze to distinguish between two poles of the face—dominated by a succession of animated features across which emotions play *and* generalized as an "immobile unity" beyond "intensive expressive movements."[47] This unity or outline assumes an abstraction which suspends individuation.

Deleuze's remarks on the "affection-image"[48] have special pertinence to the face in Bresson's cinematography, in which the willfulness of particular expressions that would constitute one pole in Deleuze's paradigm is suppressed or muted. Thus I am arguing that in *Mouchette*, as in all of Bresson's films, the "pure Quality" of the "reflexive" face,[49] the nonmimetic, nonpsychological face—the face abstracted to the state of "Entity"[50]—is so pervasive as illusorily to seem to disengage from, and almost to displace, the expressive face in Deleuze's categorical model. Moreover, in *Mouchette*, where the face lingers at the pole of outline and material surface, to say that the face reveals an absoluteness that has a metaphoric "brilliance" is to stress the congruence of the girl's face with certain shots of inanimate but palpably luminous objects: the headlights of her father's truck, the moon in the woods (fig. 4.27), Arsène's flashlight (fig. 4.28), which, like the face (for instance, fig. 4.23), are self-luminous, independent of what they might light up.

(Even when we see the partridge that Mouchette watches fly away, the viewer's gaze is mesmerized by the autonomous lure of that face [fig. 4.29], whose brightness compels absorption in the way no object of its gaze could—though, in this instance, the fate of the bird she regards is nothing less than an alternative to her own fate, rhythmically anticipated.) The odd cinematographic parallel between the bodies of artificial and natural light and the human face is underscored by the fact that, like the face, these globular objects

FIGURE 4.27

FIGURE 4.28

are framed as autonomous sources of interest, with no reverse shot of what they illuminate. The camera's privileged treatment of these objects (as though their literal brightness were alone sufficient to compel attention) thus draws these spherical shapes, with their undifferentiated surfaces, toward the outline of Mouchette's face, on whose radiance the camera dwells, in its abstract emphasis inadvertently rethinking the duality of Deleuze's prototype.

The brightness of those objects—the high beams, the flashlight, the moon, also the baby's eyes, the fire that burns near Mouchette's head while Arsène rapes her, and of course Mouchette's face—can intensify or darken, be ignited or extinguished, turned on or off, close or open, be obscured or revealed (as the moon is by the misty clouds, so that it appears, then disappears, its visibility swallowed up by night and sky), but *not*, it seems, adulterated. Rhythmically

FIGURE 4.29

drawing these objects into relation, Bresson insists that the artifactual (the flashlight, the headlights), the natural (the moon), the human (Mouchette's face, the baby's eyes), and, in another register, the animal (whose fate threatens to become the girl's) can be analogized, thus unveiling his profound indifference to taxonomies and hierarchies. In the baby's eyes (fig. 4.30) we see the same binocular image foreshadowed in the headlights (fig. 4.31).

In *Procès*, Joan's visions have a *life* and an ontology that is not our ontology. Bresson points to the disparity between what Joan can see and what we can see, without invalidating the reality of the former. Joan's vision *is*, but not for us. In distinction, in *Mouchette* something more radical is hazarded, in that Bresson makes us see that our judgment about the lifelessness of objects is a matter of vision, rather than a matter of ontology. In drawing together the light in Mouchette's face with the light of the moon, and the light of the baby's eyes with the automobile lights, Bresson effaces the line between what is animate and what is inanimate. In *Mouchette*, Bresson rewrites ontology, enlivening inert objects by canceling the "*in*" or "not," of *in*animate, much as *A Man Escaped* breathes life into objects.[51]

Certain sounds in the film also appear to have an abstract autonomy: the strains of Monteverdi's *Magnificat*, which begin and end *Mouchette*; the baby's wrathful screaming, which at one point nerve-rackingly continues off-frame long past the point where it signifies unappeasable misery. At such a moment the screaming becomes only annoying sound, detached from the infant's anguish. The Monteverdi and the infant's screaming—harmonic sound and dissonant sound, both nonlinguistic (the arrangement of sounds in time organized rhythmically as well as melodically and, their counterpoint, the baby's shrieking)—do not exist on the social plane of *Mouchette*'s world. The *Magnificat* could have no place in a universe blind and deaf to beauty, just as, when its anguish is heard only as noise, nothing could appease the infant's screech. Alain Badiou's claim that "Bresson's quest to achieve a completely inner expressiveness . . . is anti-cultural"[52] is almost correct—*almost* because the materiality of the body *conceals* that inner world even while ascribing it authority. And also *almost* because the same globed outline as the face is revealed in objects that have no interiority: the headlights, the moon, and the flashlight, however outrageous or whimsical we might assess this visual congruence.

To say that the film captures Mouchette's essential brightness, which, notwithstanding the assault, is left untainted is to recognize its alliance with corollary

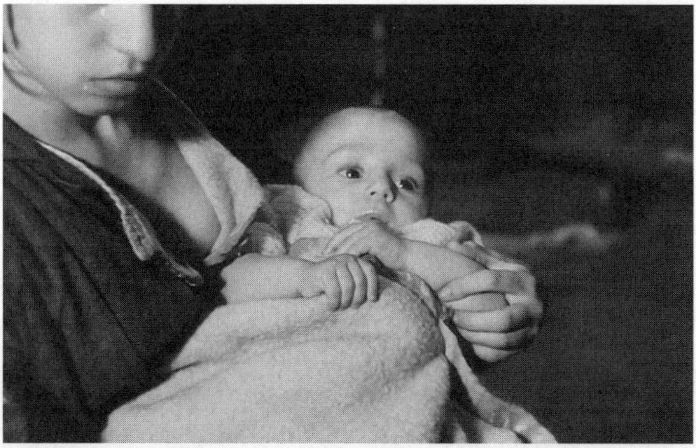

FIGURE 4.30

FIGURE 4.31

FIGURE 4.32

sounds as well as images (often other round objects) that also reveal the absoluteness I am claiming the film attributes to the face beyond its repertoire of particular expressions. In this way Bresson moves beyond *Dasein* (Martin Heidegger's term for the "Being" of the human, for the *es gibt* of Being that distinguishes *Dasein* from all other phenomena), because in *Mouchette* the human is drawn toward the inanimate, and everything else *there* also *is*.[53] What the spectator sees in Mouchette's face and in the lights, and hears in the Monteverdi and in the infant's wailing, glues these sights and sounds together through the rhythm of montage, a contact that emphasizes the formal autonomy of these pairings in contrast to the diegetic elements of the plot, which could not have such independence. In Deleuze's characterization of the "affection-image," Mouchette's face is a manifestation of light, and the linkage of that face to other objects —given to us contrapuntally, almost always in medium close-ups, which include the white of the partridge's neck and belly (fig. 4.13), as well as the white of the long-distance shot of the rabbit's legs in its death throes (fig. 4.32)—mirror that light, insisting in the camera's impartiality that any entity could be linked to another by the mere brightness of each.

Thus while another obvious way to read the film's luminous objects is as internally contrastive (how *could* the bright of the moon be analogized to that of the artificial flashlight?), they are nonetheless drawn into similitude by the starker juxtaposition of all the film's whites with the opaques, blacks, and grainy shadows of the narrative scenes whose content translates the visual and formal oppositions into ethical corollaries. Optically among the darkest of Bresson's frames in his cinematography, these shots can be so extreme as almost to efface the frame's composition, as in figure 33, of Arsène in the wood, or as to so heighten the contrast between the white and the dark shades (as in figure 34, between the flame and Mouchette's face, and the graying out of the body that will be raped) that they seem to affirm the melodrama of the diegetic.

The film gives us alternatives as a visual choice: the partridge on its back (fig. 4.13), the rabbit on its back, writhing, and Mouchette on *her* back (fig. 4.34) as Arsène rapes her are starkly juxtaposed to Mouchette's freedom from bondage through a stunning game she invents—inspired by the rabbit she sees twisting in its death throes, a vision counterpointed to the girl's fate. Her body also turns from side to side, but she terminates this agonistic rhythm. The genius of Mouchette's deadly game may appear to save her, not because there is another world, but because she slips away from this one without being mutilated.[54]

FIGURE 4.33

FIGURE 4.34

FIGURE 4.35

FIGURE 4.36

Framed in a series of medium close-ups, she is swathed in the dress that the death-obsessed old lady gave her, which she holds against her body; it becomes a winding-sheet (figs. 4.35, 4.36). In Mouchette's repetitive turnings downward, her movements rhyme with each other; she rhymes with herself. Released from any narrative exterior to her "game," she escapes into pure momentum.[55]

In these final frames, the abstraction of Mouchette's face shifts to her body as a whole, which magnetically comes to have the face's homogeneity, its integrity, and, in the rhythm of her revolutions downward, its self-agreement. In that roll downward (which internally rhymes exhilaration and horror, method and serendipity, agency and gravity that is predetermined), we see the corporealization of intention before it reaches its endpoint, as though the camera were making visible, moment after moment, in an unbroken continuity, what an intention looks like as the body discerns and realizes it. In Béla Balázs's generic description: "*The only thing that produces tempo in a scene is the mobility of the atoms of which it is composed.* This is because the spoken word can always call to mind the plot in its entirety, but it is only the momentary that enables us to see."[56]

The most inventive of all of Bresson's cinematic conclusions, Mouchette's end has an affinity with the martyrdom of Joan, with Jeanne in *Une Femme Douce*, who leaps out a window to escape her husband's petty meanness, and with the donkey in *Au hasard Balthazar* (although, unlike the last instance where death is borne by the animal, while the girl technically evades it, in *Mouchette* the girl chooses the fate that is inflicted on the animals). The critics' exegesis of these diverse calamities is that Bresson depicts such murders and "prophetic suicide[s]" to hold up the darkness of the world to the "shine" of "God's unchanging watchfulness."[57] In *Mouchette*, however, I have described a more immediate dialectic between *plus d'espérance* and *ne plus d'espérance* that in *this* world enacts a conflict, a rhythm, a trajectory, a pendulum swing in which "*plus*" turns into the negative and back again. The film pivots on that back and forth; its sweep touches everything around Mouchette: her life, the world she flees, and her suicide.

To recapitulate: we see the dialectic in the trapping and the release of the partridge, an opposition that, from the first, blurs the distinction between the two actions since both men, the one that traps and the one that releases the bird, enjoy its misery. We see it in Mouchette's gaze of tenderness at Arsène's plight, and in the inverse of tenderness when she pushes him away. We see it in Mouchette's pacification of her infant brother and in the baby's renewed screaming, a sequence that repeats itself. We see it in the song with the off-key note that Mouchette performs in the schoolroom and in her perfect key when, no longer coerced, the ditty becomes a lullaby. In Bresson's cinema, more hope and no more hope are not mind states or manifestations of subjectivity. They are words in a song; entrapment and release; involuntary expressions that break through impassivity; notes sung on- or off-key; the clasp of hands around someone's neck, or the threat to break it. Like the undiscriminated *there is* of all things and individuals and the *es gibt* of *Dasein*, the film's contrastive elements resound against each other, even at moments seeming to occupy the same space, or to have the same formal structure, albeit at a saving distance, as though their convergence or echoic recapitulation could only evanescently be contemplated.

But that equivocal relation changes in the film's final moments. In Mouchette's movement downward to freedom and to death, Bresson corporealizes one last time his vision of *plus* and *ne pas plus,* which, in *distinction* to what precedes it, is tethered in Mouchette's slide toward death *and* freedom, which the film's climax makes simultaneous, so that finally the very idea of preserving Mouchette's radiance from Mouchette's violence is derided. Violence *is* what *preserves* her integrity and her brightness. Unlike the film's apparent promissory note on an autonomy that would permit opposite states to take refuge from each other, unlike Joan's death in *Procès*, which leaves her purity intact, unlike *Un condamné à mort s'est échappé*'s uncompromised freedom, even unlike *Au hasard Balthazar*, in which beauty recoils and keeps its distance from cruelty (as rhythm in that film wards off narrative), Bresson's unanticipated insight at the end of *Mouchette* insists on the impossibility of sustaining such segregations, since it compromises the film's idea that what is innocent could remain free from blemish. In the exegesis of the country priest in *Journal*, to imagine such effaced distinction is to see the Holy Virgin's hands as those of "a poor child already roughened by hard work" and on her son, "a child's face, without the slightest radiance." More radically, still through the lens of the priest's vision, when he explains to the Countess why rage at her son's death cannot be separated from the love she squanders on him if he is its only object: "There isn't one kingdom for the living and one for the dead. There is only the kingdom of God, and we are within it."

In *Mouchette*, what could such an insight mean if not to signal Bresson's rethinking of the visual logic according to which the face, the moon, the baby's eyes, and even Mouchette's joy-ride in the bumper car remain at a formal distance from the violent cruelty that would defile them, while denying the spectator the gloss that would make such rethinking legible? For unlike the "one kingdom" of *Journal*, which holds out the salutary possibility that love could envelop all, in *Mouchette* what one *world* threatens is the privilege that has distinguished the girl, that has made her what she is in Bresson's cinematic embodiments of her. In distinction, the film's end insists: one world for the girl's innocence and for her violation of that innocence by suicide, for the peaceful baby's eyes and the screaming that transforms anguish into unheeded noise. In this way, to revector Balázs's sentence, the "tempo," the rhythm of Mouchette's roll toward death, reveals the film's re-composition of its "atoms," a reconstruction marked by Mouchette's death and the enigmatic repetition of Monteverdi's *Magnificat*.

We first hear the nonvocal part of the *Magnificat* during the initial credits. But how does *Mouchette* employ Monteverdi, which frames the film's beginning and its end? In *The Film Sense* Eisenstein writes of "childish and senseless" "correlations of . . . sound and picture" in which "*music*" is made to correspond to a film's "*purely representational elements*," in effect illustrating the latter.[58] In my view, a naïve correspondence, of the sort identified by Eisenstein, is implied by the claim that Monteverdi helps figure Mouchette's deliverance.[59] As in prescriptions like the following, Bresson implicitly agrees with

Eisenstein's general principle: "Image and sound must not support each other, but must work each in turn through *a sort of relay*" (*N* 62). "When sound and picture support each other, the sum is bland and weak."[60] Bresson's use of Monteverdi, I am arguing, has the effect of seeming to offer a musical illustration and interpretation of Mouchette's death, suggesting (in the words of one gloss like many such) that God will "exalt and redeem the humble," while simultaneously retreating from anything that could adequate the fantasy of such an interpretation.[61] The *Magnificat* holds out a consolatory possibility (of the sort quoted above), but in the film's context—a young girl's suicide—consolation is hollowed out. Mouchette's "sacrifice" does not fit into the paradigm offered it by the Monteverdi. Even Columbus's words "I will give you a world," presumably a new world, do not validate it, since the world Columbus will discover is *this* one.

When asked about Mouchette's motive, and whether he meant to celebrate her suicide with "the blast of the Magnificat," Bresson replied: "I explain nothing, and you can understand it any way you like."[62] Just as Bresson forestalls any way to make the girl's death intelligible, he also literally prevents us from *seeing* it (thus depriving us of the vision that would precipitate the illusion that we can grasp what we see): "death is like a magic trick: in a flash, the person vanishes. That is why I don't show her falling in the water. . . . there is a cut, and she is gone. . . . You must have noticed that in the film there is not one word about what her experience means."[63] In quotations like these, I take Bresson to be preempting interpretations that conceive of the Monteverdi as though it illustrated a transformative understanding of Mouchette's suicide. Meaning in fact fades away with the disappearance of the body and the passage from the *Magnificat*. Then should we recall the orchestral passage from the *Magnificat*, which appears wholly out of context over *Mouchette*'s opening credits, lending a certain symmetry—yet complication—to its more fully motivated but still arbitrary or spiritually ambiguous return, bluntly overdetermined at the end? Because any resurrectional uplift in the swell of the Monteverdi behind the credit sequence would be coded as arbitrary and hence extraneous, when the *Magnificat* reappears at the end, it has already been de-thematized. Thus, if not anti-redemptive, the Monteverdi must at least be seen as ironic, in distinction to *Journal d'un curé de campagne*, where the cross we see at that film's end leaves no room for ambiguity. Such a reading certainly contradicts the doctrinal interpretations of the Monteverdi at *Mouchette*'s ending. But Bresson, though a Catholic, was not doctrinaire. Thus about the mortal sin of suicide, Bresson insisted that—to paraphrase—he less and less thought of suicide as sinful: "Killing oneself can be courageous; not killing oneself, because you wish to lose nothing, even the worst that life has to offer, can also be courageous."[64] Is Mouchette's "game," when she rolls down that hill, to gamble on which form of courage will define *her*?

One way of understanding the Monteverdi is to see that it could not be integrated into the sense of the film's diegetic elements, and not into *any* signifying sense (including the sense that the Monteverdi "figures the disappearance of the body, and perhaps also the freeing of the soul"),[65] for such a speculation would sentimentally reintroduce a splitting—here particularized as the girl's death and the promise of her resurrection—which Bresson has taken pains to relegate to the moments that precede the film's climax. While the soundtrack does not give us mere ambience, it cannot carry the weight of *neutralizing* the suicide or compensating for it, especially since the music behind the credits at the film's beginning is, as noted, rendered irrelevant, since it precedes a context that would give it meaning.[66] In this respect, *Mouchette*'s conclusion goes beyond dialectics—very much as the final moments of *L'Argent* will do, though in an opposite direction. In *Mouchette*, the girl's purity is tarnished by the violence of her suicide, while, in *L'Argent*, Yvon's uncompromising violence dissolves before the upheaval of the vision that sees it, the climax of Bresson's last film. At the same time, in both films, violence and what sublimes violence cannot be disentangled, however the beginnings of each might promise to safeguard the structure of opposition that undergirds them. Because Bresson tethers the downward pull of suicide to the uplift of the Monteverdi, he insists her fate has an untranslatable strangeness. Say then, about the Monteverdi, to appropriate Jean-Luc Nancy's general characterization of sound, that in distinction to the meanings made legible through oppositions that have marked the film to its endpoint, "Sound has no hidden face; it is all in front, in back, and outside inside, *inside-out* in relation to the most general logic of presence as appearing, as phenomenality or as manifestation."[67] Sound is "omnipresent," "anterior and posterior to any signifying punctuation."[68] This departure from signification, however ambiguously proffered by the Monteverdi, is what Bresson emphasizes when, interviewed at the time of *Mouchette*'s first viewing, he insisted "the domain of cinematography is the domain of the unsayable."[69]

At the end of *Mouchette*, Bresson returns the spectator to a world in which meaning—like the divisions that constitute it—has been expelled or left behind. At the moment when Monteverdi floods over the image of the water and then continues while the screen fades to black, Bresson gives us a world as complex as any in his cinematography. He thus shatters the sentimentality held at bay but always threatening to emerge in the parceling of distinctions between baseness and purity and the hope and no more hope that attend these possibilities, which of course include redemption and its impossibility, a crude, but accurate, way of designating the film's alternatives. Instead, the film forces upon us a revisionary relation to the experience we thought we understood—dismissing motive, gloss, and even our capacity to *see* it ("I don't show . . . there is a cut, and she is gone"). The event, like the face, is non-penetrable. Or, say that Bresson employs the Monteverdi to supplant a set of significatory coordinates which the film first introduces, then sidesteps, and finally surpasses. In this way, as in Nancy's general description of sound, the music bespeaks "a relationship to meaning [*sens*], a tension toward it: but toward it completely ahead of signification, meaning in its nascent state, in the state of return [*renvoi*] for which the end of this return is not given . . . and hence to the state of return without end, like an echo that continues on its own and that *is* nothing but this continuance going in a *decrescendo*, or even in *moriendo*."[70] This "beyond-meaning" is how Bresson presents experience at the film's end. What meaning could there be to a state of affairs in which there is no polarity between violence and purity, self-destruction and self-preservation, so that it almost seems that differentials no longer count for anything? The shock of such a conclusion to a film repeatedly pulled back from the verge of pathos (understood as what arouses feelings of sympathy) to conceive pathos as a structure defined by mobility and transport (section III will elaborate) reveals that in *Mouchette* experience is bifurcated, it is unified, it is inassimilable. We can't read a mystery that first engages, then dispenses with, the ethical, the sentimental, and the religious—those consolatory logics for apprehending experience, which in *Mouchette*'s final moments is seen as too heterogeneous to be grasped or penetrated.

III

A Man Escaped presses on the question of how material form manifests impalpable "spirit," which can't be extricated from physical embodiment, but can't be equated with the implements that Fontaine in the Nazi prison cell uses to free himself from prison.[71] In distinction to *Procès* and *Mouchette*, which obliquely illuminate the kinship between material and immaterial phenomena, *A Man Escaped* thematizes and visually parses the relation between what is enfleshed and what could never be enfleshed, a mystery immediately specified as such in the Biblical passage that Pastor de Leyris transcribes for Fontaine after Orsini escapes ("Perhaps that's what Christ meant . . . 'Unless one is born again . . .' I copied out the passage for you") from which the film's subtitle (*Le vent souffle où il veut*: "the wind bloweth where it listeth") is extracted. In his cell, unfolding the paper, Fontaine reads:

> Nicodemus said: "How can a man be born when he is old? Can he enter his mother's womb and be born?" Jesus said: "Marvel not that I said ye must be born again. The wind bloweth where it listeth. Thou knowest not whence it cometh." (John 3:3–8 KJV)

While in the passage a distinction is made between life "born of water" (that is, of flesh) and life "born of spirit," Fontaine's ingenious use of objects to secure his freedom from imprisonment foils the idea that the two could ever be disarticulated.[72] The new life of *A Man Escaped* is first of all the new life given to objects. The film dismantles a rigid understanding of what an object is and can become; objects have a core whose principle is pliability, enabling their transformation from one form of utility to another, which also extends beyond the merely instrumental. Bresson wrote: "I was hoping to make a film about objects which would at the same time have a soul . . . to reach the latter through the former."[73] In *Escaped*, objects are "faceified." Like the face, objects can be animated. From a different vantage, in Montaigne's words, objects are "all face," because of their bare, unobstructed materiality (*N* 40). In the film's understanding, a vital force resides in objects as a life to be awakened when Fontaine discerns what each might be if it could escape the fixity of its present form.

Thus while in *Procès* essence is represented as almost autonomous, and in the plot of *Mouchette* essence is initially compromised by what lies outside it, in *Escaped* a rhythm is established that radically effaces the arbitrary distinction between inside and outside in that the aggregate of characteristics that identify an object is eradicated as it becomes something it was not designed to be. *Escaped* reveals the tangible transformation of objects in the camera's all-consuming attention to Fontaine's deconstruction of door panels with the chisel-spoon; of window frame with spoon-screwdriver, which is then made into hooks; of mattress netting twisted into rope—and of strips of cloth from a box of clothes to bind the rope—so that Fontaine can slide down the courtyard wall outside his cell and travel to the prison's outer wall. In this way, mundane objects are given a life beyond their quotidian use. The transformative change whereby one thing becomes another recalls the Biblical passage's insistence on the enigma of spirit. Invisible but perceptible ("you hear the sound"), but not perceptible in relation to any decipherable origin or end ("Thou knowest not whence it cometh"), spirit is a force that resides in matter, or uses matter as its ground, literally at the moment when Fontaine's feet touch the earth, a realization that permeates *A Man Escaped* as something like *its* spirit.[74]

The originality of Bresson's interpretation of the Nicodemus passage lies in his recognition that freedom from confinement in materiality can be realized only through another manifestation of materiality, as when Fontaine and Jost leap to freedom and land on their feet outside the prison walls.[75] Spirit does not do away with matter; that would be like abolishing one of the elements. So when Jost at the film's end marvels "If only my mother could see me," we are returned to the Biblical passage's insistence that a child can't be born twice from a mother. What Jost's mother would see, if she could see Jost now, would be a parturition that does not issue out of embodied materiality, but which is also not separated from the materiality of spoon, bed netting, window frame; strips of cloth, mattress, and pillow, the objects with which Fontaine ingeniously engineers his own and Jost's delivery by presuming their pliancy beyond their present incarnation.[76] When Fontaine takes matter into his own hands, objects that imprison are converted into objects that free. Only once is any word spoken on the subject of whose incorporeal force (human or divine) inhabits matter to make it tractable. In an exchange that contrasts two clichés for passive waiting and active assistance—here in the labor of redemption—when Pastor de Leyris says: "God will save you," Fontaine replies: "Only if we give him a hand. . . . It would be too easy if God saw to everything." In *Escaped* words *are* spoken that extol the great good fortune in the life of objects. When Pastor de Leyris, who was arrested ("at the pulpit. No time to take a thing") suddenly discovers a Bible in prison, he exclaims "I'm in luck. A miracle. Everything has changed since yesterday." But Fontaine also has a windfall. He and de Leyris are standing near each other in the room where the prisoners wash up when Fontaine spots an iron spoon (fig. 4.37). His first spoon has been bent out of shape by the joints of the door frame that secures the three boards he is trying to pry apart. "I'm in luck myself," Fontaine marvels. In Fontaine's echo of de Leyris's exultation, the Bible and the spoon are made equivalent.

Moreover, although the spoon engineers a literal out (it pries loose the panels so Fontaine can walk the hall at night), like the "miracle" of de Leyris's Bible, the spoon also lifts Fontaine's spirit: "That night I went to sleep less miserable." When Fontaine is told that his "neighbor downstairs" was "executed day before yesterday," he steadfastly continues his labor: "it prevented me from thinking." The spirit of work thus becomes the remedy for the dispirit of thought—two obverse intangibles set against each other, as matter and spirit are not.[77]

In distinction, then, to how Joan occupies her cell—her visions are the transport that effaces the material conditions that define where she is—for Fontaine, matter could be recast only by vision's reimagining of it; matter could not itself be displaced by vision. When one inmate remarks: "You can't control fate," the

FIGURE 4.37

Pastor disagrees: "*He* can." Fate can be regulated if spirit can be embodied without concern for outcome. Fontaine insists, "The door just had to open. I had no plans for afterwards"—an imperative that grasps the immediate obstacle without regard for future perils whose tangibility would be conjectural, a state of affairs similarly validated by the Biblical passage in relation to spirit, which, like matter, is only perceptible in a present.[78] In *Escaped* matter dazzles with its strangeness not only because it can be reborn in a new life (whose own sequel is uncertain in all the ways *Escaped* sensuously realizes that idea) but more directly from an experiential vantage, because to fathom matter as it is (however it is) is to be delivered to a real beyond any preconception. Bresson insisted: "if we got really close, as close as possible" to "nature," "almost penetrating things, we'd" see, and, filmically capture "the supernatural almost every time." When asked, "What is the supernatural?" Bresson replied, "It's reality, a precise reality that we get as close to as possible. That's the supernatural."[79]

Such a proposition recalls Bresson's corollary claim that in *Genesis* Adam had to speak in "a language almost no one can understand" (not "French or English"), an imperative issued to avoid the pitfall of an audience's supposition that what preceded human witness would be *recognizable*.[80] The beholders of *Genesis* must be awakened to the fact that, in Deleuze's words, what is "primordial" is "not yet a figure . . . not yet an action," could never be conceived, imagined, or remembered.[81] To see the real in the present, Bresson implies, is to see *all* things as "primordial." In the case of the never seen and the habitually seen, the principle is the same: to render the visible and the audible not immediately or even ultimately identifiable, since identification is a way of estranging the real, of *only* conceiving, imagining, or remembering it.[82] Bresson's strategies for plunging the viewer into a real that could not be anticipated emerge out of a philosophical perspective that asks the spectator to experience the disorientation of a familiar object when it is heard or seen in all its mystery—as when a sound we think we know is coupled with a sound that startles by proximity (in *Balthazar*, the donkey's braying joined to the Schubert andantino), as when an object assumes features we don't discern as *its* features (the metamorphosis of mattress netting into rope), so that in the conjunction of alien elements, our routine associations are snapped, strained, or worn away.[83]

In Bresson's films, materiality is the foreign language that the beholder is urged to see anew: the ropes and chains that bind Joan; Mouchette's magnetic face; in *Balthazar*, the great displeasure of the miser's scowl; Fontaine's ingenious hand as it employs the metal spoon to cut through wood,[84] whose sumptuous details almost displace our interest in the spirit and vision they all but dispel. For instance, in the close-ups of the door and the rope, the raw wood, the braided cloth, are illuminated against the monotone blacks and grays that frame them, rendering the sheen of the wood's grain what, by contrast, one could only call opulent. This luster is also a product of Bresson's focus: we are made to see in the striated whites of the chiseled wood a possible opening (fig. 4.38) before we see the hand holding the instrument against the door it has yet to penetrate (fig. 4.39). In the implied inversion of cause and effect, effect precedes the cause, visually inspiring it, though in the film's narrative trajectory, figure 4.39 can be glossed as the marshaling of Fontaine's assault against a second door panel. The image is temporally continuous with what precedes it, and it is also legible as the contemplated effect that inspires Fontaine's energy.

The off-center shot of the raw wood with the shards chiseled away is moreover a synecdochic promise of Fontaine's freedom, even as any achievement that could be ascribed to *him* is marginalized, much as the fragmented shot of the hand is (fig. 4.38). One way to view the subordination of hand to oak—the hand's impassioned agency fading to near-irrelevance before the ragged wood, which has become a harbinger of possibility—is to see that, notwithstanding Fontaine's effort, "the wind bloweth where it listeth," a gloss too abstract for those lines of smudgy white, even as the film's subtitle lingers in the background of frames like this when they too hopefully augur a good outcome. In the same careful way that Fontaine dismantles the door, he straightens the flexible mattress netting; cuts cloth to strips; plaits wire and cloth; maintains the tension of the weave by standing on one end of the braid (fig. 4.40); then

FIGURE 4.38

FIGURE 4.39

fashions the spine of a second rope from Jost's mattress (fig. 4.41) until coils of rope are massed (fig. 4.42), and both can flee. (In figure 4.43, Fontaine climbs down the wall with Jost behind him.) In *Escaped* the "miracle" is Fontaine's capacious vision of objects, in which the hook is born from the window frame.

Eisenstein theorizes such a transformation in which a new "quality," a new "dimension," and even a new "entity" emerge when a thing breaks free of the boundaries that have defined it.[85] In Eisenstein's analysis, this "new quality" comes into being as a "leap"—an "*ex-stasis*"—from one register to another, "*from one 'dimension' to another*," or "*from one intensity to another*,"[86] inaugurating a "transition to opposition" inherent in "all dialectical processes."[87] Eisenstein calls this leap "pathos," a phenomenon also explained in relation to the spectator's affect: "Pathos shows its affect—when the spectator is compelled to jump from his seat. When he is compelled to collapse where he stands. When he is compelled to applaud, to cry out. . . . In brief—when the spectator is forced 'to go out of himself.'"[88] In Eisenstein's analysis, pathos is thus a sudden movement—a vaulting or springing outward or upward, an outbreak in which a static condition bursts into a new dynamism—a volatility that is inherent both in film structure and in the spectator's affective experience of that structure.[89] In *A Man Escaped* Fontaine's labor inspires *object*s so they too reveal their volatility—or, rather, the film almost inspires us to think we could see the pulsing energy that lies within the ostensible inertia of solid objects.[90] Such dynamism is also apparent in Bresson's juxtaposition of "absolute silence" to the instrumentality of "silence obtained by a *pianissimo* of noises" (*N* 49). For Bresson the "quality" that is silence does not theatrically punctuate the film's diegetic elements, but emerges as their profound antithesis. Silence (like Bresson's use of the Monteverdi in *Mouchette*) has no signifying register, though it has a resonance, a style, an intensity, a haunt that inflects, by proximity, image, sound, and narrative. So when Bresson writes: "Build your film on white, on silence and on stillness" (*N* 136), he implies—again, in Eisenstein's terms—an "ex-static" movement out of hue, image, sound vibration, motion (a respite from their wealth and welter) to the achromatic, the quiescent, and the static. This is the case even as their irrelative strangeness seeps into the impossibly banished contingent states that, of course, must also constitute Bresson's cinematography. And the "*ex-stasis*" also goes in the other direction for, since every frame is still, a film is literally built on transparent pictures that are motionless. In this way Bresson asks us to rethink by opposition, intensification, and transformation how color, sound, and moving image construct a world as foreign as these apparent absolutes, these impure negations.

In Bresson's films, like the hook made out of the window frame, nothing is constituted independently, without reference to what extrinsically forms it. This is no less the case for Joan's and the dog's juxtaposed visions which *Procès* incongruently unifies. However incomparable Joan's vision of angels and the dog's vision of Joan, the space of another's sight to which access is denied is neither personal nor species-specific, a point made dramatically by the film's insistence on these incommensurate but similarly occluded visions. The paired phenomena—whether the face and the moon; purity and the violence that despoils purity; the diegetic and rhythmic; or "absolute silence" and "silence

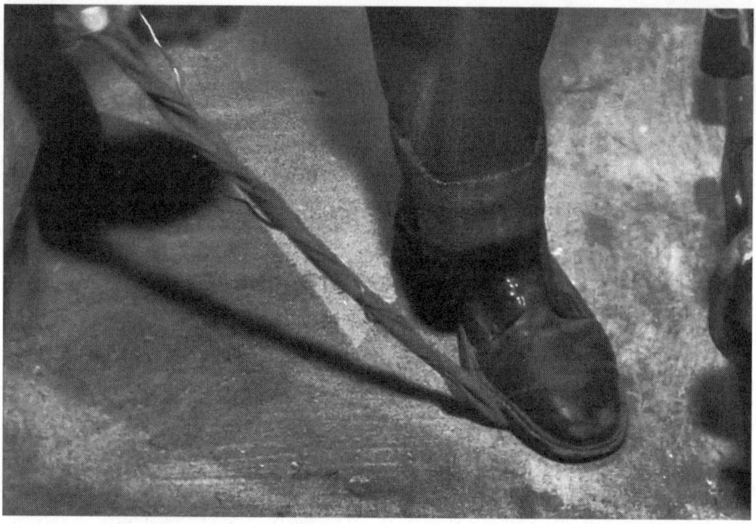

FIGURE 4.40

FIGURE 4.41

obtained by a *pianissimo* of noises" (*N* 49)—thwart expectations about what something is deemed to be, and are themselves not only discoverable within the sphere of character, or even representation, as when Bresson instructs himself: "See your film as a combination of lines and of volumes in movement apart from what it represents and signifies" (*N* 90).[91] An imperative reaches in an opposite direction, when Bresson writes, "Do not draw back from prodigies. Command the moon, the sun. Let loose the thunder and the lightning"

(*N* 128), would seem not only to extol representation but, improbably, to suggest control could be exerted over celestial bodies and bursts of radiant energy that are insusceptible to human governance, even as the irony of a word like "prodigies" contests the possibility of power or patronage. Thus, in Bresson's written imperatives, as in his cinematography, the "leap" from one perspective to an incommensurate perspective emerges even within the confines of a single statement.

FIGURE 4.42

FIGURE 4.43

IV

"Of almost all the great directors," Michael Haneke asserts, "it is said that they have always made the same film over and over."[92] To think about the film Bresson remakes is immediately to fasten on the repertoire of murder, suicide, and natural catastrophe (Balthazar is shot by a bullet meant for the hood Gérard; Mouchette, Jeanne, and Charles kill themselves; Yvon, in *L'Argent*, murders indiscriminately) and the converse: "born again" fully narrativized in *A Man Escaped* and condensed to a pivot in *Les Anges du péché* and *Procès*. These extremes converge in *Le Diable probablement*, where Charles's belief in "everlasting life" benignly accompanies his decision to kill himself. *Four Nights of a Dreamer*, in which a young girl who would throw herself into the Seine decides to live, rhymes the swing from one participle to its opposite: *désespérant* to *espérant*, while in an opposite swing of fate, Arnold in *Balthazar* celebrates the great good fortune of a family legacy, but then succumbs to a mortal inheritance when, drunk, he falls off the donkey, hits the ground, and dies.

Such far-flung endpoints are not legible only in a literal or religious context. Eisenstein's "leap" equally spans the epiphanic moments in *Les Dames du Bois de Boulogne* when Agnès's consuming passion for ballet (an "*ex-stasis*" that rapturously takes her out of herself and out of the realm of cabaret dancing, the hallmark of her life of prostitution) is succeeded by another kind of transport, as she is carried away by the impulse to renounce the very ecstasy that made her rapturous—"I'll never dance again"—and by its physical corollary when she falls to the floor in despair, as her mother exclaims, "I thought you were dead." When, after her marriage to Jean, the latter learns of her past ("You've married a tramp," Hélène tells him victoriously), and upbraids and leaves her, Agnès sinks to the ground in a blackout that rhymes with her desolate fall from dancing's rapture and with the swoon at the film's end, in which she hangs between life and death, propelled first one way and then the other by Jean's flickering love.[93] At the end of *Les Dames du Bois de Boulogne* the spectator can barely distinguish dying and reviving, though no difference could be more drastic. Narrative drives the two apart, but rhythm compels their reconciliation. In Haneke's terms: "Everything dissolves into" a "pure relationship"[94] that, after Eisenstein, I have called "ex-static", never more so than when "born again" rhymes with the extinction that must precede or be its sequel, which—notwithstanding such a sure trajectory—even on film still requires a shock to realize. Reviving and dying; swooning and regaining consciousness; dancing and no more dancing epitomize the states that Bresson affixes to each other. In these conjunctive images, Bresson gives us a whole in which nothing is excluded, and in which animate and inanimate entities break through the physical and conceptual forms that bind them—glass into shards, netting into rope, spoon into chisel, and in *Balthazar* the illegible gaze of girl and donkey into our vision of their kinship, each, however incompletely, revealed as the same kind of creature as the other, though all else between them might resist comparison.

When Bresson described his work as "a new way of writing, a new way of feeling," and further specified, "The insensible bond, connecting your furthest apart and most different images, is your vision" (*N* 37), he not only meant to draw together the dead girl and the live girl, who, though turned against each other, since they inhabit the same space, are also federated. The characterization also recalls the passage in which Bresson links objects with the preternatural: "if we got really close" to "reality," "almost penetrating things," that's "the supernatural"[95]—that's "reality" seen in its estrangement from what is remembered, boundaried, reasoned, and imagined. And Bresson would also have had in mind frictive images and sounds propelled into relation by the dynamic transfer of Eisenstein's "pathos" so that, as I've argued, the boundaries we discern around what something is are challenged by the affinity with what lies outside it (Mouchette's purity by her suicide; her suicide by the Monteverdi), disabling viewers from seeing things isolated from the range of their possibility—what they were, could become, or do become in their transformations.

Even single frames resist our ability, not to identify what we see, but to fathom what we identify—almost as though we couldn't really see it, since not to grasp what we see, in the sense of not to comprehend it, also has a physical component in which we feel we can't reach what there could be to perceive. Like the graininess of the bare wood with the fist partially effaced in figure 4.38, the blacks and grays that bleed to the edge of the frame are saturated with a vehemence that seemingly has no confines. Seemingly, because the image with its contrasts is bounded, but the camera's focus is indeterminate: is it trained on the hand, those gradations of white and black, the whole constellation, or does it beckon us to see something off-frame, as in Haneke's notion of the "dirty image" whose edge is "frayed"?[96] In figure 4.38 we see the intensity of the image itself, even in its negative blackness: the black is as saturated in tone as our retained gaze is by what we see. In Bresson's films intensity can also be read as optical voracity in that the camera pauses far longer than necessary to register images and lingers on scenes whose inclusion appears gratuitous (the truck lights, the baby's eyes). Intensity, more conventionally conceived, inheres in the camera's dwelling on the rapt expression of Bresson's models (their immersion in what they see, which we can't penetrate—absorption and impenetrability are thus made coordinate), and still further by example (though atypically): intensity presumably governs the determined gaze of the anonymous figures at the end of *L'Argent*, passersby outside the bar from which Yvon has been led away, who stare into the doorway through which he and the police have passed, though what there was to look at has vanished.

These figures epitomize something of the beholder's experience of Bresson's films—because we can't identify what they see, or precisely orient ourselves to the source of our own enthrallment, since what mesmerizes the film's beholder (nothing can be discerned in the backs of those heads) has been divested of the formula that would make the seen legible. Moreover, such a conclusion asserts an odd equality between two manifestations of blockage—odd because the witness of the passersby must be coded as incidental, while Yvon's vision, or what escapes his vision, will chart his destiny. In the rhythm Bresson constructs, what the crowd looks at is no more apparent or less important than what Yvon looks at, or than whether what transforms Yvon *could* be looked at. At moments like these *our* gaze is held by a visibility that does not beguile with the lure of an identifiable significance, or with an economy in which significance is only selectively present. Without discrimination the beholder is made to forfeit certain preemptive visual identifications that would disentangle our expectations from the welter of experience, its superfluity. No overspecified reward for the beholder's gaze in Bresson's art is allowed to dilute a generalized immersion in experience's perceptual plenitude. In all such optical insistence, the extreme—and supreme—achievement of Bresson's visionary cinema is distilled here yet again: the relentless ocular concentration on things that simply can't be seen.[97] Philosophical questions about what something is are mired in uncertainty or outright blockage in Bresson's films, but at the same time they diffuse the screen with forms, textures, and intensities whose extravagance does not just compensate for, but actively staves off, all that spiritual and psychological reductiveness of which Bresson's films deprive us.

When Bresson asserted that "The exchanges that are produced between images and images, sounds and sounds, images and sounds, give the people and objects in your films their cinematographic life" (*N* 54–55), he located "life" in differentials of black and white; in material forms (the hand guiding the spoon across the grain of splintering wood, the splintered wood itself); and in discrepant sounds. In insisting that the wood and the hand have vitality—though not the same vitality—Bresson ruptures our conceptions of what things might be, what persons are, and how life is imbued in each. He insisted: "One single mystery of persons and objects" (*N* 26), a mystery that is discernible in a tethering that confines, unifies, and quickens. "THE BONDS THAT BEINGS AND THINGS ARE WAITING FOR, IN ORDER TO LIVE" (*N* 80). Thus when Bresson writes, "'Visible parlance' of bodies, objects, houses, roads, trees, fields" (*N* 24), he means that film is the language that pulls these into relation. But not into *any* relation: "To set up a film is to bind persons to each other and to objects by looks" (*N* 23). And not into *that* relation in which persons have sight while lifeless objects passively wait to be envisioned, for the plural "looks" suggests, however cryptically, that the looking might be mutual. Further: "The persons and objects in your film must *walk at the same pace, as companions*" (*N* 79). What Bresson means by "*companions*" is almost less strange than what he means by "*walk*" and "*at the same pace*." In his threefold iterations of the intimacy between persons and objects, Bresson's imperative insists we can't separate entities in relation to a standard by which it would be intelligible to determine whether one could ascribe or withhold life from our conception of them, since, in Bresson's formulation, persons and objects converge and are enmeshed. If we don't know what it means to think of objects as animated rather than as inert, as possessed of liveliness rather than of dormancy or deathliness, something about the symmetry of the plight of persons and objects, as expressed in Bresson's formulation, prods us to realize that we may *also* not know how to think of persons as invigorated in the particular ways in which Bresson's films enliven them. That, in any case, is the effect, if not the point, of the aphorisms that implicitly bequeath flesh and locomotion to objects as well as to bodies: how otherwise could both walk companionably?

In being asked to think about what kind of life objects have (do they have life?), we are also turned back to the tough question of what kind of life persons have (how do *they* have life, and how is the life they have made visible—to themselves, and to us?). Yet "have life" is an idiom that mistakenly suggests an attribute to be possessed, while in Bresson's films vitality is not a property that belongs to some things and not to others, is not a property at all, but emerges when things are drawn into relation. (Analogously, in *Mouchette*, if from one point of view, as I've argued, it could be said that the flashlight and the moon, the truck lights and the baby's eyes share a brightness we are made to see as consonant, this is because the electromagnetic radiation in waves of light does not transport energy *selectively*, but rather interacts with the atoms, ions, or molecules of all matter—an omnipresence certain congruent images in *Mouchette* make perceptible.) The dissemination of "life" in Bresson's films could also be described phenomenologically. Bresson's films wean the viewer from his habit of attending to the face above all as though it alone were an important, a penetrable, or a revelatory surface. When Bresson effaces the expressions of his models so that thought, affect, animus remain contained, insusceptible to scrutiny, the spectator must look elsewhere in the film, must look anywhere and everywhere to discern where and how all that pent-up life is released and distributed.

5

Kafka's No-Hope Spaces

Nothing is more inescapable than certain spaces in Franz Kafka's writings, in particular, those of the human body: "people are sewn into their skins for life and cannot alter any of the seams, at least not with their own hands," Kafka writes to Felice Bauer.[1] Identifying a cosmic equivalent of this corporeal inevitability, Kafka insists: "I want to change my place in the world entirely . . . actually means that I want to go to another planet."[2] Closer to home, human anatomy is figured as an impediment to the movement of mind, so that, counterintuitively (since the mind is not palpable), even the reaches of thought violently encounter an unmovable physical obstacle: "The bony structure of his own forehead blocks his way; he batters himself bloody against his own forehead."[3] From an opposite vantage (constriction imposed not from within but from without by the perception of law), what further entraps are the determinates that characterize a species, delimiting what it can endure—an utmost extent beyond which trespass is prohibited: "I have, to be sure, experienced states . . . in which I not only felt myself at my boundary, but at the boundary of the human in general" (*DFK* 48). And, as I shall suggest, there is a counterpart to this threat, an alternative form of inescapability, associated with the menace of an outside force that continuously threatens to burst into and violate any interior space that would protect by its containment. Whether it be the frontal bone of the skull, feeling states that press against the limits of human stamina, or lures that ensnare, Kafka never tired of formulating the versatile conditions that constitute human imprisonment. In Kafka's writing there is no way to escape these narratives of imprisonment, however multifariously they are spatially plotted. Moreover, although Kafka identified the constriction that governed his own fate as extreme ("To live a human life in my surroundings is impossible"), and even unique ("I don't believe people exist whose inner plight resembles mine"), the despair he insisted on was articulated on behalf of everyone.[4] "We are nihilistic thoughts, suicidal thoughts that come into God's head. . . . our world is only a bad mood of God, a bad day of his," Max Brod reported Kafka said. When Brod intervened, offering an alternative to such nihilism ("Then there is hope outside this manifestation of the world that we know"), Kafka famously quipped: "Oh, plenty of hope, an infinite amount of hope—but not for us."[5]

If one scratches the polish of Kafka's wisecrack, a question is visible directly under the surface, less refined but serious: if hope is that boundlessness (which Ernst Bloch associates with the undisclosed possible of a utopian consciousness and thus with a utopian social vision)[6] denied in Kafka's oeuvre, is there some other infinite, counter to that of hope, but nonetheless an infinite, that emerges in its place as a plenitude? In section I of this essay I examine the representation of a phenomenological amplitude in three of Kafka's parables that are associated with certain inescapable insides. In section II I turn to "The Burrow," in which an inescapable outside puts all structures at risk.[7] In "Investigations of a Dog," examined in section III, notwithstanding the narrator's attempt to arrive at the core of experience or to thrust through it to freedom, he is alienated from both regions, and can reside only on something like a surface. Thus, in distinction to hope, which is a nonconfinement in a present state of affairs, the bodily, conceptual, and affective dwellings that Kafka's narrators inhabit can be contemplated, even plumbed, but not broken out of. The narrator is never in the right place to free himself from the experience that consumes him: he is either locked within it, expelled from it, or on a surface—regions that are split off from each other, and that might intimate the existence of an elsewhere, but that always refuse access to it.[8]

Yet at the same time that these spaces are represented as inescapable, they are also represented as almost infinitely rich, as alluring, even absorptive, and, in that sense, deep, an enchantment that is also perceptible on the surface of experience. Thus the inability to escape an inside, or, conversely, the inability to free oneself from the terrifying omnipresence of an outside, is counterpointed to and compensated by a phenomenological wealth. In one instance Kafka represents *himself* as the interior space that is penetrated. On November 2, 1911, he writes in his diary: "This morning, for the first time in a long time, the joy again of imagining a knife twisted in my heart" (*DFK* 101). Although the condensation of this remarkable sentence does not encourage comment, it could be said that bliss arises from the torque of being penetrated. The knife is a figure for a piercing intensity whose vitality is so thrilling that it renders any pain the twisting might inflict as an ecstasy. Such shocking means of experiencing vitality in the interiors that Kafka represents (or discovers he is) point to the bounty of the no-hope spaces in Kafka's writing. On December 25, 1911, Kafka experiments with an inverse imagining, access to an unthinkable outside (in distinction to representing himself as the unthinkable inside that the knife seeks out), an encounter that can only be perilous: "To run against the window and, weak after exerting all one's strength, to step over the window sill through the splintered wood and glass" (*DFK* 153).

As I shall explain, in "The Burrow" and "Investigations of a Dog" this splitting of interior and exterior regions is recapitulated in the narrators' identification with taxonomically unidentifiable animals,[9] a manifestation of Kafka's estrangement from the human community, in an alienation so extreme that only a species difference could mark it, as the following passage underscores in different terms: "What is it that binds you more intimately to these impenetrable, talking, eye-blinking bodies than to any other thing, the penholder in your hand, for example? Because you belong to the same species? But you don't belong to the same species" (*DFK* 396). To locate himself outside of human being, to renounce affiliation with the human, while, in another register, suggesting that insides and outsides could be riven so that the interior or exterior of a phenomenon or entity (a mere fragment of a whole) is nonetheless represented as virtually autonomous, as an entirety, is to undertake a metaphysical investigation of being that redefines what is actual, logical, and even possible. Kafka also posits fictional entities that, illusorily, are not beholden to recognizable categories (a state of affairs exemplified by "Odradek," a creature that looks "like a flat star-shaped spool for thread," has "no fixed abode," and "laughs . . . the kind of laughter that has no lungs behind it," and by the "curious animal" of "A Crossbreed [A Sport]," "half kitten, half lamb").[10] Illusorily, since Kafka's work is intelligible precisely because it draws on classifications like "animal" and "human," and on the idea that being can be identified within or outside a species.

If this is contradictory, the paradox does not operate by inflicting the kind of insolubility about what is occurring that governs the interpretation of narrative events in the novels. In the stories and the parables we are rarely in doubt about what is happening.[11] When this is ambiguous, Kafka directs our attention to other facets of the story or parable to which exegesis about narrative event is irrelevant. Rather, difficulty inheres in the mystery of how Kafka could ever have put one sentence in front of the other with no sense of impasse to represent states of mind and being—like senselessness, impossibility, hunger, and, especially, an alienation so extreme that it could be indicated only by Kafka's claim to reside at "the boundary of the human" (*DFK* 48), and also on its other side. In uniquely representing his dis-identification with the human species—it is a commonplace that there is nothing like it—he gave this estrangement such substance and feature that it is almost transmuted to a graspable thing, as in Kafka's implicit claim (not weakened for being figurative) that his tie to human beings is no greater than his bond with the inanimate but not miscellaneous object, the "penholder" in his "hand" (*DFK* 396).

I

Though the three parables with which I begin mute this extremity and isolation, they progressively break away from the domesticating frames that contain their narratives to establish something like an inside, where an absorptive interest is developed in states of being or states of mind that are not beholden to the narrative coordinates that introduce them. "At Night," the most conventional of the parables, redirects attention from the representation of sleep as a communal phenomenon experienced under nomadic conditions (a state of affairs presupposing some condition of risk compelling a migration from safety) to an intimation of peril that is made to hang over the state of unconsciousness itself, which unites the anonymous sleepers:

> Deeply lost in the night. Just as one sometimes lowers one's head to reflect, thus to be utterly lost in the night. All around people are asleep. It's just play acting, an innocent self-deception, that they sleep in houses, in safe beds, under a safe roof, stretched out or curled up on mattresses, in sheets, under blankets; in reality they have flocked together as they had once upon a time and again later in a deserted region, a camp in the open, a countless number of men, an army, a people, under a cold sky on cold earth, collapsed where once they had stood, forehead pressed on the arm, face to the ground, breathing quietly. And you are watching, are one of the watchmen, you find the next one by brandishing a burning stick from the brushwood pile beside you. Why are you watching? Someone must watch, it is said. Someone must be there.[12]

The lure of "At Night" resides in Kafka's capacity to move from the vast panoply of figures in an imaginary forsaken land to the unadorned human form immediately experienced, notwithstanding the assembly that Kafka's prose aggregates, as solitary. (Even the companionless narrator has only fleeting contact with the watchman who will relieve him.) At the center of the passage there is a shift from plural "people" to individual "forehead" and "arm"—singularities that are at once a general way of referring to parts of the body common to all and a specific acknowledgment that sleep comes to each alone. Moreover, if "At Night" restores sleep to its mystery—first by narrating a fable and then by splitting it open to reveal a helplessness that the sleeper's immobility makes visible and, in the press of body to earth, tangible—the passage finally enacts a transfer of attention from sleep to witnessing ("Someone must watch. . . . Someone must be there"). Watching is required not to guard the undefended state that sleep is discovered to be, since reflection could have no instrumentality, but rather to uncover the phenomenon for which protection is deemed necessary, stripping sleep of the civilized conditions that conceal its vulnerability.

While "At Night" travels backward to an imaginary past to disclose the "self-deception" of safety in ordinary, nocturnal unconsciousness, in "The Silence of the Sirens" an event thought to be marvelous is not located in any temporal imagining, for that would be too narrow to contain the experiential fullness that derives from a conjecture about all its possibilities. In Kafka's retelling of the myth Ulysses still binds himself to the mast of his ship and stops his ears with wax so that he will not be beguiled by the Sirens' spellbinding music. Yet such a characterization, with its near-fidelity to Homer's narrative, is immediately derided: "such things were of no help whatever" since "the song of the Sirens could pierce through everything, and the longing of those they seduced would have broken far stronger bonds than chains and masts" (SS 431).[13] More fatal than the Sirens' singing is their silence. Kafka adds: "it is conceivable that someone might possibly have escaped from their singing; but from their silence certainly never" (SS 431). Kafka's narrative contemplates the allure of that silence, asking: who entices, who resists silence, and what constitutes its hazard? Did the Sirens not sing "because they thought that this enemy could be vanquished only by their silence" (SS 431)? Did they not sing because they had themselves become the victims of Ulysses' counterspell, being smitten by the vision of a bliss exceeding any they could generate (the "look of bliss on the face of Ulysses, who was thinking of nothing but his wax and his chains, made them forget their singing" [SS 431])? Or was Ulysses' transport not ravishment at all but only a ploy to "shield" (SS 432) himself from their wiles?

In Kafka's iteration of these alternatives, they unfold as mutually constitutive possibilities that appear to sustain rather than to supplant each other, however they might logically be required to do so. Thus the devastating power of the Sirens (their singing could "pierce through everything" [SS 431]) is counterpointed to a rhapsodic breakdown of an alternative source of power, Ulysses' absorption, which hypnotically enthralls everyone. In fact, because what happened cannot be determined ("here the human understanding is beyond its depths" [SS 432]) or because what can be determined is only the trivial outcome ("all that had happened was that Ulysses had escaped them" [SS 432]), deliberations about what happened are displaced by the passage's immersive fascination with these ecstatic states. Moreover, when Kafka insists on the absoluteness of Ulysses' concentration ("the Sirens literally vanished before his resolution" [SS 431]) and on the absoluteness of their thrall to this vision of his obliteration of them ("They no longer had any desire to allure; all that they wanted was to hold as long as they could the radiance that fell from Ulysses' great eyes" [SS 431]), the extinction of consciousness is made central (if, in their case, conditionally so) to a rapture that destroys what it penetrates: "If the Sirens had possessed consciousness they would have been annihilated at that moment" (SS 432). I take this enigmatic sentence to imply that while consciousness is a bounded state, absorption obliterates anything that would confine it; in Ulysses' case, also liberating itself from the body as an emanation: the "radiance that fell from" his "great eyes" (SS 431). Although the narrative develops characters whose motivations it attempts to distinguish (whose lure captivated? was it a lure?), it conversely represents absorption as deeper than any singularity, whether this pertains to discrete persons or to interpretive possibilities. Rather, these states of enchantment are constituted by their affinity with each other, engrossment being variously disseminated into a resolve so unshakeable its triumph is an exaltation; into the thrill of that resolve for the Sirens who cannot penetrate it; into the longing reflected in their desiring bodies ("But they—lovelier than ever—stretched their necks and turned, let their awesome hair flutter free in the wind, and freely stretched their claws on the rocks" [SS 431]); and into Ulysses' glimpse of their transport ("their throats rising and falling, their breasts lifting, their eyes filled with tears" [SS 431]), which, too, might be called absorptive, were it not so fleeting. The spell cast by such rapt states illusorily also touches Kafka's gorgeous prose, illusorily because that prose creates the spell.

In "At Night" helplessness is the essential trait extracted from the innocuous appearance of sleep. In "The Silence of the Sirens," concentration is rendered as ubiquitous, effacing all individual expressions of it. In "An Imperial Message" something said to be imperative is shown to be impossible. The experience of impossibility is the state whose omnipresence pervades everything. In the parable a message that is ultimate, urgent, and unique, a message "sent . . . to you alone" by "the Emperor from his deathbed,"[14] a message whose meaning would make existence explicable to "you" (for "message" displaces the idea of meaning contained within it while also making the association inevitable), cannot be delivered. The conditions surrounding the sending of this message emphasize the lengths taken to ascertain the messenger's accurate understanding ("so much store did" the Emperor "lay on it that he ordered the messenger to whisper it back into his ear again" [IM 4]). Though whispered confidentially as if it were a deathbed confession, the transmission is also staged. Therefore the fact of the message (though not its content) is a fully objective and public, is perhaps even a political, phenomenon: "before . . . the great princes of the Empire . . . he has delivered his message" (IM 4–5). The communal nature of the secret, theatricalized as a spectacle, is crucial to the passage's insistence on the event's full autonomy, which remains independent of any imagining, a detail that bears on a very different characterization of the message and its delivery, called a "dream" (IM 5) in the passage's conclusion, an implicit shift in designation that is consonant with the message's nonarrival.

The messenger, "a powerful, an indefatigable man," then "immediately sets out." The muscular force with which the man presses through impediments ("now pushing with his right arm, now with his left, he cleaves a way for himself through the throng" [IM 5])—a vigor emblematically replicated on his own person ("if he encounters resistance he points to his breast, where the symbol of the sun glitters" [IM 5])—personifies him as a figure whose energy cannot fail. Yet that apparent invincibility is repudiated by the second half of the passage, which documents the certainty of his failure. The very conditions that ensure the inevitability of the message's transmission ("the way is made easier for him than . . . for any other man" [IM 5]) only give way to obstacles and to a doom that anticipates the plight of K. in *The Castle.* The message that must reach the "you" of the parable cannot do so. As in Kafka's novel, the power of the parable's prose resides in the detail that enlivens insurmountable impediments:

> the multitudes are so vast; their numbers have no end. If he could reach the open fields how fast he would fly, and soon doubtless you would hear the welcome hammering of his fists on your door. But instead how vainly does he wear out his strength; still he is only making his way through the chambers of the innermost palace; never will he get to the end of them; and if he succeeded in that nothing would be gained; he must next fight his way down the stair; and if he succeeded in that nothing would be gained; the courts would still have to be crossed; and after the courts the second outer palace; and once more stairs and courts; and once more another palace; and so on for thousands of years; and if at last he should burst through the outermost gate—but never, never can that happen—the imperial capital would lie before him, the center of the world, crammed to bursting with its own sediment. Nobody could fight his way through here even with a message from a dead man. But you sit at your window when evening falls and dream it to yourself. (IM 5)

If there is an unswerving tempo to Kafka's description of the messenger's journey, the voicing of impediments that arise to block his way has its own propulsive rhythm. Yet, oddly, no anguish is reflected in the representation of that insurmountability that is repeatedly exampled in the long sentence (a sentence equally long in German) that documents the trajectory of obstacles in such a way that their serial manifestations seem gratuitous.[15] The initial "never will he get to the end . . . nothing would be gained" hardly seems to require the parenthetical emphasis "never, never can that happen [*niemals, niemals kann es geschehen*]." It could be said that the narrator, who is also the "you" of the conclusion, whose desire will be defeated, is not alienated from the impossibilities he chronicles. Those impossibilities are grammatically hypothetical, but assume evidential certainty because of the unremitting repertoire of temporal and spatial obstacles, which, nonetheless, are enumerated with composure. The most potent assurance of impossibility—the messenger will not reach the "you" who awaits him—emerges in this final image of obstruction: "if at last he should burst through the outermost gate . . . the imperial capital would lie before him, the center of the world, crammed to bursting with its own sediment."

Sediment is matter that has been deposited by natural process on the surface of land, or the lees that settle to the bottom of a body of water. Yet the sediment in Kafka's parable is not simply a residue but rather a remainder that has expanded to become an entirety, something that does not sink, but that rather takes over, an all-pervasive, even consolidated, presence. In this astonishing image in which inert matter derives energy from its own explosive excess, impossibility is itself invigorated, though not personified, because no agency is visible behind it. Thus the messenger's last passionate challenge—supposing it could be sustained after "thousands of years" and could suddenly achieve a breakthrough ("he should burst through the outermost gate")—is immediately negated, a negation secured by a counterforce dramatically animated by Kafka's characterization of the mass "crammed to bursting [*hochgeschüttet*] with its own sediment" when assailed by the messenger's utmost effort.[16] In Kafka's parable a materiality that is inert, undeliberated, even accidental, a materiality that is like refuse, defeats intention, passion, and significance, which cannot survive contact with its pure emptiness.

Although the narrator's commitment to impossibility (his passionate testimony to its contours) might be called strange, from another point of view—that advanced by the parable—impossibility is the only state with which the "you" *could* objectively be intimate. Since even at the parable's beginning, before the messenger is thwarted, the content of the secret, though publicly transmitted, is not represented—a phenomenon seen from an insuperable distance and therefore from the outside—it remains something undisclosed and alien. At the same time, the evidence marshaled to insist on the certainty that the message will never arrive does not incapacitate the desire for it to do so: "But you sit at your window when evening falls and dream it to yourself." For the message meant for "you alone" is so crucial that it alone could give life its meaning. Yet the illusion of meaning exists in a parallel realm—that inhabited by the messenger whose fate epitomizes the dashed hope that is the centerpiece of Kafka's writing—in an autonomous outside to which there is no access. This is a state of affairs which the parable literalizes.

In progressively stronger terms, the parables I have discussed resist outsides. This is true of "At Night," which restores sleep to its mystery by dismantling superficial understandings of it as deceptive "play acting." It is true in "The Silence of the Sirens," where Kafka's transmission of Homer's story is so eccentric that any conventional or even idiosyncratic exegesis that could illuminate the myth's power or its ideology (as for instance Max Horkheimer and Theodor Adorno's claim that Odysseus, in a cunning informed by reason and restraint, can be identified as "a prototype of the bourgeois individual")[17] is repelled by Kafka's narrative which renders absorption as a state whose omnipresence is everywhere disseminated or, rather, is intersubjective. And the resistance to an outside region is decisively manifest (in different terms from those I have previously discussed) in "An Imperial Message," in that the way in which figuration operates in the parable transgresses our understanding of how figuration customarily works.

For instance, a symbol is something that means something else. Its legibility depends on a principle of substitution; it is exfoliated with reference to some other space than that in which it is posited. But in Kafka the symbol is divested of its something-elseness; his symbolizing procedures do not permit pathways to a world exterior to themselves. In Kafka's parable the space of signification (inhabited by the dying emperor and the messenger who transports his words) and signification itself (the message) never penetrates the interior where the narrator awaits it. Thus in "An Imperial Message," and in Kafka's writing generally, the symbol makes itself discernible not by an amplification of terms that would clarify it (for if the message that never arrives is a symbol, it is tautologically a symbol of something that never arrives), but by divesting itself of abstraction in a transfer of attention to the experiential feel of the impossibility the narrator embraces with fervor for a fate he recognizes as his. Kafka's most extravagant symbols do not have outside spheres of reference that would illuminate their radical strangeness. Thus in "The Metamorphosis," the "gigantic insect" Gregor Samsa awakens to find himself is understandable as nothing other than the creature which he has become.[18] Another way to understand this redundancy is to say that in Kafka's writing the literal and the metaphoric share the same term, even the same space; more than replicating each other, they are not in fact even alienated.[19]

We see an inadvertent example of this bond in a sentence Kafka writes to Milena Jesenská: "we're really standing side by side watching this being which is me down on the ground; but in that case I who am looking am then without being" (*wir [stehn] doch nebeneinander . . . und [schauen] dieses Wesen auf dem Boden [an], das ich bin; aber ich, der dann zuschaut, bin dann allerdings wesenlos*).[20] The propensity to typify an essence like "being" (*Wesen*) that could be externalized (an externality required to permit the mutual scrutiny) immediately makes contact with the implications of such an understanding: if being is outside of Kafka, he is then bereft of it; he is insubstantial: *wesenlos*. Although in the context of the letter to Milena, an insistence on the singularity of the term is a little joke (being cannot reside in two places at once), this pressure on a symbol to reveal its autonomous essence, its completeness, lies at the heart of Kafka's writing. Being is here figured in Kafka's calculation not as an emblem of an essence that retains its existence when it is metaphorized, but rather as something whose existence is forfeited so that, evacuated from Kafka, it must reside in the physical location to which the emblem transports it: "I who am looking [at being] am then without being." Yet, as noted, when Gilles Deleuze and Félix Guattari claim that "Kafka['s] *experimentation*" is "without interpretation or significance" or that his "intensive usage of language" is opposed "to all symbolic or even significant or simply signifying usages of it," that is incorrect.[21] Kafka's intensities are only uninterpretable in terms of something else. (Of course, Deleuze and Guattari are correct if interpretation requires the something else.)

While Kafka in a letter to Felice explains that it is rare to have, as "I have," "the faculty of grasping the essence of people so completely that it frightens even me. . . . This faculty, however, is almost a danger to me when I am not writing,"[22] it could be added that in Kafka's writing the faculty of "grasping . . . essence" is a completeness discovered by a heightening, an intensifying, and in that sense a deepening (rather than by a reaching outward), which does not require something else to explain it. Such independence divorces inside and outside spheres so that progressively the frames of the parables I have considered dissolve before the narrator's rapt attention to the enigmatic inner states that they first enclose and then make manifest as entireties: helplessness stripped of its civilizing explanations, absorption, and impossibility, three of Kafka's most passionately deliberated subjects. In Walter Benjamin's analysis: "The word 'unfolding' has a double meaning. A bud unfolds into a blossom, but the boat which one teaches children to make by folding paper unfolds into a flat sheet of paper. This second kind of 'unfolding' is really appropriate to the parable; it is the reader's pleasure to smooth it out so that he has the meaning on the palm of his hand. Kafka's parables, however, unfold in the first sense, the way a bud turns into a blossom. That is why their effect resembles poetry."[23] To be sealed is of course the essence of a bud, a state of being that Kafka analogized to his own inwardness. In January 1923 he wrote to Milena: "you have to be patient with me, this bud opens slowly and is really only a bud, because closed things are called buds" (*LM* 231–32), an explanation that does not venture outside the initial recognition, since the "because" that would explain what a bud is only reiterates the thing to be explained: "closed things are called buds" (*LM* 232).

II

In "The Burrow" there is no way to be immured in the insular spaces that characterize the parables I have discussed. Even so, the narrator of that story, an animal whose frenzies speak through him, is obsessed with the question of how to design a physical structure in which he can exile himself from danger and anxiety. He is not really safe within the walls of the rooms that "enclose me more peacefully and warmly than a bird is enclosed in its nest," since, in addition to "external enemies. . . . There are also enemies in the bowels of the earth" that inhabit the same place he does. Only were the burrow "transformed . . . with a giant's strength" could it actually be made "impregnable."[24] Of course peace is not only a matter of being in a certain place, but is also a mental state, with its own perilous outside. For instance, the burrow "can flood one with peace if one only remains quite open and receptive to it" (B 339), but that is a hypothetical state of affairs, not a condition of certainty. Moreover, no refuge could keep thoughts from being penetrable: ("the mere thought of the door itself, the end of the domestic protection, brings such feelings with it" [B 332]). What makes for peace is not where you are, but how you experience the place outside where you are, the narrator's most profound recognition.

For the narrator, peace can be fully intelligible only in terms of the outside that compromises it; friendship is also recognizable in terms of a trope exterior to the narrator's actual circumstances. Returning from his wanderings, he explains the consolations of the burrow by invoking this metaphor for intimacy with its passages: "I must go my long round of all the passages, but that is no hardship, that is merely to commune again with friends, as I often did in the old days . . . or as I have often heard that it was done" (B 342). The "or"s in the sentence do not recall intimate gatherings, but rather the absence of such intimacy, since "as I have often heard that it was done" (B 342) acknowledges the fictitiousness of the memories that precede it. The very category of friends is thus extrapolated by report, for friends are a solace outside of the narrator's apprehension of them. Similarly, if to fly to his own door exposes its location to an enemy, the latter is transiently hypothesized as "someone of my own kind, a connoisseur and prizer of burrows, a hermit, a lover of peace, but all the same a filthy scoundrel who wishes to be housed where he has not built" (B 337). In "The Burrow," threat could not be dissevered from what one terrifies oneself by imagining and even from an identification with "someone of my own kind," the enemy one imagines.

The story unfolds its passionate deliberations in relation to the perspectival disparity generated by the narrator's first being within a structure that he then beholds from outside its protective walls. Although scrupulous attention is devoted to making the narrator's domestic space inviolable, the distinction between the joy of his sanctuary and what lies outside its defensive fortifications is continuously compromised by his own volatile understanding. For instance, the domestic intimacies the narrator enjoys within his dwelling—the pleasures of sleep, play, the folly but thrill of gluttony ("Happy but dangerous hours" when "steeping myself more profoundly in the mingled smells, until at last I can no longer restrain myself and . . . fling myself upon my stores and glut myself . . . until I am completely gorged" [B 331, 330–31])—are sustained and, as I elaborate, even unaccountably heightened, outside the burrow. Kafka's story thus seems to be assessing whether one could separate pleasure from a place evacuated of it and, insofar as the contemplation of joy flows into the experience of joy, whether musing on joy is a form of dwelling within it. From an opposite point of view, the narrator's ruminations invite a question about how the outside peace, which is a mere reflection on it (rather than an inhabitation of it), leads to the outside peace, which is the despoiling of it, a question to which the story's linguistic patterning and its genre, but not, I shall argue, its identification with the animal, are auxiliary.[25]

Occupying a double position, the narrator's taking stock of the joyful states he describes is also yet again a partaking of them. In its exclamatory expression ("Deep stillness; how lovely it is here, outside there nobody troubles about my burrow" [B 352]), the peace that is extolled seems purely rapturous. But the same benign state is also viewed reflectively, as what occasions thought: "how have I managed to achieve this?" (B 352), a sequence that represents a bliss that is first inhabited and then glimpsed interrogatively by a perspective that is no longer an abiding within peace. When in the following passage Kafka visually literalizes the double vantage of such statements, he presses on the narrator's propensity to be both within and outside an experience as more than a function of his giving utterance to it. Outside the burrow, the narrator is drawn to gaze at its entrance: "this time from outside—for whole days and nights. . . . At such times it is as if I were not so much looking at my house as at myself sleeping, and had the joy of being in a profound slumber and simultaneously of keeping vigilant guard over myself" (B 334). The passage recalls the vigilance of "At Night," but here the unconsciousness the narrator guards is identified as his own "profound slumber" (B 334), so that sleeping and watching oneself sleep are hypothesized as coincident. The capacity to envision discordant images of one's consciousness—for if "slumber" is that state in which consciousness is lost, "looking" is that state in which, awakened and employed, it assumes a direction and an object—is replicated in the narrator's contemplation of happiness from a vantage that is exterior to it. Watching his entrance, the narrator "gloat[s]" on "how steadfast a protection my burrow would be if I were inside it" (B 335). But this immediately raises a question about how he might himself become the object of regard:

> What does this protection which I am looking at here from the outside amount to after all? Dare I estimate the danger which I run inside the burrow from observations which I make when outside? Can my enemies, to begin with, have any proper awareness of me if I am not in my burrow? A certain awareness of me they certainly have, but not full awareness. And is not that full awareness the real definition of a state of danger? . . . No, I do not watch over my own sleep, as I imagined; rather it is I who sleep, while the destroyer watches. (B 335)

At other moments the very interstices of the burrow's passages, elsewhere deemed crucial to guarantee tranquility, are peremptorily found gratuitous to that beatific state that can arise in their vicinity. Lounging at the burrow's outside, beneath "the moss covering" (B 341) at the entrance, the narrator partakes of the solace to which physical shelter is incidental (B 340). In the following ecstatic passage in which he is outside the Castle Keep, the most sanctified enclosure where food is stored (for the interior of the burrow also has its spatial divisions), the narrator imagines occupying what he calls a "free space . . . the loveliest imaginable haunt" (B 346), whose rapture is ascribed a futurity that does not deprive it of being immediately present:

> What a joy to lie pressed against the rounded outer wall, pull oneself up, let oneself slide down again, miss one's footing and find oneself on firm earth, and play all those games literally upon the Castle Keep and not inside it; to avoid the Castle Keep, to rest one's eyes from it whenever one wanted, to postpone the joy of seeing it until later and yet not have to do without it, but literally hold it safe between one's claws, a thing that is impossible if you have

> only an ordinary open entrance to it; but above all to be able to stand guard over it, and in that way to be so completely compensated for renouncing the actual sight of it that, if one had to choose between staying all one's life in the Castle Keep or in the free space outside it, one would choose the latter, content to wander up and down there all one's days and keep guard over the Castle Keep. . . . then peace would be assured there and I would be its guardian; then I would not have to listen with loathing to the burrowing of the small fry, but with delight to something that I cannot hear now at all: the murmurous silence of the Castle Keep. (B 346–47)

The visceral image that draws us up close to the fiction of Kafka's creature's anatomy half suggests a commensurability between an uncanny structure (a claw where our hand would be) and some provident capacity we can identify ("to postpone . . . yet not have to do without" [B 346], to defer but at the same time to savor, renouncing and being compensated for that sacrifice by immediately grasping the very joy renounced) is materialized. For joy can be delayed, and so relished as a future bliss, even as it is already experienced as a tactile immediacy. In this way some structure not our own, some horny, curved formation, is made instrumental to our imagining the possibility of apprehending and even palpably possessing a joy that is forestalled, from which the narrator holds back, but which he also "hold[s]" (B 346), the postponement of joy being also its utmost manifestation.

Yet in the midst of the narrative, noise, that auditory penetration of space that is peace and joy's antithesis, is suddenly perceptible "everywhere, everywhere" (B 347). The refinements of noise (sound demonized by its intrusiveness) are like those of peace and joy in their sensuous envelopment of the narrator, being in fact their inverse. Thus the narrator speculates that noise could be produced by "crowds of little beasts" (B 346) or by a "single big" beast (B 353), or by "some animal unknown to me" (B 347). But he himself becomes the beast that destroys his equanimity. Hysterical fear about the origin of the all-consuming sound drives him to damage the burrow with "wild digging" (B 349) so that at every hint of noise he finds himself "tearing out a lump of earth . . . simply so as to do something to give expression to . . . inward agitation" (B 349). At the story's end he must migrate to the labyrinth near the burrow's entrance. Only there "beneath the moss covering" is silence discoverable in "a complete reversal of things" in which "what was once the place of danger has become a place of tranquility" (B 352). The real problem of the burrow is not its anxieties (whether to store food in one rather than many cells) or its defects (the narrator's realization that the "little maze of passages" near the door once prized as "the crown of all burrows" is simply "an idle *tour de force*" [B 331]), but the "door itself" or rather the "thought of the door" (B 332). This is the case because for the narrator "merely" to "walk in the direction of the entrance" is to sense "an atmosphere of great danger, actually as if my hair were growing thin and in a moment might fly off and leave me bare and shivering, exposed to the howls of my enemies" (B 332), a sense that is less a presentiment of violence than its unmitigated outcome—"hair" that "might fly off" (B 332) being a synecdoche for an instantly experienced vulnerability: flesh open to the outside, inviting assault.

"Inner and Outer belong to each other," Kafka remarked. "Divided, they become two bewildering aspects of a mystery which we endure but can never solve."[26] The power of Kafka's story—*its* tour de force—lies in the understanding that contrary states are constitutive of each other, whether these be manifested as beholding and inhabiting; as an awareness that is one's own and that is then ascribed to an enemy; or as the metamorphic moment when bliss opens into torture and noise destroys peace.[27] "The Burrow" represents the experiential feel of this recognition. Its interest is not in disordered states of mind (though, personally, Kafka described the ravage of noise as precipitative of a breakdown),[28] but in inverse states that seem to have an incorporative relation to each other, while at the same time repelling each other, a perception that opens onto other formulations in Kafka's writing organized by that logic. For instance, Kafka's expression of fear at the loneliness that would devastate him were he to remain in Planá after Ottla, his sister, returned to Prague: "If I stayed here alone, I would be completely lonely." "I don't have to describe the outward symptoms of such a state; you too know what they are like, though you must think of the most intense form you have ever experienced, where the emotion is already on the point of reversing itself. . . . I . . . was totally preoccupied by unspeakable fear, and in clearer moments by fear of this fear." But a page later, Kafka adds: "But what is it about loneliness? Fundamentally, loneliness is my sole aim, my greatest temptation, my opportunity, and assuming it can be said that I have 'arranged' my life, it was always with the view that loneliness can comfortably fit into it."[29]

In the following passage contact with another and no possibility of contact with others gives onto the same estrangement: "He feels more deserted with a second person than when alone. If he is together with someone, this second person reaches out for him and he is helplessly delivered into his hand. If he is alone, all mankind reaches out for him—but the innumerable outstretched arms become entangled with one another and no one reaches to him" (*DFK* 420–21). In the torture of the first predicament, the "he" is at the mercy of another's presence without experiencing the intimacy of that presence to which "he" is nonetheless vulnerable. In Kafka's representation of absolute loneliness contact is differently unavailable, personified by the image of everyone reaching out to the "him" but no one reaching "him." Or, rather, the persons who reach out to "him" make contact only with each other, an understanding that underscores the solidarity of mankind as an aggregate or community from which the "he" is excluded. Thus loneliness and some not-loneliness alternative are logically or rather morphologically permeable. The outside of loneliness is the felt presence that would dissipate it and the absence which is required to constitute it. Finally, the insight about loneliness appears in a different form still in Kafka's disbelief that his "dreamlike inner life" (*DFK* 302) could be touched by an outside. But although Kafka claims that these worlds do not impinge on each other, only at the moment of a breakdown could they ever really split apart. Although there is a boundary between the human world from which, for instance, Milena exercises her magnetism and the "forsaken" world of banishment ("forsaken not by people . . . but rather by myself *vis-à-vis* people" [*DFK* 408]), however it might be emblematized by metaphors that progressively strengthen the opposition ("What used to be a dividing-thread is now a wall, or a mountain range, or rather a grave" [*DFK* 409]), the impediments that separate these incompatible spaces can precipitously dissolve. Thus the wish to "quit the world" and become a "citizen of this other world" (*DFK* 407), a plight Kafka analogizes to "Wandering in the Wilderness" away "from Canaan" (*DFK* 407), leads precipitously to the thought: "perhaps I shall keep in Canaan after all" (*DFK* 408). Thus in a flash, the antagonism between the "Wilderness" and "Canaan" can burn up, since though "I live elsewhere . . . the attraction of the human world is so immense, in an instant it can make one forget everything" (*DFK* 409).

At the same time that antithetical states can be described as constitutive of each other, the emphasis of "The Burrow" is not on their conciliation but on the constant emerging of an outside that shatters the places of safety in which the narrator lodges. Characterizing the sublime as a "break within or from aesthetics," Jean-Luc Nancy argues that the sublime gestures toward a "destiny" outside of "aesthetics," "beauty," and "the imagination."[30] I want to suggest an analogy between Nancy's representation of the "outside," which reaches beyond the aesthetic enclosures that might engender it, and Kafka's representation of a perpetual transgression of the contained spaces inhabited by his animal narrator in "The Burrow." The consequence of an erosion of limit is the "reversal" of form, "feeling and subjectivity" when the outside breaks into these as an "infinite pulsation," which surpasses even feeling.[31] In Nancy's account, if "feeling" remains, it is "first of all exposed to the unlimited totality of an 'outside' rather than related to its proper intimacy," being characterized by a transport in which the sensible and the affective are experienced without contour or limit.[32]

Although the "outside" of the sublime must be distinguished from the outside in which Kafka's narrator continuously finds himself, Nancy's distinctions illuminate the narrator's burrowing beyond the reach of structuring spaces, whether these be material, conceptual, or affective. Hence "digging, simply for the sake of digging" (B 349); "wild digging" (B 349) that will "bring me either peace or despair" (B 348); or "digging" that, like the trench the narrator plans to construct in response to the terrifying noise, could "lead to nothing at all" (B 349), in its total pointlessness shatters the dialectic that had seemed to structure Kafka's story. Such digging is less an attempt to break up, turn over, or remove earth than it is a motiveless inclination to transgress the brink where safety opens into peril. The shattering of limit might culminate in a passage "outside" (B 346) through "the door itself" (B 332) or to a space inside the Castle Keep, but it more ceaselessly conducts itself as a pressure, in Nancy's terms as an "infinite pulsation" without compelling purpose or content, against all the borders that make up the story's demarcated regions—"*beyond everything*"[33] that could picture a sufficient motive or a decisive boundary. This "unlimited unbordering," this "raising and razing of the limit," this passage beyond, is the aesthetic of "The Burrow," its freedom, and its peril.[34]

While in "The Burrow" the threat to home is both the menace of an outside and the compulsion to break through to an outside, Kafka exposes a different peril in a letter to Milena, elaborating a plight in which he can't be at home in a human realm because of something like a condition of alterity:

> It's more or less like this: I, an animal of the forest, was at that time hardly even in the forest; I was lying somewhere in a dirty ditch (dirtied only by my presence, of course) when I saw you outside in the open. . . . I forgot everything, forgot myself completely, I stood up, approached. . . . I crouched down beside you as if it were my right, I laid my face in your hand, I was so happy, so proud, so free, so mighty, so much at home, again and again: so much at home—but in essence I remained a mere animal, just part of the forest, living in the open only by your grace. . . . Although you were stroking me with the kindest of hands, you had to recognize certain peculiarities pointing to the forest, my true home and origin. . . . I remembered who I was, and saw that your eyes were no longer deceived; I had the nightmare (of feeling at home in a place one doesn't belong), but for me this nightmare was real. I had to return to the darkness, I couldn't stand the sun, I was desperate, truly like an animal gone astray; I started running as fast as I could and still could not escape the

> thought: "If only I could take her with me!" and the counterthought: "But can there be any darkness where she resides?" (*LM* 193–94)

Story and letter each distinctly ask: what does it mean to feel "at home in a place one doesn't belong" (*LM* 194) or to mistake one's home? "The Burrow" understands the idea of an outside in terms of a dwelling. The letter understands the idea of an outside in terms of a being ("an animal" of "the forest"). But dwelling can't be extricated from being. That is the letter's insight. Though the meditations on home and Kafka's story might be thought to derive from such different contexts as to invalidate comparison, their mutual identification with the animal invites us to consider their relation.

In "The Burrow" the eroded cordon between one emotion and another—the spilling over of bliss to the anxiety that lies just past it at the core of the narrator's ruminations—might be in Kafka's story the very model for the breakdown of a species determination that, for instance, governs the narrator's identification with animal essence. Thus understood, "The Burrow" would be governed by two related structuring binaries (that of inside and outside, and of animal and human being). Yet I wish differently to claim that Kafka does not elide animal and human forms of embodiment. Rather, the story reveals an identification with the *construct* of "animal" whose uniqueness lies in dwelling within an immediacy for which there is no conceptual refuge against the shifting changes that immerse him.[35] "Animal" is the name for the experience of being caught in a flux of dissolving physical and mental phenomena—of affective states whose extravagance transgresses limits in an immoderation that has no recourse to forms of sociality that would mediate, organize, or constrain it. In "animal" Kafka's narrator inhabits the fleetingness—the quicksilver transformations of one emotion to its opposite—that humans (ostensibly) protect themselves against with understanding. Just this sensuous dwelling in the affective changes that course through him constitutes the "animal" intelligence with which Kafka's narrator aligns himself.[36]

Thus while "The Burrow" seems to rely on a transparent anthropomorphism inherent in the genre of the fable, soliciting us to transpose the enmity between the narrator and the other creature he imagines to two human antagonists, the absoluteness of the estrangement at the story's foundation (the banishment of all creatures from the narrator's imaginary, or the implication that they may only be imaginary) forbids us to countenance human corollaries, which would domesticate its central, if implicit, premise. "Animal" designates a perception of detachment from every other being so acute that, from a human perspective, only a word that denotes a species difference could mark it. "Animal" embodies Kafka's pervasive feeling of being outside the dwelling that is human being ("What is it that binds you more intimately to these impenetrable, talking, eye-blinking bodies . . . ? Because you belong to the same species? But you don't belong to the same species" [*DFK* 396]).[37] "Animal" names the experience of being unrecognizable to oneself in any system of classification, of feeling so alienated from the human community that one experiences oneself as residing outside its realm, while at the same time, since one *is* human, not being at home, not encountering one's kind, among the members of any other species. Across Kafka's writing, forms of life that derive from discrete classificatory systems are treated as penetrable to each other. But they are not then treated as recognizable. They are not treated as recognizable because the animal's attributes (language, thought, claws, beard, anxiety, rapture, hair, and "my forehead, that unique instrument" [B 330], which "hammered . . . a wall for the" Castle Keep's "beautifully vaulted chamber" [B 328]) are not perceptible in any form that we could call a genus. For the same reason it could be said that Kafka represents himself as *sui generis*. In his diary he wrote: I am "Still unborn and already compelled to walk around the streets and speak to people" (*DFK* 417). Even when he identifies himself as a homo sapiens who needs nutriments, he does so in a sentence that invokes the requirements of the metabolic processes of the underground stem of a plant organism: "since I am human after all . . . my roots want nourishment" (*DFK* 408). The very choice of such a metaphor to indicate this source of nourishment interlineates attributes of plant and animal species. In Kafka's writing, the experience of hybridity implicitly lies at the heart of certain kinds of sentience, but the mixture is not then treated as identifiable as a strain or type, because, for instance, a root could not replace a throat or the complex human metabolism.

At the same time, Kafka's letters and stories insist there is no place to abide in any experience, notwithstanding its extremity, that is closed to what lies outside it, however that outside is figured. This is the corollary to the phenomenological insight expressed by a story like "The Burrow" in which experiences are intelligible only in relation to the outsides that constitute them. In the letter to Milena, the outside is troped as a forest to which the figure Kafka calls himself flees. Yet in the forest the very alterity to the human that defines the animal Kafka calls himself does not do so purely. The animal being that is Kafka also has its outside: "I had to return to the darkness, I couldn't stand the sun, I was desperate, truly like an animal gone astray; I started running as fast as I could and still could not escape the thought: 'If only I could take her with me!'" (*LM* 194). To flee the "open" Kafka calls "home" (*LM* 194) still leaves rapture, embodied in Milena, outside where he is. In the letter to Milena and in "The Burrow" not feeling at home where you are at home; "feeling at home in a place" where you don't "belong" (*LM* 194); and not being at home anywhere are nightmares from which it is impossible to awaken. Kafka required the radical identification with an alien form to validate his sense that exile, the continuous dispossession of every feeling we have and every experience we are in, is not a consequence of human relations but exists metaphysically prior to human arrangements in the nature of being itself. At the same time the very absence of human affiliation at the heart of Kafka's writing (in "The Burrow" there are no human presences; they would not count for anything) could not help but castigate the human, since, for Kafka, human forms of sociality are nonconsolatory, even incidental, to the plight he represents as excruciating.[38]

Yet this identification with "animal" to epitomize the human condition extricated from its sociality—which seems as if it marks a limit that has no further or beyond, if the operative category remains "creature"—is itself transgressed and given an outside. Three years after Kafka broke off his affair with Milena, the "belonging" that signals affinity emerges in Kafka's passionate eagerness to be welcomed by his tuberculosis. Thus the personification of the disease as an intimate who summons him: "For years I haven't written a soul; I might as well have been dead. . . . It was as if I wasn't of this world, but not from any other either; it was as if throughout the years I had done everything demanded of me just on the side, while in reality I was only listening to find out whether I was being called—until the disease actually did call from the next room and I ran in and began belonging to it more and more [*immer mehr und mehr gehörte*]" (*LM* 231).[39] To "belong more and more" to the tuberculosis (to "belong so indissolubly together," to appropriate the words of the animal for his burrow, "that in spite of all my fears I could make myself quite comfortable out here" [B 340]) is to embrace his fatal illness and hospitably to give *it* residence. Kafka called his cough "the animal," that which, like the disease of which it was a symptom, claimed him as *its* habitation, thus providing a peace with a definitive outcome. "I shall never get well again," Kafka wrote to Felice. "Just because what we are here dealing with is not a tuberculosis that can be nursed back to health in a deck chair but a weapon that remains absolutely indispensable as long as I live. It and I cannot both go on living."[40] In this way Kafka armed himself with that artillery that would decisively enable him to wrest for himself the peace that his fictional character, the animal narrator, could only covet.

Recalling the dove, another creature that could find no place to rest or set its feet because water covered all the earth's surfaces, Kafka wrote to Milena: "To want death but not pain is a bad sign. Otherwise one can risk death. One has simply been sent out as a biblical dove, and having found nothing green, now slips back into the darkness of the ark" (*LM* 205). Although in "The Burrow" what justifies the ferocity with which the narrator anxiously guards the burrow is a joy whose evanescence might leave a residue of the mental silence, for which "deep stillness" (B 352), "blissful hours" (B 340), "peace" (B 353) are tropes (the "green" the dove does not discover [*LM* 205]), "The Burrow" finally disputes that any single mind state could be sustained or even linger as a trace. Kafka's story moves into and out of these ostensibly solid mind frames—which any reflective movement, or even the mere passing of time, dissipates into a beyond, an unbordering, an outside. These enmeshed casts of mind—with their compulsions, fervors, dangerous intensities, and, most, convictions that the truth that each concentrates will not endure beyond the present—always encounter the shattering moment when something outside the mental space, credence in which has been taken as a refuge, devastates it. "Frank is unable to live," Milena wrote to Max Brod:

> Frank isn't capable of living. Frank will never recover. Frank will soon die. . . . we have all taken refuge in a lie, in blindness, enthusiasm, optimism, a conviction, pessimism or something else. But he has never fled to any refuge, not one. He is absolutely incapable of lying. . . . He lacks even the smallest refuge; he has no shelter. That is why he is exposed to everything we are protected from. He is like a naked man among the dressed. Everything he is, says, and lives cannot even be called truth; actually it is predetermined being, being in and of itself, being with nothing added that might allow him to distort his picture of the world—whether into beauty or distress. (*LM* 245)

Though issuing from a different sphere, and with a different object as a reference, from that occupied by Kafka's animal narrator in "The Burrow," Milena's reflections, like those of Kafka's letters cited earlier, obliquely illuminate a fundamental if elusive aspect of that story, which I touch on briefly. Although the narrator of "The Burrow" presumes an evolution (he sweepingly encompasses the arc of his own development from "a young apprentice" to "an old architect" [B 357]), his obsessions have nothing to do with learned forms of mastery or failure whereby experience could be ordered and made manageable. Rather, the story reveals the repeated breakdown of mental and physical barriers that would sequester rapture from torture—a breakdown constitutive of the narrator's experience in its entirety. Yet something virtually invisible is glimpsed as it emerges from this collapse—what Milena termed "being in and of itself, being with nothing added"—being that does not take refuge in this or that sequestered space or incarnation but always falls outside any form or coloring that would alloy it. In "The Burrow" being slips free of anything that would ameliorate or tinge the experience of it by casting it in this or that particularity—rapture or torture, peace and what despoils peace, "fatigue" and "ardent zeal" (B 341). The ephemerality of these states (and of all particular states) yields to something like a neutral essence in which being again and again impersonally emerges—though, without shape or coloring, we could not see it—from their dissolution. In representing a plight in which physical and mental states constantly discover their outsides and their insubstantiality, being is implicitly represented as a nothingness—"being in and of itself . . . with nothing added" (*LM* 245)—a phenomenon without meaningful attributes, a purity, in Milena's words, free from "beauty or distress" (*LM* 245), from peace or what despoils it, something like a nakedness, strangely unmarked by the duress and fascination of the intensities that compel the plenitude of Kafka's represented mind states.

III

In "Investigations of a Dog" a canine narrator rhapsodizes about a performance seen in his youth in which seven dogs who have a "creative gift for music with which the canine race alone is endowed. . . . conjured music," while also embodying it in their own movements: "Everything was music, the lifting and setting down of their feet, certain turns of the head, their running and their standing still. . . . great masters all of them, keeping the rhythm so unshakably."[41] This experience then becomes the provocation for the narrator's deliberation of questions about music and other rudimentary phenomena—the narrator calls them "senseless" (I 295), a characterization that would seem to discourage investigation. The lure of music is rapture and transport. "The artistry of the . . . dogs" (I 282) destroys the limits of the known world by intimating some beyond-logic that music makes perceptible ("I longed . . . to beg them to enlighten me, to ask them what they were doing" [I 282]). Questions arise from a like desire to break through to a region where essential mysteries (the source of food; the objects of hunger; the lure of silence, as well as of fasting, and of music itself, for which the narrator develops a hunger) could be explicated. These incommensurate topics, which can't be integrated and can't be separated, pull us into Kafka's story.[42] Because we can't sort out the questions that drive the exposition, we are in relation to the inquiry as the narrator is to the music, gripped by the proposition that experiences as visceral, and as unencryptable, as hunger, music, and silence—in effect, that "all the senseless phenomena of our existence, and the most senseless most of all, are susceptible to investigation" (I 295).

The first question, identified by the narrator as "the chief object of all our meditation" "since the dawn of time," is "what the canine race nourished itself upon" (I 286). A second asks whether food is supplied from the earth or the sky (I 303). A third concerns agency: does food grow because dogs "water the ground," since "the earth needs our water to nourish it" (I 287), or is watering the ground, urinating, a compulsion that inadvertently contributes to the soil's fertility? Is there an auxiliary method of procuring food, namely "spells, songs, and ritual movements" (I 287) that supplements the beneficial watering? The narrator's questions draw us inward as to an essence that might be penetrated, even as the categorical incommensurability of the phenomena being considered (and the stressed inadequacy of anyone to consider them) keeps us at bay, thwarting both the idea of access and the deepening associated with haecceity. When the narrator introduces a contradiction (though incantations should be directed to the soil, "the people in all their ceremonies gaze upwards" [I 304]), this is a starting point that goes nowhere, for it is less food than the management of hunger that he ultimately identifies as his consuming interest.

The narrator desires a sublime form of nourishment without material gratification. His ambition, and "often enough" his achievement, is to "have literally got my teeth into hunger" (I 309). In the redundancy of the trope, the thing that is represented (metaphorically, the biting that is hunger; the biting that assuages hunger; and the idiom *to get one's teeth into*, which exemplifies an engagement with hunger that is a firm taking hold of it) can't be clarified by the specifications that inequivalently posit it. Even if the doubling of hunger in the expressions does not refer to the same hunger, the reiteration dramatizes an incapacity to examine hunger's properties from a space that is not one's own hunger, for the formulation's only mobility is to repeat itself with variation, rather than to move outward to gain access to the phenomenon it would apprehend.[43] The impossibility of investigating hunger from a neutral space introduces the idea of fasting, which would impose distance between the hunger that devours the narrator and the hunger he would examine. Fasting is a failure because the narrator continuously falls on food "with the fury both of hunger and of disappointment" (I 305). Moreover, the very food that is renounced might assume agency: what if "the food were to come of itself from above" and "knock at my teeth for admittance"? (I 306)—macabre, if gratuitous, proof that hunger cannot be regulated. In addition, because fasting heightens auditory sensation, the only certain source of peace is to feed: "I must eat so as to reduce to silence this world rioting so noisily around me" (I 311). In the end, fasting is a privation that makes the narrator's own flesh appealing ("I was twisted with the pangs of hunger, and in my distress of mind sought relief in my own hind legs, despairingly licking and gnawing at them up to the very buttocks" [I 310]). Fasting awakens desires so archaic they are almost unrecoverable ("delicious dainties that I had long since forgotten . . .

yes, I could smell the very fragrance of my mother's teats" [I 311]). Its greatest torment is a sensibility exacerbated by the clamor ("the greatest noise of all") that arises "from my own belly" (I 311), from which it is impossible to sequester himself.

In fact, the narrator craves a state of affairs in which his questions about hunger (more essential to satisfy than physical hunger) could be shared.[44] Questions are the meat of Kafka's story—the aliment that could sustain the race, even potentially yielding their plenty without dog labor or avarice: "The hardest bones, containing the richest marrow, can be conquered only by a united crunching of all the teeth of all dogs. That of course is only a figure of speech and exaggerated; if all teeth were but ready they would not need even to bite, the bones would crack themselves and the marrow would be freely accessible to the feeblest of dogs" (I 291). Yet this "figure of speech" (I 291) for the discovery of ample food is immediately made continuous with its near-converse, when it is confessed that if a feast were laid before dog multitudes, the narrator alone would fall on it: "I want to compel all dogs thus to assemble together, I want the bones to crack open under the pressure of their collective preparedness, and then I want to dismiss them to the ordinary life that they love, while all by myself, quite alone, I lap up the marrow" (I 291). Like the rest of the diegetic in which hunger is animated from subject/object positions that slide into each other, and in which material gratification looks like its metaphysical counterpart, avarice and altruism can't be pried apart, but also can't be unified, even though these distinctions lie at the heart of the story's polemic. The "senselessness" (I 294) to be investigated is echoed in the bond of these unacknowledged antinomic formulations.

And if what the dog narrator would discover is hypostatic (a term prompted by the story's lament for the disappearance of the "true Word" [I 300]), is a foundation he calls the "marrow" (I 291), no religious apparatus could explicate it, since "the totality of all questions and all answers, is contained in the dog" (I 289–90). Dog quiddity could only be illuminated by the repository of being perceptible here, a recognition that compels a new object of voraciousness: "I wanted to feed on the marrow, not merely of a bone, but of the whole canine race itself" (I 291). Does the predatory fantasy of feeding on the whole dog race pertain to the narrator's realization that he does not care for the dogs he would seduce with questions, but only for their validation of those questions? That he is infatuated with dog essence, which is an abstraction he could contemplate, while being indifferent to dogs he could love? Some such possibilities are indicated but invalidated as glosses of the cannibalistic trope, which is never explicated. Thus the image that ostensibly gives access to the pith, the inmost part, of the presumptive object of inquiry—dog-essence—is empty. There is no inside, no "marrow" (I 291) at the center of the narrator's investigation, and there is also no outside that would free him from its confusions:

> You are yourself a dog, you have also the dog knowledge; well, bring it out, not merely in the form of a question, but as an answer. If you utter it, who will think of opposing you? . . . Then you will have clarity, truth, avowal, as much of them as you desire. The roof of this wretched life, of which you say so many hard things, will burst open, and all of us, shoulder to shoulder, will ascend into the lofty realm of freedom. (I 290)

The ultimately platitudinous effect of that release ("you will have clarity, truth, avowal" [I 290]) could not be realized outside of an exclamatory utterance, for, like the idea of glutting oneself on an object that would appease hunger, the "freedom" it postulates, also imagined as violent, has no achievable content, being a category that nothing real could occupy.

"Investigations" holds out the promise that questions could be aliment, along with the different objective that questions could release one from the conditions of "this wretched life" entirely. But access both to an inside, a "marrow" that would appease metaphysical as well as material hunger, and to an outside ("the roof of this wretched life . . . will burst open" [I 290]) figure conceptual resolutions to problems that are insoluble, even as that failure escapes narrative comment—in distinction to the state of affairs in "An Imperial Message," where failure is contemplated with relish. The story's most seductive promise emerges in the assurance that authentic questions could be isolated, a hope given voice in relation to the bewilderment the narrator experienced as a youth, but whose anxiety more directly pertains metacritically to Kafka's own story: "how, when so many questions are going about, are you to pick out the right questions? One question sounds like another; it is the intention that counts, but that is often hidden even from the questioner. And besides, it is a peculiarity of dogs to be always asking questions . . . as if in doing that they were trying to obliterate every trace of the genuine questions" (I 297). If one could extract the true questions from the fraudulent and subsidiary ones, from so many "questions" asked "confusedly all together" (I 297), it might be possible to stand in a "genuine" relation to the senselessness, the next best thing to explicating it.

The lure of Kafka's writing is that there are "genuine questions" (I 297) and that these can be discriminated from inauthentic alternatives. But no standard is available that would permit a ranking that would render a discrimination like "genuine" sensible. In the absence of hierarchy (and of differentiation) what is disabled is an understanding of how the story's questions, which have proximate, superficial, reiterative, chiasmic, and antinomic relations, bear on each other. Superficial is also a characterization that oddly describes the story's imagistic apex. When images at the heart of the narrator's questions are examined, they reveal something like their own hollowness. Hence the metaphor of feeding on "the whole canine race itself" (I 291) introduced mid-story, but the climax of the contemplation of questions about what would appease hunger illuminates a brilliant surface, like that of an M. C. Escher drawing, whose dazzle cannot be glossed (no true outside is available) or penetrated (no inside is available). Thus, inversely, the story's epiphanic image of freedom, the "roof . . . burst[ing] open," represents a stupendous violence that would liberate from the epistemological entrapments detailed by the narrator. But it is a vehemence without consequence, for there is no way to imagine a release from experience's imprisonment. Freedom, like satiety, is an insubstantiality. It can be indicated deictically, but never realized, having no dimension, no inside *and* no outside. Such failed spatializations powerfully insist: the very idea of an outside (the exploded roof) or an inside (the "marrow") of the phenomenal "senselessness" represented by "Investigations" is a placeholder for an access and an escape that are prohibited.

The trope of dog partakes of this shallowness. There is no good way to identify the figure of the narrator and his iconoclastic relation to his colleagues. On the one hand, the positions both of the questioner and of the community that rebukes his questions anthropocentrically mimic a human predicament. On the other hand, because dogs are not like this, and, however much human beings are like this, they are not dogs, "dog," like "animal" in "The Burrow," becomes a figure for a mode of being that is interpretively inassimilable to either species. At the same time, through the questions raised by the narrator's encounter with the musical dogs that are "nevertheless, dogs like you and me" (I 281), the very figure of the indecipherable dog becomes associated with the marvelous. Wonder is not therefore confined to a specific region where, for instance, the knowledge importuned by the narrator would have been located, but is rather distributed throughout Kafka's story, much like the "blast of music which seemed to come from all sides, from the heights, from the deeps, from everywhere, surrounding the listener, overwhelming him, crushing him, and over his swooning body still blowing fanfares so near that they seemed far away and almost inaudible" (I 282). The narrator's questions partake of this marvelous, for in the obdurate silence that rises up to meet them, all they have to sustain themselves is their own intense seriousness. Questions about the miraculous concert forever destroy the sense that any phenomenon actually beheld could be recognized as banal—or could be recognized at all: "Was the world standing on its head? Where could I be? What could have happened? . . . Oh, the music these dogs made almost drove me out of my senses" (I 284)—and reach their crescendo in the simple uncertainty of whether these creatures with "their music and their radiance" (I 284) are "perhaps . . . not dogs at all" (I 283).[45] For whether these are dogs, or what dogs are, is just the inscrutability that the cascade of questions has undertaken to represent as experienced. That same sense of the miraculous then encompasses all the phenomena that the narrator investigates.

In this way "dog" becomes the name for an interrogative stance inseparable from enchantment at beholding experiences so perceptually strange they cannot be classified. "Dog" is also the name for one who investigates what questions are. "Dog" is equally the name for creatures that resist the fascination of questions. In Kafka's story those pledged to silence and those pledged to investigate it are part of the same inexplicability. The community both resists questions and is required to render them intelligible, even as an investigation like the narrator's could be conducted only in a solitude experienced as exile. The perspectival relativity in which "dog" signifies the impulse to question and to resist questioning also infuses other aspects of the story. A different way to understand the story's plural subjects and its gymnastic relation to those subjects is to say that the truth sought by the narrator has no unitary manifestation. One can't identify the "genuine questions" (I 297) because only from a theoretical vantage where no one could reside could the privilege of the narrator's distinctions be meaningful. To arrive at the freedom that the narrator calls "that final consummation" (I 290) would be to pull himself out of an experiential whole whose elements are insusceptible of the kind of separation marked by a word like "genuine." All questions are genuine (and all are not), because no aspect of the experience that generates them could ever be assessed as deficient (or as sufficient). For this reason "Investigations of a Dog" juxtaposes the liberatory space of questions (which occupy an ostensible outside to the "senseless" phenomenal realm) to the phenomenal world itself, the true place of transport, whose fascination is constituted by the senselessness the questions would pacify, where ravishment and its objects dwell.

IV

"Was he an animal, that music had such an effect upon him?" the narrator of "The Metamorphosis" asks about Gregor Samsa's fascinated attention to his sister's violin-playing. What distinguishes Gregor, a "gigantic insect," from the people in the living room, also listening to his sister's violin-playing, is that he alone is stirred by what he hears.[46] In distinction to his family, who cannot see beyond the degradation of his bodily transformation ("If this were Gregor, he would have realized long ago that human beings can't live with such a creature"), his "tenderness" for the human family to which he once belonged is so pure that no sacrifice seems too great to assuage their misery: "The decision that he must disappear was one that he held to even more strongly than his sister, if that were possible."[47] The disparity between his father's ruthlessness, whose manifestations are still palpable—though in Gregor's indifference to his own suffering, they are almost also imperceptible ("The rotting apple in his back . . . already hardly troubled him")—and his own amiableness toward those who inflicted the injury is at the heart of the story's distinction between what it calls "animal" and "human" forms of acknowledgment.[48] The "such an effect" that music has on Gregor opens into mercy for the very beings whose repugnance has inflicted so much sorrow. "Was he an animal . . . ?" is thus a question whose affirmative indicates a forbearance, a mildness, even a magnitude, of which the humans are bereft, a species distinction as pronounced as "the numerous little legs which never stopped waving in all directions" of his insect embodiment.[49]

From another vantage, in Kafka's writing the estrangement from the human community that "animal" signifies could not be further developed. Its absoluteness—could only again and again be repeated. "I belong in the quietest quiet [*die stillste Stille*]," Kafka wrote Milena (*LM* 220).[50] In this superlative, which Kafka emphasizes (but does not elaborate), there is a nothing further, only a highest degree, which indicates by repetition (the echo of the noun in the superlative of the adjective "quiet") the maximum of the desired state, as if language had become impoverished so there were no outside to the root word "quiet," which, to retain its integrity, could never be supplemented, but only modified by a suffix. The same with the insularity—the apparent sufficiency to which nothing need be added—of "animal," which can seem the utmost of what Kafka could say about it.[51] In "The Burrow," the extremity of the narrator's need for what Kafka called "the quietest quiet" (*LM* 220) places him on an "unlimited unbordering"[52] beyond where others dwell. "Animal" is the name for the self-exclusion of that outer limit.

If Kafka's *sui generis* animals dwell in spaces whose attributes replicate their own features—the spaces are as estranged from each other as are the beetle and the human beings in "The Metamorphosis"—it must be because no single trope, whether isolated forms of being or isolated arenas in which beings dwell, is alone sufficient to convey the extremity of the solitude Kafka both cultivated and feared. The plenitude of Kafka's no-hope writing depends as a first premise on the segregated spaces and beings of Kafka's imaginary, specifically on the extravagant attempts of his narrators to construct boundaries that will not be pervious to threat, even as such boundaries are *conceptually* exceeded in the movement away from threat and in the figuration through which the narrators place themselves outside a community of others that constitute the threat. (Or inside a space so undiscoverable it cannot be accessed for the delivery of a message that could ameliorate the threat.) From another point of view, if in "An Imperial Message," there is no access to an outside, there is also no dispelling the hope of an outside, just as in "The Burrow" there is no escaping the fear of an outside. Similarly, in "Investigations of a Dog," if there is no breakthrough to a depth and no release upward from a surface, the mobility, unavailable in fact, drives and permeates thought. What is alien in *fact* always bumps up against its limit in *thought*, at once confirming the limit, and threatening its dissolution. Gregor becomes the most animal, and the most humane, while his family, instinctively repelled by features of his beetle incarnation—with an instinct unmediated by reason or compassion—behave like brute animals. In this way categories like "animal" and "human" are compromised, even as the rigid distinction, maintained by Gregor's human family, lies at the core of the story's agony. This haunting of the human by the animal, of the inner by the outer (in "The Burrow"), of satiation by hunger, of surface by depth that can't be penetrated, but also can't be relinquished (in "Investigations of a Dog") has the effect of illusorily depriving Kafka of the resources of language, since language insists on categories, on rhetorical, structural, and exegetical distinctions that Kafka's perceptions violate, even as, of course, his writing invents the most nuanced vocabulary imaginable for the feel and texture of those violations in which unlike states are drawn toward and almost into—but never actually into—each other, as a threat, a provocation, a challenge, an impossibility, and a revelation.

The problem (or, from another vantage, the mystery) of Kafka's writing, most generally conceived, is categorical. It presupposes a realm of Aristotelian ontological categories that point to entities into which the world divides, even as, also in that writing, conceptual categories (whether Kant's or Husserl's) are at war with such realist classifications, being rather governed phenomenologically by thought or consciousness.[53] Kafka's characters are often unsure whether to place an entity inside or outside a category (does the invasive noise come from inside or outside the burrow? is that noise emitted by a "single animal" or a "whole swarm" of animals? [B 347]), including a temporal category, when what is putatively actual and what is perceptible do not coincide, or when it's impossible to tell whether or how they coincide.[54] Kafka could not adhere to categories that exclude what lies outside of them, and he could not do so because the very attempt to render experience in terms of the divisions and taxonomies that close perceptions and beings off from each other reveal that such *kinds* or categories (as, for instance, Aristotle's "substance," "place," and "date") are always exceeded by impressions, intuitions, understandings, and, most, perceptions whose superfluities and incongruences cannot be harnessed to, or governed by, classificatory limits. At the same time that supposed ontological categories do not coincide with phenomenological categories—the two do not occupy the same region or presume the same kind of space—they also can't be relinquished, even as they remain incommensurable with lived experience. Thus Kafka's startling observation: "The outside world is too small, too clear-cut, too truthful, to contain everything that a person has room for inside,"[55] a disparity also registered in terms of dwelling in regions as disparate as "the forest" and "the open" described by Kafka's letter to Milena (*LM* 193–94). But if such regions do not coincide, may not even overlap, and therefore cannot be unified, how to communicate from one to the other? For instance, how could the essence of a pure interiority be transmitted? To Milena, Kafka writes: "I keep trying to convey something which cannot be conveyed, to explain something which cannot be explained, something in my bones, which can only be experienced in these same bones (*LM* 219) [*was ich in den Knochen habe und was nur in diesen Knochen erlebt werden kann*]."[56] How can the invasion of a pure exteriority inhabited by "ghosts"—"if one were writing, they were all benevolent spirits; when not writing, they were demons"—be thwarted? Kafka writes to Grete Bloch, Felice's friend: "they came and stayed at will, delicate birds' backs turned into the backs of monumental giants . . . huge, bony ghosts [*knochige . . . Gespenster*] they were, nameless in their multitude; a single ghost could be fought but not all those by which one was surrounded."[57] The inhabitation of such interiors ("in my bones") and the opening to such exteriors at the limit of the human, which bear on the human ("bony ghosts" that "came in through every door, forcing those that were shut")—formulations that appropriate the root of the same word to figure opposite states of threat: what is penetrable and what could never penetrate outwards—become the preemptive focus of Kafka's writing. These spaces refute integration and escape, while never quite being sealed off from each other.

If the experiences Kafka represents resist inquiry about an etiology (why the entombment in impossibility? why the visitation of the ghosts?), their absolute power is never mysterious. Nor is it only ruinous. The ghosts do not only destroy everything recognizable in their midst, they also reveal that vitality is inseparable from devastation. This is what renders "demons" indistinguishable from "benevolent spirits."[58] Kafka's project is to uncover the ways in which "this subterranean threat constitutes my life, my being; if it ceases, I cease. It's how I participate in life" (*LM* 197). (Thus Gregor Samsa discovers the humane features that define his metamorphosis at the center of the torment that has become his destiny.) Threat constitutes life because Kafka never relinquishes his sense that "the real person, unknown to all and to himself, who exists even less than others" is, nonetheless, "more real than anything" and can only "show himself" (*LM* 201–2), to adopt a formulation from "An Imperial Message," by inhabiting "the chambers of the innermost palace" (IM 5), where impossibility and its cognates dwell, or in the same space where the "ghosts" and what Kafka calls the "animals" do, even glimpsing his own features in their agonized countenances. One cannot gloss such an understanding of an interior or of an outermost region by pointing to a trope like the unconscious or to a mystical tradition like the Kabbalah that would lodge the inalienability of threat and essence (the two realms never driven apart in Kafka's writing) in this or any other explanatory system, for these stories refuse to explain—that is, they refuse to relinquish the wonder—of such a congruence. Kafka's problem in the stories is to vivify this wonder so that the reader has the same absorptive relation as his characters to its all-pervasive presence, and even to its intuitions and forebodings. To extrapolate from another context: the difficulty of explaining the premonitions discerned in these radical spaces—spaces whose relation we can see because they are incompletely riven—could be analogized to the attempt to communicate something foreign from a place of exile to one whose life in another geopolitical region would not prepare him to understand it: it is "as if I were living somewhere in Central Africa and had lived there all my life and wanted to share with you who live in Europe, in the middle of Europe, my unshakable opinions about the next political configuration" (*LM* 159), Kafka writes to Milena. He adds: "But this is just a simile, a stupid, clumsy, wrong, sentimental, lamentable, intentionally blind simile" (*LM* 159). If the referent isn't clear in Kafka's writing—perpetually, the reader's torment—what replaces that elucidation is the passion, the alienation, the invincible conviction of the defiantly indecipherable strangeness of these disarticulated spaces whose habitation Kafka represented as opening to a mode of being that, from a distance, he viewed as human.

Acknowledgments

Ross Posnock introduced me to *Au hasard Balthazar* many years after I should have been familiar with Bresson's films, and he continued to offer skeptical but encouraging comments during early attempts to formulate the connection among the essays that Bresson inspired. In 2006–7 I received a fellowship from The Dorothy and Lewis B. Cullman Center for Scholars and Writers at the New York Public Library, which enabled me to begin the essays; two sabbatical leaves from Johns Hopkins enabled me to complete them. The English Department at New York University granted me an appointment as Visiting Scholar and thus a borrower's card to Elmer Holmes Bobst Library, where Diana Greene, the Slavic Studies librarian, familiarized me with Bobst's resources in Russian literature. Gabrielle Dean, of Johns Hopkins's Sheridan Libraries, offered repeated and patient instruction on how to search electronic resources. I appreciate the exchanges with colleagues at universities where I presented early versions of two of the essays (the University of California, Berkeley; the University of Maryland; Yale University; Duke University; CUNY; and Brown University) and the readers' reports (by Brian Price and Michael Wood) that pushed me toward more rigorous formulation of key ideas.

I was able to sharpen other essays in response to the incisive comments of Jonathan Auerbach, Theo Davis, Elizabeth Falsey, Frances Ferguson, Jean-Marie Jackson, Janet Malcolm, Allan Miller, Anne Eakin Moss, Yi-Ping Ong, Samuel Otter, Nancy Ruttenburg, Rochelle Tobias, Mark Thompson, Barry Weller, and David Wills, and to the suggestions of the editorial board of *Representations* for "Animal Sentience: Robert Bresson's *Au hasard Balthazar*," which is reprinted here from *Representations* 114 (Spring 2011): 1–35.

I am particularly indebted to Nancy Ruttenburg and Anne Eakin Moss, who translated and interpreted some passages from the Russian for my essays on Tolstoy and Dostoevsky while tenaciously disagreeing when my readings of those passages struck them as implausible, and to Elizabeth Schneewind for a conversation that confirmed my hunch about the connotations in German of a single word in a Kafka story. My book is the beneficiary of their generosity.

Randolph Petilos of the University of Chicago Press agreeably answered questions about all aspects of production. Brian Cole at Johns Hopkins's Center for Educational Resources captured the Bresson stills used in this book. Hadley Leach and Kate McIntyre aided in the preparation of the manuscript. Ann Goldstein offered her expert opinion on questions of style and usage. I am grateful for their help. Beyond the call of long friendship, Barry Weller rechecked the quotations: his eye for error, his impeccable editorial sense, his substantive observations, and his generosity continue to astonish me.

Finally, I wish to thank Branka Arsić, Colin Dayan, Jonathan Goldberg, George Kateb, Neil Hertz, Michael Moon, and Garrett Stewart, friends who read all the essays, often more than once; posed questions that pressed me to think past what I believed to be my limits; and offered suggestions that touch every page. Their clear voices drifted into the solitary space of writing and made it companionable.

Notes

INTRODUCTION

1. Robert Bresson, quoted in Paul Schrader, "Robert Bresson, Possibly," in *Robert Bresson*, ed. James Quandt (Toronto: Cinematheque Ontario, 1998), 488.

Bresson's *Une femme douce* (1969) is adapted from Dostoevsky's "A Gentle Creature"; *Quatre nuits d'un rêveur* (1971) is drawn from Dostoevsky's "White Nights"; *Au hasard Balthazar* (1966) is inspired in part by Dostoevsky's *The Idiot*. The alienated youth of *Le Diable probablement* (1977) recalls the nihilists of Dostoevsky's *Demons*, a connection discussed in Brian Price's *Neither God nor Master: Robert Bresson and Radical Politics* (Minneapolis: University of Minnesota Press, 2011), 148–82. *Pickpocket*'s story of crime and redemption owes a debt to *Crime and Punishment*, and in *L'Argent* (1983) Bresson reconceived Tolstoy's "The Forged Coupon." Among the works on Bresson's adaptations of Dostoevsky, see, for instance, Mireille Latil Le Dantec, "Bresson, Dostoevsky," in Quandt, ed., *Robert Bresson*, 325–337; and Schrader, "Robert Bresson, Possibly," 485–97. On the relation of Bresson's "radical revolutionary politics" to his "chosen literary precursors, Dostoevsky and Tolstoy, and [the] Russian revolutionary culture of the nineteenth century," see Price, *Neither God nor Master*, cover. Kent Jones discusses Bresson's last film in his monograph *L'Argent* (London: British Film Institute, 1999).

Bresson made thirteen films over forty years, which also included other adaptations. *Les Anges du péché* (1943), whose dialogue was written by Jean Giraudoux, was based on an idea of R. L. Bruckberger (a French Dominican priest and a Résistance member). *Dames du Bois de Boulogne* (1945) was founded on a novel by Denis Diderot; its dialogue was written by Jean Cocteau. In *Journal d'un curé de campagne* (1951), Bresson adapted Georges Bernanos's novel of that title, and in *Mouchette* (1967) he drew from Bernanos's *Nouvelle histoire de Mouchette. Un condamné à mort s'est échappé* was grounded on an account by André Devigny.

I sometimes refer to Bresson's films by their English titles.

2. For two of the earliest and best discussions of what Susan Sontag called the "impertinence" of supposing we could have access to the inner life of characters in Bresson's films, see her 1964 essay "Spiritual Style in the Films of Robert Bresson," in Quandt, ed., *Robert Bresson*, 57–71; and Steven Shaviro, "A Note on Bresson," in *The Cinematic Body* (Minneapolis: University of Minnesota Press, 1993), 240–51. Most recently, see Jacques Rancière's chapter on *Mouchette*, in which he argues that in distinction to Georges Bernanos's novel from which the film is adapted Bresson "demolishes . . . the project of a 'language of images'" in which the girl's state of mind is

"reveal[ed]" ("*Mouchette* and the Paradoxes of the Language of Images," in *The Intervals of Cinema*, trans. John Howe [London: Verso, 2014], 61). Although Mouchette is "expected to reveal her 'inner truth' what she displays instead is a talent for opacity" (61), on Rancière's account, an effect created by Bresson's disposal of the novel's "wealth of images, sounds and movements" that constitute the "strange entropy" (48) of its "literary cinematographism" (47).

3. Fyodor Dostoevsky, *The Idiot*, trans. Constance Garnett (New York: Bantam, 1981), 55; hereafter abbreviated *I* and cited parenthetically.

4. The attributes are Dostoevsky's, quoted in Joseph Frank, *Dostoevsky: The Miraculous Years, 1865–1871* (Princeton: Princeton University Press, 1995), 304. Such impersonal conversations recall Mikhail Bakhtin's characterization of Dostoevsky's polyphony of social voices, in which the realm of ideas is not containable within solitary minds: "Everything in them that is essential and true is incorporated into the unified context of 'consciousness in general' and deprived of its individuality. That which is individual . . . is cognitively not essential. . . . From the point of view of truth, there are no individual consciousnesses" (*Problems of Dostoevsky's Poetics*, ed. and trans. Caryl Emerson [Minneapolis: University of Minnesota Press, 1984], 81).

For a discussion that moves beyond the intersubjectivity considered by Bakhtin in Dostoevsky's writing, and beyond intersubjectivity in general, to examine "cosmic connectedness," see Leo Bersani, *Thoughts and Things* (Chicago: University of Chicago Press, 2015], xiii). For instance, Bersani's penultimate chapter, "Far Out," begins with this passage from the cosmologist and theoretical physicist Laurence Krauss: "essentially every atom in your body was once inside a star that exploded. Moreover, the atoms in your left hand came from a different star than did those in your right" (77); considers an "individuality unencumbered by selfhood" (88) in Proust's notion of art, alongside Bergson's idea of "a virtual coexistence of all the levels of the past" (88); and concludes by stressing the "correspondences that most profoundly situate us outside ourselves" so that it could be said there are "material inscriptions in our body of a universe to which we belong, which we *are* before being born into it" (89). Of special interest for the essays that follow is Bersani's reformulation of the idea of "alikeness" (81). "Alikeness is absorbed into a congruence, or community, of being" (82). Some such community of being is exemplified in Bresson's films; see "Robert Bresson's Pathos."

5. Leo Tolstoy, *War and Peace*, trans. Louise and Aylmer Maude, ed. George Gibian (New York: Norton, 1966), 904, 801; see also 201. Hereafter abbreviated *WP* and cited parenthetically. I have removed the stress accents over the Russian names in this translation, since they are present only to indicate the English pronunciation of those names.

6. Fredric Jameson argues that the promiscuous "anyone" (*WP* 152) of my examples is precisely the point in Tolstoy's writing, since the sovereignty of the person is threatened by an "affective contagion, a glowing enlargement of affect well beyond the natural limits and boundaries of the individual subject . . . susceptible of modifying our current conceptions of intersubjectivity and indeed of subjectivity itself as some purely inward, private and psychological matter" (*The Antinomies of Realism* [London: Verso, 2013], 92). For this reason, what Jameson argues about a particular chapter in *War and Peace* in which Bilibin explains to Prince Andrew the partisanship of victory—"The chapter is the story of the affects themselves, and not of external events or plot developments; and vivid as the characters are, the very density of the affects themselves secures an impersonal existence for them, above and beyond those individual subjects which were once the protagonists of realism" (85)—is also claimed of Tolstoy's novel as a whole.

My considerations of the extra-individual in Tolstoy and Dostoevsky (closer to Jameson's than to Bakhtin's) have a more pointed focus than both comprehensive theses.

7. Bresson insisted images have vitality only in conjunction with each other: "Your images will release their phosphorus only in aggregating" (*Notes on the Cinematographer,* trans. Jonathan Griffin [København: Green Integer, 1997], 91; hereafter abbreviated *N* and cited parenthetically). Lone images are lifeless, while "the intimate union of the images . . . charges them with emotion" (*N* 34). Such images are drawn together "in prevision of their *inner* association" (*N* 56).

8. My essays will elaborate. To anticipate, four specific propositions in *Notes* might be said to further capture Bresson's theory of cinema: first, the insistence that "the cause follow the effect, not accompany it or precede it," an imperative exemplified by the recollection of an "approaching . . . man"; his "eyes caught something behind me, which I could not see: at once they lit up. If, at the same time as I saw the man, I had perceived the young woman and the child towards whom he now began running, that happy face of his would not have struck me so; indeed I might not have noticed it" (*N* 102); second, a passage from Pascal—appended in *Notes* to the heading "Fragmentation"—about particulars that stretch in a continuum that reveal increasing nuance so that the abstractions that conceptualize what is real dissolve into parts so endlessly miniscule they could not be anatomized ("A town or countryside at a distance is a town, a countryside; but as one approaches, those are houses, trees, tiles, leaves, grasses, ants, ants' legs, to infinity" [*N* 93]); third, a formulation about a pace that creates the effect of motility: "Slow films in which everyone is galloping and gesticulating; swift films in which people hardly stir" (*N* 89); and, fourth, a vision that locates immobility not in the object of regard but in the regard itself, whose only movement is a deepening, as though the bottom had a malleability that vigilance could make further penetrable: "Dig deep where you are. Don't slip off elsewhere. Double, triple bottom to things" (*N* 30).

9. The essays that follow the introduction chart impersonality from a different vantage from that examined in my 2007 book of that title, not as a thematized subject but rather as a multiform phenomenon that obliquely disputes the person as the highest value. *Impersonality* focused on the uncompromising nature of writing about the precariousness of personal identity captured at the moment of its disintegration. It did so without straying far across the boundary of the human, although there are moments in the works considered in those essays when the inanimate becomes a figure for subjectivity that does not look like subjectivity, as, for instance, in Simone Weil's image of the "de-creation" of the self that makes it into "dead wood" (Sharon Cameron, *Impersonality: Seven Essays* [Chicago: University of Chicago Press, 2007] ix, x) or in Melville's trope of Billy Budd as "light" (*Impersonality*, 189). The categorical disturbances in the literary texts and cinematography examined by *The Bond of the Furthest Apart* arise from ideas that more extensively challenge the demarcations that separate objects, persons, animals, and natural phenomena—such disturbances arise from an allegiance to the nonanthropocentric, to the transhuman, and even to the counterhuman, as elaborated in the text.

10. In Bakhtin's "Forms of Time and of the Chronotope in the Novel: Notes toward a Historical Poetics," the "chronotope" is defined as "a formally constitutive category of literature" in which "spatial and temporal indicators are fused into one carefully thought-out, concrete whole" (in *The Dialogic Imagination: Four Essays,* ed. Michael Holquist, trans. Caryl Emerson and Michael Holquist [Austin: University of Texas Press, 1981], 84). I distinguish such "thought-out . . . whole[s]" from the images, fragments, and philosophical interludes examined in my essays.

11. Rancière, writing of the logic of a new kind of work which contradicts the expectations of story and subject matter, named these disruptions of narrative "*opsis*—the spectacle's sensible effect" in distinction to the old Aristotelian hierarchy that privileged "*muthos*—the coherence of the plot" (*Film Fables,* trans. Emiliano Battista [New York: Berg Books, 2006], 2). In Rancière's

analysis, what counts as *opsis* is broadly inclusive. It is anything that "counter[s] art's aesthetic autonomy with its old submission to the representative regime" (10) by "the effect of the real" (17) to which story is irrelevant. Films require both *muthos* and *opsis*. Thus, for instance, of Humphrey Jennings's *Listen to Britain,* a 1941 film "meant to rally support for England's war," Rancière writes: "The peaceful moments that make up the film . . . are nothing other than the moments of suspension that punctuate fiction films and that invest the constructed verisimilitude of the action and the story with the naked truth, the meaningless truth of life" (17). Elsewhere, Rancière describes the distinction between *opsis* and *muthos* in elemental terms: on the one hand "dramatic progression," on the other "continuous movement made up of an infinity of micro-movements" (2).

12. In *Death 24x a Second*, Laura Mulvey writes that in "the frozen cinematic image" we see a "segment extracted from the flow of narrative" that "bears witness to the pull towards tableaux that has always been there in cinema" (*Death 24x a Second: Stillness and the Moving Image* [London: Reaktion Books, 2006], 80, 150). This stillness, she points out, can now be produced by anyone pausing a DVD. If we could see each frame in isolation, we would see these frozen images as a sequence of stills disarticulating the temporality of narrative. Cinema, Mulvey writes, quoting Raymond Bellour, involves "death 24x a second" because when film is paused, "the stop on the image . . . asserts the power of stillness to enthral"; "if this impression is so strong, it must be because it touches the stop of death" (32). Many aspects of Mulvey's argument owe a debt to Garrett Stewart's discussion of the relation between the single photographic image, or photogram, and the moving image, as, for instance, the notion that when there is an optic freeze, there is a "radical conflation of real time with screen (no longer plot) time" (*Between Film and Screen: Modernism's Photo Synthesis* [Chicago: University of Chicago Press, 1999], 139). For an analysis of the relation between the photogram and Barthes's "third or *obtuse* meaning," see Stewart, *Between Film and Screen*, 341–42. The capacity to pause, repeat, and return is of course what permits my close-up analysis of Bresson's films.

13. Sergei Eisenstein, *Film Form: Essays in Film Theory,* in *Film Form: Essays in Film Theory, and The Film Sense*, ed. and trans. Jay Leyda (Cleveland: World Publishing Company, 1957), 40. Eisenstein enumerates the many "*conflicts*" within and between frames, ultimately extending the notion of "*counterpoint*" to "*acoustics and optics*" "in the sound film" (39, 40).

14. Virginia Woolf also understood *her* writing in terms of rhythm. In a famous letter to Vita Sackville-West she disagreed that writing is a matter of searching for the perfect word: "Style is . . . all rhythm. Once you get that, you can't use the wrong words. But on the other hand here am I sitting after half the morning, crammed with ideas, and visions . . . and can't dislodge them, for lack of the right rhythm. Now this is very profound, what rhythm is, and goes far deeper than words. A sight, an emotion, creates this wave in the mind, long before it makes words to fit it; and in writing . . . one has to recapture this, and set this working (which has nothing apparently to do with words) and then, as it breaks and tumbles in the mind, it makes words to fit it" (Woolf to Sackville-West, March 16, 1926, Woolf Online, http://www.woolfonline.com/?node=content/contextual/transcriptions&project=1&parent=48&taxa=49&content=6344&pos=7).

Is the rhythm Woolf associates with a "wave in the mind" like the "little phrase by Vinteuil" that Swann hears at the Verdurins' ("he sought in the little phrase for a meaning to which his intelligence could not descend, with what a strange frenzy of intoxication did he strip bare his innermost soul of the whole armor of reason and make it pass unattended through the dark filter of sound!" [Marcel Proust, "Swann in Love," *In Search of Lost Time,* vol. 1, *Swann's Way,* trans. C. K. Scott Moncrieff and Terence Kilmartin (New York: Modern Library, 2003), 308, 336–37])?

For Gertrude Stein "emotion" is associated with something like the rhythm of repeated and meaningless sound, as in the astonishing exemplification of the following insight: "Sentences are not emotional but paragraphs are. . . . I found this out first in listening to Basket my dog drinking. And anybody listening to any dog's drinking will see what I mean" ("Poetry and Grammar," quoted in Ulla E. Dydo and William Rice, *Gertrude Stein: The Language That Rises: 1923–1934* [Evanston: Northwestern University Press, 2003], 399).

15. Bakhtin, describing "the basic principle of Dostoevsky's art," writes: "Everything in his world lives on the very border of its opposite" (*Dostoevsky's Poetics*, 176). In *Antinomies of Realism*, Jameson elaborates on the "mood swings" (88) and "unrelated traits" that "enter into opposition with each other" (90) in *War and Peace* until their "ceaseless variability" becomes Tolstoy's narrative (85). In my example, think of Rostov's agitated terror of dying at the battle of Enns, which flips into an emotion at the other end of the spectrum, expressed by this finality: "Oh, God, what would happen to me if the Emperor spoke to me? . . . I should die of happiness!" (*WP* 264).

16. The expression is Bakhtin's. See *Dostoevsky's Poetics*, 20.

17. The phrase is Rowan Williams's. See Williams, *Dostoevsky: Language, Faith, and Fiction* (Waco: Baylor University Press, 2008), 53.

18. See Eisenstein, *Film Form*, 166–78.

19. Dostoevsky, quoted in Frank, *Miraculous Years*, 308.

20. Tolstoy, "Memoirs of a Madman," in *Tolstoy's Short Fiction*, ed. and trans. Michael R. Katz (New York: Norton, 2008), 308. Hereafter abbreviated MM and cited parenthetically.

21. One could read Franz Kafka's fable of a dreamer awaiting an "imperial" messenger who will deliver a crucial communication as an allegory of such enclosure that permits no escape or penetration. Although the dreamer sits in a reverie by his window imagining the messenger's energy and invincibility as he presses valiantly through impediments, the dreamer has no contact with the world outside that window, and perhaps with the world outside the mind that imagines the window. Therefore the desperately awaited message cannot reach him—"Nobody could fight his way through here even with a message from a dead man" ("An Imperial Message," in *The Complete Stories*, trans. Willa and Edwin Muir [New York: Schocken, 1971], 5)—through the hermetic space that seals him off from everything he has a great need to know. While Kafka's parables foreclose on access to an illumination outside story (in Walter Benjamin's terms, they do not "unfold" in the sense of disclose or reveal their meanings ["Franz Kafka, On the Tenth Anniversary of His Death," in *Illuminations*, trans. Harry Zohn (New York: Schocken, 1969), 122)]), his animal stories deliberate the logic of such segregated spaces—of insides, outsides, and surfaces—regions whose partition does not permit escape, peace, or knowledge.

22. Kafka, *Diaries 1910–1923*, ed. Max Brod (New York: Schocken, 1976), 396.

23. Kafka, quoted in Benjamin, "Franz Kafka," 116.

24. Dostoevsky, *Demons*, trans. Richard Pevear and Larissa Volokhonsky (New York: Knopf, 1994), 236; hereafter abbreviated *D* and cited parenthetically.

25. At the same time, Kafka's naked rendering of ultimate questions, often fantastically, associates him indirectly with the tradition of Menippean satire "characterized by an *extraordinary freedom of plot and philosophical invention*" described by Bakhtin (*Dostoevsky's Poetics*, 114). Bakhtin's characterization of Dostoevsky's inheritance of the genre of Menippean satire is in one sense far afield from Kafka's dream world. Yet the description that follows recalls not just the universe of Dostoevsky, but also the heterogeneously surreal world of *The Castle*: "A very important characteristic of the menippea is the organic combination within it of the free fantastic, the symbolic, at times even a mystical-religious element with an extreme and (from our

point of view) crude *slum naturalism.* The adventures of truth on earth take place on the high road, in brothels, in the dens of thieves, in taverns, marketplaces, prisons, in the erotic orgies of secret cults, and so forth" (*Dostoevsky's Poetics,* 115). Moreover, certain phenomena described by Bakhtin as characteristic of Menippean satire—"Dreams, daydreams, insanity destroy the epic and tragic wholeness of a person and his fate," so that it might even be the case that "he ceases to coincide with himself"—bring to mind the ruptured spaces of Kafka's writing (*Dostoevsky's Poetics,* 116, 117).

26. This is the whole sentence: "There is no happiness in comfort, happiness is bought by suffering" (Dostoevsky, *Notebooks for Crime and Punishment,* quoted in Jacques Catteau, *Dostoyevsky and the Process of Literary Creation,* trans. Audrey Littlewood [Cambridge: Cambridge University Press, 1989], 228).

27. See Gilles Deleuze, "The Affection-Image: Face and Close Up," in *Cinema 1: The Movement-Image* (Minneapolis: University of Minnesota Press, 1989), 87–101.

28. See Eisenstein, *Film Form,* 166–78. Writing of the mimetic relation between the ecstatic transformation of affect in the spectator and the ecstatic transformation of "the objects of the diegesis," Jacques Aumont argues that for Eisenstein "*The laws of form could never be determined by anything other than the similarity to, and the closest relationship to, the laws of human thought*" (*Montage Eisenstein,* trans. Lee Hildreth, Constance Penley, and Andrew Ross [Bloomington: Indiana University Press, 1987], 62, 63). Bresson renders the transformation of thing and thought, of the spiritual and the material, virtually inseparable in an organicism as radical as that described by Eisenstein. For a discussion of this "organicism" see Aumont, *Montage Eisenstein,* 57–72; and Anne Nesbet, *Savage Junctures: Sergei Eisenstein and the Shape of Thinking* (London: I. B. Tauris, 2003), 179–84.

29. By postmodernist practices I mean the new critical discovery of metaphoricity underneath a textual surface; the deconstructive account of how contradictory rhetorical structures dismantle themselves; or de Man's analysis of the impasse of textual problems against which one can only knock one's head. In previous books, I also read against the grain of ostensibly closed structures: in identifying a time that disrupts story in Dickinson's lyrics; the heteroglossic relation of nonexclusive variants in Dickinson's fascicles; consciousness that is dissociated from psychology in Henry James's novels; figurations of embodiment beneath the objectively formulated exegetical questions of Melville's and Hawthorne's writing; the storyless pain of the novel *Beautiful Work.* But in distinction to the analysis of the essays that follow, each of these earlier considerations opens into an analysis that singularly accounts for the counterintuitive facets of the works that are deliberated. See my previous books. As with *Impersonality,* in the essays that follow, there is no single interpretive logic that would get at the core of the works considered.

30. For example, in Kafka's stories the question of how the animal is related to the human being can't be meaningfully addressed. His representations disallow us from denominating creatures as either animal or human, but also disallow us from interpreting the representation as some third kind of creature. Kafka has broken through the binary of these categories, much the way I will argue Bresson differently breaks through classifications, and what is given us to comprehend can't be analyzed by the categories he's broken through. Identifying the being as x or y, or undecidably neither x nor y, is not the point of the stories.

31. Roland Barthes, "The Third Meaning: Research Notes on Some Eisenstein Stills," in *Image Music Text,* trans. Steven Heath (New York: Hill and Wang, 1977), 54.

32. Barthes, "The Third Meaning," 64.

33. I am adapting Deleuze's term, "*any-space-whatever,*" which he borrowed from the French anthropologist Pascal Augé to indicate the "pure potentiality" of association between space and

affect in Bresson's films. To radically simplify Deleuze, a close-up of a face is no longer necessary to express affect: "*Any-space-whatever* is not an abstract universal. . . . It is a perfectly singular space, which has merely lost its homogeneity, that is, the principle of its metric relations or the connection of its own parts, so that the linkages can be made in an infinite number of ways. It is a space of virtual conjunction, grasped as the pure locus of the possible" (Gilles Deleuze, *Cinema 1: The Movement-Image,* trans. Hugh Tomlinson and Barbara Habberjam [Minneapolis: University of Minnesota Press, 1986], 109). My adaptation of this term stresses the contingency not of space and affect, but of the objects constellated to form a relation.

34. Benedict de Spinoza, "The Ethics," in *A Spinoza Reader: The Ethics and Other Works,* ed. and trans. Edwin Curly (Princeton: Princeton University Press, 1994), 114. In Spinoza's analysis of the fiction that everything that happens happens on our account: "men" have "explained natural things: *good, evil, order, confusion, warm, cold, beauty, ugliness*" as though they revealed "an order in things," in which "what is most important in each thing is what is most useful to them" and what is "most excellent" can be attributed to things by which men are "most pleased," whereas in fact the idea of an "order . . . in Nature" is nothing "more than a relation to our imagination" (113).

35. Kafka, quoted in Benjamin, "Franz Kafka," 116.

36. It's in the context of what would give relief, in the sense of dimension and significance, to objects in the foreground that I understand Wittgenstein's elliptical statement: "Perhaps what is inexpressible (what I find mysterious and am not able to express) is the background against which whatever I could express has its meaning." Ludwig Wittgenstein, *Culture and Value,* ed. G. H. von Wright in collaboration with Heikki Nyman, trans. Peter Winch (Chicago: University of Chicago Press, 1980), 16e.

1

ANIMAL SENTIENCE: ROBERT BRESSON'S *AU HASARD BALTHAZAR*

1. While the boy speaks these words, "Receive the salt of wisdom" (*accipe sal sapientiae*), the act's association with the ritual of baptism is undermined by the camera's miscellaneous focus on random objects that compete for attention, calling into question where importance lies.

2. Figures 1.1 through 1.16 are from Robert Bresson's 1966 *Au hasard Balthazar* (New York, 2005), DVD. Figures 1.17 and 1.18 are from Robert Bresson's 1974 *Lancelot of the Lake* [*Lancelot du Lac*] (New York, 2004), DVD.

3. One way to understand the ambiguity of sleep that looks like—but must not be—death (since her father, leaving the house, gets into his car and nonchalantly drives away) is to see it as rhythmically drawing together proximate bodily states whose near-coincidence the film contemplates. The letter reporting the girl's death is from Jacques's to Marie's father: "As I am too sad to return to this house since my daughter's death and have failed to sell the farms, why not farm yourself using modern techniques as you once said you would like to?"

4. Marie, at the film's end, may be headed for Paris and a life on the streets, but in the scene of her torment the camera records a mortification akin to that which drives Mouchette, and the pawnbroker's wife in *Une femme douce,* to suicide.

5. Robert Bresson, *Notes on the Cinematographer,* trans. Jonathan Griffin (København: Green Integer, 1997), 91, 20; hereafter abbreviated *N* and cited parenthetically.

6. This is the central narrative: In a provincial village Balthazar, a baby donkey, is acquired

by Jacques's family; passed on to Marie's family; then sold to a baker, for whom the hoodlum Gérard works; then to Arnold, a tramp; at Arnold's death, to a miser; then returned to Marie's family, where he is stolen by Gérard. Laden with contraband, the donkey is killed by a border guard with a bullet meant for Gérard. Thus Balthazar's story is a picaresque tale, with the donkey as the protagonist moving choicelessly from master to master. A second narrative line concerns Marie, a character whose suffering parallels the donkey's, and her torturous relations with Jacques, her childhood lover, and with Gérard. A third narrative line recounts charges of murder and larceny and changes in monetary fortune.

7. Steven Shaviro, *The Cinematic Body* (Minneapolis: University of Minnesota Press, 1993), 30.1.

8. Gilles Deleuze, *Cinema 2: The Time Image*, trans. Hugh Tomlinson and Robert Galeta (Minneapolis: University of Minnesota Press, 1989), 214. Strong analyses of Bresson's juxtaposed images include Amédée Ayfre's speculation that "Bresson, the erstwhile painter, may have meditated upon . . . the space of cubist paintings, where one is dealing . . . with a partitioning of facets which are entangled with each other without intermingling because they are always separated by rigid edges" ("The Universe of Robert Bresson," in *The Films of Robert Bresson*, ed. Ian Cameron [New York: Praeger: 1970], 18); Michael Haneke's assessment of Bresson's cinematic technique as one in which there is "no room for ideology or an interpretation of the world, commentary or consolation. Everything dissolves into pure relationship" ("Terror and Utopia of Form: Addicted to Truth: A Film Story about Robert Bresson's *Au hasard Balthazar*," in *Robert Bresson*, ed. James Quandt [Toronto: Cinematheque Ontario, 1998], 558); and Shaviro's amplification of a Bresson-like distinction: "In a world of mechanical reproduction, fragmentation and construction are not modes of representation, but processes of the real itself" (*Cinematic Body*, 40). "You are the cineaste of the ellipsis," Jean-Luc Godard declared in an interview with Bresson. "It is certain that with *Balthazar* you break all records" ("The Question: Interview by Jean-Luc Godard and Michel Delahaye," in Quandt, *Robert Bresson*, 457). In Colin McCabe's analysis, the "belief that images only find their meaning in their juxtaposition" is one Godard shared with Bresson (*Godard: A Portrait of the Artist at Seventy* [New York: Faber & Faber, 2003], 187).

9. Martin Heidegger, *The Fundamental Concepts of Metaphysics: World, Finitude, Solitude*, trans. William McNeill and Nicholas Walker (Bloomington: Indiana University Press, 1995), 177. The discussion is continued on 178–273.

10. Jacques Derrida, *The Animal That Therefore I Am*, ed. Marie-Louise Mallet, trans. David Wills (New York: Fordham University Press, 2008), 155.

11. See Giorgio Agamben, *The Open: Man and Animal*, trans. Kevin Attell (Stanford: Stanford University Press, 2004).

For Humberto R. Maturana and Francisco J. Varela, what defines "living beings" as a class is their "*autopoietic organization*"—"they are continually self-producing" (*The Tree of Knowledge: The Biological Roots of Human Understanding*, rev. ed., trans. Robert Paolucci [Boston: Shambhala Press, 1992], 43). Cary Wolfe considers the development of this theory (which involves a "*disarticulation* between the category of language and the category of species") as it affects our understanding of the relationship between animal and human being (*Zoontologies: The Question of the Animal*, ed. Cary Wolfe [Minneapolis: University of Minnesota Press, 2003], 38).

In distinction to theories about the animal's relation to the human, Bresson is not interested in pressing on questions of whether animals can "suffer" (Jeremy Bentham, *The Principles of Morals and Legislation* [Buffalo: Prometheus Books, 1988], 311n); "bear witness" (Jean-François Lyotard, *The Differend: Phrases in Dispute*, trans. Georges Van Den Abbeele [Minneapolis: University of Minnesota Press, 1988], 28); "respond" (Derrida, *The Animal*, 84); or have a "face" and an "ethics" (Emmanuel Levinas, *Totality and Infinity: An Essay on Exteriority*, trans. Alphonso Lingis [Boston: Martinus Nijhoff, 1979], 79–80, 194–219)—to touch on some of the questions that figure in that debate.

Nor is he interested in what links species outside of filiation, as Gilles Deleuze and Félix Guattari are when they write: "There is a block of becoming that snaps up the wasp and the orchid, but from which no wasp-orchid can ever descend" (*A Thousand Plateaus: Capitalism and Schizophrenia*, trans. Brian Massumi [Minneapolis: University of Minnesota Press, 1987], 238). In the end then, "becoming animal" is not really about animals but rather about indistinctions among species that form assemblages. This would be the opposite of any attempt to investigate the boundary between the human and the animal, being rather the erasure of that boundary: "A single abstract Animal for all the assemblages that effectuate it" (255).

12. Unlike even the most scrupulous discursive essay, which can merely hypothesize the relation between animal and human beings, Bresson's film visually anatomizes manifestations of their disparity and congruence. Derrida, in *The Animal,* for instance, would reclaim the animal from various forms of disparagement and lack—in his view constituted by Descartes's notion that the animal cannot "respond to a question" (84); by Kant's notion that the animal does not have the concept of the "first person" or "I" (93); by Levinas's notion that the animal is "outside of the ethical circuit" (106); by Lacan's that the animal might know how "to pretend" but not "to lie" (128); by Heidegger's notion that the animal cannot die but rather merely "stops living" or "croaks" (154); and, in Derrida's conclusion, by Heidegger's claim that the animal does not have access to the "as such." For, while the initial charge against the animal is that it cannot think and cannot refer to itself, a second substantial charge is that the animal cannot apprehend a thing objectively outside of its utility. Thus paraphrasing Heidegger, Derrida writes: "The lizard . . . has a relation to the stone that appears to it, to the sun that appears to it, but they don't appear to it *as* stone, *as* sun" (156). Insisting that the human also cannot see the "'as such' purely" (the human too sees from a "utilitarian, perspective-making project" [160]), Derrida suggests that the reclamation of the error in which deficiencies are attributed to the animal "would consist in pluralizing" our understanding of "the 'as such,' and, instead of simply giving speech back to the animal, or giving to the animal what the human deprives it of . . . in marking that the human is . . . similarly 'deprived' . . . and that there is no pure and simple 'as such'" (160).

Yet these subtractions from the human (of the "as such") and these additions to the animal—Derrida's greatest addition is perhaps the pluralization "*animot*," because "we have to envisage the existence of 'living creatures,' whose plurality cannot be assembled within the single figure of an animality that is simply opposed to humanity" (47)—remain abstract. Derrida cannot imagine a nonhypothetical convergence of animal and human forms of embodiment that is not based on a plus-and-minus arrangement, as, for instance, Montaigne and Bresson do, as discussed in the text. The visual immediacy of Bresson's images and of Montaigne's descriptive particularities pierce through the diagrammatic abstraction that inflects so much writing on this topic, again and again fleshing out correspondences that in Bresson's film the spectator immediately beholds with evidential certainty.

13. This would be in distinction to Bresson's other films—for instance, to *Pickpocket* and *Un condamné à mort s'est échappé ou Le vent souffle où veut*, where narrative and rhythmic factors corroborate each other.

14. Critical responses to Bresson's 1966 film, however diverse, have remained fixated on its enigmatic Christological elements, as in the following representative examples. The first full-length treatment of the film, Nick Browne's classic 1977 essay, explores Bresson's transfer of focus from an "*identification* with character" to an "*attention* to the image" ("Narrative Point of View:

The Rhetoric of *Au Hasard, Balthazar*," *Film Quarterly* [1977]: 25). Yet the upshot of this sophisticated analysis (still the strongest articulation of "the problems" posed for filmic narration when the "central depicted consciousness is not human" [21]) is an "allegory" that "has as its model . . . the story of the Christian resurrection" (29): "Bresson is not speaking of animals, but of the humble of spirit" (28). In Lindley Hanlon's 1986 scene-by-scene reading of Bresson's film, in which antinomies and disjunctions that structure *Balthazar* are complexly scrutinized, it is nonetheless the allegorical element that ultimately pervades the examination; hence Gérard is the "anti-Christ" (*Fragments: Bresson's Film Style* [Cranbury, NJ: Fairleigh Dickinson University Press, 1986], 113), while "the Christ-like nature of [his] suffering" renders Balthazar "a lamb of God" (86), associations conveyed through parataxis (see 97–98). The most recent recapitulation of this type of exegesis is Tony Pipolo's 2010 study, which fastens the identification of Balthazar as a "Christ figure" whose redemption is compromised by the film's conclusion (*Robert Bresson: A Passion for Film* [Oxford: Oxford University Press, 2010], 186, 205–8) to features of Apuleius's *The Golden Ass* (185) and to Prince Myshkin in Dostoevsky's *The Idiot*, whose own "nobility," Pipolo argues, is attributed to the animal (186).

Bresson's elusive remarks about his film ("The donkey is the entire Bible, Old Testament and New Testament") licensed the language, though not the reductiveness, of these readings, as when Bresson described Balthazar as "a living creature that is completely humble, completely holy, but happens to be a donkey" (quoted in Joseph Cunneen, *Robert Bresson: A Spiritual Style in Film* [New York: Bloomsbury Academic, 2003], 98). Because the "but" of such a sentence separates the quality of humility from the animal that instantiates it, Bresson's remark goes against the grain of the Christological readings that would fuse the two in the reading he helped promote. Other critics have realized the implausibility of a transcendental reading of *Balthazar*, arguing, as James Quandt does, that *Balthazar* relies on a "proliferation of signs" that link the donkey with Christ, such as "the donkey's death, serene and glorious," even as "Bresson's lucidity sees the death differently, as the prolonged expiry of an old, abused animal . . . too exhausted to do anything but collapse to the earth" (text accompanying the Criterion DVD disc of the film, adapted from *The Hidden God: Film and Faith*, ed. Mary Lea Bandy and Antonia Monda [New York: Museum of Modern Art, 2003]). Put differently by Shaviro in one of the most powerful analyses of Bresson's films: "The radical incompossibility of worldly and spiritual existence is what must be incarnated and materialized" (*Cinematic Body*, 249–50).

Still the best essay on Bresson's sanctity (written two years before *Balthazar*) is Susan Sontag's 1964 "Spiritual Style in the Films of Robert Bresson" (in Quandt, *Robert Bresson*, 57–71), which analyzes Bresson's style as "antiromantic" (69), antipsychological (65), "antidramatic" (62), and antireligious in any conventional sense (68). A "spiritual style" is committed to "coldness" and "emotional distance . . . because all identification with characters is an impertinence" (58–60). To negate, purify, "pare down," and disidentify is to discover what is "necessary" (71), a recognition Sontag locates at the core of the "spiritual."

My understanding of Bresson's commitment to immanence rather than to transcendence follows Sontag's, Shaviro's, and Quandt's. But my essay goes in a different direction. I argue that the oppositions of redemption and unredeemed materiality cannot withstand the dynamism of a parallel set of terms (animal eye and human eyes, beauty and cruelty), continuously held against each other through a polyrhythmia, which—in the film rather than in its frame—displaces that binary.

15. Heidegger, *Being and Time*, trans. John Macquarrie and Edward Robinson (New York: Harper & Row, 1962), 308.

16. Godard and Delahaye, "The Question," 462.

17. Godard and Delahaye, "The Question," 459. Similarly, the sound of the rain when it falls on Balthazar's hoofs as he stands outside the barn where Marie and Gérard are lovers rhymes with the sound of rain falling from the empty sky after an apocalyptic peal of thunder, and with the sound of rain around a pail from which Balthazar drinks, as well as with the patter outside the miser's door where Marie, drenched from a downpour, seeks shelter. The film also rhymes materials: hay covers the ground where the children frolic with the donkey; it is the bed of his near-euthanizing, but also the place where Marie and Gérard make love; and the burden the donkey pulls once on a cart so absurdly overloaded that it spills animal and driver onto hay that becomes a cushion that protects them from the fall.

18. Maurice Merleau-Ponty, "Indirect Language and the Voices of Silence," in *Signs*, trans. Richard C. McCleary (Evanston: Northwestern University Press, 1964), 76–77.

19. Bresson does not pan from one to the other: "*Traveling* or *panning* shots do not correspond to the movements of the eye. This is to separate the eye from the body" (*N* 99).

20. Bresson, describing the "ejaculatory force of the eye," elaborated: "To set up a film is to bind persons to each other and to objects by looks. . . . One single mystery of persons and objects" (*N* 22–23, 26). In *Balthazar* there is a third element, the animal, constellated in relation to the other two.

21. Godard and Delahaye, "The Question," 479.

22. Bresson asserted that since "the life of a donkey is a very even life, very serene," it was "necessary to find a character who would be parallel to the donkey . . . who would give the film that dramatic rise that was necessary for it" (Godard and Delahaye, "The Question," 454). Bresson linked the donkey and the girl on the basis of shared "suffering. . . . Example: in the miser's house. One refuses food to her (she is even forced to steal a pot of jam) in the same way that one refuses oats to the donkey. She undergoes the same jolts as he. She undergoes lust, too. She undergoes, not rape, perhaps, not exactly, but something that is almost a rape" (459).

23. Such containment demonstrated Bresson's conviction that the projection of affect is fictitious: "For want of truth, the public gets hooked on the false. Falconetti's way of casting her eyes to heaven, in Dreyer's film, used to draw tears" (*N* 127). "If an actor projects himself elsewhere [he] is absent even from his own image" (interview conducted by Donald Richie, Criterion disc of *Balthazar*). What Bresson sought, in distinction, was not actors who "make gestures"—not actors who are "uninhabited" (Godard and Delahaye, "The Question," 467)—but rather models who are "involuntarily expressive" (*N* 81). Of containment Bresson wrote: "Debussy himself used to play with the piano's lid down" (*N* 52).

24. Sontag's characterization ("Spiritual Style," 65). Bresson's cultivation of inexpressiveness in his models might productively be illuminated by Leo Bersani and Ulysse Dutoit's analysis of a kind of seeing in Godard's *Contempt*, in which "when subjects and objects are eliminated, the exaggerations of expressiveness lose their seductive appeal." In this account, to leave expressiveness behind is to leave subjectivity behind, to emerge into, and even "emit," a light "blocked by our expressive being" (*Forms of Being: Cinema, Aesthetics, Subjectivity* [London: British Film Institute, 2004], 70).

25. Merleau-Ponty, *The Visible and the Invisible*, ed. Claude Lefort, trans. Alphonso Lingis (Evanston: Northwestern University Press, 1968), 136. Repeatedly the camera illuminates objects from angles that exceed a person's vision of them: in the car where Marie and Gérard sit we see, from the perspective of Marie's position, the slip peek out from under her hem (though in fact she does not look at it) rather than from the perspective of Gérard's position (though he does

look at it, but out of the corner of his eye). Similarly, when the camera records Marie's regard of Balthazar's eye, it also commingles her gaze with ours, since it is our seeing of her seeing of Balthazar's ostensible seeing of Gérard in her car that constitutes vision that is interpenetrated.

26. Merleau-Ponty, *The Visible and the Invisible*, 141.

27. Merleau-Ponty, *The Visible and the Invisible*, 142.

28. He elaborated: "No actors. (No directing of actors.) No parts. (No learning of parts.) No staging. But the use of working models, taken from life. *Being* (models) instead of *seeming* (actors)" (*N* 14). In *Balthazar* even the donkey was untrained: "I wanted that animal to be even as an animal, crude matter" (Godard and Delahaye, "The Question," 478), as elaborated later in the essay.

29. See "What Remains of a Rembrandt Torn into Little Squares All the Same Size and Shot Down the Toilet," where Jean Genet writes of his realization of the "the secret . . . irreducible domain" behind the "charming or . . . monstrous appearance" in which "I was identical to this man," an identity, as indicated in the text, also discoverable in the "sightless eyes" of dead animals. "Except that a phenomenon, for which I don't even know a name, seems infinitely to divide this single man, splits him into the accidents of appearance, and makes each of the fragments foreign to us" (in *Fragments of the Artwork*, trans. Charlotte Mandell [Stanford: Stanford University Press, 2003], 95, 94, 97).

30. Richie interview, Criterion disc. Systematically preventing the models from thinking about how they appeared, Bresson explained: "They don't know how they are doing on screen. They aren't shown the previous day's rushes . . . so they won't watch themselves on screen and try to correct themselves as most actors do. . . . I ask the actors to learn their lines ignoring their meaning, as if they didn't have a meaning, as if the words were just syllables. As if sentences weren't made of words but of syllables. The meaning comes upon them unaware . . . when I set them loose in the film."

31. Deleuze elaborates on automaticity in the films of Eric Rohmer, Carl Dreyer, and Bresson in language that echoes Bresson's *Notes on the Cinematographer*: "The automatic image demands a new conception of the role or of the actor but also of thought itself" (*Cinema 2*, 178). The point about automatism in Deleuze's understanding of it is its alienation from the world as we know it: "The automaton is pure, as bereft of ideas as of feelings, reduced to the automatism of segmented daily gestures, but endowed with autonomy" (178). Or in Bresson's own characterization of his models' suppression of thought and intention: "The thing that matters is not what they show me but what they hide from me, and above all, *what they do not suspect is in them*" (*N* 15).

32. Bert Cardullo, "Spirituality as Style: Robert Bresson in Conversation, June 1983, part 2," in *The Films of Robert Bresson: A Casebook*, ed. Bert Cardullo (London: Anthem Press, 2009), 212. In *Notes on the Cinematographer* Bresson adds: "'Tout mouvement nous découvre' (Montaigne). But it only reveals us if it is automatic (not commanded, not willed)" (131).

33. In "Of the Power of the Imagination" Montaigne writes: "We do not command our hair to stand on end or our skin to shiver with desire or fear. The hand often moves itself to where we do not send it. . . . As for our will, . . . does it always will what we would will it to will? Doesn't it often will what we forbid it to will?" (in *The Complete Essays of Montaigne*, trans. Donald Frame [Stanford: Stanford University Press, 1965], 72, 73; hereafter abbreviated *E* and cited parenthetically).

34. With respect to the question of animal communication, Montaigne writes: "How could they not speak to one another? They certainly speak to us, and we to them" (*E* 335). Thus Montaigne, for instance, extols the "pure logic" of the dog deducing the path taken by his master

(*E* 339); the "ratiocination" of the fox who puts his ear to the ice to hear whether the water beneath it is near or far away (*E* 337); the intelligence of the elephant who can reveal to the master that the keeper is robbing him of "half the ration ordered for him" (*E* 342) by using his trunk to divide his barley into two portions.

35. This is the whole passage: "We would know no more than a stone, if we did not know there is sound, smell, light, taste, measure, weight, softness, hardness, roughness, color, smoothness, breadth, depth. These are the base and the principles of the whole edifice of our knowledge. . . . Knowledge is nothing else but sensation" (*E* 443–44).

36. Since animal senses are more acute than ours, Montaigne adds, "To judge the action of [our own] senses, then, we should first of all be in agreement with the animals" (*E* 452). Maybe, he speculates, some animals perceive the true nature of objects not only on the basis of more sharply honed senses but also on the basis of a superior physiology: "When we press our eye, we perceive the bodies that we are looking at as longer and more extended. Many animals have an eye thus pressed. So this lengthiness is perhaps the real shape of this body, not that which our eyes assign to it in their ordinary position" (*E* 452).

37. Derrida, *The Animal*, 12.

38. "The things one can express with the hand, with the head, with the shoulders!" (*N* 124). What is expressed is "the enigma peculiar to each living creature" (*N* 43).

39. "Maybe I'm your man, the killer," Gérard, the hoodlum, says to the police provocatively when he is brought in for questioning about a murder. But as they are on the verge of booking him, he insists, "I'm innocent." "You're the killer," he taunts Arnold.

40. Charles Barr argues that there is a conflict between Arnold's willing not to drink and his compulsive alcoholism (as there is a conflict between Marie's "conscious will and the way she finds herself acting"), while, "in contrast," Gérard is a character who wills the torment he inflicts, as when he slicks down a road and causes a car to skid ("*Au hasard, Balthazar*," in Cameron ed., *Films of Robert Bresson*, 110–11).

41. In *Balthazar* characterological distinctions are consistently elided, most dramatically when the camera rhythmically juxtaposes shots that separate Marie from the miser (she sits in his kitchen on a chair across from his chair) and shots that join her to him (she sits on his lap with her back to him). Bresson at once makes Marie and the miser perfect opposites (Marie with her back to the miser iconically illustrates that each does not see what the other sees: there is a frictive relation between her idealism and his cynicism) and illuminates what brings them together: each has a vision deformed by a passion whose persuasiveness does not regard the reality that ostensibly sets it into motion. "What do you see in that boy?" Marie's mother asks, wondering how Marie can be in thrall to a figure so small and brutal. But Marie is indifferent to Gérard's stature and his sadism, as the miser, mopping his brow with an excruciated look as he whips the animal, is indifferent to his own sadism, to any pain but his own, which alone commands his respect. In Bresson's film we are repeatedly shown characters who have nothing in common but are nonetheless authentically linked at a depth by cruelty.

42. Fyodor Dostoevsky, *The Idiot* (1869), trans. Constance Garnett (New York, 1981), 53; hereafter abbreviated *I* and cited parenthetically in the text. In "Bresson, Dostoevsky" Mireille Latil Le Dantec alludes to "the conscious or unconscious impregnation of *The Idiot* and *The Insulted and the Injured*" in *Balthazar* and *Le Diable probablement*: the "progression toward absurdity and catastrophe, mixing several stories that revolve around the donkey, appears to be the poetic equivalent of the Idiot's universe" (in Quandt, *Robert Bresson*, 335–36). As indicated, I see a more specific connection. Among the passing references to *Balthazar* and *The Idiot*, see

Keith Reader, *Robert Bresson* (Manchester: Manchester University Press, 2000), 78; Cunneen, *Robert Bresson: A Spiritual Style in Film*, 98; and, more extensively, Pipolo, *A Passion for Film*, 186–207 passim.

43. Godard and Delahaye, "The Question," 478. Although Bresson discounts *The Idiot* as the "idea" for his film, he comments on the passage in which Myshkin is brought to his senses by the bray of the ass: "To have an idiot transformed by an animal, to have him see life through an animal, who passes for an idiot but is of an intelligence . . . to compare him to an animal that passes for an idiot . . . that is magnificent. . . . That is genius" (Godard and Delahaye, "The Question," 477–78). Further linking the donkey in *Balthazar* with that in *The Idiot* is Lizaveta's retort to Myshkin: "One of us may even fall in love with an ass. . . . It's happened in mythology" (*I* 53), which is echoed by Gérard's watching Marie gaze rapturously at Balthazar: "She may love him and he her. In mythology. . . ."

44. Dostoevsky, *Crime and Punishment*, trans. Richard Pevear and Larissa Volokhonsky (New York: Vintage Classics, 1993), 55–56.

45. Even if Bresson had not frequently drawn on Dostoevsky for his films, one would see an analogy between the torture of Balthazar and that of the gray mare (also noticed in passing by Hanlon, *Fragments*, 86) because of the relentlessness of each, both leading to the animals' deaths, and because of the senselessness of each, made more horrific by Dostoevsky's depiction of the communal participation in the violence ("Several fellows . . . drunk, seize whatever they can find—whips, sticks, a shaft—and run to the dying mare" [*Crime and Punishment*, 58]), a communal violence reiterated in Bresson by Gérard's, Arnold's, his gang's, and the miser's repeated beating of the donkey. The beating of a donkey or horse is also a topos in John Gay's *Trivia*, William Hogarth's *Stages of Cruelty*, Henry Fielding's *Champion*, Charles Dickens's *Oliver Twist* and Joseph Conrad's *The Secret Agent*.

46. Dostoevsky, *Crime and Punishment*, 56.

47. Bresson's use of the Schubert has been variously interpreted, for instance, as "the narrator's musical 'voice'" (Browne, "Narrative Point of View," 28); as Balthazar's voice, in that the donkey can't speak "except through the music of Franz Schubert" (Donald Richie, "Bresson and Music," in Quandt, ed., *Robert Bresson*, 302); and, in its lullaby quality, as a conveyor of "nostalgic reminders of childhood" (Cunneen, *Robert Bresson: A Spiritual Style in Film*, 100).

Bresson said about the Schubert: "I did not know how to fill the silences. I used this piece as a kind of language for the donkey's soul, a *leitmotiv*" (Godard and Delahaye, "The Question," 507), but such a claim produces the sentimental ascription of human attributes to the animal that the film in fact avoids. If, once the film begins, the sections of Schubert's sonata are also used as a transition from one scene to another; as music that accommodates the emotional shift from one mood to another; or as punctuation to intensify sadness, anger, or danger, these functions remain subordinate to the film's more primary correlation of animal and human sounds.

The second time we hear the Schubert in conjunction with the donkey's braying, Balthazar, having run away from men chasing him with a pitchfork, returns to Marie's barn. In a third instance of their proximity, Gérard steals Balthazar and, loading him up with contraband, leads him toward the border. In other scenes the braying without the music and the music without the braying recall each other like complementary voices. Thus, when Bresson wrote: "Bring together things that have as yet never been brought together and did not seem predisposed to be so" (*N* 51), he might have been speaking (though he wasn't) of this remarkable congruence.

48. Thus, Bresson would have agreed with Agamben's claim that "in identifying himself with language, the speaking man places his own muteness outside of himself, as already and not yet human" (*The Open*, 34–35).

49. Roland Barthes, "The Third Meaning: Research Notes on Some Eisenstein Stills," in *Image Music Text*, trans. Stephen Heath (New York: Hill and Wang, 1977), 61, 62, 63. An obvious meaning is what "comes to seek me out" with clarity, that "which presents itself quite naturally to the mind," whereas an obtuse meaning, "at once persistent and fleeting, smooth and elusive" (54), is "supplementary" (64). Barthes adds: "What the obtuse meaning disturbs, sterilizes, is metalanguage (criticism)" (61). Writing of Eisenstein's films in particular: obtuse meanings are the subversion of narrative but also "a seal endorsing the whole of the work" (64). Obtuse meanings have "a quite different analytical segmentation to that in shots and sequences."

50. Philippe Lacoue-Labarthe, "The Echo of the Subject," in *Typography: Mimesis, Philosophy, Politics* (Cambridge: Harvard University Press, 1989), 196, 160, 201. Lacoue-Labarthe bases his startling conclusions on Emile Benveniste's discussion of the etymology of *rhuthmos*, the latter defining rhythm as something that cannot be grasped. According to Benveniste, as glossed by Lacoue-Labarthe, "If *skhema* designates 'a fixed, realized form posited as an object' (a *stable* form, therefore a figure or *Gestalt*), *rhuthmos*, on the other hand, is 'the form at the moment it is taken by what is in movement, mobile, fluid, the form that has no organic consistency.' It is, Benveniste adds, 'improvised, momentaneous, modifiable' form. . . . Repetition in its difference . . . conditions [*rhuthmos*'s] possibility'" (200–1). In Lacoue-Labarthe's analysis, Benveniste's characterization of rhythm—of a mobility that preempts figuration and unity—applies not only to music, it equally applies to autobiography, because such self-division and vacillation also become "the condition of possibility for the subject" (195). Since "there is no 'proper image' with which to identify totally," the subject's "only chance of 'grasping itself' lies in . . . oscillating *between* figure and figure." This destabilizing division of the figural connects "musical obsession" with "autobiographical compulsion" (175). See also Emile Benveniste, "The Notion of 'Rhythm' in Its Linguistic Expression," in *Problems in General Linguistics*, trans. Mary Elizabeth Meek (Coral Gables: University of Miami Press, 1971), 281–88, 312.

51. Sergei Eisenstein, *Film Form: Essays in Film Theory and The Film Sense*, ed. and trans. Jay Leyda ([1957]; Cleveland: World, 1968), 40, 37, and *Selected Works*, vol. 2, *Towards a Theory of Montage*, ed. Michael Glenny and Richard Taylor (London: British Film Institute, 1991), 236, 229. In Deleuze's understanding of this effacing of conflict in the work of a figure whom he called a "cinematographic Hegel": "If Eisenstein is a dialectician, it is because he conceives of the violence of the shock [of the cinematographic image] in the form of opposition and the thought of the whole in the form of opposition overcome, or of the transformation of opposites" (*Cinema 2*, 210, 158).

52. In other Eisenstein formulations rhythmic and narrative elements are also treated as compatible, sometimes as conciliatory ("The rhythmic construct is always dogged by a cautious concern not to lose the narrative [and] the narrative . . . must always be taking account of the rhythm" [*Selected Works*, 2:229]), even as collaborative, not, therefore, as frictive in any ultimate effect, as when Eisenstein described the rhythmic elements in a series of shots in *The Strike* as "embodying a generalisation of the entire scene" (233), or as when of *Potemkin* he wrote that "rhythm functioned . . . as the supreme mode of expressing the inner tension of an emotion . . . integral to the [film's] plot" (238). In Eisenstein the frictive is subsumed by the depictive, though not exactly erased by it, whereas it remains unassimilated to narrative in Bresson.

53. "Un metteur en ordre: Robert Bresson," a 1966 French television show about *Balthazar*, featuring Bresson, Godard, Louis Malle, and members of *Balthazar*'s crew and cast; Criterion DVD of film.

54. In the stunning details of the two close-ups, sentience and its extinction are thus given to us with more tactile immediacy—with more intensity—than in any comparable images of the

armored human counterparts (and than of the tournaments and wars as recounted by the film's narrative). For the extreme states the warriors suffer are not visibly experienced by them, but in the resistant sheen of that metal are obstructed from being viewed as experienced.

55. Bresson is referring to the suicides in *Mouchette*, *Une femme douce*, and *Le Diable probablement*. Quoted in Paul Schrader, "Robert Bresson, Possibly" in Quandt, ed., *Robert Bresson*, 489.

56. "What no human eye is capable of catching, no pencil, brush, pen of pinning down, your camera catches without knowing what it is, and pins it down with a machine's scrupulous indifference" (*N* 36).

Of the mechanical exercises that suppress intention, will, and even consciousness in his models Bresson wrote, "Reduce to the minimum the share [the model's] consciousness has. Tighten the meshing within which he cannot any longer not be him" (*N* 58). In this way the camera captures the ontic and even the "constant, the eternal beneath the accidental" (*N* 56). Bresson elaborated: "THE BONDS THAT BEINGS AND THINGS ARE WAITING FOR, IN ORDER TO LIVE" (*N* 80).

57. Bresson adds: "And to make what you understand be understood, through the intermediary of a machine that does not understand it as you do" (*N* 79).

58. Godard and Delahaye, "The Question," 478, 479.

59. "Un metteur en ordre: Robert Bresson."

2

"OUTSIDE CHRIST": DOSTOEVSKY'S JOY

1. Fyodor Dostoevsky, *Crime and Punishment,* trans. Richard Pevear and Larissa Volokhonsky (New York: Vintage Classics, 1993), 55, 57; hereafter abbreviated *CP* and cited parenthetically.

2. Dostoevsky, *The Brothers Karamazov*, trans. Richard Pevear and Larissa Volokhonsky (New York: Vintage Classics, 1993), 580; hereafter abbreviated *BK* and cited parenthetically.

3. When Alyosha, to whom she has confided her monstrosity, leaves, she slams her finger in the door—"crushed it with all her might" (*BK* 585)—another stage in the economy in which pleasure at another's torture unsuccessfully wards off the masochistic enjoyment of one's own suffering. In Raskolnikov's mathematics, the old crone's death will also avert others' suffering: "Kill her and take her money, so that afterwards with its help you can devote yourself to the service of all mankind. . . . One death for hundreds of lives—it's simple arithmetic! And what does the life of this stupid, consumptive, and wicked old crone mean in the general balance?" (*CP* 65).

4. Dostoevsky, quoted in Jacques Catteau, *Dostoyevsky and the Process of Literary Creation,* trans. Audrey Littlewood (Cambridge: Cambridge University Press, 1989), 228.

5. I am not suggesting that the passages I consider are free of an economy. As Jacques Derrida demonstrates, all narrative, and in fact all language, is a "giving-taking" (*Given Time: I. Counterfeit Money*, trans. Peggy Kamuf [Chicago: University of Chicago Press, 1992], 81). But in the exchanges I consider, joy is not calculated as restitution for suffering; joy is not compensatory.

6. Dostoevsky, *The Idiot*, trans. Constance Garnett (New York: Bantam, 1981), 213; hereafter abbreviated *I* and cited parenthetically.

7. In Russian the words for happiness and joy are *radost'* (joy) and *schast'e* (happiness). Although in general *schast'e* evokes something caused, hence concrete and secular (corresponding

to the happenstance of the English "happiness"), and *radost'* something transcendental, in Russian the two words can pertain indiscriminately to either context, or they can even be evoked simultaneously. While in absolute instances Dostoevsky invokes *radost'* to signify joy, he also employs *schast'e* to indicate the less quotidian meaning. I distinguish between the quotidian and the transcendental senses according to the context; in quotations from the text, however, I adhere to the translation of the edition I am citing.

In an extraordinarily generous email reply (which I have edited) to my question about the distinction of the two words, dated August 15, 2007, the late James Rice writes: "That *schast'e* evokes something concrete and secular that is caused or bestowed, *radost'* something abstract and possibly spiritual, which emanates from an inward state, is buttressed by Max Vasmer's *Russisches Etymologisches Wörterbuch,* 3 vols. (Heidelberg, 1953–58). But Vasmer always offers two or more sides to [any] controversy. The famous *Dahl Dictionary* [1862] of provincialisms, archaisms, and much more (e.g. proverbs) serves up something more satisfactory. [Among other definitions, it associates] '*radost'* with any event or object giving rise . . . to inward spiritual feelings.' Two proverbs collected by [Vladimir] Dahl are these: 'Sow with tears, reap with joy (*radost'*)'; 'Joy (*radost'*) is not eternal, grief is not without end.' *The Soviet Academy of Sciences Russian Dictionary,* 17 vols. (Moscow, 1950–65), which gives meticulous definitions and specimens, quotes a minor nineteenth-century writer to illustrate that the words have a certain overlap as near-synonyms: 'An inexpressible sensation of *radost'* and *schast'e* took hold of me.' And Nikolai Chernyshevskii distinguishes the words, while drawing them together. 'In my *radost'* there were tears of *schast'e*.'"

But though, in the examples and sources provided by Rice, common usage both maintains and blurs the distinction between the two words, at the extreme—as in *The Brothers Karamazov* when Alyosha, his faith restored by Grushenka's kindness, returns to the hermitage where his elder lies dead, finds the smell that had shattered him two chapters earlier stronger than ever, and falls "down before the coffin as if it were a holy thing . . . joy, joy was shining in his mind and in his heart" (*BK* 359). The word Pevear and Volokhonsky translate "joy" is Dostoevsky's *radost'* ("*radost', radost' siiala v ume ego i v serdtse ego*"). The example is James Rice's. Rice's email concludes: "*Radost'* stands at the pivotal center of *The Brothers Karamazov*."

8. Dostoevsky, *Demons,* trans. Richard Pevear and Larissa Volokhonsky (New York: Knopf, 1994), 236; hereafter abbreviated *D* and cited parenthetically.

9. Joseph Frank, *Dostoevsky: The Miraculous Years, 1865–1871* (Princeton: Princeton University Press, 1995), 325, 317.

10. Hannah Arendt, *Love and Saint Augustine,* ed. Joanna Vecchiarelli Scott and Judith Chelius Stark (Chicago: University of Chicago Press, 1996), 7.

11. Dostoevsky, quoted in Joseph Frank, *The Mantle of the Prophet, 1871–1881* (Princeton: Princeton University Press, 2002), 712. I am therefore arguing with Rowan Williams's claim that, for Dostoevsky, "outside Christ" refers to worldly fact in distinction to a different kind of truth (see *Dostoevsky: Language, Faith, and Fiction* [Waco, TX: Baylor University Press, 2008], 30–31). There is not a "truth" of will and history outside of Christ and some superior "truth" ("more comprehensive than any given ensemble of facts" [26]) when it is allied with Christ. There are not two truths. That is what is so shocking about Dostoevsky's proposition. The shock is to someone who assumes Christ is equivalent to truth; the implication is that He might not be, while still being preferable to truth.

12. Arendt, *Love and Saint Augustine,* 14.

13. Dostoevsky wrote: "time is the relationship of being to non-being" (quoted in Catteau, *Dostoevsky and the Process of Literary Creation,* 372).

14. Although Myshkin is depicting his mental state during a period of idiocy, something about his characterization—leaving aside the violent fits—recalls the preoccupied state of an ordinary mind. This congruence between the idiot's mind and the ordinary mind (at least with respect to anxiety and inattention) is not the point of the description. But the effect is to insist on the efficacy of the remedy for all who are listening to Myshkin's narration. On such a premise, Aglaia asserts: "You might teach us, even [how to be happy]" (*I* 55). When Alexandra observes, "I've always been interested to know how people go out of their minds and recover again" (*I* 54), we can say that what sparks such interest is not the extremity of a plight beyond compare with her own, but rather a fascination with its near-recognizability.

15. "One minute . . . a flash of light . . . passed like a flash . . . the very second" (*I* 218–19). Just as the falling away of time ("*no more time*" [*I* 219]) must be represented by temporal marks, so, too, the passage's rendition of ecstatic consciousness necessarily avails itself of a sentience that, amplified, is reconceived. Myshkin thinks "if the condition [he experiences] was to be expressed in one word" it would be "quickening of self-consciousness . . . and at the same time of the direct sensation of existence in the most intense degree" (*I* 219); Pevear and Volokhonsky translate this word as "self-awareness and at the same time a self-sense immediate in the highest degree" (Fyodor Dostoevsky, *The Idiot,* trans. Richard Pevear and Larissa Volokhonsky [New York: Vintage Classics, 2003], 226). The words being translated are "*samosoznanie*" and "*samooshchushchenie*" (my thanks to Anne Eakin Moss for imparting the Russian words). But such consciousness, shaped by "serene, harmonious joy and hope" (*I* 218), could only surpass and render unrecognizable finite self-perception. Myshkin's expression of supreme gratitude ("for this moment one might give one's whole life!" [*I* 219]) is not voiced by a delimited self, for whom such a sacrifice would be calamitous. And if the rapturous state Myshkin describes is "filled with reason and ultimate cause" (Pevear and Volokhonsky's translation [225–26]), "reason" could not imply analytic or logical thought. The words "reason and ultimate cause" are omitted from Garnett's translation.

16. It has been claimed that Dostoevsky, appalled at Kirillov's perspective, parodies rather than endorses "Everything is good": "Kirillov stretches Panglossian optimism to its ultimate absurdity . . ." (W. J. Leatherbarrow, *Dostoevsky's* The Devils: *A Critical Companion* [Evanston: Northwestern University Press, 1999], 91). Yet Kirillov's indiscrimination might rather be understood in relation to Markel's "life is paradise" (*BK* 288), even as Markel's beatitude (a response to his own illness, rather than an acquiescence to others' violence) is not quite comparable to Markel's implicit embrace of "everything," which fails to register the shock of what "everything" might include.

17. Williams, *Dostoevsky: Language, Faith, and Fiction*, 53.

18. Williams, *Dostoevsky: Language, Faith, and Fiction*, 53.

19. Williams, *Dostoevsky: Language, Faith, and Fiction*, 54, 53.The phrase cited by Williams is Leatherbarrow's. But Williams extends the analysis: "the only figures ever shown in profile are demons and—sometimes—Judas Iscariot" (*Dostoevsky: Language, Faith, and Fiction*, 53). In Léonide Ouspensky and Vladimir Lossky's earlier formulation: "the icon is a likeness . . . of a deified prototype . . . an image . . . of flesh transfigured. . . . Consequently, everything which reminds of the corruptible human flesh is contrary to the very nature of the icon" (*The Meaning of Icons,* trans. G. E. H. Palmer and E. Kadloubovsky [Crestwood, NY: St. Vladimir's Seminary Press, 1982], 36).

Julia Kristeva touches on what "probably legitimized" the painting in the eyes of its purchasers—an "edging bearing the inscription *Jesus Nazarenus Rex Judaeorum*," which "includes, between the words of the inscription, five angels bearing the instruments of the martyrdom: the shaft, the crown of thorns, the scourge, the flogging column, the cross"—since this edging "recovers the evangelical meaning that [the painting] did not insistently contain in itself" ("Holbein's *Dead Christ*," in *Black Sun: Depression and Melancholia*, trans. Leon S. Roudiez [New York: Columbia University Press, 1989], 114–15).

Kristeva explores the painting's "originality," which "lies . . . in a vision of Christly death devoid of pathos and Intimist on account of its very banality" (115); its "*irony* toward transcendence" (118) in that it "maintains grief while humanizing it, without following the Italian path of negating pain and glorifying the arrogance of the flesh or the beauty of the beyond" (117); its "compositional asceticism" (123); and most especially its capacity to capture a "*melancholy moment* . . . an actual or imaginary despair, an actual or imaginary razing of symbolic values, including the value of life" (128). The essay is especially powerful in identifying Holbein's "minimalism" (138), which Kristeva situates "between classicism and mannerism" (137), and understands as at once the expression of Holbein's personality, and more broadly also a reflection of "the spirit of his time" (124). Finally, the chapter is remarkable in identifying the numerous vantages—psychoanalytic, religious, aesthetic—from which the "unbearable moments when meaning [is] lost" must be grasped (133).

20. For instance, Robert Hollander ("The Apocalyptic Framework of Dostoevsky's *The Idiot*," *Mosaic* 7.2 [1974]): 123–39) and David M. Bethea (*The Shape of the Apocalypse in Modern Russian Fiction* [Princeton: Princeton University Press, 1989], 96–104) identify figures of a Christ and anti-Christ in the scenes discussed above. Yet Dostoevsky's enigmatic figures precisely defy this symmetry.

21. The phrase "Rogozhin in the flesh" (*I* 398) prompts us to realize that what Ippolit sees is Rogozhin *out* of "the flesh," but utterly enveloped in the concreteness of anti-transcendence (like the "spiders in . . . the corners" of Svidrigailov's "eternity" [*CP* 289]). Such apparitions both assume and renounce materiality. That is what situates them between the vital and the spectral. Malleability in which flesh can metamorphically be put on and taken off is the ground on which the exchange of properties between the Christ and the "dumb beast" that kills Him is made intelligible. In each of these instances what mortifies life is made to seem indistinguishable from the life that is mortified.

22. Ippolit's inability to discern the difference between the semblance and the man inspires the same disgust as the transfer of "eternal Power" (*I* 396) from the Christ to the beast that crucified Him and retrospectively to the creature that "wriggl[ed]" (*I* 378), since in each instance, what mortifies life is drawn into appalling intimacy with the life that is mortified.

23. Norman Cohn, *Cosmos, Chaos, and Death: The Ancient Roots of the Apocalyptic Faith* (New Haven: Yale University Press, 1993), 219.

24. Georges Bataille, "Sacrifice, the Festival and the Principles of the Sacred World," in *The Bataille Reader*, ed. Fred Botting and Scott Wilson (Oxford: Blackwell Publishers, Inc., 1997), 215, 212. Joy, like "the sacred" in Bataille's account of it, "is that prodigious effervescence of life that, for the sake of duration, the order of things holds in check" while at death or some other threat to workaday arrangements, "this holding changes into a breaking-loose, that is, into violence" (214).

25. Bataille, "Sacrifice," 212, 215.

26. Like Myshkin's prisoner, Ippolit is reprieved, albeit comically, when the gun he fires to kill himself does not go off, so that he eventually dies not of a self-inflicted wound, but rather of his disease.

27. For instance, the Countess Du Barry on the verge of being guillotined, who "fell to screaming, '*Encore un moment*'" (*I* 190); "Stepan Glyebov in the eighteenth century. . . . impaled in the time of Peter . . . fifteen hours on the stake" (*I* 506); the man waiting to be executed who

"kissed the cross greedily" that the priest held up to him (*I* 61); the unhinged General about to have a stroke who cries from the middle of the street: "When you bury me, write on the tombstone: 'Here lies a dead soul!' 'Disgrace pursues me!'" (*I* 489).

28. Dostoevsky, *The Notebooks for* The Idiot, ed. Edward Wasiolek, trans. Katharine Strelsky (Chicago: University of Chicago Press, 1967), 233–34.

29. "He was an *indispensable* image to Aglaia. . . . He dominated Rogozhin. . . . He dominated Ganya. . . . He stirred up the Prince" (Dostoevsky, *The Notebooks for* The Idiot, 234).

30. Apollon Maykov to Dostoevsky, quoted in Catteau, *Dostoevsky and the Process of Literary Creation,* 397. Maykov analogizes the illumination in Dostoevsky's novel to the light cast on the figures in Karl Briullov's enormous canvas (1830–33), which depicts the eruption of Vesuvius in AD 79.

31. Dostoevsky, quoted in Mikhail Bakhtin, *Problems of Dostoevsky's Poetics* (Minneapolis: University of Minnesota Press, 1984), 97. This is the quotation in context: "Only one verification of [my convictions] exists—Christ. But this is no longer philosophy, it is faith, and faith is a red color."

32. Of course, the interludes of joy and suffering are also technically narrated. Yet Dostoevsky emphasizes the incongruity of the ostensible audience for these expressive fragments. Stavrogin has no feeling for the epiphany Kirillov unfolds for him. Myshkin reveals his joy to the brutish, brooding, uneducated Rogozhin, his demonic counterpart, who is unprepared to understand it. The polite bourgeois Epanchin establishment barely knows what Myshkin is talking about. One could argue that my reading underplays the novel's dialogism: Myshkin's idealism prompts Aglaia to fall in love with him. At the novel's end, Myshkin and Rogozhin lie together on the same bed next to Nastasya Filippovna, whom Rogozhin has murdered with a knife. Drawing the characters together in an ultimate intimacy, we are told, Myshkin's "tears flowed from his eyes on to Rogozhin's cheeks" (*I* 594). At the same time, while the two are structurally and diegetically interwoven, Myshkin's disquisitions—on how to be happy, on the joy that precedes the epileptic fit—might originate in dialogism, but reach outside of it in the evocation of an absolute state that can't be fully associated with character or situation because it *is* absolute. Such passages are self-contained, even soliloquy-like—external to the contexts that ostensibly situate them.

33. Roland Barthes, *Roland Barthes by Roland Barthes,* trans. Richard Howard (Berkeley: University of California Press, 1994), 94.

34. In *Revelation: Vision of a Just World* (Minneapolis: Fortress Press, 1991), Elizabeth Schüssler Fiorenza writes: "The author of Revelation does not separate the narrative structure into clear-cut segments or logical sequences, but he joins individual visions and cycles together by interweaving them with each other through the techniques of intercalation and inclusion" (34).

35. Barthes, *S/Z: An Essay,* trans. Richard Miller (New York: Hill and Wang, 1974), 177.

36. Ptitsyn is a usurer "trying to make his fortune by lending money at high interest" (*I* 86); Ferdyshtchenko explains he will ask to borrow money, while instructing Myshkin not to lend it to him (*I* 89). At Nastasya's nameday party Rogozhin drunkenly insists he will buy up Ganya ("I can buy the whole of you and your live-stock too" [*I* 108]). The captain's widow, Ippolit's mother, procures money from the general and lends it at exorbitant interest. Burdovsky, one of the nihilists, claims he is the illegitimate son of Pavlishtchev, Myshkin's benefactor, and comes to blackmail Myshkin to conceal it ("We demand, we demand, we demand, we don't beg" [*I* 260]). Ivolgin steals a pocketbook from Lebedyev (*I* 475–78). These monetary negotiations suffuse the novel, complementing the expenditures of affect with expenditures of capital so that there is no relation among *The Idiot*'s characters free of them.

37. Leonid Grossman, quoted in Bakhtin, *Problems of Dostoevsky's Poetics*, 15.

38. But also in Pevear's enumeration: "the demons . . . are ideas, that legion of isms that came to Russia from the West: idealism, rationalism, empiricism, materialism, utilitarianism, positivism, socialism, anarchism, nihilism, and, underlying them all, atheism" (*D* xvii).

39. That "topsy-turvy" (*I* 275) state of affairs is exemplified in *The Idiot*'s notion that "Socialists, both here and abroad, are nothing more than Liberals from the landed gentry of the serf-owning days" (*I* 324). "Liberals . . . are . . . the most stupid and dangerous of Conservatives" (*I* 325). In *Demons*, Shigalov explains his politics and those of the revolutionaries: "I got entangled in my own data, and my conclusion directly contradicts the original idea. . . . Starting from unlimited freedom, I conclude with unlimited despotism. I will add, however, that apart from my solution of the social formula, there can be no other" (*D* 402).

40. When Verkhovensky admits to Kirillov, "I never could understand why you want to kill yourself" (*D* 614), Kirillov replies: "God is necessary, and therefore must exist. . . . But I know that he does not and cannot exist. . . . Don't you understand that a man with these two thoughts cannot go on living?" (*D* 615). Elsewhere, Kirillov attributes his divinity to a "Self-will" that can be realized only if he kills himself (*D* 619).

41. Dostoevsky, *The Notebooks for* The Idiot, 233.

42. Kirillov confesses to killing the student Shatov (*D* 620). But there will be widespread implications, as Verkhovensky elaborates: "they'll figure out for themselves that it's Skvoreshniki. . . . once they find the corpse—it means what's written here is true, and so it's also true about Fedka. And what is Fedka? Fedka is the fire, he's the Lebyadkins; so everything was coming from here, from Filippov's house, and they didn't see a thing . . . that will put them into a real whirl! It won't even enter their minds about *our* people; it's Shatov, and Kirillov, and Fedka, and Lebyadkin; as for why they killed each other—there's another little question for them" (*D* 622).

43. This state of "exemption" must be distinguished from Raskolnikov's, who, above the law, does not care about his actions. Kirillov is indifferent not to his actions but to the uses to which others put them.

44. Martin Heidegger, *What Is Called Thinking*, trans. J. Glenn Gray (New York: Harper Colophon Books, 1968), 41.

45. Heidegger, *What Is Called Thinking*, 41.

46. Heidegger, *What Is Called Thinking*, 172, 173–74.

47. Heidegger, *What Is Called Thinking*, 237.

48. Dostoevsky's repeated association of death with joy, his suggestion that the perception of death precipitates joy, leads me to wonder whether the presence of death instigates a completely different way of relating to affect (as when the irascible Ippolit uncharacteristically asks: "what do you think would be the best way for me to die?" [*I* 507]). Death might thwart the propensity to identify with affect, and even reveal consciousness and unconsciousness to be crude ways of distinguishing where precisely joy might be situated when it is not delimited, when it can't be recognized as *ours*.

49. Heidegger, *What Is Called Thinking*, 237.

50. Georges Bataille, "Hegel, Death and Sacrifice," in *The Bataille Reader*, ed. Fred Botting and Scott Wilson (Malden, MA: Blackwell Publishers, Inc., 1997), 284.

51. Philippe Lacoue-Labarthe and Jean-Luc Nancy, *The Literary Absolute: The Theory of Literature in German Romanticism*, trans. Philip Barnard and Cheryl Lester (Albany: SUNY Press, 1988), 48.

Lacoue-Labarthe and Nancy examine the fragment—specifically as exemplified by Friedrich Schlegel's *Athenaeum*—as a romantic ideal, a romantic genre, and, revealed in Schlegel's practice, as a theory of romantic form. The fragment is an "essential incompletion" (42), but also a "totality" (44), and therefore "complete in itself" (43). Its most important attribute is "*Witz*" which "is a doublet of *Wissen*, knowledge . . . the French *esprit* and . . . the English *wit*." Essentially "*Witz* is . . . knowledge that is other than the knowledge of analytic and predicative discursivity" (53).

I should immediately acknowledge that in light of the characteristics too briefly sketched above, the passages I have identified as fragments in Dostoevsky's novels would not be considered as such by Nancy and Lacoue-Labarthe. They are too coherent, too intact, too fully narrativized, and too tangential to the plotted stories from which they are set off, while not being free of them. However, in their condensation, their epiphanic rendering of suffering and joy, these limit-point expressions of melancholy and ecstasy (which also exemplify a philosophy of time) are energized by a spirit and an intuitive understanding analogous to that described in relation to the fragment. So while Dostoevsky's passages are not governed by the interruptive grammar of "anacoluthon" and "asyndeton" that "short-circuits" utterance in Barthes's characterization of the fragment (Barthes, *Roland Barthes*, 93), nor are they self-contained—like Raskolnikov's dreams or the Elder Zosima's narrative transcribed by Alyosha; these passages disrupt the plot. They do so because they are so immersed in the affective states they express as momentarily to be constituted by those states, pulling away from character, context, and even content, since the extremity of the affect they manifest has the feel of surpassing any content that could account for it.

52. Lacoue-Labarthe and Nancy, *The Literary Absolute*, 53.

53. Tikhon, the monk to whom Stavrogin reveals both his dream of joy and his criminality, comments: "Certain places in your account are stylistically accentuated; as if you . . . seize upon every little detail just to astonish the reader with an unfeelingness that is not in you" (*D 706*). Such hyperbole suffuses the language of Stavrogin's confession.

54. Lacoue-Labarthe and Nancy, *The Literary Absolute*, 48.

3

THE SIGHT OF DEATH IN TOLSTOY

1. Rainer Maria Rilke, *Letters of Rainer Maria Rilke 1910–1926*, trans. Jane Bannard Greene and M. D. Herter Norton (New York: Norton & Company, 1972), 149.

2. The first and third quotation are from "The Memoirs of a Madman," in Leo Tolstoy, *Tolstoy's Short Fiction*, ed. and trans. Michael R. Katz (New York: Norton Critical Editions, 2008), 307, 308; hereafter abbreviated MM and cited parenthetically; the second is from "The Death of Ivan Ilych," in Leo Tolstoy, *The Death of Ivan Ilych and Other Stories*, trans. Aylmer Maude and J. D. Duff (New York: Signet Classics, 1960), 130; hereafter abbreviated II and cited parenthetically.

3. After the death of his youngest son, Ivan, Tolstoy wrote: "One must always live as though a favourite child is dying in a room nearby. He is always dying. And I am always dying" (*Tolstoy's Diaries, Vol. II 1895–1910*, ed. and trans. R. F. Christian [New York: Scribner, 1985], 402).

4. Tolstoy, *Resurrection*, trans. Anthony Briggs (New York: Penguin, 2009), 423. In Simonson's opinion: "We have come to define the earth, after observing only its crust, as inorganic matter. Not true" (417).

I have learned from critical discussions of both strains of writing, especially from Lydia Ginzburg's analysis of contradiction in Tolstoy's representation of character in *On Psychological*

Prose (Princeton: Princeton University Press, 1991); E. B. Greenwood's "Tolstoy and Religion," in *New Essays on Tolstoy*, ed. Malcolm Jones (Cambridge: Cambridge University Press, 1978), 149–74; Inessa Medzhibovskaya's *Tolstoy and the Religious Culture of His Time: A Biography of a Long Conversion, 1845–1887* (Lanham, MD: Lexington Books, 2008); Richard F. Gustafson's *Leo Tolstoy: Resident and Stranger* (Princeton: Princeton University Press, 1986); Donna Tussing Orwin's *Tolstoy's Art and Thought, 1847–1880* (Princeton: Princeton University Press, 1993); Caryl Emerson's "Tolstoy's Aesthetics," in *Cambridge Companion to Tolstoy*, ed. Donna Tussing Orwin (Cambridge: Cambridge University Press, 2002), 237–51; Douglas Robinson's "Zarazhenie: Tolstoy's Infection Theory," in *Estrangement and the Somatics of Literature: Tolstoy, Shklovsky, Brecht* (Baltimore: Johns Hopkins University Press, 2008), 1–75; and Gary Saul Morson's writing about Tolstoy in general and about *War and Peace* in particular. See especially *Hidden in Plain View: Narrative and Creative Potentials in* War and Peace (Stanford: Stanford University Press, 1987).

5. Tolstoy, *A Confession* (1882), in *Leo Tolstoy: A Confession and Other Religious Writings*, trans. Jane Kentish (New York: Penguin, 1987), 75, 64; "An Appeal to the Clergy" (1902), in *Last Steps: The Late Writings of Leo Tolstoy*, ed. Jay Parini (New York: Penguin, 2009), 173.

Tolstoy's denunciation of the twelve articles of belief formulated at the Council of Nicaea opens into an invective about the Church's teaching on Christianity, which emphasizes "miracles, the movement of a star, songs from the sky, talks with the devil, the turning of water into wine, walking on the water, healings, calling people back to life, and, finally, the resurrection of Jesus himself, and his flying up into the sky" ("An Appeal to the Clergy" [1902], in *Last Steps*, 173).

In "What Is Religion and of What Does Its Essence Consist?" (1902) Tolstoy continues his invective: "There can be nothing as immoral as those dreadful teachings according to which an angry and vengeful God punishes everyone for the sin of Adam, or that he sent his son to earth to save us, knowing beforehand that the men would murder him and be damned for it" (*A Confession and Other Religious Writing*, 95). Also included in the list of the "immoral" and "absurd . . . teachings" (95) is the idea that "the son of God was killed in order to save people and that those who do not believe it will be punished by God with eternal torment" (96). The perversions of sacraments and rites are equally abhorrent to Tolstoy: "I reject all the Sacraments" as "coarse, degrading sorcery" ("A Reply to the Synod's Edict of Excommunication" [1901], in *Last Steps*, 145). Finally, he challenges the clergy: "You believe you ought to say. . . . that God is One and Three; that Jesus flew up into the sky and will come back from there to judge those who will rise in their bodies" but "you do not believe" these things. "One may utter words that have no sense, but one cannot *believe* what has no sense" ("Appeal to the Clergy" [1902], in *Last Steps*, 182).

True faith requires an emancipation from the hypnotism of Christianity's manifestos and an adherence to its clear and simple "principles . . . that there is a God . . . that in man dwells a spark from that Divine Origin, which man, by his way of living, can increase or decrease in himself; that to increase this divine spark man must suppress his passions and increase love in himself; and that the practical means to attain this result is to do to others as you would they should do to you" (*Last Steps*, 156–57). Tolstoy writes: these "principles" are also common to "Brahmanism, Confucianism, Taoism, Hebraism, Buddhism, and even Mohammedanism" (*Last Steps*, 156). In his diary Tolstoy adds, "people of advanced views . . . pointing the way to an eternally remote state of perfection" include "Christ, Buddha, yes, and Kant and Emerson" (*Diaries*, 599).

6. Tolstoy, "A Reply to the Synod's Edict of Excommunication," 145.

7. The disparate tenets of this story cannot be assimilated to each other by the conventional gloss that would make them compatible (though there is death, it can be succeeded by something like life's residue in virtuous acts), for Tolstoy's language ("if this [poverty] was not, then

neither was there death . . . tearing asunder within me" [MM 313]) is more radical because it literally goes beyond the platitude that virtue bestows its own afterlife.

It is generally assumed that Tolstoy's *A Confession* (1882), begun in 1878, marks the date of his conversion. But both *War and Peace* (1863–1869) and *Anna Karenina* (1873–1878), which well precede it, attest to his characters' beliefs in a God, a belief that coexists with a terror of death, while the biographical incident on September 2, 1869, that it has been said provided the foundation for "Memoirs of a Madman" (1883), anticipates the deathlessness theorized in *On Life* (1887). My point is that Tolstoy's anomalous spirituality cannot be documented in a straight-line chronology; as Medzhibovskaya explains in *Tolstoy and the Religious Culture of His Time*, it did not occur in a "crisis-begotten tragic moment" (xv), but "offers a glimpse into a process that is overly long, laden with suffering, and punctuated by painful setbacks" (xv). Complicating the understanding of this crisis, she writes: Tolstoy's "thoughts on death and immortality . . . are considered inauthentic sources of conversion in Russian contexts—in Tolstoy studies, Orthodox theology, and Russian religious thought" (xiv–xv).

8. See Tolstoy, *Life* (1887), in *What Is to Be Done and Life* (New York: Thomas Y. Crowell Co., 1899), 381; hereafter abbreviated *L* and cited parenthetically. All citations are to this edition, but I refer to Tolstoy's work as *On Life* in keeping with Aylmer Maude's translation (1934, 1959) and the title frequently used in the critical literature, for instance, in Medzhibovskaya's biography.

9. "He whose understanding mattered would understand" (II 152), Ivan Ilych thinks when he means to say, but does not say, "forgive," while in "Master and Man," Vasily Andreevich feels himself summoned: "He came and called him; and it was he who'd called him and told him to lie down on Nikita" (Tolstoy, "Master and Man," in *Tolstoy's Short Fiction*, 232).

10. In *On Life* Tolstoy expresses skepticism that death could ever be thought other than illusory: "there is nothing more fantastic than discussions of the development of life in time" (*L* 323). Since "true life *is* . . . it cannot either begin or perish" (*L* 354). Before such alien claims, Turgenev expressed his own incredulity: "He has plunged headlong into another sphere: has surrounded himself with Bibles and Gospels in nearly all languages, and has written a whole heap of papers. He has a trunk full of these mystical ethics and of various pseudo-interpretations. He read me some of it, which I simply do not understand. . . . I told him, '*That* was not the real thing'; but he replied: 'It is just the real thing'" (quoted in Aylmer Maude, *The Life of Tolstoy: Later Years* [New York: Dodd, Mead and Company, 1910], 19–20).

11. My essay does not discuss that writing of Tolstoy's which treats ethics as an independent subject, unlinked to the belief in death or deathlessness, though that writing, often overtly Christian, implicitly makes such a connection. "Letter on Non-Resistance" (1896), enjoins its readers ("you, who today live and tomorrow will die" [*Last Steps* 83]) to attend to the urgency of ethical action. On February 2, in *A Calendar of Wisdom: Daily Thoughts to Nourish the Soul*, Tolstoy returned to the topic several times, as in this reflection: "*There are two different states of human existence: first, to live without thinking of death; second, to live with the thought that you approach death with every hour of your life*" (*A Calendar of Wisdom: Daily Thoughts to Nourish the Soul*, trans. Peter Sekirin [New York: Scribner, 1997], 45).

12. This is Prince Andrew's characterization of his reflections on death—distinguishing something that is thought from an experience that is visceral and instantaneous. Tolstoy, *War and Peace*, ed. George Gibian, trans. Aylmer Maude (New York: Norton Critical, 1966), 1090; hereafter abbreviated *WP* and cited parenthetically. I have removed the stress accents over the Russian names in this translation, since they are present only to indicate the English pronunciation of those names.

13. Tolstoy, *The Gospel in Brief,* trans. Isabel Hapgood (Lincoln: University of Nebraska Press, 1997), 115–16.

14. Tolstoy, "Father Sergius," in *Tolstoy's Short Fiction*, 262–63.

15. Tolstoy, "Father Sergius," 263.

16. "How Much Land Does a Man Need?" (1886) (Tolstoy, in *Collected Shorter Fiction,* vol. 2, trans. Louise and Aylmer Maude and Nigel J. Cooper [New York: Alfred A. Knopf, 2001], 196.) Pahom, "too cramped to be comfortable" on the estate that is his, tries to acquire virgin land owned by a mysterious tribe, the Bashkirs, who "neither tilled the ground, nor ate bread" (195, 199). The price is said to be "one thousand rubles a day" for "as much [land] as you can go round on your feet in a day" (201), though Pahom must return to the starting place by the time the sun sets, or all his money will be forfeited. As the day wanes, his ambitions grow. Though "his breast was working like a blacksmith's bellows, his heart was beating like a hammer" (206), he repeatedly shrugs off failure until, still dreaming of more land, he falls to the earth, "blood . . . flowing from his mouth" (207). Asleep the previous night, Pahom has another kind of dream of a man "prostrate on the ground, with only trousers and a shirt on . . . he saw that the man was dead, and that it was himself!" (202). Yet the dream that is a wild hope inflames Pahom more than the dream that is a foreboding. "'What things one does dream,' thought he" (202) when he awakens, as if good-natured disdain could vanquish an actual threat.

17. Tolstoy, *Anna Karenina,* trans. Louise and Aylmer Maude (New York, Norton: 1970), 718.

18. Tolstoy, *Resurrection*, 358.

19. Nekhlyudov's question, which intimates some such displacement, is then itself displaced by vacuities: "Instead of answers he got arguments about whether man has, or has not, free will. Can criminality be determined (or not) by skull measurements and the like? What part does heredity play in crime? . . . What is temperament? . . . What is society? . . . And so on, and so forth. These deliberations reminded Nekhlyudov of an answer he once got from a little boy walking home from school. Nekhlyudov asked him if he was good at spelling. 'Oh yes,' replied the boy. 'All right. How do you spell the word "paw"?' 'What kind of paw—a dog's paw?' asked the little boy. . . . It was answers like these, in the interrogative, that Nekhlyudov discovered in scientific works, when he asked his one basic question" (Tolstoy, *Resurrection,* 358–59).

The analogy of the bogus questions to the spurious ambiguity of the spelling of "paw" by the boy whom Nekhlyudov interrogated when a child could also obliquely be analogized to the sophistry that lurks behind Tolstoy's characters' belief that if only they could be ingenious—could demonstrate their special torment or their uncontested individuality—such uniqueness, or such casuistry, would release them from a universal outcome. Moreover, the presumption in both contexts is that type or kind—of paw, of life—makes a difference, respectively, to orthography and mortality. Yet "paw" would be spelled the same no matter what kind of paw it was, and death will come to all, no matter what kind of life precedes it.

A like claim of exception lies behind Nicholas Rostov's famous question in *War and Peace,* "Can they be coming . . . . to kill me? No, there's some mistake. . . . They can't have wanted to kill me" (*WP* 201), while the commander at Schön Grabern, urging Prince Bagration to take cover from "the bullets whistling, singing, and hissing continually around them. . . . spoke as if those bullets could not kill him" (*WP* 195).

20. Tolstoy, "A Prisoner in the Caucasus," in *Tolstoy's Short Fiction*, 59.

21. Tolstoy, *Hadji Murad,* in *Collected Shorter Fiction*, 737. The anxiety that wells up for Hadji Aga, who "placed his foot on the back of the corpse and with two blows cut off the head" is only that, "roll[ing] it away with his foot," the "crimson blood" that "spurted from the arteries of the

neck," also "black blood" that "flowed from the head, soaking the grass," might "soil his shoes" (737–38), for horror can no longer be experienced on behalf of Hadji Murad.

22. Tolstoy, "Master and Man," 234.

23. The story's two dominant critical interpretations were initially propounded by Georg Lukács, for whom Tolstoy's realism specifically assaults the bureaucratic dehumanization of a "nascent Russian capitalism" which results in living badly and dying painfully ("Tolstoy and the Development of Realism," in *Tolstoy: A Collection of Critical Essays*, ed. Ralph E. Matlaw [Englewood Cliffs, NJ: Prentice-Hall, 1967], 88) and by Lev Shestov, whose existential argument could be summarized thus: only up against the "miraculous, inconceivable, enigmatic change we call death" (a characterization specifically elicited by "Master and Man," but applying to all of Tolstoy's late writing) could anyone see how to live well ("The Last Judgment: Tolstoy's Last Works," in *Tolstoy*, 171).

In Lukács's Marxist analysis, "the isolation of the dying Ivan Ilych" is represented as "an island of horror, of a horrible death after a meaningless life" and every object associated with his living and dying "eloquently and poetically expresses the soul-destroying emptiness and futility of human life in a capitalist society" (85). In a twist on this assessment, John Bayley argues that Tolstoy *imposes* on Ivan Ilych the revelatory understanding that his life has been empty; the bourgeois character Tolstoy invented would have been incapable of this realization. See Bayley, "The Death of Ivan Ilych," in *Tolstoy's Short Fiction*, 415.

Objecting to the claim that Ivan Ilych's dying is horrible because his life has been meaningless (which Lukács finds compelling and Bayley does not), N. K. Mikhaylovsky takes issue with Tolstoy's implication "that the right kind of life will preserve us from death" ("*Master and Man* and *The Death of Ivan Ilych*," in *Tolstoy's Short Fiction*, 452), though of course Tolstoy never suggested that conclusion.

In a compelling essay, Natalie Repin extends Shestov's diagnoses—only the fear of death inverts the nightmare of misunderstandings that underlie the quotidian—by linking Tolstoy with Heidegger (*Being and Time* contains a footnote to Tolstoy's story) to argue that "the logic of everydayness and the logic necessary to understand death are different and incompatible" ("*Being-Toward-Death* in Tolstoy's *The Death of Ivan Il'ich*: Tolstoy and Heidegger," *Canadian-American Slavic Studies* 36.1–2 [2002]: 130). Death's proximity is necessary to reveal the inauthenticity of everydayness. See Repin, "*Being-Toward-Death*," 119.

Above, I examine the ways in which Tolstoy's representation of Ivan Ilych's suffering opens to a perspective that breaks down the distinctions fundamental to the existential and the Marxist arguments.

24. Timothy J. Clark, *The Sight of Death: An Experiment in Art Writing* (New Haven: Yale University Press, 2006), 22, 119, 150–51. Poussin's painting is dialectical, rhythmically bringing together life and death, but it is also threatening, since "any true dialectic has to contain the moment at which the contraries threaten to whirl apart" (97). Conversely, Clark argues, these extremes are also pulled into each other: "Painting at its most intense *revels* in its deathliness, its freezing of movement into pose and of form into flat shape: it revels but it also recoils. . . . The doubleness is everywhere. Even the bloodless, rigidified corpse is reanimated by the slithering black coils surrounding it" (236).

25. Clark, *Sight of Death*, 139, 50.

26. Tolstoy does not simply juxtapose Ivan Ilych's horror at dying with that of his family, whose repugnance has a different object—dying's indecorousness, "as if someone entered a drawing-room diffusing an unpleasant odour" (II 135) —he triangulates this contrast in the

figure of Gerasim whose freedom from falsity ("he alone understood the facts of the case and did not consider it necessary to disguise them" [II 135]) is the counterweight to that repugnance.

If the reader can neither identify with Ivan Ilych's family nor, precisely, with the dying man, Gerasim's vantage is the one we are least equipped to occupy. I would therefore agree with Gary Saul Morson's assessment that "The only person in the story to whom its lesson does not apply is the one who could not read it, the peasant Gerasim" ("The Reader as Voyeur: Tolstoi and the Poetics of Didactic Fiction," in *Tolstoy's Short Fiction*, 395). But I would disagree with Morson's assertion that the ethical charge of the story arises in relation to a frame-breaking in which "Involuntarily, the reader *of* the fiction becomes an actor *in* the fiction" (381) when he understands that the "conclusion of [the] syllogism" in "The Death of Ivan Ilych" is not "that 'Caius is mortal' but that *you* will die" (394), since, as elaborated above, the drama is Ivan Ilych's. We are drawn close to Ilych's fate, but our plight diverges from his, in that we can refuse to read, in effect resisting Ilych's experience, by saying *not that*: *I don't want to experience that*. But Ivan Ilych can't say *not that* about dying. See Nancy Ruttenburg's discussion of "*ne to*" in a different context in *Dostoevsky's Democracy* (Princeton: Princeton University Press, 2008), 17–24, specifically in relation to Dostoevsky's *House of the Dead*.

27. Clark, *Sight of Death*, 139, 150.

28. Tolstoy's word here is not *stradanie* or *stradat'* (suffering), but the sharper, more nuanced, *muchit'sia* (torment or torture).

29. "The pain in his side . . . would begin its own gnawing work. Ivan Ilych would turn his attention to it and try to drive the thought of it away, but without success. *It* would come and stand before him" (II 130).

"The clear antecedent of *It*," David Danaher writes, "is the pain [*bol'*]. . . . In the critical literature on the story, *It* has been identified with pain (*bol'*), life (*zhizn'*), and death (*smert'*), all of which are grammatically feminine in Russian" ("The Function of Pain in Tolstoy's *The Death of Ivan Il'ich*" [*Tolstoy Studies Journal* 10 (1998): 25]). But in the contrast between the roman lowercase "it" and the italicized capitalized "*It*," I think Tolstoy rather means to isolate "it," the pronoun that refers to pain (which is immediately recognizable), from "*It*," the pronoun whose antecedent is death (which could never be recognized). In the text to which this note refers, there is no ambiguity: death is the antecedent to the italicized *It*.

In her analysis of Tolstoy's repertoire of devices for signifying the *unheimlich*, incognizable quality of such visitations, Kathleen Parthé examines the range of personal pronouns that defamiliarize death in Tolstoy's writing: "(*ona* 'it [fem.],' *ono* 'it [neuter]'), indefinite pronouns (*chto-to* 'something'), demonstrative pronouns (*eto* 'this,' *to* 'that'), and certain third-person verb forms with 'something' or the neuter 'it' in subject position or with no subject at all" indicating death. She adds: "'It' (*ono*, a neuter form used to refer to death, a feminine noun) is used to give death an eerily neuter animacy" ("Tolstoy and the Geometry of Fear," in *Tolstoy's Short Fiction*, 408). That neuter *ono* directly corresponds to one connotation of the English pronoun when it indicates a lifeless thing that could not be gendered.

30. In *War and Peace* the very attempt to trace the history of a cause ("Why did Kutuzov . . . not do this or that?" [*WP* 921]) is understood as ludicrous. Just as there is no single moment when Kutuzov could have decided "to abandon Moscow or defend it" (*WP* 922), rather "moment by moment the event is imperceptibly shaping itself" (*WP* 922), a "coincidence of occurrences" (*WP* 919) is never an accurate way of understanding what determines why "a cold wind blows in late spring" (*WP* 919) or how "the hands of the watch" or "the valves and wheels of the engine" move (*WP* 919). Instead, we should study "the infinitesimally small elements by which,"

in Tolstoy's example, "the masses are moved" (*WP* 920). Are the laws that explain the cause of a man's suffering less complex? When Ivan Ilych looks at his family and discovers in their "false[ness] . . . the awful truth" (II 149) (the mirror in which he sees his own countenance), it would seem so, but the story belies this simplification, for if guilt has a basis, guilt is also part of the agony, being an irrelevance about what is required in the moment's immediacy.

31. William James, "A World of Pure Experience," in *Essays in Radical Empiricism* (Cambridge, MA: Harvard University Press, 1976), 45, 25. In James's definition: "To be radical, an empiricism must neither admit into its constructions any element that is not directly experienced, nor exclude from them any element that is directly experienced" (22).

32. Michael Katz translates this differently, explaining in a note: "Ivan misspeaks: he means to say *Prosti* (Forgive me), but utters the word *Propusti* (Let me through) by mistake" (*Tolstoy's Short Fiction*, 128). Like Aylmer Maude, Richard Pevear and Larissa Volokhonsky translate the mistake as "forgo." There are radically different connotations to these translations. The didactic "forgo" suggests a model for us to follow, while "Let me through" suggests nothing prescriptive, just a plea to move past an obstacle.

33. Clark, *Sight of Death*, 236.

34. Tolstoy's words for "suffering" (*stradanie*), "pain" (*bol'*), "torment" (the noun is *muchenie*, the verbal perfective form *muchit'*, and the reflexive form of *muchit, muchit'sia*, so that the word has the sense of suffering that is a consequence of tormenting the self) recur throughout the story. It might look as if "suffering" (*stradanie*) pertains to mental, and "pain" (*bol'*) to physical, anguish, but in Russian as in English both words can apply to either. And in "Life, a series of increasing sufferings . . . the most terrible suffering" (II 147), *stradanie* is used to refer to both mental and physical sufferings; the reference is not indeterminate, even if which is not specified: the word applies to both. Moreover, physical pain has nuances, as for instance when "agonizing physical suffering" (II 150) (*uzhasnye fizicheskie stradaniia*) is counterpointed to a something "new" (II 150) that is happening: breathing [this is the subject, the something "new"] began to (*stalo*) tighten (II 150) [the way a screw is tightened], and to produce a shooting pain [no distinctive word for pain exists here or elsewhere in the sentence—all that follows the comma after "tighten" is a one-word verb, in the infinitive form "to have a shooting pain" (*streliat'*), and "to squeeze" (*sdavlivat'*)]; all the verbs in the sentence are in the imperfective, indicating something ongoing that is affecting Ivan Ilych's breathing. In distinction, when Ivan Ilych struggles in the black sack into which he is thrust, Tolstoy's word, translated by Maude as "agony" (II 151), is the same word (in noun rather than verb form) that appears at the end of the paragraph: "torment" (II 151). (The noun is *muchenie* and the verb *muchat'*.) Torment here must be the mental suffering of being unequal to the force of death.

While the distinction between physical and psychic suffering is iterated, it is also thus continuously effaced. For example, in the first paragraph of section 8, which Maude translates as "the gnawing, unmitigated, agonizing pain" (II 136), the word is *bol'*, which, in its unisyllabic simplicity suggests physical pain, even as it immediately gets entangled with the dread and the despair of experiencing such sensations. Similarly, when Ivan Ilych asks, "What do I want?" and answers "To live and not to suffer?" (II 144; Tolstoy's word is *stradat'*, the verb form of the noun *stradanie*), again, mental and physical suffering are both implied. And when Ivan Ilych realizes: "All you have lived for and still live for is falsehood and deception, hiding life and death from you" (II 150), this assessment is so devastating that it would be foolish to discriminate between the types of agony that afflict him. I am indebted to Nancy Ruttenburg for these translations and assistance with the commentary.

Danaher's "The Function of Pain" provides a helpful analysis of the variety of words for pain in Tolstoy's lexicon. The exegesis is especially illuminating in pointing out how vision and pain are drawn into a continuous relation that "de-automatizes perception" (27).

35. Tolstoy, *Diaries*, 587.

36. Pierre's beliefs are fluid. He accepts Karataev's notion of an "immortal soul" (*WP* 1130). But he is also a pantheist, and he was once a Freemason, and at a different time still supposed Napoleon to be the Antichrist. Though Pierre believes in God, that belief is never the foundation of his ethical understanding, nor is faith the ground of his equanimity on the march away from Moscow, which is explicitly contrasted with his earlier efforts to *achieve* serenity under more auspicious conditions: "He had long sought in different ways that tranquillity of mind, that inner harmony that had so impressed him in the soldiers at the battle of Borodino. He had sought it in philanthropy, in Freemasonry, in the dissipations of town life, in wine, in heroic feats of self-sacrifice, and in romantic love for Natasha; he had sought it by reasoning—and all these quests and experiments had failed him. And now without thinking about it he had found that peace . . . only through the horror of death, through privation, and through what he recognized in Karataev" (*WP* 1122).

37. Thus Pierre reflects that the *experience* of terrible suffering does not require a proportionate correlative ("when he had put on tight dancing shoes he had suffered just as he did now when he walked with bare feet that were covered with sores" [*WP* 1176]). Moreover, if freedom can be enjoyed without reference to external conditions, it can also be predicated on an illusory understanding of those conditions: "when he had married his wife—of his own free will as it had seemed to him—he had been no more free than now when they locked him up at night in a stable" (*WP* 1176).

38. When Karataev falls ill with fever, when Pierre sees his friend halt; "when he smelled the odor emanating from him which was now stronger than before, Pierre moved farther away and did not think about him" (*WP* 1176). The transfer of attention away from the pain of Karataev's plight, however initially shocking, has in fact been gleaned from Karataev. After Pierre has witnessed the meaningless executions "committed by men who did not wish to commit them" (*WP* 1072), Karataev restores his spirit by his own equanimity (*WP* 1073). Like the Russian commander Kutuzov, Karataev is a hero of *War and Peace* by virtue of his indifference to circumstance, which is fundamentally irrelevant to his own serenity: He "loved and lived affectionately with everything life brought him in contact with" (*WP* 1078). His wisdom is incarnated both in the precept "The great thing is to live in harmony" (*WP* 1075), and in a story he tells of a merchant unjustly jailed for a murder. Although the merchant is ultimately vindicated, both the wrongful imprisonment and the Tsar's order that rectifies it become no more than contingencies. The merchant autonomously escapes the injustice by his liberal interpretation of what has befallen him: "I . . . am being punished for my own and other men's sins" (*WP* 1179). He is equally exempt from the Tsar's decree to "free" him, because "God had already forgiven him—he was dead!" (*WP* 1179).

39. Ivan Ilych's "Oh! Oh! Oh!" (II 150) (a prelude to his agreement to "'Let the pain be'" [II 152]) and "the dog's howl" (*WP* 1182) at Karataev's death (an anguish that is pointedly coincident with Pierre's freedom from feeling it) are manifestations of suffering that coexist with equanimity, which cannot be extricated from each other.

40. Rilke, *Letters*, 150.

41. I am indebted to Nancy Ruttenburg and to Anne Eakin Moss for translation of the Russian words discussed in this passage.

42. In sleep "we have already lost both our body and our consciousness many times" (*L* 397); even when we are awake "consciousness is not a unit" but a "series of successive states" (*L* 396).

43. Happiness based on the fulfillment of individual wants (which satisfy the personality and even constitute it) is impossible, because, as Tolstoy's hermit, Fëdor Kuzmich, realizes: "while my wishes were being fulfilled or becoming impossible, new wishes arose, and so it went on and goes on to the end" ("Fëdor Kuzmich," in *Collected Shorter Fiction*, 777).

In the treatise Tolstoy thus disputes that life lies in pleasures, activities, and achievements, and he amasses a list of diverse objects of interest and forms of engagement to sweep away their pertinence to anyone's intuitive understanding of existence's fundamentals: "We pierce mountains, we fly round the world; electricity, microscopes, telephones, wars, parliaments, philanthropy, the struggle of parties, universities, learned societies, museums,—is this life?" (*L* 317).

44. Tolstoy, *Last Diaries*, ed. Leon Stilman, trans. Lydia Weston-Kesich (New York: G. P. Putnam's Sons, 1960), 45.

45. Tolstoy, *A Confession*, 55.

46. Martine de Courcel, quoted in Robinson, *Estrangement and the Somatics of Literature*, 10. In Robinson's analysis this "autism" is underscored by Tolstoy's claim in *A Confession* that he needed to "reject" humanity's "faith" in "collective decisions" about religion (Robinson, 61), thus positing his own logic for an ideal "universal brotherhood of man" (64), which, Robinson argues, is "grounded experientially, by inversion, in Tolstoy's . . . own depressed isolation turned imaginatively inside out" (64).

47. Tolstoy, *A Confession*, 55.

48. "Portions of the original Russian text were published . . . in Russian periodicals as early as 1889, but the first full Russian-language edition of the text . . . was not published until 1891, and then not in Russia but in Switzerland" though a "French translation of the text under the title *De la vie* . . . appeared in March 1889 in Paris" (James P. Scanlan, "Tolstoy among the Philosophers: His Book *On Life* and Its Critical Reception," *Tolstoy Studies Journal* 18 [2006], 53).

Scanlan points out that unlike Kant in *The Critique of Practical Reason*, who argued that "since moral perfection is commanded by God, but is impossible to attain in earthly life, there must be a future life in which the eternal soul advances in the quest. . . . Tolstoy's eternal self . . . makes progress toward perfection in *this* life only and in the afterlife is seemingly frozen in a state of moral incompletion—unless (to engage in one of Tolstoy's 'guesses') the self should continue its journey upward by becoming . . . another bodily individual" (58). Scanlan's essay superbly lays out the background, the philosophical thesis of *On Life*, and the reception Tolstoy's contemporaries gave to his "rationalistic foundationalism" (56).

To summarize some key points in Scanlan's analysis of that reception: In 1890 three major essays on Tolstoy's book appeared in response to the French translation. Each "raise[d] substantial objections to the book, ranging from serious to devastating" (59). In the first, the philosopher Prince Dmitrii Nikolaevich Tsertelev attacked Tolstoy's reworking of the Gospel directive to love your neighbor as yourself, because in Tolstoy's reconception what was required was to love your neighbor *rather* than yourself, a transposition that had neither fidelity to the original nor rationality (59). In addition, Tsertelev argued: "Tolstoy makes no distinction . . . among *degrees* of love appropriate to different persons but equates all love with the extreme of self-sacrifice" (59). Yet, citing Christian doctrine, Tsertelev argues: "The Gospel commandment demands love and benevolence toward all people . . . not that this love be identical for all" (59).

In the second philosophical analysis, Petr Evgen'evich Astaf'ev dismissed Tolstoy's rational and "impersonal" critique of human beings (60), because the consequences of rejecting personality and individuality (and the affiliations of "family, the economy and law, state and society, science and art") amount to a "reject[ion]" of "all human culture" (61). Astaf'ev also savaged Tolstoy's notion that "impersonal reason outside space and time is the only truth, goodness, and reality. Only in a true idealism such as Hegel's . . . might one hold such a view of reason" (61). The third review, by Aleksei Aleksandrovich Kozlov, "a personalist and panpsychist strongly influenced by Leibniz" (62), assaults *On Life*'s vague, contradictory, and even incoherent definitions of "reason," "self," and "life" (62) as well as Tolstoy's "bloodless 'love'" (63).

For a fleshed-out analysis of these three critiques and of the scathing criticism of Tolstoy's "devaluation of individuality" and of the "miraculous metaphysical foundation" of Christianity (65) by Akim Volynsky, one of the book's *supporters*, see Scanlan's essay in its entirety. Scanlan concludes: "when the philosophers examined [Tolstoy's] efforts, the consensus was decidedly negative: neither his ideas nor his arguments for them were judged rationally defensible" (67). In Volynsky's words, Tolstoy's belief in the "insignificance of the individual" turned "the Russian man . . . into a speck . . . a little black spot" (65).

49. That "special relation" is analogized as follows: "If I know the special and various races of animals . . . I know them, not so much by their external marks, as because each one of them—the lion, the fish, the spider—presents a general peculiar relation to the world. All lions, as a rule, love one thing, and all fish another, and all spiders a third; only because they love differently are they distinguished in my imagination as different living creatures.

"But what I do not yet distinguish in each of these creatures, his special relation to the world, does not prove that it has not existed, but only that the peculiar relation to the world which constitutes the life of a single individual spider is remote from that relation to the world in which I find myself, and that therefore I have not yet understood him as Silvio Pellico understood his individual spider" (*L* 399). The spider, an emblem of love, makes an earlier appearance, in the young Tolstoy's diary: "The powerful means for achieving true happiness in life is—and without any dogmas—to spread out from oneself, in every direction, like a spider, a whole spider's web of love and to catch in it everything that comes along—whether it is an old woman or a child, a girl or a policeman" (quoted in T. A. Kuzminskaya, *Tolstoy As I Knew Him: My Life at Home and at Yasnaya Polyana*, trans. Nora Sigerist et al. [New York: Macmillan, 1948], 61).

50. See "What Counts as Love: Jonathan Edwards's *True Virtue*," in Sharon Cameron, *Impersonality: Seven Essays* (Chicago: University of Chicago Press, 2007), 21–52.

51. *On Life* continually alludes to the Gospels: only if man renounces the goal of satisfying his animal personality "will all the sap of his life pass into the one ennobling shoot of genuine love . . . the doctrine of Christ is the graft for this love" (*L* 379). Yet the core principles of Christianity are also proclaimed by other faiths (see note 6). *On Life* adds to this list "Lao-dzi," the "Stoics," and "all the true thinkers of mankind" (*L* 368). In *What Is to Be Done,* Tolstoy makes a list of "artist-producers of spiritual food" that includes "Solon, Socrates, . . . Homer, Isaiah, David" (in *What Is to Be Done and Life*, 232).

52. "People prefer faith to consciousness, because faith is firmer and easier, as firm and easy as following a custom, and it easily passes into habit" (Tolstoy, *Last Diaries,* 136). "Man . . . learns all things through his reason, and not through faith" (*L* 440).

53. Since *On Life*'s publication, critics have echoed the assessment of Tolstoy's contemporaries who claimed that *On Life*'s rendition of Christianity violated its fundamental metaphysical basis, a future life beyond the grave. Thus Irving Howe writes of Tolstoy's "Christian anarchism" ("The Old Magician," *New Republic,* April 27, 1992, 32); Medzhibovskaya elaborates on the strands of such a heresy: "Tolstoy's Christ the Redeemer requires no sacrifice other than

trading one's delusion for the right understanding" (212). For Tolstoy "right understanding" is verified "in self-accountability bordering on apostasy and anarchy that will be visited on the old-fashioned moral law" (212). Finally, Tolstoy "rejects [resurrection] because resurrection in the body will mean the triumph of the temporal life" (213), which defies *On Life*'s thesis.

54. The reduction of the denominator can make love for others swell, very like the drops on which the Swiss geography teacher discourses: "each drop tries to expand" to reflect the divine "to the greatest extent" (*WP* 1181). From Tolstoy's diary: "The error of . . . philosophers is that they admit only the consciousness of oneself as an individual (the so-called subject), whereas in fact the consciousness of the entire world, of the so-called object, is as undoubtedly true as individual self-consciousness" (quoted in Lisa Steiner, *For Humanity's Sake: The Bildungsroman in Russian Culture* [Toronto: University of Toronto Press, 2011], 133). Anne Eakin Moss called my attention to the geography teacher's lesson as *On Life*'s precursor.

For one who fails to augment the degrees of love—who remains "in that degree of love to one thing and dislike to another, with which he entered upon existence"—there is only death "visible and terrible to him, not only in the future, but in the present" (*L* 404). Pages later, however, Tolstoy rethinks that verdict, proclaiming love's entitlement for all: "the life of all men is one and the same, and, like every life, it has no beginning and end" (*L* 418). Death can even rescue the doomed from an insufficient aggregation of love by facilitating a better chance for happiness in another earthly incarnation. Thus death's efficacy: "A man dies only when it is indispensable for his welfare" (*L* 419). That is, he dies "because the happiness of his true life cannot be enhanced, in this world, and not because his lungs pain him, or because he has cancer, or because a bomb has been thrown at him" (L 419). Such inconsistencies punctuate Tolstoy's theory.

55. In addition, "all that by which I live has been formed from the life of those who have lived before me," just as "every man who fulfills the law of life, submitting his animal personality to reason, and manifesting the power of love, has lived and does live in other people after the disappearance of his corporeal existence" (and here mark the specification of purpose in the following) "in order that the clumsy and alarming superstition of death should never again torment me" (*L* 410). Also notable about this claim is the ambiguous relation between a collective and an individual karma ("this life of my dead brother . . . enters into me. His . . . relation to the world, becomes my relation to the world" [*L* 408]), since earlier in the treatise nothing ameliorated individual karma.

56. Tolstoy, quoted in Kuzminskaya, *Tolstoy As I Knew Him*, 61.

57. Although "Coupon" reveals *On Life*'s polemic most schematically, many of Tolstoy's late fables demonstrate the same understanding that life considered as one's own can have no rational meaning: In "Esarhaddon, King of Assyria," the protagonist is instructed that "Lailie [the enemy] is you, and the warriors you put to death were you also. . . . And not the warriors only, but the animals which you slew when hunting and ate at your feasts, were also you. You thought life dwelt in you alone." But your life "is but a portion of this same common life" (in *Collected Shorter Fiction*, 746).

58. Ilya Kliger and Nasser Zakariya understand the bipartite structure of "Coupon" in relation to an especially powerful insight about "the elective affinities between metaphysical principles and narrative organizations" ("Poetics of Brotherhood: Organic and Mechanistic Narrative in Late Tolstoi," *Slavic Review* 70, no. 4 [2011], 763).

In "Coupon," the authors argue, Part I is "mechanistic" in that "part-by-part relations unfolding in successive time" are "organized through external, diachronic causation" (759), while Part II is structured in relation to the "organically conceived ethics" (757) of a harmonious whole which "begins to verge on the marvelous . . . in a strictly generic" sense (771) as a "narrativization of brotherhood" (771). The two parts thus operate within "the dichotomy of the Russian formalist distinction between *fabula*," a "chronological or causal sequence of narrated events" (758), and *siuzhet*, a "meaningful" sequence (759). Of the rival logics that structure Tolstoy's story, Kliger and Zakariya assert: "the experience of death as such, the individual's dread of annihilation, is inconceivable within a thoroughly organic worldview" (763), a claim issued from a different vantage than that of the analysis above, but compatible with my argument about Tolstoy's polemical writing.

59. Tolstoy, "The Forged Coupon," in *Collected Shorter Fiction*, 905, 903, 905; hereafter abbreviated FC and cited parenthetically.

Ivan Mironov has in fact "persuaded" Gerasim, "a skilful young fellow," to do the actual dirty work, rewarding him with "pie and vodka" (FC 904). Before Stepan strikes the final blow, a crowd of villagers beat Mironov. When he falls to the ground, provoking his fate, he goads them: "You barbarians . . . beat me to death then. I'm not scared of you" (FC 905).

60. Ivan Mironov, the man Stepan kills, has himself been cheated by Yevgeny Mikhailovich, who passes on a forged coupon as payment for the former's firewood. (The coupon was given to Yevgeny's wife by two schoolboys at his photographic store; they commit the forgery because the father of one of the boys, "a man of incorruptible integrity" [FC 875], has been accused of acting "dishonestly," and he, in turn, snaps at his son "you will end up as a swindler" [FC 876], a prediction whose sting precipitates the schoolboy's boast, "I'll be a swindler now" [FC 879], and of course the chain of crimes.) So Ivan Mironov, like the wronged schoolboy, becomes a thief.

61. "If you killed a man, you killed a man," musing: "It's his turn today, tomorrow it may be mine" (FC 906). Moreover, like Vasily, who is corrupted by his own act of perjury, Stepan justifies his killings by brooding on the discrepancy between how the gentry and merchants are treated for unlawful actions (they "could get away with it") and how the muzhiks are treated (they "got sent off to prison to feed the lice on account of any little thing whatever" [FC 907]). In much the same way, after he executes a plan to steal Dapple and Beauty, the horses of Pyotr Nikolayevich, Ivan Mironov "on his binge . . . was thinking incessantly not just about the individual who had wronged him, but about all the masters, some of them worse than others, who only lived by what they could filch from the likes of him" (FC 894)—the incentive for crime being in each of "Coupon"'s vignettes the plight of first having been its victim. By light of such resentments one could argue that Tolstoy wants to focus his blame on a classed society (and its institutions), especially on the gentry, and that Stepan's actual agency in the murders he perpetrates is therefore diffused.

But, notwithstanding the vector of the muzhiks' resentment and the chain reaction of evil, crime as Tolstoy represents it in "Coupon" has no single class origin. Thus Pyotr Nikolayevich, robbed by Ivan, had been sympathetic to the peasants (he "observe[d] the strictest fairness in his dealings with them" [FC 892]), but after the robbery he could only exclaim, "Filthy peasants! . . . From now on you're going to get different treatment from me" (FC 893). The "different treatment" begins when Pyotr Nikolayevich begins to suspect an innocent man of the horse theft (FC 896), and this unfairness blossoms into loathing for all the peasants indiscriminately, a sentiment they reciprocate: "Before a year was out they had . . . burned down the barn and the threshing-floor" (FC 910). When Pyotr Nikolayevich impounds "their livestock" for being let out "on to the manorial meadows" (FC 911), they start a "general riot" in which "Pyotr Nikolayevich was crushed to death. And five minutes later his mutilated body was dragged away and thrown into a ravine" (FC 912). As in *War and Peace*, it is impossible to separate victim and victimizer, and thus to identify "who" is doing these things (*WP* 1070).

62. Tolstoy's story emphasizes the contagion of such a theory. When Vasily, the yardman, is asked by his master Yevgeny Mikhailovich to testify deceptively in court "that they never bought firewood from muzhiks" (FC 887), and when he is believed, "it seemed as if the whole affair had ended well for Yevgeny Mikhailovich and for Vasily the yardman." But "something had actually happened which no one could see, something far more serious than anything merely human eyes could perceive" (FC 889). An omniscient point of view cedes to Vasily's when the narrator puts it this way on his behalf: "Before the court case with the coupon Vasily had still not believed that the upper classes had no law governing the way they lived. . . . But this court hearing over the coupon, and most of all, his own perjury, which . . . had actually earned him an extra ten roubles, convinced him that there were no laws at all, and that a man should simply live for his own pleasure" (FC 890). So he begins to pilfer. After several successful escapades, thrown out for stealing his master's wallet, obsessed with the thought "that the beginning and the end of everything was to have money" (FC 902), he burgles the shop owned by his former employer, is imprisoned and then sentenced to exile.

63. Michel Ciment identified Yvon in Bresson's adaptation, the filmic Stepan, as an "exterminating angel" ("I Seek Not Description But Vision: Robert Bresson on *L'Argent*," in *Robert Bresson*, ed. James Quandt [Toronto: Cinematheque Ontario, 1998], 508. The epithet is unconnected to Buñuel's 1962 film of that title about guests who arrive at a dinner party and are unable to leave it.

64. Virtually, because in "Coupon"'s second half, Prokofy, a prisoner who was unjustly accused of stealing horses (FC 897), dies in the prison hospital (FC 951) and two men are hanged on orders of the Tsar by "a cruel and bestial murderer" (FC 947). These deaths are marginalized.

65. Identifying himself as the serial killer, Stepan grows meek and obedient (FC 925). In prison the "Our Father" is the primer through which he becomes literate (FC 932); he reads the Gospels to the prison executioner, Makhorkin, who—ravished by what he hears—declares "never again would he be carrying out the duty of executioner" (FC 933). Stepan's "moral level" (FC 934) so surpasses that of Makhin (one of the schoolboys who passed off the forged coupon, who has now become the magistrate judging Stepan) that Makhin comes to understand a "new world of spiritual aspirations which had formerly seemed to him so strange and alien" (FC 937), while Mitya, the other delinquent school boy ("now . . . an engineer on a large salary in the Siberian gold-mines" [FC 954], who takes Stepan with him on a prospecting mission), "fell to thinking for the first time about his own life" (FC 954)—an anomaly producing an "upheaval" (FC 954) leading him to rethink his vocation—and awakening a burning desire "to serve the common people" (FC 954). But first he "decided to make things up with his father," who "recalled the many, many occasions" (FC 955) he had wronged his son. So the domino effect of love comes full circle from the other direction.

66. Stepan, in prison, listening to Chuyev reading Matthew 15:31–46 and Luke 23:32–43 (FC 929–30), immediately understands what he hears. Specifically, he "realized that the overall meaning of this teaching was that men were brothers, and ought to love and pity each other, and then it would be well with all of them" (FC 931). This instantaneous conversion through rational understanding of scripture is also the one-legged tailor's who "was lost in wonderment for" Mariya Semyonovna's life (FC 909). When she reads the Sermon on the Mount, he "kept thinking about what he had seen in Mariya Semyonovna's house, and about what she had said to him and read to him" (FC 910). The crippled tailor then converts Chuyev by reading "five chapters from the Gospel of Matthew" (FC 913). "Ivan Chuyev . . . really took it in. And he took it in to such an extent that he began trying to live his whole life according to God's way" (FC 913).

67. In prison Stepan has one pre-reflective moment. To ward off the devils, he recites "the Hail Mary and the Our Father. . . . As he recited the prayers he would start to recall his past life: his father and mother, his village, the dog Wolfcub, his grandad asleep on top of the stove . . . the girls and their songs, and the horses, how they had been stolen and how they had managed to catch the horse-thief, and how he had finished the thief off with a stone. And . . . the fat innkeeper and the drayman's wife and the children, and then once again he would recall *her*. And he would feel hot all over, and throw off his prison robe . . . and start pacing rapidly up and down his cramped cell like a wild animal in a cage" (FC 926). This moment almost brings to mind Ivan Ilych's recollection of his childhood. But while reminiscence goads the former to near-insight, Stepan can only "feel hot" and pace his cell—as though perception were so foreign to this story that it is instantly converted into bodily agitation. Subsequently, in prison, what converts Stepan from being a murderer to being a repository for benevolence is not only prayers, or penitence (though when "he dreamt that she came towards him with her scraggy, wrinkled throat, all cut open" [FC 927] he asks forgiveness), and not the gospel alone, but rather the "sun of reason" (*L* 353)—miraculously realized in a series of inexhaustible acts of charity—whose basis is conceptual.

68. Fyodor Dostoevsky, *Crime and Punishment,* trans. Richard Pevear and Larissa Volokhonsky (New York: Vintage Classics, 1993), 492.

Tolstoy may himself be signaling a link between the works, for the first two words of "Coupon" are "Fyodor Mikhailovich," Dostoevsky's name and patronymic. Tolstoy certainly was reflecting on the difference between his conception of crime and punishment and Dostoevsky's when in 1883, after reading the latter's novel, he dismissed "all those Idiots, Adolescents, Raskolnikovs, and the rest of them" to exclaim that "it is all much simpler, more understandable" than Dostoevsky makes it (quoted in Maxim Gorky, *Reminiscences of Tolstoy, Chekhov, and Andreyev* [New York: Viking Press, 1959], 42).

Unlike Raskolnikov in *Crime and Punishment,* who is inspired to kill when he embraces an intellectual theory that commits "extraordinary" people to becoming outlaws, Stepan, an ordinary peasant, kills out of common rage. While Raskolnikov cannot say the words "I killed," which "froze in him" (*Crime and Punishment,* 525) ("Was it the old crone I killed? . . . the devil killed the old crone, not me" [*Crime and Punishment,* 420]), Stepan, in the bar, immediately identifies himself: "I'm the one who cut all those people's throats" (FC 924). Moreover, Stepan is not redeemed by a long and solitary Raskolnikov-like process of personal torment that only begins to culminate in the flicker of understanding that "instead of dialectics, there was life" (*Crime and Punishment,* 550–51); he is instead redeemed by an expeditious ethical insight whose foundation is "communal," like the "cell" (FC 927), in which all of "Coupon"'s prisoners dwell.

Bresson (whose film *Pickpocket* is explicitly linked to *Crime and Punishment*) perhaps draws the two models together in *L'Argent.* Thus his murderer looks nothing like a peasant, but more like a Raskolnikov-like student. In *L'Argent,* as in "Coupon," crime is the effect of a chain reaction, not of a philosophical theory. And, for Tolstoy, redemption is a communal not personal enterprise. In distinction, Bresson renders the strangeness of Yvon's redemptive vision all his own, though it excites a communal fascination, as touched on above.

For pressing me to think about the connections between *Crime and Punishment* and "Forged Coupon," I am grateful to Barry Weller and Diana Greene. Lyubov Golburt noticed that the first two words of Tolstoy's story call to mind Dostoevsky, as well as suggesting that in "Coupon" Tolstoy might be rethinking the Dostoyevskian paradigm of crime and its redemption.

69. Alberto Moravia, "*L'Argent*," in *Robert Bresson*, 408. The film alters "Coupon"'s details. When Yvon delivers fuel to a photographic shop, he is paid with the counterfeit bills that two schoolboys have palmed off on the wife of the couple who run that shop. Yvon's downward spiral begins when he uses the counterfeit money to pay his check at a café. Defending himself by insisting that he was himself the victim of fraud, he returns with the police to the photographic shop, where Lucien, the assistant at the shop, asked by its owner to perjure himself, replies that he has never before seen Yvon. (In "Coupon," Vasily, the yardman, also asked to perjure himself by his master Yevgeny Mikhailovich, turns into a crook who steals from his own master; in the same way, Lucien steals first from a customer. Then, when he is caught and fired for cheating the customer, he also steals from the owner of the photographic shop by breaking into his safe. Thus the man who taught him to lie and cheat becomes Lucien's victim.) Ultimately, Vasily and Lucien become magnanimous crooks who give stolen money to their corrupting masters.

As with Stepan in "Coupon," Yvon, released from prison, murders first the couple at a hotel (we see them welcome, then close the doors behind him; in the next shot blood is rinsed away in a sink), then he murders the saintly woman's entire family. In Bresson's summary "I simplified everything, first by elimination on paper and then, much more so, during shooting" (quoted in Ciment, "I Seek Not Description But Vision," 503). Bresson combines several characters into one, and he also draws certain characters closer together, for instance, strengthening the connection between perjurer and victim by counterpointing Lucien's arrival at prison to the exact moment that Yvon returns there from the hospital where he recovered from a botched suicide attempt.

For a detailed analysis of Bresson's film, see Kent Jones, *L'Argent* (London: British Film Institute, 1999). Specifically focusing on "the type of 'sensation'" (16), the intensity of perception, and especially on how rhythm and sound (and the "*sensual* impact of Bresson's art" [39] in general) unusually figure in *L'Argent*, Jones isolates aspects of the film that differentiate Bresson from other film makers; from his own previous films; and from "every other film ever made about murder" (73).

70. Bresson, quoted in Ciment, "I Seek Not Description But Vision," 503.

71. Translations from the French are from the subtitles of Bresson's 1983 *L'Argent* (New Yorker Video, 2005), DVD. Figures 3.1–3.13 are also from this DVD version of the film.

72. Bresson, quoted in Ciment, "I Seek Not Description But Vision," 508.

73. Bresson, quoted in Ciment, "I Seek Not Description But Vision," 507.

74. Bresson, quoted in Ciment, "I Seek Not Description But Vision," 510.

75. Bresson, quoted in Ciment, "I Seek Not Description But Vision," 507.

76. Throughout *L'Argent*, Bresson tethers and untethers image and sound. In *Film, A Sound Art* Michel Chion calls the phenomenon of off-screen sound "acousmatization" in which "at some crucial moment in the plot . . . we are made to hear without seeing, after having first been allowed to see and hear at the same time." When "we hear sounds without seeing their cause or source," we must "imagine what is happening"; that is "acousmatic sound" (Michel Chion, *Film, A Sound Art*, trans. Claudia Gorbman [New York: Columbia University Press, 2009], 465). When Bresson cuts away from the dog to juxtapose the image of the axe with the sound of its barking, the harsh sounds are at once contained and uncontained, affective and unaffective, seeping into the scene—issuing from the animal, but also seeming to diffuse into a disembodied cry—the victim's? the murderer's? no one's at all?

In this way, in *L'Argent*, sound is both bound to the diegetic, and disseminated beyond it in "a bath of affect," a phrase Claudia Gorbman coined in *Unheard Melodies: Narrative Film Music* (Bloomington: Indiana University Press, 1987) to indicate how in the audio portion of a film sound unconsciously washes over listeners to cue them to the fact that they are on a different ontological plane than the characters in the film who don't hear what we do (6).

Although Bresson wrote that he used "sound" in *L'Argent* "to move from one scene to another" (quoted in Ciment, "I Seek Not Description But Vision," 504), these "musical connections" not only link the "large number of locations" in the film, they also establish a fluid connection among the scenes of intimacy between Yvon and the woman he kills and the scenes of violence. In the former, we hear the swooshing of water generated by the woman's washing her clothes while she and Yvon speak, as well as the rustling of the stream, which we hear but do not see, while Yvon picks fruit for her to eat. In the latter, we hear running water before we see the sink in which Yvon washes blood off his hands after the murder of the hotel keepers; following the murder of the family, we both hear and see the splash of the axe in the stream, around which the water closes; and we hear but do not see the murmuring of water—from that same stream?—outside the bar where Yvon stands immobile. In *L'Argent*, water is the fluid medium that neutrally mingles affinity and rage—extremes that aurally dissolve into each other.

Bresson wrote: "The eye (in general) superficial, the ear profound and inventive" (*Notes on the Cinematographer*, trans. Jonathan Griffin [København: Green Integer, 1997], 81).

Jonathan Auerbach drew my attention to the importance of sound in Bresson's films in general, and in *L'Argent* in particular.

77. Bresson, quoted in Ciment, "I Seek Not Description But Vision," 507.

78. Bresson, quoted in Ciment, "I Seek Not Description But Vision," 508.

79. This exemplifies Morson's notion of frame breaking ("The Reader as Voyeur," 381) in a different context. See note 26.

80. Bresson's focus at the climactic moment is not visual because *L'Argent* is a screen adaptation of Tolstoy's narrative—a conclusion that would confuse *L'Argent*'s representational medium with Bresson's reinterpretation of Tolstoy's story, marked by his replacement of Stepan's awakening to "the Gospels" (Bresson, quoted in Ciment, "I Seek Not Description But Vision," 503) with an immanent (nongospelized) vision on which ethics is grounded. Bresson told Ciment, his interviewer: "I seek not description but vision. A sense of motion comes from building a series of visions and fitting them together." He continued: "with *L'Argent* it became almost a working method . . . to communicate the impressions I feel" (506).

In speaking of these interlocking visions, Bresson would surely have been thinking of the montage at the film's end in which Yvon, at the bar's back door, looking downward, must retrospectively be glossed by the viewer in relation to the crowd at the bar's front door, looking at Yvon as he is led away, and then into the lit space behind him. What Bresson called "the omnipotence of rhythms" (*Notes*, 68) is discernible in the penultimate and ultimate frames—in perspectives shrouded in mystery—which conclusively intersect to underscore a question about the genesis of the ethical act, its catalyst.

81. Bresson, quoted in Ciment, "I Seek Not Description But Vision," 503.

82. Bresson, quoted in Ciment, "I Seek Not Description But Vision," 506.

83. Alain Badiou, *Saint Paul: The Foundation of Universalism*, trans. Ray Brassier (Stanford: Stanford University Press, 2003), 66. Badiou writes: "Grace . . . is pure and simple *encounter* . . . we are the beneficiaries of certain graces, ones for which there is no need to invoke an All-Powerful" (*Saint Paul*, 66). If grace, rather than vision, marks the break between the murders and Yvon's confession, it could not be linked to an image.

In Badiou's account, the crisis of the "event" ("a hazardous . . . unpredictable supplement" to anything that precedes it) "vanishes as soon as it appears" (*Ethics: An Essay on the Understanding of Evil,* trans. Peter Hallward [New York: Verso, 2001], 67). Ethics depends on "fidelity" to the rupture of the event, on a decision for "a *new* way of being . . . by *thinking* . . . the situation 'according to' the event" (*Ethics,* 41). Yvon's surrender could thus be construed in terms of such fidelity.

I'm grateful to Luka Arsenjuk for prodding me to think through the differences between these two understandings.

84. Badiou, *Ethics,* 43. In the preface to the English edition of *Ethics*, Peter Hallward writes: "there can be no ethics in general, but only an ethic of singular truths, and thus an ethic relative to a particular situation" (lvi).

85. The moment in Tolstoy's story that precedes Stepan's confession—to which Yvon's standing outside the bar door corresponds—is marked by Stepan's "reliving over again everything he had done to her" (FC 923). If Bresson is adhering to Tolstoy's sequence, Yvon would be recalling the murders: seeing them. If Bresson is not adhering to that sequence, no logic, image, or impression explains what precedes his ethical action.

Bresson, frequently identified as a Jansenist (an affiliation that might privilege the film's representation of an evental ethics), in a discussion of *L'Argent* vehemently insisted he wasn't one: "I've been called a Jansenist which is madness. I'm the opposite. I am interested in impressions" (Bresson, quoted in Ciment, "I Seek Not Description But Vision," 501).

86. Ludwig Wittgenstein, "Lecture on Ethics," in *Philosophical Occasions 1912–1951,* ed. James C. Klagge and Alfred Nordmann (New York: Hackett Publishing, 1993), 38.

87. Wittgenstein, "Lecture on Ethics," 39–40. To demonstrate the unassailable divide between the propositional and the ethical, Wittgenstein proposes this example: "Suppose one of you were an omniscient person and therefore knew all the movements of all the bodies in the world dead or alive and that he also knew all the states of mind of all human beings that ever lived, and suppose this man wrote all he knew in a big book, then this book would contain the whole description of the world." But "this book would contain nothing that we would call an *ethical* judgment. . . . It would of course contain all relative judgments of value and all true scientific propositions and in fact all true propositions that can be made" ("Lecture," 39). These facts and propositions would not be ethical because "there are no propositions which, in any absolute sense, are sublime, important, or trivial" ("Lecture," 39).

Earlier in the *Tractatus Logico-Philosophicus* Wittgenstein had elaborated: "In the world everything is as it is, and everything happens as it does happen: in it no value exists. . . . If there is any value that does have value, it must lie outside the whole sphere of what happens and is the case. For all that happens and is the case is accidental" (*Tractatus Logico-Philosophicus* [Seven Treasures Publications, 2009], 6.41). "So too it is impossible for there to be propositions of ethics. Propositions can express nothing that is higher" (*Tractatus,* 6.42).

88. Wittgenstein, "Lecture," 40.

89. Wittgenstein, *Tractatus,* 6.522. Anat Biletzki's interpretation of the *Tractatus* explores the claim reiterated in "Lecture" that "only factual states of affairs which can be pictured, can be represented by meaningful propositions" ("Ludwig Wittgenstein," *The Stanford Encyclopedia of Philosophy,* revised March 3, 2014, Available at: http://plato.stanford.edu/entries/wittgenstein/; accessed August 9, 2015). Biletzki writes: This "leaves out of the realm of sense a daunting number of statements which are made and used in language." Biletzki continues, glossing Wittgenstein's statement that "there can be no representatives of the logic of facts" (*Tractatus,* 4.0312): "This is not a happenstance thought; it is fundamental precisely because the limits of sense rest on logic. Tautologies and contradictions, the propositions of logic, are the limits of language and thought,

and thereby the limits of the world. . . . they do not picture anything and do not, therefore, have sense," because the meaning of a sentence is its capacity to picture a possible situation which is or could be true. "Since only what is 'in' the world can be described, anything that is 'higher' is excluded, including the notion of limit and the limit points themselves. Traditional metaphysics, and the propositions of ethics and aesthetics, which try to capture the world as a whole, are also excluded . . . for [they are] not 'in' the world but at its limit."

The analysis of the distinctions between sense, senselessness, nonsense, and especially the question of whether ethics is inexpressible, is amplified by James Conant's "What 'Ethics' in the *Tractatus* is *Not*," in *Religion and Wittgenstein's Legacy*, eds. D. Z. Phillips and Mario von der Ruhr (Aldershot: Ashgate, 2005), 39–88.

90. Wittgenstein, "Lecture," 41.

91. Wittgenstein provides a second experience that also embodies an ethical absolute: "the experience of feeling *absolutely* safe. I mean the state of mind in which one is inclined to say 'I am safe, nothing can injure me whatever happens'" ("Lecture," 41). These expressions are "nonsense . . . misusing language," Wittgenstein continues, since to "'wonder at such and such being the case' has only sense if I can imagine it not to be the case" (41). And one could only feel "safe [if] it is physically impossible that certain things should happen to me" and therefore it is "nonsense to say that I am safe *whatever* happens" (42). "A third experience of the same kind is that of feeling guilty . . . described by the phrase that God disapproves of our conduct" (42).

Counter Wittgenstein, one could argue that there could be the perception of such absolutes without positing the allegory of God as their origin, even though the experience of nonreligious transcendence might have an incredibly brief half-life (like a Higgs boson, as Neil Hertz suggested to me), absorbed in the moment by a character, by the reader, while being unavailable for further moralizing. A Higgs boson would explain how elementary particles are imbued with mass, therefore would explain why there is both mass and life, and would thus be foundational in a different register, as wonder at God's universe is foundational.

92. Wittgenstein, "Lecture," 44, 42–43.

93. Wittgenstein, "Lecture," 41, 43.

94. Tolstoy, *Anna Karenina*, 724. In *A Confession*, Tolstoy wrote: "It became apparent to me that to say that in the infinity of time and space everything is developing, becoming more perfect, complex and differentiated, is really to say nothing at all. They are all words without a meaning, for in the infinite there is no simple and complex, no before and after, and no better or worse" (36). Attributes are relative and the infinite is absolute. Wittgenstein specifies a corollary opposition between the realm of facts and a realm that facts can't comprehend: "even when all possible scientific questions have been answered, the problems of life remain completely untouched" (*Tractatus*, 6.52). The "problems of life," like its "miracles," have nothing to do with the scientific or the factual. As is well-known, Tolstoy was Wittgenstein's hero. The latter wrote to Ludwig von Ficker: "Are you acquainted with Tolstoy's *The Gospel in Brief*? At its time, this book virtually kept me alive" (quoted on the back cover, Tolstoy, *The Gospel in Brief*).

95. Tolstoy, *Anna Karenina*, 720. The word is in the comparative form. Levin literally says: "What could be said that would be more senseless than what he said?" For Tolstoy, the "senseless" (*bessyslennee*) has nothing to do with the nonpropositional language that elicits Wittgenstein's characterization "nonsense," but rather indicates what lies outside of reason. Levin, whose logic dictates the question of why he should live if death is a limit (*Anna Karenina*, 711–12), discerns intuitively rather than through ocular or argumentative proof the "rounded vault" of sky become an "infinite" (*Anna Karenina*, 724).

The deontological versus the teleological or utilitarian nature of both Tolstoy's and Wittgenstein's understandings of ethics is elaborated in E. B. Greenwood's "Tolstoy, Wittgenstein, Schopenhauer; Some Connections." Specifically, Greenwood juxtaposes sentences from *Anna Karenina* ("If goodness has a cause . . . [or] a consequence . . . it is . . . not goodness") to ones from *Tractatus* ("ethics has nothing to do with punishment and reward in the usual sense of the terms . . . the *consequences* of an action must be unimportant") to argue that, for each, "ethics" is "independent of ulterior aims and consequences" (in ed. W. G. Jones, *Tolstoi and Britain* [Oxford: Berg, 1995], 242). Greenwood is of course characterizing only Tolstoy's earlier writing. See also Emyr Vaughan Thomas, "Wittgenstein and Tolstoy: The Authentic Orientation," *Religious Studies*, 33, no. 4 (1997), 363–77. Tolstoy's relation to Kant's deontological ethics is discussed in Gary Jahn's "Tolstoj and Kant," in *New Perspectives on Nineteenth-Century Russian Prose* (Columbus, OH: Slavica Press, 1982), 60–70.

96. Tolstoy, *Anna Karenina*, 720.

97. Wittgenstein, "Lecture," 44.

98. Tolstoy, "Alyosha Gorshok," in *Collected Shorter Fiction*, 959; hereafter abbreviated AG and cited parenthetically.

99. Literally translated, "was surprised," without the "looked as if" or "looked": "He asked for something to drink, and was surprised by something. Was surprised by something, stretched out, and died."

In Katz's translation: Alyosha "merely asked for something to drink, and felt a growing sense of wonder. Suddenly, overcome with wonder, he stretched out, and died" ("Alyosha Gorshok," in *Tolstoy's Short Fictions*, 284). In the first of these sentences, "wonder" is in the imperfective form, indicating an ongoing action, and in the second of the sentences, in the perfective form, indicating a completed action. My thanks to Anne Eakin Moss for the translation and explanation of the grammar.

Archibald J. Woolf's 1920 translation renders the word as "wonderment," and retains the "looked as though" ("he looked as though marveling at something, then he stretched out his limbs and died" ["Alyosha Gorshok," in *Posthumous Works: The Wisdom of Children*, trans. A. J. Woolf (New York: New York International Book Publishing Co., 1920), 204]).

The Maudes' translations generally have a literary resonance, as, for example, in: "This event had to do with his astonishing discovery" (AG 962), while Katz's late twentieth-century revision of S. A. Carmack's translation of "Alyosha Gorshok" renders the same sentence fragment in the matter-of-fact key of vernacular English: "This event was as follows: much to his own surprise, he discovered" (282). Against type, therefore, it is the Maudes, rather than Katz, who translates *udivlenie* as "surprise," and Katz who translates it as "wonder."

100. "If we take eternity to mean not infinite temporal duration but timelessness, then eternal life belongs to those who live in the present" (Wittgenstein, *Tractatus*, 6.4311). In *The Gospel in Brief* Tolstoy wrote: "one must live without time, in the present alone" (156).

101. Resistance would be demonstrated by pushing away the unexpected or by prematurely understanding it (another way of being tripped up). Instead, Alyosha is literally tripped in the fable's initial paragraph in which he falls "and smashe[s] a pot" (AG 959), his first misstep (his last is to trip on the roof). Of course, from another point of view, Alyosha's fall and his death could not be disassociated.

102. "*I wonder at the existence of the world*. And I am then inclined to use such phrases as . . . I am safe *whatever* happens," which are a "misuse" of language or "nonsensical" (Wittgenstein, "Lecture," 41, 42, 44).

103. Wittgenstein, "Lecture," 40.

104. Wittgenstein, "Lecture," 40.

105. Tolstoy, *Anna Karenina*, 646.

106. "Reason sets a man upon that sole path of life which, like a cone-shaped, widening tunnel, inclosed in the center on all sides by its close walls, opens to him afar off the indubitable immortality of life and its happiness" (*L* 421).

107. Wittgenstein admired *Hadji Murad*, and commented: "I once tried to read 'Resurrection' but couldn't. You see, when Tolstoy just tells a story he impresses me infinitely more than when he addresses the reader. When he turns his back to the reader then he seems to me *most* impressive. . . . It seems to me his philosophy is most true when it's *latent* in the story" (quoted in Norman Malcolm, *Ludwig Wittgenstein: A Memoir* [Oxford: Oxford University Press, 2001], 38). William Dean Howells wrote: "The ethics which are not aestheticized are of less permanent impression than the aesthetics which are ethicized" ("Lyof N. Tolstoy," *North American Review* 192, no. 661 [1910]: 744).

108. Bresson, quoted in Ciment, "I Seek Not Description But Vision," 502–3.

109. One topic taken up in this debate is whether in *Tractatus* logic and ethics can be separated in the way Biletzki, the editor of the entry on Wittgenstein and ethics in the *Stanford Encyclopedia,* suggests (see note 89). In distinction to Biletzki, Conant, Cora Diamond, and Piergiorgio Donatelli argue that for Wittgenstein the two topics cannot be pulled apart. A second topic instigated by Wittgenstein's claims that "ethics cannot be put into words. Ethics is transcendental" (*Tractatus,* 6.421) is what Wittgenstein meant by distinguishing between what can be said and what must be shown. (*Religion and Wittgenstein's Legacy*, ed. D. Z. Phillips and Mario von der Ruhr [Burlington, VT: Ashgate], 2005).

110. Conant, "What 'Ethics' in the *Tractatus* is *Not,*" 68, 71.

111. Cora Diamond, "Ethics, Imagination and the Method of Wittgenstein's *Tractatus*," in *The New Wittgenstein,* ed. Alice Crary and Rupert Read (London: Routledge, 2000), 168.

In Iris Murdoch's analysis, which insists on differences among moral outlooks that need not be confined to prescriptive linguistic or universal rules, it is "pointless to crush at all costs" these distinct "kinds of moral outlook . . . into the universal rules formula" (R. W. Hepburn and Iris Murdoch, "Symposium: Vision and Choice in Morality," in *Proceedings of the Aristotelian Society, Supplementary Volumes: Dreams and Self-Knowledge* 30 [1956]: 46). Specifically, Murdoch contrasts "people whose fundamental moral belief is that we all live in the same empirical and rationally comprehensible world and that morality is the adoption of universal and openly defensible rules of conduct" with "other people whose fundamental belief is that we live in a world whose mystery transcends us and that morality is the exploration of that mystery in so far as it concerns each individual. It is only by sharpening the universality model to a point of extreme abstraction that it can be made to cover both views" (47).

Diamond discusses a corollary distinction in relation to G. K. Chesterton's 1908 *Orthodoxy*, between "an ethical conception of the world as marvel" and ethics understood in relation to "logical necessity" (*The Realistic Spirit: Wittgenstein, Philosophy, and the Mind* [Cambridge, MA: MIT Press, 1991], 9).

112. The image is Murdoch's (see "Symposium: Vision and Choice in Morality," 40–41), but Diamond discusses it in relation to Hare's and Chesterton's opposed moral visions of the world: Hare's is predicated on "a concept"—the example is "*courage*"—tethered to "certain sorts of situation and to certain evaluations," while Chesterton's view of "moral thought and moral agency" is not related to "any particular descriptive content" or to "certain sorts of situations"; also not

"to any linguistic convention" and, most important, is not dependent on a predetermined "*conceptual choice*" since, for Chesterton, there is a "genuine variety . . . in the forms taken by moral thought" that could not fit preconceived moral concepts ("We Are Perpetually Moralists: Iris Murdoch, Fact, and Value," in *Iris Murdoch and the Search for Human Goodness*, eds. Maria Antonaccio and William Schweiker [Chicago: University of Chicago Press, 1996], 93–94).

Diamond ultimately locates Murdoch's understanding of a moral core in what she calls a "quality of consciousness" (95) that specifically manifests "moral awareness" as "*visual* awareness" (107). In a sentence inadvertently pertinent to the conclusions of "The Death of Ivan Ilych" and *L'Argent*, Diamond writes: "We *take in* the visual world, and how we take it in depends on the quality of our attention" (107). In other words, "the visual world" presents "moral colorings . . . hence the importance of the quality of our attention to reality" (107).

113. Repin, "Being-Toward-Death," 119. Repin cites Heidegger's footnote: "In his narrative (*Erzählung*), *The Death of Ivan Il'ich* (*Der Tod des Iwan Iljitsch*) L. N. Tolstoy has presented (*dargestellt*) the phenomenon of the shattering and breakdown of (that) 'one dies/people die' (*man stierbt*)" (101). She argues that these incommensurate realities are vivified by Tolstoy's story, and, commensurately, that the story is illuminated by Heidegger's reflections.

114. Repin, "Being-Toward-Death," 120.

115. Repin, "Being-Toward-Death," 126.

116. Repin, "Being-Toward-Death," 130.

117. See Garrett Stewart's *Death Sentences: Styles of Dying in British Fiction* (Cambridge, MA: Harvard University Press, 1984), a book-length analysis arguing that death does not have its real-world force without narrative. See also Peter Brooks, *Reading for the Plot: Design and Intention in Narrative* (Cambridge, MA: Harvard University Press, 1992); and Walter Benjamin, "The Story-Teller," in *Illuminations*, ed. Hannah Arendt, trans. Harry Zohn (New York: Schocken Books, 1969), 83–110.

118. Tolstoy, *Diaries*, 499, 506, 518, 536, 541, 566, 596, 652.

119. Tolstoy, *Diaries*, 518.

120. Tolstoy, *Diaries*, 547.

121. Tolstoy, *Diaries*, 541.

122. Tolstoy, *Diaries*, 541.

123. Tolstoy, *Diaries*, 487.

4

ROBERT BRESSON'S PATHOS

1. Michel Ciment, "I Seek Not Description But Vision: Robert Bresson on *L'Argent*," in *Robert Bresson*, ed. James Quandt (Toronto: Cinematheque Ontario, 1998), 504.

2. The dismantling is most obvious in Bresson's editing of shots so they are parceled—as when in *Lancelot du Lac*, we see a horse's flank, chest, abdomen, knee, buttock, but not its hoof, head, or entire body—a feature of Bresson's cinematography that has been well discussed.

But the fragmenting and recombination of visual and aural elements that determine the contours by which we recognize the relation of a thing to its parts, or two manifestations of a single phenomenon, can be more complex. In *Le Diable probablement* passengers on the bus are arguing about "who is it that is making a mockery of humanity"? Who is "driving us against our will" to destroy ourselves? Is it "the government"? Is it the "masses"? Is it "obscure forces whose laws are unfathomable"? "The devil, probably," one man replies. (Translations of the French from Bresson's 1977 film are from the subtitles of the DVD *The Devil, Probably* [Artificial Eye, 2008].) The bus crashes just at the instant that the driver, irritated at the passengers' analysis, turns his back to the road to glare at them, a wreck that raises a question about the relation between the fender-bender caused by the driver's carelessness and the negligence precipitating global self-destruction, whose particulars the film documents (the annihilation "of birds and insects beneficial to agriculture"; "rivers and oceans contaminated by seepage"; tankers leaking oil into the ocean; "oxides are released" that are "destroying the ozone layer"; "the destruction of entire species for profit"; the bombing of Hiroshima), though, of course, the traffic accident and the global tragedy are incomparable.

At the same time the menace of not looking—at the road, at what threatens the earth's survival—joins the two in an association underscored by Bresson's juxtaposition of the passengers' conversation with the image of the bus's outside rearview mirror, whose reflection benignly shows no danger, and of a second rearview mirror that captures the jumble of plastic, metal, glass of the bus interior. Both are lenses through which to see the relation of the minor crash and the planetary cataclysm.

In this way Bresson's montage rhythmically draws together and rends the elements of what we see so they are at once identified and dis-identified. Such a strategy is in keeping with Bresson's respect for the enigma of the relation between outcomes and origins. Bresson told his interviewer: "As Dostoevsky frequently does, I present the effect before the cause. I think this is a good idea because it increases the mystery; to witness events without knowing why they are occurring makes you desire to find out the reason" (Charles Thomas Samuels, "Encountering Robert Bresson," in *Robert Bresson (Revised)*, ed. James Quandt [Toronto: TIFF Cinematheque, 2011], 681).

In the montage I have described, effect and cause, the traffic collision and the global catastrophe interpenetrate in lieu of any genuine understanding of how one moves from the accidental to the calamitous and intentional evil that Hiroshima is.

3. Bresson's rethinkings of filmic traditions, from the illegible face to elliptical montage, which reveal phenomena outside the conventions that easily classify them, are articulated in *Notes of a Cinematographer* and explicated in a range of critical essays. Commonly discussed features of Bresson's innovative cinematography are his use of untrained actors rather than professionals; his technique of blanking out the willfully expressive face so there is no illusion that a transparence could reflect the inner life (in the text, and in "Animal Sentience," I elaborate); fragmented close-ups of legs, feet, and hands that compel attention with the same magnetism Bresson's inexpressive faces do, while the body as a whole is rendered at a distance in medium shots; the subordination of dialogue to involuntary gesture; the alternation of sound and image that Bresson insisted must register contrastively; the rhythm of fractured images in tension with an often discontinuous narrative.

More recent criticism has situated Bresson within the cinematic traditions he is revising. See, for example, David Bordwell's discussion of how Bresson's "cuts [of] scenes in *A Man Escaped* and later films [owe] a great deal to Soviet constructive editing in the silent era. His denial of establishing shots and his recourse to eyeline-match cutting rely upon the Kuleshov effect. But this tactic doesn't simply replicate the silent-film device. In building scenes that never show characters sharing the frame, Bresson provides a sense of adjacency and environment through offscreen sound. In effect, he revises the schema he inherits from cinematic tradition" ("The

Exchange: Narration and Style in *Les Anges du péché*," in Quandt, *Robert Bresson (Revised)*, 234–35).

4. Translations of the French from Bresson's 1951 *Journal d'un curé de campagne* are from the subtitles of the Criterion Collection DVD (2004). In the DVD of *Journal*, and in other DVDs discussed in this essay, where the subtitles are unidiomatic, I have edited them.

5. Robert Bresson, *Notes on the Cinematographer*, trans. Jonathan Griffin (København: Green Integer, 1997), 67; hereafter abbreviated *N* and cited parenthetically.

6. In the interview with Ciment, Bresson indicated the "close shot" of "the wet floor with the sound of the sponge. That is music, rhythm, sensation" ("I Seek Not Description But Vision," 505).

7. Martin Scorsese, quoted in "Film Makers on Bresson," in Quandt ed., *Robert Bresson*, 579. Scorsese added: "in Bresson you get a true dynamism generated by the most elemental relationships between image and sound" (579).

8. In the phrase *being without admixture* I am trying to get at an illusion created by Bresson's cinematography that there is a certain way of capturing human and animal bodies, as well as the material life of objects, that reveals what is essential to their existence, so that we see the nature of being outside of human personality, species distinction, and even sentience. As discussed in Giorgio Agamben's analysis of Gilles Deleuze's essay "Immanence: A Life," "*a life*" is "the figure of absolute immanence"—the opposite of Aristotle's "nutritive life." It is "what can never be attributed to a subject, being instead the matrix of infinite desubjectification," pointing to "a principle of virtual indetermination, in which the vegetative and the animal, the inside and the outside and even the organic and the inorganic, in passing through one another cannot be told apart" (Giorgio Agamben, "Absolute Immanence," in *Potentialities: Collected Essays in Philosophy*, ed. and trans. Daniel Heller-Roazen [Stanford: Stanford University Press, 1999], 232–33). Bresson's peeling away of inessentials encourages us to think we could arrive at a vantage from which "*a life*" might be apparent.

9. Sergei Eisenstein, *The Film Sense*, in *Film Form: Essays in Film Theory and The Film Sense*, ed. and trans. Jay Leyda ([1957] Cleveland: World, 1968), 168, 172; 166–78.

10. Bresson, quoted in Ciment, "I Seek Not Description But Vision," 508.

11. Bresson, quoted in Ciment, "I Seek Not Description But Vision," 510.

12. This sense of seeing outside the conceptual grids that domesticate vision is inherent in Bresson's understanding of the relation between technique and intuition: "I don't think much of technique, or making technique a big part of things. If you find a new way to catch life, nature, this could change details, but not the whole. I don't think so much of what I do when I work, but I try to *feel* something, to see without explaining, to catch it as nearly as I can—that's all" (Paul Schrader, "Robert Bresson, Possibly," in *The Films of Robert Bresson: A Casebook*, ed. Bert Cardullo [London: Anthem Press, 2009], 163–64). He elaborated: "I think you must think a lot in the intervals between working and writing, but when you work, you mustn't think anymore. Thinking is a terrible enemy. You should try to work not with your intelligence, but with your senses and your heart, with your intuition" (164).

13. "Models" is Bresson's idiosyncratic designation for persons who have no prior training in film or theater. For an elaboration of his theory of the model, see notes 23 and 28 of "Animal Sentience."

14. In note 14 of "Animal Sentience," which examines the inadequacy of an opposition like immanence/transcendence to discuss Bresson's films, I outline that critical history.

15. Marcel Proust, *Swann's Way: In Search of Lost Time*, vol. 1, trans. C. K. Scott Moncrieff and Terence Kilmartin (New York: The Modern Library, 2003), 341.

16. Philippe Lacoue-Labarthe, "The Echo of the Subject," in *Typography: Mimesis, Philosophy, Politics* (Cambridge, MA: Harvard University Press, 1989), 201. "Animal Sentience" elaborates.

17. She reads: "My daughter was born of a legitimate marriage. I had her baptised and confirmed. I brought her up to fear God and respect the Church within the limits of her age and simple condition. She did not think, plot or do anything against the faith. But envious people who wished to harm her, her parents and the good of princes and peoples, tried her for heresy. They accused her of false crimes, condemned her with iniquity and burned her."

18. Figures 1 through 9 are from Bresson's 1962 *Procès de Jeanne d'Arc* (Artificial Eye, 2004). Figures 10 through 35 are from Bresson's 1967 *Mouchette* (the Criterion Collection, 2006). Figures 36 through 42 are from Bresson's 1956 *A Man Escaped* (the Criterion Collection, 2004, 2013). Translations of the French in my text cite the subtitles of the above DVDs, except for in *Trial of Joan of Arc* and *A Man Escaped*, where there are two DVDs with varying translations; I have drawn from both of these, sometimes in a single quotation.

19. For a detailed history of how Joan came to hear the counsel of voices that dictated her mission; how she was "admitted into the presence of Charles VII" and convinced him to dismiss the claim that she was a "crazy visionary"; how Joan's voices accurately prophesied her fate, as well as that of the English (she asserted that "within seven years' space, the English would have to forfeit a bigger price than Orléans" and in fact "Paris was lost to Henry VI . . . six years and eight months afterwards"), see *The Catholic Encyclopedia,* s.v. "Joan of Arc, Saint," http://www.newadvent.org/cathen/08409c.htm (accessed August 6, 2015). Its narrative of Pierre Cauchon's "unscrupulous" treatment of Joan (she was not allowed an advocate, and "though accused in an ecclesiastical court, she was throughout illegally confined in the Castle of Rouen, a secular prison") confirms Bresson's adherence to documentary evidence.

20. Sometimes she refuses to answer: "'On whose advice [were you wearing men's clothes]?' . . . 'Next question.'" Though her face is unvarying in its guilelessness, she repeatedly weighs what can be said against what must be withheld: "It would be perjury for me to say what I have sworn not to say."

21. Pauline Kael, quoted in Scott Nye, "On the Hulu Channel: Robert Bresson's 'Trial of Joan of Arc,'" June 4, 2012, Available at: http://criterioncast.com/column/on-the-hulu-channel-robert-bressons-the-trial-of-joan-of-arc. Accessed August 8, 2015.

22. For an elaboration of Bresson's antipsychological vision identified in 1964 by Susan Sontag ("Spiritual Style in the Films of Robert Bresson," in *Robert Bresson,* 57–71), see Steven Shaviro's penetrating "A Note on Bresson": Bresson's films "destroy all our myths of depth, interiority and psychological integrity. We cannot attribute identity to either the actors or the characters, just as we cannot read their blankness psychologically, as a sign of reticence, despair, or alienation" (in *The Cinematic Body* [Minneapolis: University of Minnesota Press, 1993], 244). In his 1967 "*Le Journal d'un curé de campagne* and the Stylistics of Robert Bresson," André Bazin anticipates such characterizations when he writes that Bresson "would have us be concerned here not with the psychology but with the physiology of existence. . . . There is no development of character. Their inner conflicts, the various phases of their struggle as they wrestle with the Angel of the Lord, are never outwardly revealed." Thus while "Bresson strips his characters bare," what this means is that he "is only concerned with the countenance as flesh" (in *What Is Cinema?,* vol. 1, trans. Hugh Gray [Berkeley: University of California Press, 2005], 133–34). Self-consciousness, character, personality, and affect do not obstruct the models' countenances.

23. "The transcript's most famous exchange is an exercise in subtlety: asked if she knew she

was in God's grace, she answered: 'If I am not, may God put me there; and if I am, may God so keep me!' The question is a scholarly trap. Church doctrine held that no one could be certain of being in God's grace. If she had answered yes, then she would have convicted herself of heresy. If she had answered no, then she would have confessed her own guilt" (Catholic Online, "St. Joan of Arc," http://www.catholic.org/saints/saint.php?saint_id=295 [accessed August 6, 2015]). Bresson, like George Bernard Shaw before him, repeats this piece of the dialogue.

24. Although this inexpressiveness characterizes all of Bresson's models, its effect could not help but be particularized by each film's narrative context. Delay's serenity in response to the assault of the churchmen's questions; their shackling and surveillance of her even when she sleeps; their threats; and their attempts to sicken her with poisoned food can be read as equanimity in the presence of the multifarious conditions that would defeat it, in distinction to Carl Theodor Dreyer's Joan, who theatrically suffers her fate, and in distinction to Marie in *Au hasard Balthazar*, whose inexpressiveness proclaims her a helpless thrall to Gerárd's manipulation.

Léonce-Henri Burel's cinematography of Delay's face and erect posture, often in medium close-ups, illuminates her evenness in virtually every mood and scene, including the one in which she expresses concern for her inquisitor—with a detachment that engages him without a trace of rancor: "Be on guard. God sends me and you're in great danger."

25. Stressing Joan's isolation from a different angle, Richard Suchenski writes that when we see her, "half-visible figures are stacked around Joan, spilling outside the frame to make it clear that we are seeing only slices of a much larger environment, but there is never a cut to a shot depicting Joan and her adversaries in the same contiguous space during any of the courtroom scenes, making her literal and metaphoric isolation palpable" ("'The Sum of a Mysterious Operation': Bresson's Joan of Arc," in Quandt, *Robert Bresson (Revised)*, 363).

26. "I paint the human soul in all its depth" (Bresson, quoted in Mireille Latil Le Dantec, "Bresson, Dostoevsky," in *Robert Bresson*, 325). Schrader, in the commentary on the Criterion Collection DVD of Bresson's 1959 *Pickpocket*, speaks of Michel at the film's beginning as "a soul that can't find a place," and at the film's end, as "a soul . . . leap[ing] . . . to the transcendent" (2005). But to say that the soul stands free of the body or transcends the body is bluntly contradicted in all of Bresson's films: for instance, by the camera's focus on Michel's hands in *Pickpocket*, and by Agnès's ecstatic ballet dancing in *Les Dames du Bois de Boulogne*. In *Journal d'un curé de campagne*, when Chantel impenitently divulges her sins to the young priest notwithstanding his protests—it is improper for her to do so, since she is outside the confessional ("The extraordinary force building up inside me. Life itself won't be long enough to let it all out")—it's not the soul that breaks through material confines of the confessional cubicle, or that escapes through her speech, but rather something more featured and dangerous: the "force" of hatred and rage made palpable as a knife.

27. Gilles Deleuze, *Cinema 1: The Movement-Image*, trans. Hugh Tomlinson and Barbara Habberjam (Minneapolis: University of Minnesota Press, 1989), 88.

28. One could argue that short of voice-overs all film prohibits access to inwardness. But the inexpressiveness and automaticity Bresson cultivates in his models exaggerate that inaccessibility, as when Bresson defines the model as an ideal whose only pertinent movements are physical: "Model. Two mobile eyes in a mobile head, itself on a mobile body" (*N* 39). More explicitly dictating the suppression of affect that could illusorily transport the viewer to an interior, he writes: "Models. No ostentation. Faculty of gathering into himself, of keeping, of not letting anything get out" (*N* 83). The inexpressiveness stands out as a special case in *Procès* because the very question of access to Joan's inner world, to what she sees—which is indispensable to the film's

interest in her—is precisely what is withheld. At the same time, what is invisible is not something like a Platonic spirit or Christian soul encrypted within the body. It can't be extracted, isolated, or witnessed, though as indicated above it is reflected on by an aggregate of perspectives, and is itself associated with a perspective, with what Joan sees, hears, and obeys.

29. The characterizations are Maurice Merleau-Ponty's in "Interrogation and Intuition," in *The Visible and the Invisible,* ed. Claude Lefort, trans. Alphonso Lingis (Evanston: Northwestern University Press, 1968), 84. His analysis is of the imaginary status of an abstraction like "'pure' being," and does not refer to Bresson's film. In Merleau-Ponty's account, "no essence, no idea" can be separated from "the domain of space and time. . . . of history and geography" (115) and from one's own experience of it: the very idea of such an essence is not "*before me,* but surrounding me and in a sense traversing me, and my vision of Being not forming itself from elsewhere, but from the midst of Being," from "the generality of my body, and the ideas . . . already encrusted in its joints" (114).

30. Merleau-Ponty, "Interrogation and Intuition," 113.

31. Agamben, "Absolute Immanence," in *Potentialities,* 232. Merleau-Ponty, "Interrogation and Intuition," in *The Visible and the Invisible,* 84. "The spark of life" is exemplified in Agamben's discussion of Charles Dickens's character Riderhood, who, when reviving after an incident of near-drowning, hovers between life and death in *Our Mutual Friend* (Agamben, "Absolute Immanence," 228–29). Riderhood's near-drowning is initially discussed by Deleuze in "Immanence: A Life," in *Pure Immanence: Essays on A Life,* trans. Anne Boyman (New York: Zone Books, 2001), 28–29. As noted, "'pure' being" is Merleau-Ponty's term in "Interrogation and Intuition," 84. Simone Weil writes: "what is sacred in a human being is the impersonal in him" ("Human Personality," in *The Simone Weil Reader,* ed. George A. Panichas [Wakefield, RI: Moyer Bell, 1977], 317).

32. At the same time, it must be stressed: Joan is not a visionary in the sense of perceiving something not real or not present. She is not seeing phantasms. What is involved is not fancy or reverie. What is disclosed to her is *there*—though what is there for *her* is not what is there for the Bishop or for us.

33. In Marjorie Levinson's Spinozistic reading of William Wordsworth's "A Slumber Did My Spirit Seal," Levinson suggests that when Lucy dies she has "undergone an ontological or substantive change, from person to thing" ("A Motion and a Spirit: Romancing Spinoza," *Studies in Romanticism* 46, no. 4 [2007]: 390). She "perishes as that individual, but assumes another conatus," becoming "part of the planet's rolling course" (391), a body very graphically and materially in the earth, which "adds to" its "mass" (392). Levinson thus posits a consolatory Spinozistic physics or metaphysics to ground her reading of Wordsworth's poem, in which there's a change of state, but not a loss. Though Bresson would not have had a Spinozistic view of the life/death divide, one could see an analogy between the claim that when Lucy dies an equivalence is maintained between what she is and was and a claim about Joan's vision before and after she is burned alive. In negative terms: Joan's vision can no more perish than it can be preserved—both attributes being inassimilable to the immateriality of Bresson's representation of vision.

34. She is of course culpable of sedition; her disparagement of the churchmen's divinely authorized power is antinomian.

35. *Mouchette* looks backward to *Procès,* the purity of whose heroine remains unconceded, and forward to *L'Argent,* Bresson's last film, in which virtue (purity framed in an ethical context) is realized in a character's acknowledgment of his own violence. To summarize the plot: in a provincial French village, Mouchette cares for her infant brother and for her mother, who is

dying. Her alcoholic father is seen with his eldest son illegally delivering bottles to a provincial village bar. Ignored by her family, Mouchette is also taunted by her classmates; humiliated by her teacher; and raped by Arsène, a poacher, whom she meets one night in the woods. Though she offers Arsène an alibi when he fears he has killed the gamekeeper, Mathieu, his nemesis, Arsène abandons her. Mouchette's mother dies. When her father, who sits by his wife's body looking clueless, reprimands Mouchette ("Stop staring at me," he coolly orders), she leaves in search of milk for the baby's bottle. Treated with hostile curiosity by the townspeople she encounters, Mouchette wanders toward a quarry, where she watches hunters shoot a rabbit, which writhes from side to side, while the girl observes its death throes. She herself rolls down a nearby hill toward the quarry pond. On the third attempt she drowns. Even within the genre of films about adolescent misery (for instance, François Truffaut's roughly contemporaneous 1959 *The Four Hundred Blows*), the apparent melodrama of *Mouchette*'s plot seems hard to beat.

36. According to Peter Brooks, although melodrama acts out the conflict between a spiritual world of light and an evil material world of darkness, it ultimately affirms the value of innocence and "the existence of a moral universe which . . . can be made to assert its presence and its categorical force among men" (*The Melodramatic Imagination: Balzac, Henry James, and the Mode of Excess* [New Haven: Yale University Press, 1976], 20). In line with such an understanding Joseph Cunneen identifies *Mouchette* as a film that contains both tragedy and uplift, since "its poetic realism succeeds in giving the girl's 'suicide' the overtones of liberation" (*Robert Bresson: A Spiritual Style in Film* [New York: Continuum, 2003], 112). In distinction, Jacques Rancière argues that Bresson thwarts melodrama; he "demolishes" a narrative line that could be read in terms of such "liberation" or the triumph of innocence ("*Mouchette* and the Paradoxes of the Language of Images," in *The Intervals of Cinema*, trans. John Howe [New York: Verso, 2014], 61).

37. Amédée Ayfre suggests that Bresson is less likely to "classify beings according to their most general characteristics: Man, Animal, Living, Being; or Commerce, Industry, Justice" than he is to discover the abstraction that would reveal what "makes a being what he is, his essence" ("The Universe of Robert Bresson," in *The Films of Robert Bresson*, ed. Ian Cameron (New York: Praeger, 1970), 7. In the text, I argue that in *Mouchette* the autonomy of such essences is challenged.

38. In French "plus d'espérance!" is ambiguous. It could either mean "more hope" or be an oblique rendering of the French double negative meaning "no more hope," since in conversation or poetry the normal double negative is often omitted. Given the genitive *d*, we also hear the ghostly overtone for "despair" in the lettering "desespérance!," an echo that Bresson makes explicit when "espérant/désespérant" rhymes in *Four Nights of a Dreamer*, released in 1971, five years later. The lyrics below are adapted for Bresson's film from nineteenth-century verses of Casimir Delavigne's (1793–1843) "Trois Jours de Christophe Colomb":

Espérez! Plus d'espérance!
Trois jours, leur dit Colomb,
En montrant le ciel immense,
Le fond de l'horizon.

Trois jours et je vous donne un monde,
A vous qui n'avez plus d'espoir.
Sur l'immensité profonde,
Ses yeux s'ouvraient pour le voir.

39. Georges Bernanos, *Mouchette*, trans. J. C. Whitehouse (New York: New York Review Books, 2006), 40.

40. He writes: Mouchette "is caught, just as the partridges are caught, in a trap" (Bresson, quoted in Samuels, "Encountering Robert Bresson," in Cardullo, ed., *The Films of Robert Bresson*, 110). Images of the trap and of imprisoned animals fill Bernanos's novel: "Arsène . . . had all the ease of the wild animals in their cages in Belloc's menagerie" (27); Mouchette "ran, moaning feebly like a hunted animal" (55); Arsène accuses Mouchette of being "crafty as a partridge" (29). When Gustave, Mouchette's infant brother, wails, the source of his suffering is said to be "his mouth . . . full of straw" (79), a plight that is an animal's.

41. Theodor Adorno and Hanns Eisler, *Composing for the Films* (London: Continuum, 2007), 50. Adorno and Eisler write: "Motion-picture music corresponds to the whistling or singing child in the dark. The real reason for the fear is not even that these people whose silent effigies are moving in front of one seem to be ghosts. The captions do their best to come to the aid of these images. But confronted with gesticulating masks, people experience themselves as creatures of the very same kind, as being threatened by muteness" (50–51).

42. Adorno and Eisler, *Composing for the Films*, 51.

43. Adorno and Eisler, *Composing for the Films*, 51.

44. Bresson equivocates when he describes Mouchette as playing a child's game, and, in her several tries, only succeeding on the third attempt; nonetheless revealing her deliberation, her meaning it: "when I read the book I immediately knew how the film should end. . . . I wanted her to make three attempts so that we know what she wants before anything decisive happens. But it's a game. There are many ways of committing suicide and Russian roulette is one. Rolling downhill is a little girl's game that is her equivalent" (quoted in "Robert Bresson in Conversation with Ronald Hayman," in Cardullo, ed., *The Films of Robert Bresson*, 142–43).

45. Even if a host of affectively identifiable intensities play across the model's face, they do so fleetingly, insisting that to see penetratively is to discern emotion as shallow, conditional, and transient. This insubstantiality of emotion also pertains to Mouchette's outbursts, as when she says to the old lady who macabrely "love[s] the dead. . . . I talk to them and they answer me" "You disgusting old thing," or "Merde" to her father when he tells her to stop staring at him (he repels her gaze as he would any intimacy). Even her attempt to get back at the smirking girls, who after school twirl on a rail and flaunt their white underpants, by throwing dirt at them, is child's play, an action almost devoid of enmity.

46. When Bresson described the model as "All face" (*N* 40), he was quoting from a passage in Montaigne, in which a man, asked about how he could go about with "*your face all bare*" in the cold of winter and with "nothing but his shirt about him," replies: "*Imagine I am all face*." To be "*all face*" is to be stripped bare, while that nakedness only exposes itself, revealing nothing further of substance beyond its materiality.

47. Deleuze, *Cinema 1*, 87.

Deleuze distinguishes between the "intensive face" defined by a series that carries us "from one quality to another" (89), essentially referring to the play of particular expressions, as from "love" to "hate" (91), and the "reflecting face" (90), which is nonmimetic, defined by the "life of the mind or spiritual nonpsychological life" (92), and that is "*abstract*[ed] *from all spatio-temporal co-ordinates*" (96) and "raise[d] to the state of Entity" (96). When the face "pass[es] from intensification to reflection," then it is "phosphorescent, scintillating, brilliant, a being of light. Brilliance emerges out of the shadows" (92).

Deleuze called the combination of these two poles (between which there is a movement) the "affection-image," and elaborated: "it is a matter of two poles, sometimes one prevailing over the other and appearing almost pure, sometimes the two being mixed in one direction or the other" (88). The "affection-image" not only applies to the face, but equally to any close-up, and also to things: "why is expression not available to things? There are affects of things. The 'edge,' the 'blade,' or rather the 'point' of Jack the Ripper's knife, is no less an affect than the fear which overcomes his features and the resignation which finally seizes hold of the whole of his face" (97).

In my discussion of *A Man Escaped* I will argue that the versatility of objects, their capacity to evolve into different forms, with different appearances, different textures, different functions, suggests a vitality, a versatility, even an expressivity that, in Deleuze's word, confers on them "faceicity" (97)—that gives them the mobility and animation of the human face—even as Bresson privileges the extreme pole of the nonexpressive face on his models.

48. Deleuze, *Cinema 1,* 87–88.

49. "The reflexive face expresses a pure Quality, that is to say a 'something' common to several objects of different kinds" (Deleuze, *Cinema 1,* 90).

50. Deleuze, *Cinema 1,* 96.

51. At the end of Terence Davies' *The Long Day Closes*, Bud shines a flashlight at the moon. "If you shine a torch up into the night sky, the light goes on forever," he unexpectedly says of the *flash*light, rather than of the *moon*light. Was Davies recalling the flashlight in *Mouchette* that seems to be the same kind of thing as the moon, much as the car lights reflected in the brightness of the baby's eyes could be said to share the vitality of those eyes? If so, the flashlight and moonlight in *The Long Day Closes*, as in *Mouchette*, would exemplify Deleuze's "pure Quality . . . common to several objects of different kinds" (*Cinema 1,* 90). In Deleuze's examples, "a snowflake caught on an eyelash, the spiritual white of an internal innocence, the dissolved white of a moral degradation, the hostile and searing white of the iceberg where the heroine will wander" in D. W. Griffith's *Orphans of the Storm* all "express white" (90).

In "The Intertwining—The Chiasm" Merleau-Ponty anatomizes red ("the red dress . . . the tiles of roof tops, the flags of gate keepers and of the Revolution . . . robes of professors, bishops, and advocate generals," to cite only a few of the page-long examples of reds that form "a constellation. . . . If we took all these participations into account, we would recognize that a naked color, and in general a visible, is not a chunk of absolutely hard, indivisible being . . . but is rather a sort of straits between exterior horizons and interior horizons. . . . less a color or a thing, therefore, than a difference between things and colors, a momentary crystallization of colored being or of visibility" [*The Visible and the Invisible,* 132]).

The look of things, like the look of faces—and like the *light* of things, and the *being* of things—which Bresson, Davies, Merleau-Ponty, Deleuze, albeit differently, draw into relation, points to something *between* "the alleged colors and visibles," namely: "the tissue that lines them, sustains them, nourishes them, and which for its part is not a thing, but a possibility, a latency, and a *flesh* of things" (Merleau-Ponty, *The Visible and the Invisible,* 132–33). Like all those "reds" and "whites" (and like the flood of whites in Melville's *Moby-Dick*), the brightness that Bresson and Davies iterate and make tangible spills over the boundaries of these things, including the face, which, as a life-form, is a kind of thing, so that we experience the mystery of things as no less alive than the face, and no less enduring than the flashlight illuminating the moonlight. In Davies' shot who could precisely locate the boundary between the thing illuminating and the thing illuminated?

52. Alain Badiou, *Cinema*, ed. Antoine de Baecque, trans. Susan Spitzer (Malden, MA: Polity, 2013), 25.

53. Martin Heidegger, "Letter on Humanism," in *Basic Writings,* ed. David Farrell Krell (New York: Harper Perennial, 1977), 238. Heidegger specifically distinguishes *es gibt* from the *there is* of things (238) and individual beings (252) since "Being" is "essentially broader than all beings"

(240). Heidegger uses the term *Dasein* only about human beings and their ontological status, which is being thrown into the world and then answerable for responding to it with "care" (246). *Dasein* applies to beings that are unique, in that Being is a question for them, just as the "guardianship" (246) of Being is an obligation.

54. Critics have glossed Mouchette's salvation in terms of redemption and a Christian iconography. See, for instance, Tony Pipolo, *Robert Bresson: A Passion for Film* (Oxford: Oxford University Press, 2010), 216–17, though Bresson's film resists such an axiomatic understanding. In distinction to such interpretations, see Charles Barr's "*Mouchette,*" in Cameron ed., *The Films of Robert Bresson*, 115–25, and the analysis in the text.

55. Thus Mouchette is released from all "time-space" and even from what Deleuze calls "Entity," an idea he attributes to Béla Balázs. "As Balázs has already accurately demonstrated, the close-up does *not* tear its object from a set of which it would form part, of which it would be a part, but on the contrary *it abstracts it from all spatio-temporal coordinates*, that is to say it raises it to the state of Entity" (*Cinema 1*, 95–96).

56. Béla Balázs, *Béla Balázs: Early Film Theory:* Visible Man *and* The Spirit of Film, ed. Erica Carter, trans. Rodney Livingstone (New York: Berghahn Books, 2010), 73.

57. The words are Badiou's, who writes about a structural dialectics he associates with "theological reactionism" in relation to the suicide in *Le Diable probablement*: "In the night of negativity there rises a pale star so old that, in actual fact, its light won't reach us, however empty and dark Bresson may make his screen, ever again" (*Cinema*, 49).

58. Eisenstein, *Film Sense*, 158–59.

59. For instance, Donald Richie: "The girl has decided that life has no answer for her, yet the *Magnificat* tells us otherwise" ("Bresson and Music," *Robert Bresson*, 301). Pipolo identifies the Gospel passage that makes this explicit: "since the text of the *Magnificat* is the canticle of the Virgin Mary in the Gospel according to Luke . . . it lends both dignity and salvation to Mouchette, particularly since the passage we hear is relevant to her situation: 'He hath put down the mighty from their seats, and exalted them of low degree'" (*A Passion for Film*, 231).

60. Bresson, quoted in Ciment, "I Seek Not Description But Vision," 501.

61. Writing that in Bresson's film the *Magnificat* "affirm[s] the possibility of another life after death," Lindley Hanlon is glossing words from Matthew 23:12 ("Sound as Symbol in *Mouchette*," in Quandt, *Robert Bresson (Revised)*, 405).

62. Bresson, quoted in Samuels, "Encountering Robert Bresson," 687.

63. Bresson, quoted in Samuels, "Encountering Robert Bresson," 687.

64. Bresson, quoted in Samuels, "Encountering Robert Bresson," 687.

65. Keith Reader, *Robert Bresson* (Manchester: Manchester University Press, 2000), 96.

66. Or if we are meant to see what precedes the credits—a woman, retrospectively recognized as the children's mother, who says "What will become of them without me?"—as a context, it does not clarify. If the mother's death and Mouchette's death are indistinguishably transfigured by the Monteverdi, this uniform treatment of death would inexplicably efface the differential representation of mortality we see in Bresson's other films. It is implausible that Bresson would erase the distinction between suicide and natural death so that resurrection always mitigates earthly torment.

67. Jean-Luc Nancy, *Listening*, trans. Charlotte Mandell (New York: Fordham University Press, 2007), 13.

68. Nancy, *Listening*, 15, 27.

69. Bresson, quoted in Cunneen, *Robert Bresson: A Spiritual Style*, 112.

70. Nancy, *Listening,* 27.

71. Bresson took Fontaine's story from an historical account of an imprisoned French Resistance leader "charged with planning a bomb attack . . . and espionage," who escaped from a Nazi prison camp in Lyon, 1943. Before the credits, we are shown the image of a prison structure. These words move down the screen: "The following is a true story. I present it as it happened, without adornment." Behind the words, the rapturous *Kyrie* of Mozart's *Grand Mass in C Minor* is sounded out. In a plaque-like text, a memorial inscription in a narrative key, in translation, reads: "At this site, under German occupation, 10,000 men suffered, victims of the Nazis. 7,000 passed away." Only then are the title and alternative title displayed.

We immediately see Fontaine's attempt to break out of custody when he unsuccessfully bolts from the car in which he is being driven to prison. He no sooner gives an official his word that he will accept defeat than he resolves, "I was determined to escape at the first opportunity," and methodically sets about conceiving how to transform the objects in his cell into implements that will free him. From the film's beginning, then, "spirit" is associated with Fontaine's resourcefulness in deliberating how to wield matter so that substances are remade, until, though still solid masses composed of specific properties, they are transformed in shape, function, and identifying characteristics.

72. The two sentences from the Biblical passage that introduce both a conditional and a futural, otherworldly, dimension to the understanding of spirit are excised from the quotation Pastor de Leyris copies for Fontaine. Omitted from the note are the sentences: "Verily, verily, I say unto thee, Except a man be born of water and of the Spirit, he cannot enter into the kingdom of God. That which is born of the flesh is flesh; and that which is born of the Spirit is spirit" (John 3:5–6). In *Escaped,* as discussed above, spirit cannot be exorcised from matter, and is nowhere if not present.

73. Bresson, quoted in Quandt, "Introduction," *Robert Bresson,* 10.

74. The film is thus not only, and not even primarily, a parable (another manifestation of its fidelity to the material life of objects), in that Fontaine's willed attention to how matter can be altered to ensure his escape (without which a new life could only be spectral) is independent of the life reborn in Christ that is glossed by the Biblical passage.

75. Jost is the traitorous young French boy (he has gone over to the German side, and also accidentally killed a German; hence his imprisonment) Fontaine discovers in his cell right before the planned escape. In explaining to Jost that the Germans will not win, and in also taking Jost with him (rather than killing the boy), Fontaine gives him another chance, promising, "I will help you to make the most of your freedom."

76. The wrong way to interpret the relation between the material and the spiritual registers is to see the latter as a compensation for the humiliation of the material world. The logic of segregation is Allen Thiher's in "Bresson's *Un condamné à mort:* The Semiotics of Grace," in *Robert Bresson,* 223–33. Thiher interprets the *Kyrie* of Mozart's *Grand Mass in C Minor,* which accompanies the images of the prisoners emptying their waste buckets into the cesspool in the prison courtyard, as providing a "religious drama of spiritual elevation" that contrasts with "the present drama of absurd degradation" (229). Rather, the film stresses the impossibility of segregating the cesspool and the *Mass,* which are drawn toward each other and specifically made congruent in Eisenstein's notion of vertical montage. François Truffaut characterizes the Mozart, "far from symbolizing liberty," as rather providing "a liturgical aspect to the daily flushing of waste buckets" ("On *A Man Escaped,*" in Cardullo, ed., *The Films of Robert Bresson,* 190).

77. When Blanchet, the cynical older man (who tried to kill himself, but the nail broke), asks Fontaine, "Why bother?" Fontaine responds: "To fight the walls, to fight myself, to fight the door.

You too, Mr. Blanchet, should fight and hope. . . . To go home, to be free." When Blanchet replies that there's no one waiting for him, Fontaine insists: "Fight anyway. Fight for everyone here. . . . I think of you, Mr. Blanchet, and it gives me courage." The obduracy that is the door, like the obduracy that is the self (whose intractability is epitomized by Blanchet's despair), provokes the same defiant resoluteness. Both must be worn away with muscular effort.

78. In distinction, Orsini's "too much hope for a new life" supersedes his deliberation of a good plan, though he is nonetheless called "courage incarnate"—the strategy that fails, like the one that succeeds, indiscriminately realizing valor. Orsini's failed attempt will become the precondition of Fontaine's freedom: from Orsini's miscalculations, Fontaine learns he'll need hooks to scale the prison walls.

79. Bresson, in "Bresson Without a Trace," *A Man Escaped*, DVD, disc 2, the Criterion Collection, 2013. The interview is from a 1965 episode of the television program *Cinéastes de notre temps* in which Bresson gave his first on-camera interview.

The exchange takes place in the context of Bresson's comparison of the "'naturalism' of theater" to the "'nature' of 'cinematography.'" He continues: "It reminds me of the two ways a camera sees things, close up or distant. Perhaps this is the way to see nature, to get closer to things, to reality. . . . If we got really close, as close as possible . . . we'd create the supernatural almost every time."

80. Bresson, quoted in Ciment, "I Seek Not Description But Vision," 510.

81. Deleuze, *Cinema 2: The Time-Image*, trans. Hugh Tomlinson and Robert Galeta (Minneapolis: University of Minnesota Press, 1989), 201. Deleuze, writing of the "disturbance" of the "visible" in cinematography, which "contradicts all natural perception," paraphrases and then quotes Jean-Louis Schefer in *L'homme ordinaire du cinéma*: "the object of cinema is not to reconstitute a presence of bodies, in perception and action, but to carry out a primordial genesis of bodies in terms of a white, or a black or a grey (or even in terms of colours), in terms of a 'beginning of visible which is not yet a figure, which is not yet an action.'" Deleuze then asks: "Is this what Bresson's project, *Genèse*, is?" (201).

82. For instance, Bresson's rope owes an obvious debt to the escape film (one classic is Alfred Hitchcock's *North by Northwest*), but it revises that genre, since its thrill has less to do with liberty than with what enables it when the rope becomes what it is in the dismantling of materials that constitute its weave.

83. Bresson claimed that "poetry . . . penetrates unaided through the joins (ellipses)" (*N* 37). However, the "poetry" of Bresson's unusual couplings is not aesthetic, but is rather ontological. In Haneke's words, Bresson has an "almost physical aversion to any type of lie, especially to any form of aesthetic pretence," including his "almost manic rejection of the 'beautiful'" (Michael Haneke, "Terror and Utopia of Form, Addicted to Truth: A Film Story about Robert Bresson's *Au hasard Balthazar*," in Quandt, *Robert Bresson (Revised)*, 389.

84. Fontaine says: The door "was made of two panels of six oak boards held within a frame of the same thickness. In the gap between two boards, I saw that the joining wood was not oak, but wood of another color, beech or poplar. There would surely be a way to take the door apart." To identify the type of wood is to discern that it is penetrable.

85. Eisenstein, *Film Form*, in *Film Form: Essays in Film Theory and The Film Sense*, 165, 170.

In relation to this transgression of boundaries Eisenstein discusses *Potemkin*, where what "looks like a chronicle (or newsreel) of an event . . . functions as a drama" (*Film Form*, 162). The "drama" is created by the structure of the work, which depends on "transition. . . . And it should be further noted that the transition within each part is not merely a transition to a merely *different* mood, to a merely *different* rhythm, to a merely *different* event, but each time the transition is to a sharply opposite quality" (164–65).

One such example of a transition to an "opposite quality" is the music composed by Edward Meisel for *Potemkin*. Eisenstein insisted that the music "reject customary melodiousness for this sequence of 'Meeting the Squadron,' relying entirely on a rhythmic beating of percussion" (177); in other words, his "demand" was that music break away from its customary role of mere illustration, and contribute to the "unity" achieved by "musical and visual images" when they "fused" (177). Thus the music was not a mere accompaniment, but shaped "by the same . . . laws and principles of construction that govern the work as a whole" (178). A passage from one condition to another is differently exemplified by an abrupt transition in which "a tense performance of the dialogue" becomes "*real* physical tension," when in Alexander Ostrovsky's *Enough Simplicity in Every Sage*, the character Golutvin "spoke his lines" while "balancing and running along" a "tight-rope." And demonstrated by a third example in which emotion surges into a physical manifestation, as when Mamayev, another character in that play, who, "angry with his nephew for a caricature he had made of him, threw himself at him head first, breaking through the paper of the portrait in a flying somersault beyond the frame" (175).

In other words, whether the transgression of limits works by opposition (as with Eisenstein's first example) or by an intensification created when feeling in one register (linguistic or affective) is transferred to a material register (as in Eisenstein's second and third examples), in each, this "leap" (or, it could be, literal breaking of the frame) transforms a static condition into a dynamic one, and, by dint of that dynamism, becomes "inseparable from the organism of the theme" (178). In *A Man Escaped*, dynamism is differently constitutive of organicism because the new life of objects cannot be separated from the new life of the spirit that transforms them.

86. Eisenstein, *Film Form*, 172, 166, 170. Whether, for instance, from "the figurative to the physical" (171); "chaos" into "rhythm"; "*downward* rushing movement" into "movement—*upward*" (170); a "*narrative* type of exposition" into the "structure of *imagery*" (171); from "quantity to quality" (173), or, in Bresson's film, from the object that frames a window to the object that enables an escape.

87. Eisenstein, *Film Form*, 173.

88. Eisenstein, *Film Form*, 166.

89. In "The Invisible Text as a Universal Equivalent: Sergei Eisenstein," Mikhail Iampolski anatomizes the "line or scheme" that, in Eisenstein's conception, "represents 'relations in the most generalized form'" (226), a form whose "Platonism" (228) ultimately enables Eisenstein to posit Tiresias as a "mythic teacher" leading him "into a hidden world beyond the visible" where lies "the 'basic' text of universal connections and equivalences" (*The Memory of Tiresias: Intertextuality and Film*, trans. Harsha Ram [Berkeley: University of California Press, 1998], 235). One example of this "equivalence" would seem "pathos" that commensurately applies to the spectator's ecstatic response and to the ecstatic movements in a film's structure. To radically simplify: for Eisenstein such "equivalence . . . is possible only when form has disintegrated, and all that remains is its bare scheme, the skeleton" (241). This shattering is not metaphoric, but, in Iampolski's argument about the "Platonic sphere of pure ideas" that enables Eisenstein's vision of resemblances, it involves the "physiognomic discovery of something hidden in the body—a thing, a text or line, a 'skeleton' . . . visible only to the initiate" (242–43).

90. Recent theorists have differently conceptualized the life of objects. In her Deleuzian analysis, *Vibrant Matter: A Political Ecology of Things* (Durham: Duke University Press, 2010), Jane Bennett argues for a "vital materialism" that "conceives of matter as intrinsically lively (but

not ensouled)" (xvii), while in *Tool-Being: Heidegger and the Metaphysics of Objects* (Chicago: Open Court, 2002), Graham Harman provides a revised Heideggerian analysis of that vitality in the context of what he calls an object-oriented ontology. In *Tool-Being*, Harman insists that "human Dasein" is not the only "star in the theater" (1): "objects themselves, far from the insipid physical bulks that one imagines, are already aflame with ambiguity, torn by vibrations and insurgencies equaling those found in the most tortured human moods. It is mistaken to follow a literal reading of *Being and Time* and assume that only human being is filled with riddles" (19). Harman's argument stresses the physical actuality of things outside of our use and consciousness of them. For instance, objects have the same "dual structure" of "presence-at-hand and readiness-to-hand," which "belongs to *every entity*" (4).

Although Fontaine transforms objects so he can use them to engineer his escape, the point I want to stress is that for Bresson's film, as for Harman, "no entity ever exhausts the reality of another, never makes contact with the darkest residues of its heart" (283). Harman argues there is not an "opposition between a brute realm of effects and a starry, windy space of transcendent vision" (294). Rather, "each thing" is "a galaxy of parts" in an "electrified whole" (294) of vibrating particles. Some such dynamism—realized through the movement Eisenstein calls "pathos"—is implicit in *Escaped*, in which something like our awareness of what Bresson called the "soul" of "objects" is gleaned, or imagined as realized, in the vicissitudes of their materiality (quoted in Quandt, "Introduction," in *Robert Bresson*, 10). *Imagined* because, following Alfred North Whitehead, in Harman's characterization, "The actuality of the object belongs always and only to a vacuum" (290).

91. For instance, representation and abstraction intersect at the conclusion of *Les Anges du péché* when, opening the door to the police, Thérèse presents her crossed hands to be cuffed, visually embodying the cross whose outline Anne-Marie marks with her hands as she lies dying, and whose burden Thérèse assumes as she assents to the arrest she has been fleeing. For a discussion of this scene, and others like it (for instance, one in which the "muting" of "facial expressions" converts "rows of bodies into striated patterns"), see Bordwell, "The Exchange, 245. Bordwell examines the film's structural symmetries, fades, and framing patterns, as well as an "abstract visual rhythm set up by overlapping black, white, and grey surfaces," which, among other strategies, contribute to the "pictorial abstraction" (245) in *Les Anges du péché*, in which Bresson juxtaposes the fallen woman to the would-be saint.

Bazin observed that for Bresson "getting to the heart of a story or of a drama" involves "the most rigorous form of aesthetic abstraction" ("*Le journal d'un curé de campagne*," in Cameron, ed., *The Films of Robert Bresson*, 55).

92. Haneke, "Terror and Utopia of Form," in Quandt, *Robert Bresson (Revised)*, 393.

93. The nexus that connects dying and reviving is of course the swoon. Bresson reveals the concatenation of these states when in the film's penultimate scene Agnès's mother warns Jean: "She's very ill. She's fainted three times. Her heart may fail any minute." Translations of the French from Bresson's 1945 *Les Dames du Bois de Boulogne* are from the subtitles of the Criterion Collection DVD (2003).

94. In context: "Everything dissolves into pure relationship, and it is up to the viewer to draw conclusions from the sum of the arrangement. Reduction and omission become the magic keys to activating the viewer. . . . Left out is the gesture of persuasion of models with whom we can identify emotionally. Left out is the (all too) condensed meaning of the connections of sociological and psychological explanations. . . . Left out is the pretence of any kind of wholeness. . . . Left out is the unusual, because it would defraud the misery of everyday existence of its dignity.

Left out, finally, is happiness, because its depiction would desecrate suffering and pain. And it is precisely this universal retraction . . . that conceals in its gesture of refusal more utopia than all the bastions of repression and cheap consolation" (Haneke, "Terror and Utopia of Form," 393).

95. Bresson interview, in "Bresson Without a Trace," *A Man Escaped*, DVD, disc 2, the Criterion Collection.

96. Haneke writes: "Bresson invented the 'dirty' image in the field of art cinema. Alongside the ever perceptible desire to show things as clearly and simply as possible, an infallible instinct saves him from the danger of sterile stylization; for all the precision of their framing, his pictures always give the impression of being frayed, ready for when reality breaks the rules" ("Terror and Utopia of Form," 389–90).

97. In *Arts of Impoverishment: Beckett, Rothko, Resnais* (Cambridge, MA: Harvard University Press, 1993), Leo Bersani and Ulysse Dutoit describe film as what characteristically "protects" "*our* inviolability . . . in assuring us that we can approach, know, even take possession of the real by an act of pure apprehension in which we need not be implicated" (157).

The artists on whom Bersani and Dutoit train their inquiry thwart such mastery, it's argued, by renouncing authority over the real and the meaningful (2) in their writing, painting, and cinematography. For instance, in Alain Resnais's *Mon Oncle d'Amérique*, the viewer can no longer feel in command of what he sees, but rather is made to attend to certain disorienting "moves of a cinematic composition" (179), a strategy that disables him from orienting his attention on "characters' psychology" within the work's fiction or removing himself to a interpretive position "outside" the "work" (178) that would be free of its confusions. Moreover, in *Mon Oncle d'Amérique*, Resnais provides no unified perspective; rather, what impedes a viewer's integrated appropriation of what he sees is a proliferation of vantages that reveal "formal variations of each moment" (177), so that all perspectives are relativized. "Resnais thus dissociates seeing from domination" (178).

What strikes me about the pertinence of this analysis to my discussion of Bresson is a commensurate disempowerment of vision and identification in Bresson's cinematography.

5

KAFKA'S NO-HOPE SPACES

1. Franz Kafka to Felice Bauer, September 12, 1916, in *Letters to Felice*, eds. Erich Heller and Jürgen Born, trans. James Stern and Elisabeth Duckworth (New York: Vintage, 1999), 529.

2. Kafka, *The Diaries of Franz Kafka 1910–1923*, ed. Max Brod, trans. Joseph Kresh, Martin Harry Greenberg, and Hannah Arendt (New York: Schocken Books, 1976), 405; hereafter abbreviated *DFK* and cited parenthetically.

3. Kafka, *The Great Wall of China: Stories and Reflections*, trans. Willa and Edwin Muir (New York: Schocken Books, 1948), 264–65.

4. Kafka, quoted in Nicholas Murray, *Kafka* (New Haven: Yale University Press, 2004), 312, 330.

5. Kafka, quoted in Walter Benjamin, "Franz Kafka, On the Tenth Anniversary of His Death," in *Illuminations*, ed. Hannah Arendt, trans. Harry Zohn (New York: Schocken Books, 1969), 116.

6. Ernst Bloch writes: an "attempt is made in *this book* to bring philosophy to hope, as to a place in the world which is as inhabited as the best civilized land and as unexplored as the

Antarctic" (*The Principle of Hope*, vol. 1, trans. Neville Plaice, Stephen Plaice, and Paul Knight [Cambridge, MA: MIT Press, 1986], 6). The "Not-Yet-Conscious" associated with hope, which is "anticipatory" (113), is also utopian. Specifically, "Everything that is non-illusory, real-possible about the hope-images leads to Marx" whose works are "part of" a "socialist changing of the world" (17).

7. In section I, an inside is exemplified by sleep that is witnessed but not experienced by another; by an absorption so pervasive that it singularizes the affective states that characteristically distinguish others; and by a narrator's confinement in a dwelling whose inner space cannot be accessed by another. In the essay as a whole "inside" and "outside" are terms that variously refer to spatial regions, to species classifications (humans, animals), and to discrete category systems.

8. My suggestion of an inescapable inside represented in Kafka's writing calls to mind Gilles Deleuze and Félix Guattari's assertion that signification is averted in Kafka's writing by intense forms of expression that abolish it: "What interests Kafka is a pure and intense sonorous material that is always connected to *its own abolition*—a deterritorialized musical sound, a cry that escapes signification" (*Kafka: Toward a Minor Literature,* trans. Dana Polan [Minneapolis: University of Minnesota Press, 1986], 6). Signification is missing in Kafka's writing because it would require a negotiation between the very internal and external regions that have been driven apart. In Kafka's parables there is no access to an autonomous space on which exegesis could be based, as discussed subsequently in this essay in relation to "An Imperial Message."

Maurice Blanchot links the "outside" (outside the world, rather than outside signification) to the aesthetic. For Kafka, who defines his writing against the bourgeois world of his family and his work, "there exists . . . only the outside, the glistening flow of the eternal outside," which is art ("Kafka and the Work's Demand," in *The Space of Literature,* trans. Ann Smock [Lincoln: University of Nebraska Press, 1989], 83). In my discussion, the outside has a more pointed reference to the penetrability of one phenomenon by another at the heart of "The Burrow" (a perception Blanchot voices in passing: "The more the burrow seems solidly closed to the outside, the greater the danger that you be closed in with the outside, delivered to the peril without any means of escape" ["The Outside, The Night," in *The Space of Literature*, 168]), and to Kafka's identification with his animal narrator.

In delineating these inner and outer spaces that pull apart from each other in Kafka's writing, and that, at the same time, paradoxically, may also be insufficiently segregated, as in a story like "The Burrow," I draw on Kafka's diaries and most especially on *Letters to Milena*, whose concerns are continuous with those of the stories. Milena Jesenská was Kafka's Czech translator with whom, at the age of thirty-six, four years before his death, he had a love affair.

9. John Updike's characterization, "the untaxonomic inhabitant of the 'The Burrow,'" refers specifically to that story, but, in his foreword to Kafka's stories, he also writes briefly about Kafka's other "zoömorphs" ("Foreword," in Franz Kafka, *The Complete Stories*, ed. Nahum N. Glatzer [New York: Schocken Books, 1971], xvii). All but one of the works from that volume discussed in my essay are translated by Willa and Edwin Muir. "At Night" is translated by Tania and James Stern.

10. Kafka, "The Cares of a Family Man," in *Complete Stories*, 428, and "A Crossbreed (A Sport)," in *Complete Stories,* 426.

Speculating on how Kafka may have come upon the word "*Odradek* . . . . a word . . . [that] belongs as little to German literature—or any other national literature—as the words and sentences of *Finnegans Wake* belong to English literature," Werner Hamacher suggests possibilities for Kafka's derivation of that word. Among them: "Odradek is the 'od-radix': the one 'without roots'; in Czech, *odrodek*, the one without its own kind, the one who 'steps out of the lineage' (*odroditi*—to degenerate, to be uprooted)." Quoting a fascinating group of words from Kott's Czech dictionary that might have been contributive to the alienation Kafka imagined in constructing the name Odradek, Hamacher recalls "the remark of Malcolm Pasley that Kafka would always speak of his writings as 'patchwork,' fragments soldered together, little bits of a story running around without a home" ("The Gesture in the Name: On Benjamin and Kafka," in *Premises: Essays on Philosophy and Literature from Kant to Celan*, trans. Peter Fenves [Stanford: Stanford University Press, 1999], 321n27).

In one of the best essays on Kafka, Hamacher thus extends the list of things in relation to which exegesis is hindered (in his recapitulation of Benjamin's analysis: genres are undecidable [302], history is "untransmissible" [303], the meanings of "doctrine," "rule" and "law" are "blocked" and "unpresentable" [304]) to the names of Kafka's imaginary creatures, each of which "no longer appears as a nominal unit but as a virtually asemantic bundle of markings" (316).

11. In *The Trial* and *The Castle* paradoxes fascinate by the unremitting energy with which they promise and then withhold explication of what is occurring. For example, in *The Castle*, where the metaphysical and the bureaucratic are indistinguishable from each other, temporalities that implicitly preclude each other because they cannot occur simultaneously are nonetheless all simultaneously indicated: "the terrible thing is that one never knows for sure what this slowness means; it can mean that the official procedure has begun, but it can also mean that the official procedure has not yet even begun" and finally, "it can also mean that the official procedure is already over" (Kafka, *The Castle*, trans. Mark Harman [New York: Schocken Books, 1998], 173).

The criticism of Kafka's novels is also mesmerized by insolubility, as in Blanchot's notion that "the essential aspect of K.'s peregrination—consists not in K.'s going from place to place, but from exegesis to exegesis and from commentator to commentator, listening to each of them with impassioned attention, then breaking in and arguing according to an exhaustive method of examination that could easily be compared with certain turns of the Talmudic dialectic" ("The Absence of the Book," in *The Infinite Conversation*, trans. Susan Hanson [Minneapolis: University of Minnesota Press, 1992], 393). In distinction, in the stories I discuss, the blockage of meaning and ambiguity about what happens is trivialized for the reader, as in "The Silence of the Sirens": "all that had happened was that Ulysses had escaped them" (*Complete Stories*, 432; hereafter abbreviated SS and quoted parenthetically).

12. Kafka, "At Night," in *Complete Stories*, 436.

13. In his consideration of Kafka's revision of Homer's myth, Matthew Olshan writes that "in *The Odyssey* . . . the wax is for" Odysseus's "crew, not for himself" (Matthew Olshan, "Franz Kafka: The Unsinging Singer," in *Modern Jewish Mythologies*, ed. Glenda Abramson [Cincinnati: Hebrew Union College Press, 2000], 185). Moreover, Kafka "has utterly reversed the polarity of the legend: his Sirens, impotent even to attract the hero's attention . . . are overcome by" his "blissful invulnerability" (188). In Stéphane Moses's analysis, Kafka, rather, revises Homer's myth by orchestrating an internal tension between opposing interpretations: for Odysseus to be saved he must either be "the most cunning of mythologic heroes" (he deludes the Sirens into thinking he does not know they are silent) or stupendously naïve (he thinks the Sirens are singing, when in fact they are silent) ("Franz Kafka: The Silence of the Sirens," *University of Denver Quarterly* 2, no. 11 [1976], 78). In distinction to these understandings of Kafka's revision, which emphasize transpositions, reversals, and additions, the analysis above explores one of the myth's elements, absorption—represented as a shared state.

14. Kafka, "An Imperial Message," in *Complete Stories,* 4; hereafter abbreviated IM and quoted parenthetically.

15. "Aber statt dessen, wie nutzlos müht er sich ab; immer noch zwängt er sich durch die Gemächer des innersten Palastes; niemals wird er sie überwinden; und gelänge ihm dies, nichts wäre gewonnen; die Treppen hinab müsste er sich kämpfen; und gelänge ihm dies, nichts wäre gewonnen; die Höfe wären zu durchmessen; und nach den Höfen der zweite umschliessende Palast; und wieder Treppen und Höfe; und wieder ein Palast; und so weiter durch Jahrtausende; und stürzte er endlich aus dem äussersten Tor—aber niemals, niemals kann es geschehen—, liegt erst die Residenzstadt vor ihm, die Mitte der Welt, hochgeschüttet voll ihres Bodensatzes" (Kafka, "An Imperial Message," in *Great Stories by Kafka and Rilke/Meistererzählungen von Kafka und Rilke: A Dual-Language Book*, ed. and trans. Stanley Appelbaum [New York: Dover, 2003] 12, 14).

16. In the context of the passage's subjunctive, "*stürzte*" could be translated as: to plunge or break through; "*hochgeschüttet*" as heaped up, filled to the brim. The Muirs, Kafka's translators, employ a form of the same word ("*burst* through the gate/crammed to *bursting*") in a repetition absent from the original, even as their linkage of the two verbs faithfully intuits a connection between the violence with which the messenger would break down the gate and the violence of a plenitude whose excess almost exceeds its limit.

17. Max Horkheimer and Theodor W. Adorno, *Dialectic of Enlightenment,* trans. John Cumming (New York: Continuum, 2001), 43. See also 45–51.

18. Kafka, "The Metamorphosis," in *Complete Stories,* 89.

19. In Stanley Corngold's analysis, "metamorphosis," rather than literalization, "dismantles, and hence destroys metaphor" (*Franz Kafka: The Necessity of Form* [Ithaca: Cornell University Press, 1988], 97). In Kafka's writing, the movement from "tenor to vehicle and then in reverse order . . . is chiastic" (101). Henry Sussman offers a related understanding when he writes that Kafka's metaphors do not "bridge" the two entities they draw into relation. Rather, composite entities (like the "man/insect" of "The Metamorphosis" or the "kitten/lamb" of "A Crossbreed [A Sport])" are "*both* of the elements they combine and *neither*" (*Franz Kafka: Geometrician of Metaphor* [Madison, WI: Coda Press, 1979], 33). In the example I discuss, however, neither chiasm nor indeterminacy accounts for the literal displacement of Kafka's "being" when it is objectively regarded.

20. Kafka to Milena Jesenská, September 1920, *Letters to Milena,* trans. Philip Boehm (New York: Schocken Books, 1990), 208; hereafter abbreviated *LM* and cited parenthetically. For the German original, see *Briefe an Milena,* ed. Jürgen Born and Michael Müller (Frankfurt: Fischer Verlag, 1983), 281.

21. Deleuze and Guattari, *Kafka: Toward a Minor Literature,* 7, 19.

22. Kafka to Felice, April 20, 1914, in *Letters to Felice,* 439.

23. Benjamin, "Franz Kafka, On the Tenth Anniversary of His Death," 122. For something to unfold as a bud does is for it to extend itself in a maturity in which, albeit mysteriously, the bud becomes what it has the potential to be in the development of a single entity, while for a boat to unfold into a piece of paper is for it to reveal something to the understanding about how one entity is related to another thought to be exterior to it. Even if what is revealed is only that the boat *is* the paper, such a perception draws two entities together into a concurrence that amounts to a discovery Benjamin associates with meaning.

24. Kafka, "The Burrow," in *Complete Stories,* 340, 326, 332; hereafter abbreviated B and cited parenthetically.

25. Sussman's deconstructive analysis of "The Burrow" identifies the "voice of the animal" as "also the voice of construction" and "the voice of language in general" (*Franz Kafka: Geometrician*

of Metaphor, 153), whose "bifurcations" (158) and "oppositions" (159) instigate "the repetitive cycle of disturbance and pacification" (158). But if the central passages I discuss do not escape the design of such patterning, their curiosity about how immediate experience could be regarded from outside the immediacy has a unique focus, as Sussman recognizes. See 163–66.

26. Kafka, quoted in Gustav Janouch, *Conversations with Kafka*, trans. Goronwy Rees (New York: New Directions, 1971), 33. At the same time that "Inner and Outer belong to each other," they are incommensurate, and can never be fitted to each other. In November 1912, Kafka wrote to Felice: "The outside world is too small, too clear-cut, too truthful, to contain everything that a person has room for inside." Quoted in Reiner Stach, *Kafka: The Decisive Years*, trans. Shelley Frisch (Princeton: Princeton University Press, 2013), 205.

27. One way of understanding this conversability is in psychological terms. Thus Kafka to Milena: "torture is extremely important to me—my sole occupation is torturing and being tortured" (*LM* 214). But Kafka's insight is deeper than the psychological. It is also other than what follows from Emmanuel Levinas's project of revising the phenomenological description of the world in light of the experience of other minds, which exceeds the singularity of the psychological. The claim therefore in the Levinasian account that "'The Burrow' can be read as a comment upon the meaninglessness and anxiety of a life lived for the self alone" with no interest in "communication," or "community," socializes Kafka's concern (Laura Stahman, "Franz Kafka's 'The Burrow' as Model of Ipseity in Levinasian Theory," *Mosaic* 37, no. 3 [2004]: 20, 19).

28. See especially Kafka's letter of July 12, 1922, to Max Brod: "Enemies everywhere. Children outside this room . . . lovely-looking children, but the noise . . . was the same. . . . For the past few days some two hundred Prague schoolchildren have been quartered here. A hellish noise, a scourge of humanity. . . . the whole margin of these lovely woods is infested. . . . And the writing? . . . constantly endangered by noise" (*Letters to Friends, Family, and Editors,* trans. Richard and Clara Winston [New York: Schocken Books, 1977], 338–339). Four days later on July 16, 1922: "Planá is beautiful, but . . . I have experienced there such days of noise, that I have cursed my life and needed many days to recover from the fear of noise, from my invariably successful lying in wait for the noise, from the confusion in my head, the pain in my temples, and afterward all of Ottla's measures—she who takes the greatest care of me—had lost all efficacy and new and terrible noise was lying in wait" (342). On September 11, 1922, Kafka claimed that this noise precipitated a "breakdown" (357).

29. Kafka to Brod, September 11, 1922, *Letters to Friends, Family, and Editors*, 359, 358–59.

30. Jean-Luc Nancy, "The Sublime Offering," in *Of the Sublime: Presence in Question,* trans. Jeffrey S. Librett (Albany: SUNY Press, 1993), 25, 26, 39. The "something other than art" is "truth, or experience, the experience of truth" (27). Concretely, it is "that which indefinitely trembles at the border of the sketch, the suspended whiteness of the page" (42).

31. Nancy, "The Sublime Offering," 46, 42.

32. Nancy, "The Sublime Offering," 47. He elaborates: "one would have to construct a double analytic of feeling. . . . it is the intimacy of the 'to feel' and the 'to feel oneself' that produces itself here, paradoxically, as exposition to what is beyond the self, passage to the (in)sensible or (un) feeling limit of the self" (47).

Although the idea of a "*delimiting and unlimiting*" "*of all figures*" that occurs "*in a single gesture*" (41) suggests an economy of the sort Roland Barthes proposes in "Contract-Narratives" when he designates narrative as a "system" of "exchange" (*S/Z: An Essay,* trans. Richard Miller [New York: Hill and Wang, 1974], 88, 89), in Nancy's description of the interrelation of these elements, the figure and what surpasses it might require each other but they remain inequivalent, since the imagination is defined by "the *Bildung* of the *Bild*," while the sublime escapes image, structure, and calculation: "The sublime totality is beyond the maximum, which is to say that it is *beyond everything*" (39). Hence the "outside" that Nancy describes as the "vanishing of the limit . . . into unlimitedness, that is, into nothing" (42) is not dialectical.

33. Nancy, "The Sublime Offering," 42, 39.

34. Nancy, "The Sublime Offering," 45, 39.

35. This is the case even though the narrator's defensive strategies are based on innumerable calculations, since the reason that underlies these is constantly represented as collapsing before the bliss that trivializes it and before the terror of actual danger that dispels the thought of danger, and that demolishes the efficacy of reckoning.

36. In distinction to the kinship between animal and human being represented in Robert Bresson's cinematography, in Kafka's writing there is no benign or even curious acknowledgment of the forms of other being onto which human being actually opens. There *could* be no such acknowledgment, since, for instance, the word "animal" has been appropriated to designate an affective excess that makes human being unrecognizable to itself.

Of course such a surfeit reaches deep into, draws upon, and even seems to dwell at the spring of all human affective possibilities, to tap their utmost—whether of terror in "The Burrow" or, in "Investigations of a Dog," of an insatiable craving for an epiphany before which the narrator's metaphysical questions would crumble; it alone would provide sustenance, for lack of which that eponymous hunger artist in Kafka's cognate story chooses starvation. To Milena, Kafka wrote: "the only truth is longing, which cannot be exaggerated" (*LM* 195).

37. To characterize Kafka's therophily comparatively as Benjamin does ("of all of Kafka's creatures, the animals have the greatest opportunity for reflection" ["Franz Kafka," 132]) or substitutively as Adorno does ("Instead of human dignity, the supreme bourgeois concept, there emerges" in Kafka "the salutary recollection of the similarity between man and animal" ["Notes on Kafka," in *Prisms,* trans. Samuel and Shierry Weber (Cambridge, MA: MIT Press, 1983), 270]), or in terms of an advancement, as Sussman does ("Animalism is . . . not merely an anticipation of humanity, a precursor on an evolutionary ladder, but is reached only after humanity has been lived, penetrated, and disqualified" [*Franz Kafka: Geometrician of Metaphor,* 149]), or, most especially, to domesticate Kafka's "animal," as Updike does ("the untaxonomic inhabitant of 'The Burrow' represents the animal in all of us" [*Complete Stories,* xvii]) is to neglect the fact that Kafka's animals are *sui generis.* There are no such creatures. "Animal" is an imaginary construction of a creature that is forced to pursue its obsessions stripped of socialized human features. I would thus agree with Hamacher's claim that "The protagonists of Kafka's parables are no longer the species-beings that inhabit Lessing's fables; they . . . come to themselves—only by abandoning their classificatory and socializing function" ("The Gesture in the Name," 316). Deleuze and Guattari's conclusion that "becoming-animal is an immobile voyage that stays in one place; it only lives and is comprehensible as an intensity" (*Kafka: Toward a Minor Literature,* 35), to whose phenomenological insight all critics of Kafka are indebted, fails to take up the fact that in this story these intensities are not immobile, but represent a phenomenon opening onto what lies outside it—a movement that has relevance to the disaffiliation of Kafka's animal narrator with a human corollary, as discussed here.

38. More: the human beings who could not ameliorate—who could not even see—the dissolving physical and mental boundaries that held Kafka's rapt attention could fatally interfere with his own absorptive attention to those states, an absorption he implicitly represents as inseparable from vitality: "Alone I am still alive, but whenever a visitor comes by he literally kills me, just so he can then revive me with his own power, except he isn't powerful enough" (*LM* 204).

39. See *Briefe an Milena,* 262.

Milena echoing Kafka's own sentiment—that the tuberculosis aided, even saved him—in her obituary of Kafka wrote: "He had been suffering a lung disease for years, and although he worked to cure it, he also consciously nourished it, and fostered it in his thoughts. He once wrote in a letter: when heart and soul can't bear it any longer, the lung takes on half the burden, so that it is distributed a little more evenly—and that's the way it was with his disease. . . . Franz Kafka loaded his entire intellectual fear of life onto the shoulders of his disease" (*LM* 271). A weapon, a support, an object of yearning, even ardor, as well as the physical malady that killed him, tuberculosis occupied a range of positions, in effect becoming everything to Kafka.

40. Kafka to Felice, September 30, 1917, quoted in and translated by Ernst Pawel, *The Nightmare of Reason: A Life of Franz Kafka* (Toronto: Collins Publishers, 1984), 363. For the translation of the same passage by Stern and Duckworth, see *Letters to Felice,* 568.

41. Kafka, "Investigations of a Dog," in *Complete Stories*, 281; hereafter abbreviated I and cited parenthetically.

42. Music is at once said to be an alternative to food; a kind of food; and a form of response (characterized as an answer) that has nothing to do with food. "Incantation" is described as the "border region" between food and music (I 315), while other distinctions rend topics that had been sutured: "the science of music" "admits of more objective inquiry . . . while in the province of food the main object is to achieve practical results" (I 315). Thus the narrator proposes a nexus of affiliations that mystify music but do not render it, or its relation to the other questions, intelligible as a single object of inquiry.

Other questions disseminated across the story are also incomparable. Some are rhetorical ("why won't you let me lie here?" [I 313]); some metacritically interrogate the communal response to the narrator's questions (referring to "the fact that the world of dogs . . . is pledged to silence," Kafka asks, "'How long will you be able to endure it?' That is the real great question of my life, before which all smaller ones sink into insignificance" [I 291–92]). Of course as discussed above, "real" could not identify a category of question, but is an intensifier.

43. In another example of the narrator's incorporation within the thing he would examine: "I wanted to convince myself that my hunger and I were still two things and I could shake it off like a burdensome lover; but in reality we were very painfully one, and when I explained to myself: 'That is my hunger,' it was really my hunger that was speaking and having its joke at my expense" (I 308–9).

Michael G. Levine discusses the inseparability of such figures in relation to his notion that, in "Investigations" as a whole, hunger is not simply a phenomenon that "has speech as its *object* . . . it is hunger itself that is the *subject*, hunger itself that *speaks*." And the narrator does not simply have a longing for nourishment, but he also has a longing for "the 'true word' that, according to Kafka's dog, 'hovered on the tip of the tongue'" ("'A Place So Insanely Enchanting': Kafka and the Poetics of Suspension," *MLN* 123, no. 5 [2008]: 1057, 1060). Levine examines "modes of suspension" and doubling that might be "resistant to narrative development" (1051), but are compellingly shown to constitute the essence of Kafka's narratives. What Levine describes in different terms is key to my sense that there is no outside to the diegetic in Kafka's writing.

44. Attempting to situate "my own bout of questioning" (I 297) within the matrix of the dog community, the narrator states that "Only with the assistance of the whole dog world could I begin to understand my own questions" (I 289). In response to his appeal, however, there were only "vacant stares, averted glances, troubled and veiled eyes" (I 290). The association of food with obliviousness and hunger with excruciating awareness, with an exteroception responsive to the affliction of sound, explains why questions (which engage enigmas with their own unpleasant

din) are experienced by the community as an assault that food could still. The best answer they can give to the narrator is "If you haven't enough to eat, we'll give you some of ours" (I 288), because "they would rather do the impossible . . . than endure my questions" (I 289).

45. "But how should they not be dogs? Could I not actually hear on listening more closely the subdued cries with which they encouraged each other . . . could I not see the last and youngest dog, to whom most of those cries were addressed, often stealing a glance at me as if he would have dearly wished to reply, but refrained because it was not allowed? But why should it not be allowed?" (I 283).

46. Kafka, "The Metamorphosis," 130, 89.

47. Kafka, "The Metamorphosis," 134, 135.

48. Kafka, "The Metamorphosis," 135. At the end of *The Trial* it is not possible for Joseph K. to separate the lone figure from the abstraction that keeps solace at bay. Of the "human figure, faint and insubstantial" that appears at "the casements of a window," K. asks: "Who was it? A friend? A good person? Someone who cared? Someone who wanted to help? Was it just one person? Was it everyone? . . . He raised his hands and spread out all his fingers" (Kafka, *The Trial*, trans. Breon Mitchell [New York: Schocken Books, 1998], 230–31).

The passage renders indeterminate something as central as number in the figure K. sees. Although the abstraction "everyone" has a grandeur, the inclusiveness empties it of the possibility of actual consolation, for an appeal (whether a request for a new hearing or a more all-encompassing supplication) can be made in the name of a universal but could only be granted by a specific person or persons. Whether K. sees one or one and all, a single person or an aggregate, is an enigma that slips into the insult of a deliberate category mistake. When human being *is* recognizable in a discrete form it is in the flesh-and-blood brutality manifested by his killers' failed recognition that Joseph K. belongs to the human family. To be killed "like a dog!" (K.'s exclamation at the cruelty of the men who "thrust the knife into his heart and turned it there twice" [231]) is to be killed like a creature perceived as so foreign to their kind that his life is worthless. In this way, the impossibility of K.'s imploring mercy and of his killers' extension of mercy is based on a distinction of kind or classification, which rivals the initial discrimination between "one person" and "everyone" in the extremity of its consequence.

49. Kafka, "The Metamorphosis," 92.

50. *Briefe an Milena*, 250.

51. A different manifestation of extremity is registered in the alienation of "human" and "animal" kinds that is almost, but not, effaced in the two-page story "A Crossbreed (A Sport)," in which the narrator inherits "a curious animal, half kitten, half lamb" (*Complete Stories*, 426). Though the animal can't express itself, the narrator discerns the creature's despondency ("I happened to glance down and saw tears dropping from its huge whiskers. Were they mine, or were they the animal's? Had this cat, along with the soul of a lamb, the ambitions of a human being?" [427]); he shares the cat's desolation (they inhabit the same domain; have co-extensive fates; are united to bodies from which each seeks release), yet each is ultimately incomprehensible to the other. The most compelling crossing is not of "cat" and "lamb" but of animal and human narrator, for the blurred origin of tears ("mine" or "the animal's?" [427]) expresses a grief discerned as common ground, as communicative as language, even as tears are not a language, and, for all the narrator knows, not, for the animal, an expression of grief.

52. Nancy, "The Sublime Offering," 45.

53. Amie Thomasson provides a lucid overview of the distinctions between Aristotle's "realist" categories, which enumerate the "highest genera of entities . . . so that a system of categories

undertaken in this realist spirit would ideally provide an inventory of everything there is"; Kant's "categories of our conceptual system . . . the categories that are *a priori* necessary for any possible cognition of objects" which are "limited to phenomena, not the thing itself"; and Husserl's "categories of meanings and objects alike" that, quoting Husserl, "'arise . . . solely in relation to our varying thought functions'" ("Categories," *Stanford Encyclopedia of Philosophy*, last modified January 23, 2013, accessed January 29, 2016. http://plato.stanford.edu/entries/categories/). See also Thomasson's characterization of what "Brian Carr . . . calls 'categorical descriptivism,'" which delineates "the categorial structure that the world would have *according to* our thought, experience, or language, while refraining from making commitments about whether or not these categories are occupied." Needless to say, in another context, such terms would be elaborated and supplemented by an account of additional category systems.

For cognate thoughts about the construction of taxonomies that separate animal and human being, see Giorgio Agamben's essays on "the shadowy kinship between animal macrocosm and human microcosm" revealed across a range of documents from ancient Greek thinkers to twentieth-century humanists (Giorgio Agamben, *The Open: Man and Animal*, trans. Kevin Attell [Stanford: Stanford University Press, 2004], 3). In Agamben's analysis (which directly engages with Heidegger's claim that the animal has "no world" [49–56]), such classifications are generated by an "anthropological machine which" produces a state of affairs "in which the outside is nothing but the exclusion of an inside and the inside is in turn only the inclusion of an outside" (37), a machine that works differently in ancient and modern times, but to the same end of separating humanity and animality. In distinction, Kafka's identification with the animal could not be explained by the history Agamben charts since for Kafka *animal* is not precisely the antithesis of *human*, but nor could it be assimilated to *human*, since *animal*, like *dog*, like the affiliation with "the penholder" in Kafka's "hand" (*DFK* 396) or with plant "roots" (*DFK* 408), designates the torture of being unclassifiable.

54. Recall the passage quoted in note 11: "the terrible thing is that one never knows for sure what this slowness means; it can mean that the official procedure has begun, but it can also mean that the official procedure has not yet even begun" and "finally, it can even mean that the official procedure is already over" (Kafka, *The Castle*, 173). I would therefore say that the rhetorical, logical, and exegetical complexities of Kafka's writing, as, for instance, discussed by Corngold's analysis of the "chiasm" (Corngold, *Franz Kafka*, 99), Sussman's analysis of Kafka's "*both*" and "*neither*" logic (Sussman, *Franz Kafka: The Geometrician of Metaphor*, 33), and Benjamin's analysis of the "precautions" Kafka takes "against . . . interpretation" (Benjamin, "Franz Kafka," 124) stem from his response to a philosophical enigma: his unique relation to ontological categories that are fixed when they encounter phenomenological categories that are not. My analysis is most in sympathy with Werner Hamacher's claim that the "protagonists of Kafka's parables" are "entities" that "come to themselves" by "abandoning their classificatory and socializing function" ("Gesture in the Name," 316).

55. Quoted in Stach, *Kafka: The Decisive Years*, 205.

56. See *Briefe an Milena*, 296.

57. Kafka to Grete Bloch, June 8, 1914, *Letters to Felice*, 463. See also *Briefe an Felice und andere Korrespondenz aus der Verlobungszeit*, eds. Erich Heller and Jürgen Born (Frankfurt: Fischer Verlag, 1967), 597.

58. Kafka to Bloch, June 8, 1914, *Letters to Felice*, 463.

Index

Page numbers in italics refer to images.